Brother
of Mine

Brother of Mine

THE CIVIL WAR LETTERS OF
Thomas and William Christie

Hampton Smith

MINNESOTA HISTORICAL SOCIETY PRESS

The publication of this book was supported, in part,
by a gift from the George A. MacPherson Fund.

The Introduction previously appeared as "The Christie Brothers' Civil War:
A Reflection of Minnesota's Experience" in *The State We're In: Reflections on
Minnesota History*, edited by Annette Atkins and Deborah L. Miller (St. Paul:
Minnesota Historical Society Press, 2010) and is reproduced here by the
editors' kind permission.

Cover images: Top: Fair Oaks vicinity, federal battery, 1862 (LC-B811-2510A).
Bottom: Gun crew, Company K, Second New York Artillery, at Fort C. F. Smith, August
1865 (LC-B817-7675). Both Library of Congress, Prints & Photographs Division.

www.mhspress.org

The Minnesota Historical Society Press is a member of the Association of
American University Presses.

Manufactured in the United States of America

10 9 8 7 6 5 4 3 2

♾ The paper used in this publication meets the minimum
requirements of the American National Standard for Information Sciences—
Permanence for Printed Library Materials, ANSI Z39.48-1984.

International Standard Book Number
ISBN: 978-0-87351-781-2 (paper)
ISBN: 978-0-87351-810-9 (e-book)

Library of Congress Cataloging-in-Publication Data

Christie, Thomas.
Brother of mine : the Civil War letters of Thomas and
William Christie / Hampton Smith.
p. cm.
Includes bibliographical references and index.
ISBN 978-0-87351-781-2 (paper : alk. paper) — ISBN 978-0-87351-810-9 (ebook)
1. Christie, Thomas—Correspondence. 2. Christie, William, 1830–1901—
Correspondence. 3. United States. Army. Minnesota Light Artillery Battery, 1st
(1861–1865) 4. Soldiers—Minnesota—Correspondence. 5. Minnesota—History—
Civil War, 1861–1865—Personal narratives. 6. United States—History—Civil War, 1861–
1865—Personal narratives. 7. Minnesota—History—Civil War, 1861–1865—
Regimental histories. 8. United States—History—Civil War, 1861–1865—
Regimental histories. 9. United States. Army—Military life—History—19th century.
10. American letters—Minnesota. I. Christie, William, 1830–1901.
II. Smith, Hampton, 1949– III. Title.
E515.81st .C47 2011
973.7′8—dc22
2010030625

Contents

Introduction 3

The Collection Story 21

1   "A Part in this Great Struggle"
October 21, 1861–March 17, 1862 25

2   "The Bullets Came like Hail"
March 22–August 15, 1862 39

3   "Your Poor Soldier Correspondent"
September 21, 1862–April 8, 1863 73

4   "No Glory in It"
April 11–October 2, 1863 123

5   "This Dull, Idle Existence"
October 20, 1863–March 19, 1864 173

6   "Enough Fighting to Satisfy Us"
March 25–September 9, 1864 213

7   "We Had a Lively Time for Awhile"
September 15–May 27, 1865 261

Bibliography 313

Index 315

Eastern States

c.1862

CANADA

ME

MN

VT
NH

Fort Snelling •

WI

NY

MA

Winona •

MI

CT
RI

Clyman •

IA

Chicago •

PA

New York •

Philadelphia •

NJ

IL

IN

OH

MD

DE

Washington, DC •

Alexandria

MO

• St. Louis

WV

VA

KY

Cairo •

NC

Goldsboro

TN • Shiloh

Bentonville •

Memphis • Corinth •

• Huntsville

• Columbia

AR

SC

Atlantic
Ocean

• Atlanta

Lake Providence •

MS

AL

GA

• Vicksburg

Savannah

TX

LA

New Orleans •

FL

Gulf
of
Mexico

Union States

Border States

Confederate States

Brother
of Mine

Introduction

Among the many collections of Civil War letters and diaries in the Minnesota Historical Society holdings, the letters of William and Thomas Christie stand apart. As a group these letters provide a detailed account of two brothers' personal experiences in the war. They also tell the story of their unit, the First Minnesota Light Artillery. The war letters, however, are part of a much larger family collection beginning in the 1830s in Scotland and continuing on to the American West in the 1890s and to Turkey in the early 1900s (where Thomas became a missionary).

Most of the Civil War letters are those of William and Thomas Christie, half brothers thirteen years apart in age who held decidedly different worldviews. (A third, younger brother, Alexander, or "Sandy," joined the army very late in the war.) The fact that William and Thomas were in the same unit, one that took part in most of the major campaigns in the western theater of the war, adds further to their interest.

Like most Minnesota soldiers, the Christie brothers were originally from somewhere else. The family originated in Scotland, where the boys' father, James, worked in the jute mills of Dundee. William was born there in 1830, the only child of James's first marriage. When his wife, Elizabeth Gilchrist, died in 1832, James moved to Sion Mills in County Tyrone, Ireland, leaving William in the care of his wife's parents. James remarried in 1836 to Eliza Reid, with whom he had three children: Thomas 1843, Sarah 1844, and Alexander 1846. William joined his father's new family in 1840. In 1848, the entire Christie clan, including in-laws, made a carefully planned migration to America, ending up in Clyman Township, Dodge County, Wisconsin.[1]

1. The great Irish potato famine does not seem to have caused the family's emigration.

For the next ten years, the family, and particularly William, worked hard to develop their farm. Another child, David, was born to James and Eliza, but Eliza died in a subsequent childbirth in 1850, and James married neighbor Persis Noyes a few years later.

Being an important worker on the farm, William missed the opportunity afforded his younger siblings to attend a township school. Although his letters suggest he had little formal education, he was well read and familiar with the Bible, with Shakespeare, and with other British writers. His writing skills were poor, however, and William self-deprecatingly joked in his letters about his penmanship and made-up grammar and spelling. He was keenly aware of the shortfall in his education because his siblings were intelligent, even brilliant writers.

By 1855, when William's younger brothers Thomas and Alexander were old enough to help their father farm in Wisconsin, William acquired land in Minnesota. He appears in the 1860 federal census as a farmer in St. Charles Township, Winona County, although the exact location of his farm is unknown.

∽

William soon found that farming solo was a difficult undertaking. The market economy following the financial panic of 1857 was poor, and William probably lacked capital for animals and equipment. He also seems to have gotten himself into debt. Thomas joined him in the summer and fall of 1860 and again in 1861 to help with the harvest, but even the two working together had a tough go of it. Thomas wrote optimistic letters home, full of promise for a good wheat crop, but when their sister Sarah joined them in October 1861 to keep house, she put the family wise to the boys' situation. Their shanty was "the most miserable looking place ever I looked at," and William's wheat harvest was poor and his expenses many, "so you see he is pretty hard set, and then he has to buy a new stove for this is so smashed up it will not do, and buy beef and potatoes and butter for the winter for he had nothing, and there is no ploughing done. If he has any more debts I do not know." To make matters worse William had lost a legal dispute with a neighbor and owed a judgment of thirteen dollars. So "hard set" was he, Sarah wrote, that he was "going to leave his claim and go away out west where he would never be heard of again if we had not come just when we did."[2]

2. Only William's letters were saved, so it is hard to know specifics of the financial problem. No tax default judgments against William appear in Olmsted County court

Meanwhile, news of the escalating Civil War was a constant pull for Thomas. In fact, his father had sent him to work with William hoping to keep Thomas out of the war. Although Thomas worked diligently for his older brother, the war remained on his mind. As Thomas recounted many years later, matters came to a head one day as he was walking to Winona and met a former neighbor, James Strachan, who had recently enlisted in the Minnesota Light Cavalry, later known as Brackett's Battalion. The sight of Strachan, who was home on leave, in his new cavalry uniform with accoutrements was too much for Thomas. He resolved on the spot to enlist. That evening he informed William that nothing would stop him. William contemplated this situation for a moment and decided that since he could not prevent Thomas from signing on, he would join him. Thomas's insistence gave William an honorable out from a difficult financial situation on the failing farm.[3]

Thus it happened that on an October day in 1861, a month that had begun "with a most gloomy and forbidding countenance" and days of heavy rain that continued "with great persistency," William and Thomas Christie walked into the lobby of Winona's Huff House Hotel intending to enlist in a company of recruits being formed for the Third Minnesota Regiment. They found the recruiters, "Captain Dawley and Second Lieutenant Clayton," readily enough, and soon their names were added to the roster of men from the country "back of Winona" volunteering their service in the war to preserve the Union.[4]

Within a few days they had arranged their affairs with the farm, had sent Sarah on her way back to Clyman, and were off to Fort Snelling. In a letter to their father, James, sent home with his sister, Thomas explained his reasons for enlisting and apologized for his disobedience:

> Now you know, Father, that you would enlist if you were in my place. You
> have taught me to hate Slavery, and to love my Country . . . I shall not deny

records. Sarah Christie to James Christie, Oct. 25, 1861, James C. Christie papers, Minnesota Historical Society (hereafter, MHS).

3. Unpublished reminiscences of Thomas Christie, 19–21, in Thomas and Carmelite Christie Papers, MHS.

4. *Winona Republican*, Oct. 19, 1861, 1. The ranks were strictly honorary. Dawley was probably Richard L. Dawley, who later served as an officer in the Second Minnesota Battery but who does not seem to have accompanied the "McClellan Rifles" to Fort Snelling. Thomas Christie reminiscence, 21.

that motives other than strictly patriotic have had an influence upon me; but I don't think these other motives are *wrong*. I do want to 'see the world,' to get out of the narrow circle in which I have always lived . . . I feel sure, even as I write, that you will not only give me your blessing—but be glad to have your son enrolled among the Defenders of the Union. But whether that be so or not, I must go.[5]

This was the first of many letters from the brothers to their family at home, some 274 altogether. The recipient of most of the correspondence was their father, James, followed by younger brother Alexander and sister Sarah.

Typically, the content of the letters varied according to the intended reader. Those addressed to James dwelled on army life, including its less savory aspects, the politics of the war, details of combat, and, occasionally, family business. Alexander received similar letters with more graphic descriptions of battles. Sarah seems to have gotten the most self-reflective letters since she was her older brothers' confidant. William often expressed his self-doubts to her, and Thomas worked through a long, sometimes contentious examination of religious belief. Since William's mother and Thomas's mother had died, Sarah was probably the primary female figure in the brothers' lives at this time. She heard their troubles and doubts but also received their advice, sometimes unsolicited and overbearing from Thomas, and almost avuncular from the older William. The boys were also Sarah's strongest advocates at home, arguing with their father that she should receive a proper education and even pledging their soldier's pay to help send her to college. Although relations with their stepmother seem to have been cordial and respectful, neither Thomas nor William ever wrote to her directly. Most of the letters were probably meant to be read by all, since side notes with messages to other family members frequently appeared. This was particularly true when the brothers were on the march and had few opportunities for writing.

Early November 1861 found the Christie boys at Fort Snelling, the place of rendezvous for Minnesota recruits. Nominally, they were part of the McClellan Rifles, recruited to form a company in the newly created Third

5. Thomas Christie to James Christie, Oct. 21, Christie papers. According to Thomas's reminiscence, Sarah left for home on the twenty-second and the company arrived at Fort Snelling on the twenty-sixth.

Minnesota Regiment. In the standard recruiting practice of the day, anyone could gather a group of men to form a company of militia to meet the
state's recruiting goal, but, in practice, recruiters were often political figures or well-known businessmen able to draw in enough recruits to form
the standard infantry company of eighty-four men. The newly formed company would then elect their recruiter as captain.[6]

The Christies' recruiting officer was William Z. Clayton, remembered by
Thomas as "the first of the heroes of my hero-worship . . . a very bright,
active, energetic, courageous man." Like most men entering the service, he
had no previous military experience. Born in Maine, Clayton had moved
in the 1850s to Minnesota, where he took up farming as well as teaching.
He seems to have been popular but not prominent and, as one of several
recruiters active in Winona, had a hard time filling his company.[7]

At Fort Snelling, the Christies' group spent their time learning infantry
drill while waiting for their company to fill up. This proved to be a slow
process since many other companies of the Third and Fourth regiments
were also recruiting. Meanwhile, the Christies and their companions en-
dured the usual bad food, lack of equipment, and ennui common to new
soldiers. How long, they wondered, would they be in military limbo?

Fortunately, the U.S. government had authorized raising two batteries of
artillery in Minnesota. Clayton, still hoping for a commission, persuaded
his squad to combine with another group of Winona men to form the Second Minnesota Battery of Light Artillery. A competing unit from Taylors
Falls and New Ulm had already formed the First Minnesota Battery, but
since neither had the necessary number and the Mississippi River would
soon close for the season, stranding them all at the fort while the war went
on without them, the two groups merged as the First Minnesota Battery.
While this left Clayton out of the picture for a commission, it allowed the
battery to muster in on November 21, 1861.

Command of the new battery went to Emil Munch, a Prussian who had
arrived in Minnesota in 1852 and been elected to the legislature. Like most
of the men in his command, Captain Munch had no previous military experience, but he would prove an able officer.[8]

6. For an excellent discussion of recruiting in the "Northwest," see Woodworth, *Nothing but Victory*, 3–20.
7. Thomas Christie reminiscence, 22. The company numbered about thirty men,
according to Thomas Christie, half of the minimum for an infantry company.
8. Emil Munch papers, MHS.

The First Minnesota Battery arrived in Benton Barracks in St. Louis, Missouri, on December 20, 1861. Long an important frontier post, Benton Barracks had become a vital center for the national war effort in the West because it was located near strategic waterways and railroad connections. Newly formed units from western states were gathered, equipped, and trained for national army service there. At Benton Barracks, the First Minnesota Battery received its advanced training as an artillery company.

Drill and training were especially important for Civil War–era artillerymen because the men had to learn not only the skills required for firing large guns but also the techniques and intricacies of maneuvering horses, carts, and limbers, the wagons used in pulling the guns. To function in combat, they needed to be skilled enough to carry out complex team maneuvers automatically in the chaos of battle.

Like most batteries, the First Minnesota functioned as three two-gun sections, each commanded by a lieutenant. Each gun crew was under the charge of a sergeant, or gunner, who was also responsible for aiming the gun. Each gun was joined to a two-wheeled cart, called a limber, that carried an ammunition chest, and both were pulled as a unit by four to six horses with a mounted driver for every pair. Other horse-drawn carts, known as caissons, carried extra ammunition chests, a spare wheel, and other parts.[9]

Each man in a seven-man crew had a number assigned with very specific duties in combat. As Thomas Christie wrote on October 18, 1862, to his father, James:

> My duty was as No. 1. Nothing is so exciting as working a gun in real action. The sound of the discharge almost raises us off our feet with delight. Before the smoke lifts from the muzzle I dash in, dip the brush in the sponge bucket and brush out the bore using plenty of water, then seize the sponge staff and sponge it out dry. No. 2 then inserts the cartridge which I ram home, then the shot, shell, or canister . . . is sent home, then I spring out beside the wheel and fall flat. "Ready," shouts the Gunner. No. 3 . . . now pricks the cartridge, No 4 jumps in and inserts a friction primer, to which his lanyard is attached, in the vent, springs outside the wheel and straightens his lanyard. The gunner gives a turn or two to the elevating screw taps . . . and then [shouts] "Fire." The gun rushes back with the recoil. The other numbers run her forward at the command, "By hand to the front," while I load [again].

9. The information on battery organization is from U.S. War Department, *Instructions for Field Artillery;* Gibbon, *Artillerist's Manual;* Thomas, *Cannons.*

Well-drilled men could carry out the complex and dangerous job of loading and firing amid the noise, smoke, and confusion of battle and fire two rounds per minute, three in a really desperate situation. In addition, thoroughly trained artillerymen, serving as drivers or ammunition carriers, could take the place of fallen men on the gun crews.

While at Benton Barracks, the Christies had decidedly different reactions to army life. Thomas clearly enjoyed and romanticized being a soldier, and he approached his duties with an enthusiasm bordering on zeal. While William, like most soldiers, regarded guard duty as tedious, unpleasant, and occasionally dangerous, Thomas saw it as an adventure. He studied every aspect of a sentry's duty in his manual, and in a long letter home he described night guard duty at Benton Barracks, complete with a description of the passwords, routine, and inspection.

Similarly, Thomas found his new comrades fascinating and entertaining. "We have all kinds of Characters in our Battery . . . 3 men have been members of the legislature, 3 were in the Crimea, 1 served under Lieutenant, now Commodore, Dupont, 1 was with Fremont in his first Expedition west of the Rocky Mountains, and 6 or 7 were in the Mexican War. So you see we have thrilling stories told around our Campfire and more interesting than those related by Novelists Characters."

Continuing, he wrote, "I have discovered things to be just as I had imagined them to be. The immense Prairies of Illinois . . . looked exactly as I knew they must look. It is so with our military life, I adapt myself to it much more readily than the most of our men do . . . [who] cannot leave off those habits of Independence, which are so meritorious in the civilian but so pernicious in the Soldier."[10]

William had a less romantic view of life in St. Louis. "Mud, Mud, Mud! Black sticky mud everywhere. Mud up to the ankles the moment you go out of doors; two or three pounds of it sticking to each foot. So drill is out of the question, and time hangs heavy on our hands." He noted that out of boredom men were "spending their money very foolishly, I am sorry to say. I fear that before the next pay-day they will be over head and ears in debt to the sutlers." As for guard duty, William noted that "not a few wounds and some deaths have come from men's trying to get by the guards and go into the city for Whisky . . . I am to be on guard tonight; but I hope I shall not be called on to fire at a fellow soldier."[11]

10. Thomas to Sarah, Dec. 24, 1861, Christie papers.
11. William to James, Jan. 9, 1862, Christie papers.

In January 1862, the battery moved to the nearby St. Louis Arsenal, where they received their guns: two twelve-pound Napoleon smoothbores, particularly lethal against massed infantry formations; and four James rifles, six-pound brass guns that had been retooled with rifled bores for greater range and accuracy, especially effective against enemy artillery and fortifications.

For the next two months the First Minnesota Battery continued to train while helping guard the nearby St. Louis Arsenal. They experienced the first episodes of disease and sickness that would follow them throughout the war, causing far more death and disability than Confederate bullets. Seven men died during January and February 1862 and at times as many as twenty-two men were on the sick list.[12]

When the battery was finally ordered to General Grant's army, the men reacted with enthusiasm and relief. Leaving on March 10, they went by steamboat down the Mississippi to Cairo, Illinois, and then up the Tennessee River to an obscure landing on the border of the two states bearing the rivers' names, where they were assigned to Buckland's Brigade of Sherman's Division and sent to camp at a crossroads near a country church called Shiloh Chapel.

While Grant was gathering his newly formed Army of the Tennessee, the men of the First Minnesota Battery spent the last days of March training with their guns and horses.

By early April, Union commanders were aware of increased activity of Confederate cavalry along their front, but they were not anticipating an attack and had not ordered their lines fortified because they felt it might make their new recruits "timid." As often happens in war, comfortable assumptions can be dangerous. Far from retreating, Confederate general Albert Sidney Johnston was steadily gathering troops from throughout the South at Corinth, Mississippi. His army was larger than Grant's command, and he intended to attack the Union Army at Pittsburg Landing and destroy it. This counteroffensive might force northern troops to abandon Tennessee and possibly Kentucky.[13]

12. First Battery Company Morning Reports, Jan. and Feb. 1862, First Minnesota Light Artillery, Reports and Record, MHS.

13. Sherman, *Memoirs*, 1:257.

The First Minnesota Battery was shifted from Sherman's Division to the newly formed Sixth Division on April 4 and posted several miles south of Sherman's troops near an opening in the woodlands along East Corinth Road. The Minnesota battery had been camped with its new command for less than two days when the Confederates attacked early on April 6, 1862.

In the battle that followed the First Minnesota performed exceedingly well. Despite losing Captain Munch and other officers to severe wounds, they withstood repeated Confederate assaults and inflicted heavy casualties on their attackers. Forced to retreat with the rest of the Sixth Division, the battery found itself part of a strong defensive position along a sunken road, known later as the "Hornets' Nest." Here the battery fought from midmorning until late afternoon. During these hours the First Minnesota helped repel attack after attack as the Confederates fought desperately to take this key strong point. The Minnesotans extracted a heavy toll on the southerners but not without costs. As Confederate troops finally flanked and closed in on their position, the battery came under withering rifle fire. Two battery men were killed and many more wounded. Virtually everyone was hit, including Thomas, who was struck by a spent bullet, and William, by flying wood splinters. As the Hornets' Nest position collapsed the First Minnesota, along with other batteries, escaped to a new defensive line along the river bluffs. There they helped repel the final Confederate attacks. Many of the other men of their division were surrounded and captured. The First Minnesota Battery could not have had a more trying baptism by fire than that day at Shiloh.

During the night the Union Army was reinforced and General Grant ordered a counterattack which drove the exhausted Confederate Army from the field. The Minnesotans took no part in the fighting on April 7, but the stand of the Sixth Division in the Hornets' Nest, in which the Minnesota battery had played an important part, gave time for Grant's army to reorganize and was an important factor in the eventual Union victory.

In letters home, the Christie brothers gradually recounted details from the Battle of Shiloh, or Pittsburg Landing. On April 10 Thomas informed the family that both brothers had survived and gave a list of killed and wounded from the battery. Letters from both William and Thomas on April 15 provided many more details, and later letters described the fight in the Hornets' Nest and their brushes with death there. While both would have other close calls, especially during the Atlanta Campaign, no other experience seems to have had quite the impact as those hours in the Hornets'

Nest, one of the Civil War's most ferocious engagements. Years later the brothers would refer to Shiloh almost as a touchstone experience for them. Writing his father nearly two years after the battle, Thomas noted, "I tell the new men not to be too anxious to get into a fight; that before Shiloh we used to talk as they do, but never after!"[14]

After Shiloh, the First Minnesota Battery remained part of the Sixth Division. Because of its heavy losses, new units joined the Sixth Division; among them was the Seventeenth Wisconsin, a regiment that included a number of the Christies' friends and acquaintances from the Clyman area.[15]

General Halleck assumed direct command of all the armies in the Department of the Mississippi, undertaking a slow and careful siege of the Confederate base at nearby Corinth, Mississippi. So careful, in fact, that he allowed General Beauregard to escape with his army and most of its supplies.

The Christies' battery remained on occupation duty at Corinth through the summer and early fall of 1862. Training continued, and wounded men rejoined the unit. In September they were sent out as part of the force trying to trap the Confederates at Iuka, Mississippi.

On October 3 troops defending Corinth received word that a large Confederate force under General Van Dorn was advancing on Corinth. The section of twelve-pound Napoleons from the First Minnesota Artillery, in which Thomas was a cannoneer, was detached from the battery and assigned to a brigade ordered to make contact with the enemy force on the road from Corinth to Chewalla, Tennessee. About three miles outside of Corinth, the brigade found itself confronting a superior force of Confederate infantry and artillery. They were soon forced into a fighting retreat. During this one-sided struggle, the section of guns from the First Minnesota Battery distinguished itself.

In late October General Grant, now commanding the Department of the Tennessee, began an offensive against Confederate forces in northern Mississippi with the objective of eventually capturing the strategic city of Vicksburg. The First Minnesota Battery spent the early weeks of 1863 guarding Grant's communications at Moscow, Tennessee, then moved to Memphis and eventually to winter quarters at Lake Providence, Louisiana, in February.

14. Thomas to James, Mar. 25, 1864, Christie papers.
15. Welcher, *Union Army*, II:233.

At Lake Providence engineers attempted to dig a canal that would allow the navy transports to bypass the Vicksburg fortifications and land troops south of the city. During their two-month stay, the Christies' battery resumed its old training routine but began to suffer more losses due to disease. The Mississippi River was running at an unusually high level, and many levees in Louisiana and Mississippi, which had not been repaired since the war began, broke under the high water and flooded hundreds of miles of lowlands. Under these conditions, Grant could only bide his time, keeping his men busy with largely futile canal projects while waiting for the waters to recede.[16]

The months of relative inactivity at Corinth and Lake Providence allowed William and Thomas more opportunities to write home. While the letters usually related news of the army and camp life, certain themes emerged. Thomas continued his long-distance debate with Sarah about religion, sparked specifically by his sister's concern for his moral welfare. "To tell the truth," he wrote, "our mode of life is not favorable of moral development, and there is a decided antagonism between the feelings that prompt us to direct our shot and shell where they tear off the most heads and limbs, and those teachings that tell us all men are brothers, and should be treated with Christian charity and Kindness." A month later, however, he described a prayer meeting in the camp of the Eighteenth Wisconsin: "It was so romantic and heart-softening, this meeting of Christians in the Louisiana swamp, far, far, from all the advantages of the home worship, that I really enjoyed it much, and will go again tomorrow evening."[17]

Music, and especially singing, seems to have been an important morale booster for the brothers and others in the First Minnesota Battery. Thomas frequently asked for copies of sheet music of both patriotic and religious themes, George Root's "Battle Cry of Freedom" being a particular favorite. He described the men keeping step as they sang the words, "Rally round the flag, boys, Rally once again," and reflected that "these words sound all the more inspiring to me, after hearing them shouted amid the din and smoke of a terrible battle, as at Shiloh." All the group singing in camp lacked, he confessed, was "a female voice or two."[18]

Writing to his father about the loss of comrades from disease, Thomas said that the battlefield deaths "have had a good effect upon the men,

16. Grant, *Personal Memoirs*, I: 458.
17. Thomas to Sarah, Feb. 13 and Mar. 11, 1863, Christie papers.
18. Thomas to Sarah, Feb. 27, 1863, Christie papers.

making them feel kindlier and more brotherly towards each other. We are no longer a mass of discordant elements thrown together and called a Company, but we are now bound together by common bereavements and common danger into one body. The feeling of isolation here in the South, and the dependence upon each other strengthens the bond."[19]

Older brother William continued to see the darker side of military life. "There is much to be learned in the army to take the gloss off from the thing called 'military glory,'" he wrote his father. He then related how army surgeons were helping themselves to food and delicacies sent from the North for wounded soldiers. "Taking these good things for their own use, and actually selling what they cannot eat themselves! And then the farce! They have the audacity to get up meetings and pass votes of thanks to the Sanitary Commission!"[20]

Ever the farmer, even on campaign, William kept up a running commentary on the deficiencies of southern agriculture. Much of this he blamed on the evil of slavery, which he saw as hindering the development of the region.

By mid-April 1863, water levels on the river had fallen far enough to allow Grant's army to begin a circuitous march toward Vicksburg with the goal of surrounding it. The Christie brothers' battery missed much of the fighting in this part of the campaign, but once the actual siege began, the battery was heavily engaged, particularly during the assaults of May 19 and May 22, when Grant tried unsuccessfully to break through Confederate lines. With the First Minnesota Battery firing every day, and most nights as well, the Christies' letters from this period are vivid as they recount the incessant, grinding labor involved in fortifying, firing, and maintaining the guns.

Following the surrender of Vicksburg, on July 4, 1863, the First Minnesota Battery remained in or near the city for nearly nine months as part of the occupation forces. Sixteen months of campaigning had greatly reduced the battery's strength; only fifty-nine enlisted men were fit for duty by July 1863, barely half the original complement. The First Minnesota operated as a four-gun, rather than a six-gun, battery during much of this time.

19. Thomas to James, June 20, 1862, Christie papers.
20. William to James, June 15, 1862, Christie papers.

As the winter of 1863–64 wore on, the men of the battery amused themselves in various ways, some more wholesome than others. A number of the brothers' letters, particularly William's, report the easy availability of liquor—which William hints at as one of his weaknesses—and constant gambling among the soldiers. The brothers also participated in a literary society, organized by soldiers with the help of the Christian Commission, with Thomas as secretary and William as a speaker.

A major issue facing the men of the battery at this time was reenlistment. Most Minnesotans had enlisted for three years, and their terms would expire in 1864. Various incentives, including a thirty-day furlough, were used to entice the veterans to remain in service. A majority of the First Battery in fact did reenlist, allowing the unit to remain together, and when Captain Clayton returned to Vicksburg with seventy recruits in February 1864, the battery was able to operate at full strength. Thomas, now a corporal, spent much of his time training and drilling the new men. The battery's armament changed when the brass Napoleon guns and James rifles were exchanged for the superior wrought-iron Three Inch Ordnance Rifles, known to the men as Rodmans for their resemblance to the cast-iron, heavy-artillery pieces of that name.[21]

The First Minnesota Battery departed Vicksburg on April 4 for Cairo, Illinois, where veterans who had been on furlough rejoined the battery. From Cairo they went up the Tennessee River and then overland to Huntsville, Alabama. There the corps was reorganized again, and the First Minnesota Battery found itself part of the Fourth Division leaving Huntsville on May 25, and, after an arduous march through northern Alabama and Georgia, it joined Sherman's forces at Big Shanty, Georgia. Through June and early July they took part in the hard-fought advance on Atlanta, including major fighting at Kennesaw Mountain and Nickajack Creek. They witnessed the dramatic events of the Battle of Atlanta, particularly the stand of the Iowa Brigade, where their army commander, James McPherson, was killed. After the Confederates abandoned Atlanta and Confederate general Hood took his army toward Tennessee in late September 1864, the First Minnesota Battery was divided; Thomas's section remained in Atlanta while William's pursued Hood's army.

21. Ripley, *Artillery and Ammunition*, 162.

In November the battery reunited in Atlanta and prepared with the rest of the Seventeenth Corps for Sherman's famous March to the Sea. They reached the outer defenses of Savannah on December 10, and after the Confederates abandoned Savannah, the battery celebrated Christmas and New Year's 1865 in the port city.

In January Sherman initiated a campaign to give the Carolinas the same treatment he had given Georgia. On February 16 his men approached Columbia and captured the city the following day. The Minnesota battery was among the first federal troops in the South Carolina capital, firing a salute as the U.S. flag was raised over the capitol building. The city was burned on February 17.[22]

Moving on through South Carolina, the battery captured a large store of Confederate supplies, including many artillery pieces. Among the latter was an English-made Blakely gun that Seventeenth Corps commander General Blair presented to the First Minnesota Battery in recognition of the battery's fine service. (Thomas was ultimately charged with seeing that it be shipped back to Minnesota as a war trophy, which proved frustrating because he wanted to get home quickly once the war ended.[23])

Sherman's forces had marched through South Carolina with very few challenges. In North Carolina, however, Sherman faced the most determined opposition since the Atlanta campaign. Battles at Bentonville and Goldsboro were the last engagements for the First Minnesota Battery. For the Christie family, they were significant. On March 21 William and two others ran into Confederate cavalry while foraging and were captured. Fortunately, he was soon exchanged and went home on leave by April 15, having spent time in the Confederate capital at Richmond. During the Georgia and Carolina campaigns, letters from the Christies were sporadic but a frequent topic was foraging. Thomas particularly seems to have enjoyed the activity, writing detailed accounts of his adventures as a "bummer." The fact that this was a dangerous activity—Confederate cavalry and guerrilla forces often killed Union foragers out of hand as "banditti"—seldom entered into Thomas's accounts. He depicted it as a lark, a grand game of "hide and seek."

22. Welcher, *Union Army*, I:641.

23. On furlough after the end of hostilities, Thomas was able to accompany the gun as far as Baltimore, Maryland, where he left it to the State of Minnesota to ship to St. Paul. The Blakely eventually made it to the St. Paul arsenal, and, according to the battery's first historian, it "is yet in existence somewhere in our state, though badly neglected and used up." *Minnesota in the Civil and Indian Wars*, I:648.

Following the surrender of the Confederate armies, Sherman's forces marched northward through Virginia to Washington, DC, with the First Minnesota Battery arriving in Alexandria, Virginia, on May 19. Many of the veterans who had been on furlough, including the Christies, rejoined the battery while the unit was camped on the Potomac River across from the capitol. There, William and Thomas reunited with their younger brother Alexander, who was serving in the Second Minnesota Infantry, also part of Sherman's forces. He had joined the unit at Fayetteville, North Carolina, just days before William's capture and Thomas's departure on furlough. They had not seen him for nearly four long years.

On May 23 and 24, 1865, the two great Union armies, the Eastern forces under Grant and the Western armies under Sherman, marched through the main thoroughfares of Washington and down Pennsylvania Avenue past the reviewing stand on the White House grounds, a magnificent event stirring to both spectators and participants, according to the Christies' letters. In the weeks following the review, the First Minnesota Battery had spare time and leave, but its members were restless and anxious to return home. Finally, on June 12 they received orders to turn over their horses, guns, and equipment, and they began their journey back to Fort Snelling to be mustered out.[24]

Traveling home by rail through Pittsburgh, Cleveland, Detroit, and Milwaukee, the men boarded a steamboat at Prairie du Chien, Wisconsin, for the final leg of the journey. Along their route, "citizens turned out en masse and gave us the great ovations of their grateful hearts," especially in Winona, which many in the battery called home. Back at Fort Snelling on July 1, the men received their final pay as soldiers and were released from the service of the United States. Thus the First Minnesota Battery ended its career.[25]

The Christies had seen action in some of the major battles of the Civil War in the West: Shiloh, Corinth, Vicksburg, Kennesaw Mountain, and Atlanta. They had followed General Sherman through Georgia and the Carolinas, campaigns that ended any hopes of Confederate victory. They had seen thirty-eight of their comrades die for their country: one officer and seven enlisted men as a result of enemy action and one officer and twenty-nine enlisted men from disease. During the war at least thirty-three more

24. See particularly the letters of Private Albion Otis Gross, one of the men in Thomas's section, manuscript collection P2323, MHS.

25. Henry Hurter, "Narrative of the 1st Battery of Light Artillery," *Minnesota in the Civil and Indian Wars*, I:649.

were discharged for disability, either due to wounds or, more frequently, disease. The Christies wrote about most of these events directly or indirectly.[26]

∽

After returning from the war, William, Thomas, and Alexander set out on a campaign of their own. With their youngest brother, David, the three veterans journeyed by wagon through southern Minnesota and northern Iowa looking for potential homestead sites. During this trip William slowly recovered from his brief ordeal as a prisoner of war. Alexander later stated that William had been "debilitated and in low spirits. The rebels had run him fifteen or twenty miles after capture . . . and his lungs had not yet recovered from the strain." (He also had serious varicose veins in both legs and suffered from rheumatism and piles.) Although the brothers did not acquire any land on this mission, the venture may have provided closure to their war experiences. In later years their letters reminisced fondly about the "expedition."[27]

In December 1865 William married, and the following February he purchased a farm in Olmsted County, Minnesota, near the spot where he had tried to farm before the war. This time he was successful. Upon his death in 1901, the community remembered him as "a man of strictest integrity, a tender father and a kind neighbor."[28]

Thomas Christie also quickly took up a new life after the war. He enrolled at Beloit Preparatory School in 1866 and continued at Beloit College, graduating in 1871 and teaching for a time at the University of Wisconsin and at Beloit College. The religious conversion he experienced during the war did not fade in civilian life, and after marrying the daughter of a Congregationalist minister he entered Andover Seminary.

In 1877 the couple moved overseas to Turkey, where they spent the next sixteen years as missionaries. In 1893 Thomas became president of St. Paul's Institute, a privately funded college in Tarsus, Turkey. Witnessing the Armenian massacres of 1895, 1909, and 1915, during which Thomas and his wife provided refuge and relief to many victims, they returned to

26. Dyer, *Compendium*, 1294–95.

27. Notarized letter of Alexander Christie to Commissioner of Pensions, July 18, 1883, Civil War Pension Applications, William Christie, No. 255203, National Archives, Record Group 15, Washington, DC.

28. William A. Christie to Minnesota Adjutant General in Pension Office, Widow's Pension Claim 787462; *The St. Charles (Winona County) Union*, Sept. 26, 1901.

the United States in 1920. Settling in Pasadena, California, Thomas died in 1921.

The brothers continued their sometimes contentious correspondence while they lived, and their postwar letters reflect the dynamics of their family as well as the history of their times. But their war letters bear particular witness to the conflict that shaped their adopted country and the experiences of one band of Minnesotans in that struggle.[29]

29. For a fascinating examination of the Christies, see Annette Atkins, *We Grew Up Together: Brothers and Sisters in Nineteenth-Century America* (Urbana: University of Illinois Press, 2001), 154–68.

The Collection Story

In the fall of 1959, the Minnesota Historical Society received several boxes of captivating papers from the family of W. L. Stevens, some of it dealing with Stevens's businesses in Mankato but also some particularly interesting letters from the family of Stevens's wife, Sarah Christie. Librarian James Taylor Dunn explored matters further, asking donor George W. Monahan if there were more materials, noting that the society's manuscript curator, Lucile Kane, "will be more than delighted to see" them.

In the realm of manuscript collecting, patience truly is a virtue, if not a necessity. Families usually don't consider what to do with piles of old papers until the immediate owner dies or the boxes and trunks get in the way. In this case, Dunn and Kane waited for nearly six years, but the result of Dunn's simple inquiry was an archivist's dream. In May 1965, the society received a letter from George Monahan's wife, artist Jean Ritchie Monahan, stating that her husband had tried to go through the "trunkfulls" of family papers but had made little progress before his death the previous January. Her children were living in various parts of the country, and she considered the materials to be "more than I am able to handle." The family agreed that the MHS should have the papers, "if you are interested." By early June, Kane had traveled to the little northern Minnesota town of Nisswa to retrieve the papers. What she found confirmed earlier expectations, and she soon reported "About one thousand letters have been unpacked thus far . . . we have already seen data on the Civil War, zinc business in Arkansas, stock raising in Montana, farming in Wisconsin, teaching in Minnesota . . . We have no fears that the collection will be dull!"[1]

1. Jean Ritchie Monahan to MHS, May 12, 1965; Lucile M. Kane to Mrs. G. W. Monahan, June 4, 1965, Acquisition Files, No. 9920, Christie papers.

As sometimes happens with materials from extended networks, when family members learn of the existence of a central collection, especially one that will be well cared for, additions come forth from far-off attics and closets. Such was the case with the Christie papers. As early as 1968, family members were contacting Monahan about additional materials. She, in turn, referred them to the Minnesota Historical Society.

As catalogers worked with the collection and the new accessions to it, they titled it to match the bulk of the materials, which related to the James C. Christie family. By the early 1970s, the primary cataloger involved with the Christie collection was Bonnie Palmquist. Like many of her colleagues, Palmquist took more than a passive attitude toward her work. She recognized the richness of the Christie collection and sought to continue developing it. As Christie relatives came forward with additional materials, she worked with them to identify potential contacts for still more papers. A particularly rich source was the Cyril Nute family of California. Nute's mother was Mary Christie Nute, a daughter of Thomas and Carmelite Christie. Enthusiastic contributors to the project, the Nutes donated a substantial collection of Thomas Christie's papers—enough to justify creating a separate collection. "Cy" Nute in particular took a great interest in the Christie papers, providing many contacts with his branch of the family and promoting the project at family reunions. Eventually, he wrote, "Even tho it may take a while to pick up all of the remaining bits and pieces of the Christie files, every member of the family thoroughly approved of putting all of the papers into your custody."[2]

These acquisitions not only filled in gaps in the existing collection, they greatly expanded the scope of papers, bringing them forward several generations and including the fascinating careers of James's children, most particularly Thomas's activities as a missionary in Turkey.

The letters transcribed here represent selections from the two collections. Boxes one and two of the James C. Christie Papers include a long series of letters received from Thomas and William and written while they served in the First Minnesota Battery. These are supplemented by a series of letters transcribed by Thomas sometime after 1901 and found in the Thomas and Carmelite Christie Papers. Near the end of his missionary career, Thomas began to write reminiscences of his service in the Civil War.

2. Kane to Monahan, June 4, 1965; Bonnie Palmquist to Cyril Nute, Nov. 13, 1975; Cyril Nute to Bonnie Palmquist, Nov. 23, 1975, Acquisition Files, No. 9920, Christie papers.

Apparently he used an extensive group of letters—his own and William's that had been in his father's possession and came to Thomas after James died. At first his memoirs merely quoted from the letters, but eventually he began transcribing them in full. A comparison with the few duplicates from his father's papers indicates that Thomas edited freely, particularly William's letters, which featured a unique system of grammar and punctuation. In his own letters, he seems to have edited out some information deemed extraneous to the war and corrected spelling and syntax. Thomas's transcriptions fit perfectly with the chronology of the letters in James's papers; regardless of his editorial changes, they help carry forward the narrative of the brothers' experiences.

Finally, four letters from William to his brother Alexander, or "Sandy," as the family called him, written between May and July 1861 were in the possession of Louisiana State University. Staff there kindly provided photocopies of the originals to the Minnesota Historical Society: these letters are reproduced here by permission.

1

"A Part in this Great Struggle"
October 21, 1861–March 17, 1862

Thomas Christie to James Christie[1]

Winona, Oct. 21, 1861

My Dear Father:—

Please don't be angry when I tell you that I have enlisted today in 'the McClellan Rifles,' a Company of Sharpshooters for the 3rd Minnesota Regiment. Indeed, my dear father, you know I ought to have gone long ago. Our Country needs my services. I have good health, and am used to 'roughing it.' My brothers are at home, to take care of you and Mother, and the farm. There is therefore no reason why I should not go. Mr. Clayton[2] is to be our Captain, under whom I enlisted an hour ago. He is a man worthy of your confidence and mine. I liked him from the moment I set eyes on him.

The Regiment which we hope our Company is to join is one of the crack regiments of the state. It is now jist about filled up to the maximum strength; and we hope to leave for the front in about a week. Tomorrow our squad of recruits takes boat for old Fort Snelling, the rendezvous of the Regiment.

Please direct a letter to me at the Fort, to tell me that you forgive me for this disobedience; and then I shall try to get a short furlough, and come down to see you all for a day, before I go South.

Now you know, father, that you would enlist if you were in my place. You have taught me to hate Slavery, and to love my Country. I am only carrying

1. Transcribed in Thomas Christie reminiscence.
2. William Z. Clayton, originally from Freeman, Maine, came to Minnesota in 1857 and eventually became commander of the First Minnesota Light Artillery. "Minnesota Biographies," 128–29.

out these principles, in coming now to the help of the Country when she is attacked by a Slaveholders' rebellion.

I shall not deny that motives other than strictly patriotic have had an influence upon me; but I don't think these other motives are *wrong*. I do want to 'see the world,' to get out of the narrow circle in which I have always lived, to 'make a man of myself,' and to have it to say in days to come that *I*, too, had a part in this great struggle. I lay all these workings of my mind frankly before you; it is for you to say if they are wrong. You know, my dear father, that I have never concealed anything from you. Do forgive me, and have Mother forgive me, for acting now in a way to pain you. I feel sure, even as I write, that you will not only give me your blessing—but that you will even be *glad* to have *your* son enrolled among the Defenders of the Union. But whether that be so or not, I must go.

My friends, Southwick[3] and Tilson,[4] have enlisted with me. Please give my best love to all at home. And *do* write me a good letter at once!

Your Affectionate Son,

T. D. Christie[5]

༄

Thomas Christie to James Christie[6]

FORT SNELLING, MINNESOTA THURSDAY, NOV. 7TH 1861.

Dear Father:

How I long for a letter from you. To assure me that I am forgiven! We are now in the service of Uncle Sam. The McClellan Rifles have been transformed into the Second Battery of Minnesota Light Artillery. We were sworn in on the 4th, and are to go South as soon as the Battery in full, which will be, they say, in ten days. Our commander is Captain Roderick,[7] an old Artillerist, and one of the best Drill-Masters in the country.

3. Charles W. Southwick, a native of Massachusetts, listed Minneapolis as his residence at the time of enlistment. *Adjutant General's Report*, 786.

4. Richard O. Tilson, born in New York, resided in Winona in 1861 and was eighteen when he enlisted. *Adjutant General's Report*, 786.

5. Thomas and Carmelite Christie Papers, M542 frame 0029.

6. Transcribed in Thomas Christie reminiscence.

7. No officer by this name appears on any muster rolls for Minnesota regiments nor in the army register. From Thomas's description, the commander in question may be Captain William Hotchkiss, who had served in the Third U.S. Artillery in the Mexican War and soon became commander of the Second Minnesota Battery. *Minnesota in the Civil and Indian Wars*, I:654.

I should have got a furlough and gone down to see you, only there are so many on furlough now that the officers do not want to grant any more till some of the others are expired. Besides, I do not know what sort of welcome I should receive! I do not wish to go down before I receive a letter from you; there will be time, I hope, to see you before the Battery goes south.

Perhaps you wonder at our joining the Artillery in preference to the Infantry. But it is the best branch of the service, with no marching on foot to do. We are getting along first rate and like soldiering very well.

Now do write on receipt of this, and tell us how Sarah got home; and what you think of this step of mine. I feel sure it is just what you would have done in my place.–Your Loving Son, Tom.[8]

ᐁ

Thomas Christie to Alexander Christie

FORT SNELLING, DEC. 6TH, 1861,

Dear Brother.

I have intimated to you so often that "this would be the last letter from the Fort," that I am almost ashamed to put pen to paper again under this post mark. However, you can join us in execrating Adj. Gen Sanborn[9] to whom is to be ascribed our detention here.

We have been ready to start at five minutes notice for the last two weeks, drill 4 hours per day with Knapsacks Haversacks Canteens and Blankets all packed and slung. We are improving in discipline fast and expect soon to begin the Saber Exercise in which the Non Commissioned officers are perfecting themselves.

I wrote you in my last not to send any more letters here, but I have since ascertained that letters with the following address will be forwarded to us anywhere.

_____ First Minn.
Battery, Fort Snelling Minn
Care of Capt Munch.

8. Thomas and Carmelite Christie Papers, M 542 frame 0044.

9. John Benjamin Sanborn served as Minnesota's Adjutant General in 1862. He was appointed colonel of the Fourth Minnesota Infantry in 1862, rising to the rank of brigadier general in 1863 and brevet major general in 1865. He also served in the state legislature. "Minnesota Biographies," 667.

So write on receipt of this and let us know how things are going on in Clyman. I will write the day we start and hope to see some of you at the Station.

We are under marching orders now and all that stops us is the condition of the River. Even as I write I hear a cry of surprise from the Loungers on the north wall and going out I am shown a black hole in the ice where a span of horses and Sleigh have just gone down, the driver barely escaping with his life.[10]

This is the first accident of the kind this winter.

It is getting dark so good Bye for the present.

Thomas D Christie

[postscript] William and I are well, I weigh 152 Lbs. Studying Algebra[11]

Thomas Christie to James Christie[12]

BENTON BARRACKS, ST. LOUIS, MO. SATURDAY, DEC. 21. 1861.

Dear Father,

I seize the first opportunity to write you that we are at length in the Land of Dixie; all well and in good health—as an Irishman would say. We arrived at Chicago on Thursday evening, 19th and took supper at the Massasoit House: then boarded the cars for Mattoon, on the Illinois Central. Here our train was switched off on to the Chicago, Alton, and St. Louis R. R. On Friday 20th (yesterday) morning we were at Belleville, opposite this city. Stayed there till afternoon, when we were ferried across the Mississippi, and marched through to city to our quarters here.

The utmost enthusiasm was shown by the people along the whole route from La Crosse; and when we marched into camp here, tired and dusty from the four miles under Knapsacks, it was very inspiring to hear 25,000 blue-coated men cheering for "the Minnesota Boys !"

Imagine a square of about 200 acres, enclosed all around by wooden barracks for the men; with stables (very similar) behind them for the horses and mules. The inclosed space is used for a drill-ground, and for parades.

10. For a full account of this incident, see "A Team Drowned," *St. Paul Daily Press,* Dec. 7, 1861.

11. Christie papers, M539, roll 1.

12. Transcribed in Thomas Christie reminiscence.

On this some thousands of men are marching to and fro as I write. Imagine all this, and you have Camp Benton[13] before you.

St. Louis is by far the dingiest, blackest city I ever saw. It is always covered by a black cloud of smoke from the countless furnaces and factories, and from the long line of steamers lying at the wharves. They burn soft coal here, and the smell of it is in the air day and night.—It is not likely that we shall see any active service in Missouri, unless the Rebels here are reinforced soon. Everybody thinks the war in this State will be ended in a month. For Sigel[14] has now got Price[15] where he will either have to fight or be taken prisoner; his favorite alternative—running away—being entirely precluded by Sigel's advance on Warrenton.—The Battery has not a man on the sick-list. But we are apparently the only Company here so favored. About 20 men are buried from the Camp each week.—The things you sent by William are just what we wanted. I have now brought for fifty cents a nice portfolio with a package of paper and envelopes, a pen and holder,—a pencil and some brass jewelry being thrown in! Wasn't that a bargain? Will has a traveler's inkstand—so you see we are provided for in the way of stationery. You may expect another letter soon, when I have time to write. Our address now is,

"The First Minnesota Battery,
Capt. Emil Munch,
Camp Benton,
St. Louis,
Mo.

☙

Thomas Christie to Sarah Christie

CAMP BENTON, MO. DEC. 24/61

Dear Sister,

In my present life I have plenty of leisure, as we do not drill any yet untill we get our guns. So more from a feeling of *ennui* than anything else have I been prompted to devote a half hour to the delineation of some part of the scenes of Camplife.

13. Benton Barracks was primarily a training center or "camp of instruction" for Union troops in the western theater. It operated from September 1861 through December 1865.
14. Brigadier General Franz Sigel.
15. Confederate general Sterling Price.

Our Company is quartered for the present in a room about 60 feet, by 30, all around this room are the Bunks for the men, three tiers in hight, formed of uprights, crosspieces joining them together, and boards laid on the crosspieces on these the Bedtick is laid two men sleeping together. William and I are to be Bedfellows after tomorrow.

As I write, a peddler is gathering a crowd around him at one end of the room, by his glowing description of his wares, "So Sheep Shentlemen" and as large a crowd is gathered around his clever imitator who is holding forth in the same style at the other end.

We have all kinds of Characters in our Battery, some of whom I hope to describe to you someday, 3 men have been members of the Legislature,[16] 3 were in the Crimea, 1 served under Lieutenant, now Commodore Dupont, 1 was with Fremont in his first Expedition west of the Rocky Mountains, and 6 or 7 were in the Mexican War. So you see we have thrilling stories told around our Campfire, and more interesting than those related by Novelists Characters.

And here let me remark that I have discovered things to be just as I had imagined them to be. The immense Prairies of Illinois did not appear in the least strange to me, for they looked exactly as I knew they must look. It is so with our military life, I adapt myself to it much more readily than the most of our men do, who have not yet realized that they are no longer independent Citizens but *Soldiers* bound by certain rules and Regulations, and subject to all the privations, fatigues and dangers consequent to a Soldiers life in time of War. A great many of our men—and the Americans especially—cannot leave off those habits of Independence, which are so meritorious in the civilian, but so pernicious in the Soldier. Hence there are daily in our company instances of insubordination and misconduct which, if the laws were executed would be severely punished.

The picture I send you is a pretty correct representation of St. Louis. you can see the City with its brick buildings, it coal Chimneys, and its Courthouse, the finest building of its kind in America. The Levee with its piles of goods and four horse teams. The River with its Steamers and their clouds of smoke, and on the other side, Belleville with its Depots and Railroad trains. It has only the faults—the River is not wide enough and the City not black enough.

16. Three former members of the Minnesota Legislature can be identified from the muster rolls: Emil Munch, Eli Burrows, and Moses Bixler.

Remember that the best Christmas Box you can send us will be a long letter. So A Merry Christmas to you, and to all our friends.

Thomas

∾

William Christie to James Christie[17]

From William, (Jan'y 9.)

You ask if we have seen the new gunboats. No, they are down the river about four miles from here. No one can get out of barracks without a pass; and very few passes are given. Comrades who have seen the boats say they are very good things of their kind, and are furnished with heavy guns, able to batter down the wall of any ordinary fort.—But two weeks ago last Sunday I had a view of General Hunter.[18] He was riding a very ordinary looking horse. The General is about five feet eight inches in height, and of dark complexion. He doesn't look very much like a fire-eater! He was dressed in a dark blue coat; and his hat was a black, low-crowned one, with three fine plumes on it. His epaulets were of fine gold cord and quite prominent. Altogether, he made a fine appearance, and I liked him at first sight. Not only that, I had the honor of speaking to him, and he answered me very civilly. Some of the boys and I were questioning whether we would not be in the way of the cavalry that were manoevoring around us. So, as I was near the General, I asked him respectfully whether he thought the cavalry were going to come our way. He answered very kindly that he thought they would. Now see,—he did not command us to get out of the way, as some officers would have done; he simply advised us. Thus you see he is a gentleman.—Mud, Mud, Mud! Black sticky mud everywhere. Mud up to the ankles the moment you go out of doors; two or three pounds of it sticking to each foot. So you see drill is out of the question, and time hangs heavy on our hands. The papers you forwarded are a godsend. Not only to us two: nearly all our comrades read them, and they are pretty well worn out before they come back to us.—I began the Sword Exercise yesterday: so did Tom. Our Captain instructs us. We have mastered some of the "cuts" so at to give them with force and precision.

17. Transcribed in Thomas Christie reminiscence.

18. Probably General David Hunter, who briefly succeeded the controversial Fremont as commander of the West. Although Hunter was an early favorite of Lincoln's, his subsequent military career, spent mostly in the East, was not particularly distinguished. He presided at the trial of the Lincoln assassination conspirators. *Dictionary of American Biography* 5:400–401.

By what is said around us, we shall have our six guns and our horses in a week or so. There is not much sickness among our boys, although a few have bad colds. I advise them to do as I do,—go hungry occasionally, and rub the chest every morning with a cold wet towel. This keeps me in excellent health. Some of them are spending their money very foolishly, I am sorry to say. I fear that before the next pay-day they will be over head and ears in debt to the sutlers. In the big hospital just outside the gate they say there are sixty deaths every month. They are caused by the change of Climate mostly; and very largely by the imprudence of the men themselves. I must tell you, however, that not a few wounds and some deaths have come from men's trying to get by the guards and go into the city for Whisky. A man of the Third Michigan Cavalry was killed in this way at dusk on Sunday evening. I am to be on guard tonight; but I hope I shall not be called on to fire at a fellow-soldier.

Your aff. Son, William G. Christie

∼

Thomas Christie to Alexander Christie
For Sandy

CAMP BENTON. JAN. 14TH 1862

Dear Brother,

Rejoice with me. I am to be a Cannoneer. You know that each platoon is composed of 25 men including the Sergeant and two Corporals. Of these there are 8 men for Cannoneers to work the gun and the rest are Drivers and Super-nummeraries. We have just been organized, and I am to be one of the gun detachment, the Sergeant says. I believe William is to be a cannoneer also but I am not sure just yet,

Yesterday must have been a very cold day in Wis. And Min. for it was a Sneezer here. For the past two weeks, Mud and Rain have reigned supreme making it almost impossible to go out of doors. But night before last "A Change came o'er the spirit of our Dreams" and we woke up to find that we were almost friz. However the change has been beneficial to us, as is shown in the *decrease* of the number sick with Colds. The warm weather which we have had since we came here has been very injurious to us. We were as healthy a set of men as you could have picked out when we arrived, and now we have 8 men in the Hospital, with Rheumatism, Lung Fever and

Erysepilas,[19] while 12 more are kept in bed here with severe colds and the *Mumps*. Only 45 of us drilled yesterday, the rest being excused on account of inability.[20] We hope this cold weather will continue until the company attains again its Minnesota health, I hope Father got the money which we sent on Thursday. No more from Camp Benton, T. D. Christie

Minn. Battery

∼

William Christie to James Christie

ST. LOUISE ARSENALL MISSOURIE JANUARY 17TH, 1862

Dear Father,

I got your kind letter this day, and now I take this opportunity, Of Aunser you. You will see By the time We have made a change of quarters. We came here last Wedensday, and have got to do guard duty. So they have given muskets, to drill withe. I have not much time to write now and realy don't feel like. you know how a Body will feel sometimes. not capable. of writing or doing anything that requires thought or mental exertion. I will give you a long letter soon. Telling you a great many things. The man I spoke of, was actually shot in the act of runing past the sentry I will send you six dollars in this letter, and explain to you. how I have it.

Jan: 18th I have again taken pen in hand. to give you as true a picture of our Present mode of life. We are living in tents, and it a very good method of living; the tents are pitched inside the walls of the Arsenel under some very hansome trees. down from us, towards the river are the buildings where they have machinery for repairing arms of all kinds: they make nothing new: only cartridges, and sabots[21] for shot and shell: filling shell making Balls: for muskets. they allso make grape, and cannister shot; they make 100,000. muskets Balls per day. so one of the men told me. and I beleive it. for you should see them sitting round there Baths of molten lead casting twenty each time. one man can make 18:000 per day of 12 hours. I will now

19. Erysipelas is an acute form of cellulitis, often caused by a staph infection. *On-line Medical Dictionary,* http://medical-dictionary.com/ (accessed February 2008).

20. According to the battery's morning reports, five men were reported sick on January 1, 1862, but by the end of the month more than thirty were on the sick list and seven had died of disease. First Battery Company Morning Reports, Jan. 1862.

21. A short wooden cylinder to which artillery shells were attached and which provided contact between the shell and the charge, insuring proper alignment of the shell in the barrel. Gibbon, *Artillerist's Manual,* 302–3.

tell you how I have the money you will find enclosed in this letter I sent you a very little to much, in the first Place. so when I got into the tent. we all concluded to have a sheet Iron stove that with the pipe and three wash dishes cost us fortfive cents each; nine of us. well I had no change, so I tried to Borrow some money, but could not get less than ten Dollars. So you see my credit is good. Tom and I has got us a Book entitled Field Artillery Instruction[22] in I should be first. it cost $2, so I will have 7 to send home to you, you may think my writing looks nervous, but if you had to do as I do you would look so to. Thinking by what you say in your letter to me, I will answer you by saying that I am not giving way to any of my Passions, any more than I did at home. I may be bad myself but I could not happy if I was the means of making any of a certain class of beings worse than they are or should be but I am thankful for your good advice: And believe me I will think of all these things, you have been so kind to mention We have had one Death in the company the Person was germain he died of Asthma yesterday he will be buried today.[23] We have quite a number on the sick list but very few of them are serious cases: There are a few caces of Mumps, one or two of lung fever the last mentioned are serious one of measels, as for the Balance of the company, they are well since we came here we have to do guard duty. it takes 23 men each day to mount guard; out of our Body of men: I have not been intoo any of the work shops yet only where they cast Balls, but I will try to get in, and then I will write at greater length have Sarah write to me

your loving son W.G.C.

∾

William Christie to Alexander Christie

ST. LOUIS ARSENAL JANUARY 22/62

Dear Brother.

I received your letter yesterday and am very happy to learn you are all well, and likely to remain so. give me every facility to know why they do not let us out to the city and I will tell you. But I suppose: it is because there would be to much trouble with unruly men. You want to know who puts us through our sword exercise: well our captain does some times: And

22. Probably *Instructions for Field Artillery*.
23. Mathias Wechsler. First Battery Company Morning Reports, Jan. 1862.

Corporal Hanks:[24] does a good deal of it of his own accord since we came here we have not drilled much of any kind on account of having so much guard duty to do. We will get rid of a great deal of that now for their has come two installments: of five hundred troops; which are to remain here they are Missouiri home guards: the fifth rigment they have been in the service six months and has got no pay yet. so you see Uncle Sam is better than Aunt Missouir any day. In my last letter to you I told you some things about the Place. I can now tell some more, for I have had better opportunity to look around. They have a building here where they have a gauge to gauge the shot after they are passed through that operation. thay are wheeled out to a building and painted, with a brush by hand. the shell are served in the same way: the smaller ones are immersed [. . .] hot [. . .] they glaze over nicely. they are rolled over on to Bars to dry. I stood guard over 4 members of sesseia at Presen[t] members of Uncle Sam's guard house, at the Arsenal. They are well fed and have as good a place to stay as our own troops: But they are a dirty set of good for nothing set of fellows. Lousey Lank, light men: Falstaff might have made the same remark about them he made about Justice Shallow: they look like forked radish an so it is there were two of them got released yesterday.[25] if they should turn Traitor to there country again, they will be able to tell a good deal about this place to the enemy.

I cannot give you much account of the men that were with Fremont. Although I have seen a good many: some of them. Also a great many that were at the Battle of Lexington. But you have read as much of those then as I can tell you. Now for the weather, and then I will let this long foolish letter come to an end for you see I have not much to say. I am sorry to here that you were froze [. . .] but use is every thing. We have had an Ir[i]sh winter, ask father and he will tell you and save me some trouble in not writing it. Ah Now when I think of it there are a lot of the men taken with the mumps new hands; one or two more have got the measles: but as a general thing they are getting along very well. there is one more thing I have not told you before. our head Bugler has deserted.[26] he left after he got his pay.

24. N. K. Hanks of Minneapolis, originally from Vermont. *Adjutant General's Report,* 783.

25. ". . . when a' was naked, he was, for all the world, like a forked radish, with a head fantastically carved upon it with a knife." William Shakespeare, *Henry IV: Part II,* 3.2.

26. Henry Rippe. *Minnesota in the Civil and Indian Wars,* I:652; First Battery Company Monthly Report, Jan. 1862.

he was dissatisfied with his pay: he did not get as much as he expected so he having got the letters to put in Post office (that being his duty assigned him by the Captain) he forgot to come back again. he has gone to Germany our Officers think. I had a drill today with the sword. the motions were first draw sabre sec. come to guard. 3'd right moulinet (Prounounced moulinea) 4th then left, then rear ditto, 5th right cut against [. . .] then the reverse, reare cut then these all combined: which being in right left and quarte and tierce cut. I cannot give you an account of all the motions fa it would not be Possible to give you a correct idea of the thing in such a space so having nothing to say to more than I want you to tell Sarreh to write me a letter, to me. so that I can write to her in r[e]turn. Thomas says he will write when the spirit moves him he's so laizey he cant Bother himself just now. he had a letter from Willie he is not gong to answer it he says. I told him I always answer it Sarah said to him that Hellen[27] was going to write to him, but she has not done it. I had a letter from Micheal Dempsey[28] yesterday. I answered him. If you see Jessie Amiers[29] tell her to write to me for I have sent her two letters, to Emmet Postoffice, so I will expect a letter from her soon. give my love to all.

tell Grand mother Bertie[30] I will certainly write to her soon.

good bye

William G. Christie

∽

Thomas Christie to James Christie[31]

SAVANNAH, TENN., MARCH17. 1862;

Dear Father,

As you are no doubt anxious to hear from us I write to say we are in good health, and enjoying ourselves as well as is possible in our circumstances. We left Saint Louis a week ago today, in the evening and came swiftly down to Cairo. I looked with great interest at the Cape Girardeau bluff, near which there is always fighting going on. At Cairo the Ohio comes into the Mississippi. There we saw some of the gunboats, and a big supply-boat,

27. Helen Reid, a cousin.
28. The Dempsey family were neighbors of the Christies in Wisconsin.
29. A cousin, and William's future sister-in-law.
30. Janet Bertie, née Smith, James Christie's mother.
31. Transcribed in Thomas Christie reminiscence.

between which and the gunboats a fiery little tug with young naval officers on board was continually going and coming. The Ohio was in flood. As we came up we saw some houses being carried down. The woods on the Kentucky shore were full of water. A whole family was perched on the roof of their house, waiting for boats to come and take them off. Be thankful you don't live in that country! We passed Paducah in the night; and on Thursday reached Fort Henry.[32] Here we went ashore to stretch our legs, for our steamer is terribly crowded. (I pity our poor horses, that have not got off yet.) I saw the big Rebel gun that burst, killing and wounding a lot of their own men; and the one that was dismounted by one of our shells. It was thrown clear back, crushing two men in its fall. The whole work, inside and out, is torn and marked by the missiles that rained so fiercely upon it. It is a wonder that a single man was left alive.—The Tennessee is a dark, sinister-looking stream. Its current is swifter, even that that of the other two rivers. Dark thick woods come down to the water's edge. Our pilot has to steer carefully to dodge the floating trees. The river is simply full of steamers coming and going. Here at Savannah there are nearly twenty tied up to the bank: most of them are loaded with troops. The playing of the bands, the shouts of the men, the shrieks of the steam whistles, and the loud playing of a "Calliope"—a musical (?) instrument that goes by steam—, fill our ears continually. This is the biggest picnic I ever saw! Only, we all feel there is serious work ahead. We have been talking with our friends from Saint Charles in Birge's regiment of sharpshooters.[33] They are in camp here. How we envy them! For they helped to take Fort Donelson.[34] They told us how they lay behind stumps and fallen trees and picked off the rebel gunners. I must confess it was not with unmixed pleasure that I heard these stories, for I am a gunner myself!

This is all I have time to write now. I don't know when it will go, as we hear no letters are allowed to leave this region. Do not worry if you don't hear from us often; the fact is, our season for letter-writing is over for the present. Our military life is just now beginning. The enemy is within 16 miles of us in force; we may be engaged with him any day now. But troops are rapidly concentrating here; and we have good hopes that the road will soon be open to Memphis at least, if not to New Orleans. In the meantime,

32. Captured by Grant's Army of the Tennessee on February 6, 1862.

33. Birge's Western Sharpshooters, assigned to the Fourth Brigade, Second Division (Charles F. Smith): see Welcher, *Union Army*, II:292, 575.

34. Fort Donelson fell to Grant's forces on February 16, 1862.

please do not borrow trouble on our account. Both of us have a sure faith that we shall come through all right. You will hear of us in the newspapers soon. We have not disembarked as yet, and expect to go further up tonight. Direct all letters to the Saint Louis Arsenal, and they will be sent after us.

    Yours aff'ly,

    T. D. Christie

2

"The Bullets Came like Hail"
March 22–August 15, 1862

Thomas Christie to James Christie[1]

CAMP MINNESOTA, AT SHILOH CHURCH, 3 MILES S. W. OF PITTSBURG
LANDING, TENNESSEE, SATURDAY, MCH.22.1862.

Well, here we are, in camp at last! You should have seen how glad both men and horses were to get off that old steamer! Some of the horses could scarcely use their legs at first. The landing is on the west bank of the river, 9 miles above Savannah, and not far from the Mississippi line. This is a very small place, made up of two or three log houses. A fight took place there a few weeks ago; and we saw the bodies of some of the men killed. They had been very hastily buried in a shallow grave, and the heavy rains had washed away the earth from above them. Poor fellows! It was a grewsome sight, and made a man stop and think. I don't wonder the rebels tried to defend the landing; for the bank is higher than any where else: it is a good place for a battery.

We reached the Landing on Tuesday the 18th, but did not get ashore till the next day. We had to cut a road for our guns up the steep bluff; and then cut down bushes and small trees on the top to make a place for the battery and the baggage etc. A big fleet of steamers lined the bank for a mile or so. We moved out here day before yesterday: have been setting up tents, policing camp, and getting settled, ever since. We are close to the little log church, just this side and to the right of it as you come out from the river on the Corinth road. There are woods all around, with an occasional clearing.

---

1. Transcribed in Thomas Christie reminiscence.

We belong to Sherman's Division, Buckland's Brigade.[2] Right in front of the Battery are the tents of three infantry regiments, Ohio men. A part of the Fifth Ohio Cavalry also belongs to the Brigade. Ours is the most advanced brigade in Tennessee. Our cavalry went out today foraging, and brought in thirty bales of cotton, three prisoners, and a quantity of grain. I wrote you at Savannah, but carried the letter for some days in my pocket before there was a chance to post it. Have patience with us if your mail from here comes somewhat irregularly for a time. Nothing has come to us, either, since we left the Arsenal. Our officers tell us we leave this camp soon for a forward movement. They have standing orders to keep us ready to start at an hour's notice. There is much bowel trouble among the men, owing to the bad water and bad food. Hard tack and raw salt pork have been our diet now for two weeks. Don't you envy the boys who wear the eagled button? Today, a party of us armed with revolvers went out into the woods and brought in six fine specimens of the Southern pig. These run perfectly wild, and are scarcely seen by their owners till the day when these latter go out, gun in hand, to provide meat for their families. The animals are nearly all of such leanness that a knot must be tied in their tails to keep them from going through a fence; but their meat is simply delicious; it tastes like game—which indeed it is. The boys had quite a feast when we came in. We are having pretty cool weather for this latitude; but the grass is green, and the woods are full of your Northern songsters resting here on their way toward you. I wish I could send a message by one of them!

A slower mail goes out tomorrow or the next day . . .

∽

Thomas Christie to James Christie

APR. IOTH. 1862

FIELD OF BATTLE, PITTSBURG.

Dear Father,

Knowing how anxious you will be to hear from us, I take the first chance I have had, to write. Well, in the first place (to your mind) Wm. and I are both well although both of us were hit. He by a ball glancing off a limb was

2. This assignment was temporary: on March 26 the battery was assigned to the Second Brigade of the new Sixth Division under General Benjamin M. Prentiss. Welcher, *Union Army*, II:231.

struck on the calf of his leg. The ball tore his pants and left a black scar. I was touched on my right arm, the bullet left a scar which pains me yet. Our list of Casualties is a follows

Killed, + R. O. Tillson[3]

. . . . . . + O. J. Taxdal[4]

Wounded . . . . Capt. Munch

. . . . + Lieut. Peebles.

. . . . + Sergt. Clayton

. . . . + Sergt. Connor

. . . . + Corp. Davis.

. . . . + J. Johnson.

. . . . G. Lammars.

. . . . H. Blood.

Those marked with + are from my Section of two guns, which were in the heaviest of the fight on Sunday. As you know the Rebels surprised us in our Camp, and the first of our fight was just outside of our tents. All our Baggage was taken and we are without a change of shirts. But that is nothing, we whipped them, and are only anxious to advance and help clean them out utterly. We know nothing of the details of the Battle, and hear all kinds of Rumors. Please save carefully all the Newspaper accounts of the Battle. I saw Gen. Hardee's[5] body, and got some lace from his sleeve.

All the descriptions of Battle Scenes I ever read fall short of what I have *seen* since Sunday morning.

The 16th and 18th Wisconsin suffered pretty severely.[6] Charley Visgar of the 16th is wounded in the head.

No letters yet, and they say that our letters will not be allowed to go away. However, I have done my duty in writing No more at present.

T. D. Christie

3. Richard O. Tilson. See page 26, note 3, Thomas to James, Oct. 21, 1861.

4. Ole J. Taxdahl, age thirty-three, a native of Norway. *Adjutant General's Report,* 787.

5. A case of mistaken identity: Confederate general William J. Hardee, present at Shiloh, was not killed there. He died in 1873. Wakelyn, *Biographical Dictionary of the Confederacy,* 216.

6. The Sixteenth Wisconsin had some of the heaviest casualties at Shiloh: 40 killed, 188 wounded, 26 missing. Fox, *Regimental Losses,* 428.

William Christie to James Christie[7]

CAMP ON THE FIELD OF SHILOH, APRIL 15, 1862

My Dear Father,

I suppose you have heard of the great battle on the 6th and 7th of this month. You will be proud to know that we were in the front of the battle, and that our Battery did its duty nobly and well. On Sunday morning very early the enemy drove in our pickets. At 7 o'clock we were ordered to the front. Nobody thought that it was anything more than a skirmish; we supposed that soon we should be back again in camp. We had marched only about 10 minutes when we were ordered to get into battery, "action front." We did so as soon as possible for the enemy were with[in] 20 rods of us. Just at this moment one of our men belonging to the right section was fatally shot as he was turning his team. The bullets were pouring upon us like a hail storm. Just as soon as we got our guns into position we began to give them our compliments with shell and canister. But we had not been there long when the regiments that were supporting us broke and fled; the[y] had suffered terribly in a few minutes. So we had to get out of that place as fast as we could. Stinson[8] was killed as we came into battery. Our captain was severely wounded in the thigh.[9] His horse was killed; T. D. helped him to mount another. Another man was shot through the ankle (died of the wound.) and many other were hit by the bullets. We limbered-up and fell back a short distance; unlimbered again, and poured the canister into them. Lieut. Pfaender[10] was then in command; he acted with the greatest skill and courage. Having fallen back half a mile through the camp of the 16th Wis., we had a little rest. But soon we were posted in a new position. While we were waiting for orders here the shot and shell from the rebel guns fell all around us, but without doing us much harm. At about 10 o'clock we were again ordered forward and took our position in front of the 25th Missouri, 12th Mich., and other regiments, or fragments of regiments, from

7. Transcribed in Thomas Christie reminiscence.

8. Colby Stinson, age twenty-two, a native of Maine and resident of Minneapolis. *Adjutant General's Report*, 786; Minnesota Light Artillery, First Battery, Muster Rolls, MHS.

9. Captain Munch never fully recovered from this wound. He returned to active duty for a few months but poor health compelled him to resign his post. For most of 1863 and 1864, he served as a captain in the Invalid Corps, finally returning to active duty as major in the First Minnesota Heavy Artillery in 1865. Munch papers.

10. William Pfaender. *Minnesota in the Civil and Indian Wars*, I:650.

our Division. when I say "we," I mean our left section.[11] The right section
was a little distance to our right, with the 8th, 12th and 14th Iowa. Our Center Section had been disabled and was ordered back to the Landing. Our 4
guns were all right; we got a high compliment from gen Prentiss;[12] he said
he was—"proud of the Minn. Battery." I tell you we raked down the rebels
to some purpose; you would have thought so if you had seen the ground
there after the battle. After some hours of this work and the repulse of several attacks, the enemy evidently saw that our guns were few in number.
(I am speaking now of our own section, the left)—; they crept up through
the heavy brush and timber, and suddenly poured upon us a terrible fire.
Ten of our horses were instantly killed. Of the men, No. 3 on our gun and
No. 1 on the howitzer were shot dead. Lieut. Peebles[13] was shot through
the throat; Sergeant Clayton in the thigh; Sergeant Conner[14] in the side; Joe
Johnson,[15] an old friend of mine in Minn., was shot through arm and
shoulder. Our two slain heroes, Taxdahl and Tilson, fell with their faces to
the foe. The balls flew fast and furious, Both my horses were killed while I
was holding them. Not a horse belonging to the other gun was left alive.
In the two gun— detachments every man but one was hit. T. D. got a rap
on the arm with a heavy bullet that passed between his arm and his body;
I had a still more severe contusion, on the calf of my left leg; if it had not
been for the tree top that I stood in (the tree had been felled by the infantry
that lay behind us), I would have got a serious wound. The infantry shouted
to us to fall back, and then they poured in their fire and heaped the ground
with rebel dead and wounded. I cannot tell you how everything went on
around us; but we saved our guns, losing only our limbers; but even these
we found the next day, after Beauregard was driven from the field. We left

11. Like many batteries, the First Minnesota was divided into three two-gun sections.
These were referred to as "left," "center," and "right." The Christies' "left" section con-
sisted of two twelve-pound, smooth-bore guns, either Model 1841 howitzers or the Model
1857 "Napoleon" howitzer which became a standard field piece. The other sections were
"James rifles," six-pound bronze cannons that had been rebored as rifled guns. James
Morgan, "The Most Common Field Pieces of the Civil War," *Camp Chase Gazette* 23.7.

12. Benjamin Mayberry Prentiss. The First Minnesota Battery had originally been
assigned to Sherman's Second Division, but on Saturday, April 5, they were attached to
Prentiss's newly formed Sixth Division and shifted their camp the night before the battle
began. See "Reports of Lieut. William Pfaender," *Minnesota in the Civil and Indian Wars*,
II:91.

13. Ferdinand E. Peebles. *Minnesota in the Civil and Indian Wars*, I:650.

14. Jesse Conner. *Minnesota in the Civil and Indian Wars*, I:650.

15. Joseph Johnson enlisted from Olmsted County. *Adjutant General's Report*, 785.

our limbers because all the horses were killed; and when Gen. Prentiss ordered us back, we had to fasten the trails of the guns to the rear of the caissons, and so drew them back towards the Landing. Col. Webster showed us a place for our four guns and one from the Center Section on the bluff near the left of his line of artillery. There were some guns there heavier than ours; also some 13-inch Mortars. The two gun-boats in the river also helped us to drive the rebels back that evening. We were greatly cheered by hearing that Buell had come up and that he would let us rest on the morrow. The fight was kept up until dark. Beauregard occupied our camp-ground, sure of victory in the morning; in fact he told his men that they would water their horses in the Tennessee after only two hours of fighting next day. He was so sure of victory that he did not destroy any of our tents; but his men despoiled us of everything else, clothing, letter-paper, etc.; in fact everything that they could carry away, thus leaving us nothing but the clothes we had on. On the next day we found many of their dead with three pair of pantaloons on. Nearly 20,000 of our men were killed, wounded or taken prisoner; we think the rebels lost even more than that. What I have written is only a small part of what I saw; and that was very little in comparison with the whole. We faught a winning fight on Monday, from daylight in the morning till about half past two in the afternoon, when they left the whole battlefield to us.

I will close by saying that I more fully appreciate the blessing of life after my many narrow escapes on Sunday.

Thomas Christie to James Christie[16]

CAMP ON THE FIELD OF SHILOH, APRIL 15, 1862

My Dear Father,

Your conjecture as to the cause of our silence for so long after leaving St. Louis was correct. Our letters were detained at Cairo by military authority; at least that is the impression among the Troops here. I wrote you immediately on arriving at Savannah, and it seems you had not yet received the letter when you wrote on the 26th of March. Your letter received to day were most welcome. The contrast between "snow two feet deep" and our semi-tropical scenery here is indeed great; how much greater is the

16. Transcribed in Thomas Christie reminiscence.

difference between the works of man in the two regions! Looking from your door you see nothing but the fruits of peaceful labor, herds of cattle, and now I suppose, fields smiling with the springing grain. We behold here a very different scene. Great trees torn by cannon shot, smaller ones cut clean in two, old muskets, pieces of harness, torn clothes spattered with blood, canteens with bullet-holes through them, and all the other debris of a great battle. The air is already loaded with the stench from unburied horses and half-buried men. This is nothing, however, compared with what I witnessed during and just after the battle. Somehow, it did not shock me as much as one would expect. You yourself will be shocked to learn that even in sight of the long lines of dead men laid out for burial I ate my supper with almost as much relish as if I had been at home. But as W. has described the battle I shall not repeat. Of all my losses I deplore the most that of my diary and note-book. I had kept the former very carefully written-up ever since leaving home to go to Minn. It was full of descriptions of scenes and incidents which I did not send in letters. And now some rebel mess are enjoying themselves over it! It makes me "madder than a setting-hen."

Please in your next letter give us some account of how the war stands; we know less of it than the citizens of St. Petersburg. It is useless to send us newspapers, for no care is taken of anything except letters. In order to write this letter I have had to borrow paper, ink, pen, envelope, and postage-stamp. You see correspondence at this end is not without its difficulties. Our Division, the Sixth, is now commanded by Gen. McKean;[17] address your letters accordingly. The 17th Wisconsin have just come, and are at the Landing . . .

∼

Thomas Christie to James Christie[18]

CAMP NEAR SHILOH, APRIL 26, 1862

My Dear Father,

Letters are once more sent back and forth with some regularity. But how long this will continue no one can tell, as we have now begun the advance on Corinth. The Battery moved camp yesterday two miles to the South; so

17. Thomas Jefferson McKean took over command of the Sixth Division after Prentiss was captured at Shiloh. Warner, *Generals in Blue*, 301, 385–86.

18. Transcribed in Thomas Christie reminiscence.

that we are now 5 miles from Pittsburg and about fourteen from Corinth. Our health is pretty good; but on account of the hardships we have passed through we are not quite so robust as when we left the Arsenal. I think not a man in the Battery has lost less than 10 pounds in weight since we came here; some have lost a great deal more than that.

Let me give you now a few details omitted in W's letter about the battle. When we first went out to meet the enemy we were in high spirits, for we [heard nothing] of the fact that they had completely surprised us and were advancing on us with their whole army. We supposed we were to take part in a little skirmish at the outposts. But we had marched only about sixty rods when the bullets began to "zip" "zip" past our heads in lively fashion; just then we saw a poor fellow lying behind a tree weltering in his blood. After holding the enemy in check beside a little field[19] for a quarter of an hour we were ordered to retreat; this was necessary, for we had no supports. We went back about half a mile, and after a rest the Battery was divided, our right section taking up a position farther to the right, our Center section going to the Landing on account of its guns being disabled, and our section taking position about the center of our whole line of battle.[20] It was not long before the enemy made his appearance on a little hill, or ridge just opposite. At first we thought they were our own men, for they were much hidden by the bushes and trees. Soon however, we found out who they were, and our guns immediately opened upon them with such effect as to make them disappear over the hill. This was repeated three times at somewhat long intervals, without our Infantry (that lay in a sunken road behind us) firing a shot. The fourth time the enemy came around on our right in a bushy ravine,[21] and were within 2 rods of us before we saw them. Then the bullets came like hail. We fired two rounds of canister in their very teeth, when nearly all of our men fell around the guns. The ball that passed through poor Taxdahl's breast threw the rags from his blouse right into my face. I was bent over at the time to the left delivering a cartridge, or

19. This is probably the Spain Field. See Minnesota Light Artillery, First Battery, Muster Rolls and Historical Data. This small collection contains a map of the Shiloh battlefield published by the Shiloh National Military Park Commission in 1900 and annotated by Thomas Christie in 1912 to describe the positions held by the battery on the first day of the battle. The First Minnesota is identified as "Munch" on the map.

20. This line was the Hornets' Nest according to the map mentioned above; the battery was on East Corinth Road at the southwest corner of Duncan Field.

21. A branch of Tilghman Creek ran through Duncan Field to the right of the battery's position.

it would have killed me. I started immediately for another round, and while near the limber-chest a heavy ball struck my right arm, benumbing it so that I thought it was shot through. The Infantry close by were cocking their guns and calling to me to come inside. At two bounds I cleared their line and sat down behind a small tree, out with my handkerchief and off with my blouse. I soon found that my hurt although painful was but slight. I got up and looked at our guns; not a cannoneer was there; all were away with the wounded. Our infantry were holding the rebels at bay by continuous volleys from their rifles. When the combat lulled a little we got our guns inside the lines and with the help of the Infantry gave the enemy another round or two. Then under orders from Gen. Prentiss we dragged the guns back to the caissons, to which we fastened them and brought them down to the bluff over-looking the Landing where they were put in position again, and as W. has told you took an effective part in the repulse of the enemy late in the afternoon. I did not accompany the guns, for I thought that W. had been killed; and crawled back again through the Infantry line to the front to find his body. There was poor Taxdahl lying on his back, stone-dead; Tilson's body had been carried away; there were our dead horses literally heaped upon one another; but greatly to my joy, W. was not there.

No more room on this sheet and no more time at present . . .

Thomas Christie to James Christie[22]

LINES BEFORE CORINTH, MAY 13TH, 1862.

Dear Father,

We are within four miles of Corinth, in the advance so we sleep beside our guns fully dressed and equipped; The guns are unlimbered and ready for immediate action; they stand behind a breast work made of bushes and earth, which we threw up last night. Yesterday we heard for the first time the trains running and the engines whistling on the rebel rail-road. Their pickets are being driven in every day; so they must evacuate, or give battle very soon—if indeed they have not already done the former.

You are, I think, mistaken in your opinion that if Buell had not come up that night at the Landing we should have been lost. It seems to be the general impression throughout the north that Buell's army saved Grant's.

22. Transcribed in Thomas Christie reminiscence.

Now I do not wish to underrate the importance of his very timely aid. Still I think that too much is claimed for him, as you will see from these facts. In the first place, our position that evening was far better than any we had occupied during the day. Wallace's Division had just come up; our lines were shorter and therefore more compact. Again, the enemy would have had to advance over ground commanded by the gunboats, and by batteries placed where they overlooked the whole country. So I know we would have given them a tremendous reception the next day, if Buell had *not* come up. still, it was a great relief to our feelings that evening, when we saw his strong battalions crossing the river and marching up the hill to our support.

You ask me abut my feelings in action. They were very much mixed; but I can say without boasting that they never interferred with the doing of my duty,—which was to get solid shot shell, and canister to the gun as fast as they were required. This was very hard work, for nos. 5 and 6 who should have assisted me were absent; the former skulked, not being very well, poor fellow; and the latter was badly wounded early in the day. No. 5's case was the only exception that I saw to the universally good conduct of our men. Tillson[23] was shot through the head while gallantly sponging his piece preparatory to loading; Taxdahl[24] was shot through the body just as he began to serve the vent; although mortally wounded, *he finished his duty,* then staggered back and fell dead. I was close behind him when he was hit, so close that the rags torn away from the back of his blouse by the ball flew in my face; I was leaning over to the left at the time delivering a cartridge to no. 2 or the ball would have killed me also. When Stimson[25] fell, some of the men were going to carry him to the rear; "boys" he said, "nevermind me, stand to your posts like men!" and there he died.

Our battery has been reduced to four guns on account of our losses at Shiloh and the large number who are sick. We get a gill of whiskey of the best quality every day. I tried it for a day or two, but finding that I did better without it I dropped it and shall have nothing more to do with it. Brother William and I enjoy better health than any other two men in the Battery. So much for temperance!

. . .

⌒

23. Richard O. Tilson. See page 26, note 3, Thomas to James, Oct. 21, 1861.
24. Ole J. Taxdahl. See page 41, note 4, Thomas to James, Apr. 10. 1862.
25. Colby Stinson. See page 42, note 8, William to James, Apr. 15, 1862.

William Christie to Alexander Christie

MAY THE 31 1862

CAMP NEAR CORINTH MISSISSIPPI

Dear Brother

I received your letter yesterday and am happy to know you are all well: The most Important news: I hope to send is that Corinth was evacuated yesterday in the morning. By the last of the troops who have kept us so long here where we are where they have gone to is only a matter of conjecture to us every one I have heard or seen of our troops says they would have liked to have whipped out the rogues here: so that the matter should have been ended here, and not have caused us to hunt them up as it is now likely we will have to do, Before they left they Blew up some of there powder magazines and destroyed; a great quantity of molasses and sugar: also a good Deal of other commissary stores, besides the Railroad Depot, for the past few days we had been harrassing and Driving in there Pickets and had got Possesion of a rising Piece of ground, and so the latter end of the army had to leave sooner than they would have done: It is now quite evident that they have not Been intending to give us Battle here: and they have been working night and day to get every thing off frome this Place: ever since they found out we had an intention to invest it. I verily beleive that all our leaders are just as much taken aback as we are: I would except Pope[26] from this statement, Who has been wanting to attack Corinth long ago: and I don't know a man in the whole army that aint sorry we did not give them a try a least two weeks ago; It is realy to Bad to think we have been lying here this, we cant say how many days before wooden guns, and almost empty Breast works; for it is said Beauregard has gone this six or eight days at least; some say to Virginia: and some saz towards the junction or Jackson; Perhaps Best as it is. Now in connnection I would state to you that it must be only some 4 or five days since I was Impressed or rather had it written to me that we would find Corinth was not a very hard thing to take. Sandy if I was not so skeptray I beleive I would be a great deal happier than I am: tis a fact. I am one of the most skepting and unbeleving fellows you or any one else ever

26. Major General John Pope, commander of the Army of the Mississippi, part of Henry Wager Halleck's forces attacking Corinth. At this stage of his career he enjoyed a reputation as an aggressive and successful commander. *Dictionary of American Biography*, 8:76.

saw: Beating the unbeleiveing Thomas all out. I have but Poor skill at drawing or I would give a slight sketch of our Positiion on the Battle of Shiloh,
or Pittsburgh landing. Now I believe I could do so But don't like to try. you
are right there is favoritism in regard to the accounts given in the Papers:
about the conduct of several Batteries; you don't hear I presume that Water-
houses Battery[27] lost two howitzers that they never got Back, also taylors
Batery[28] lost some of there Pieces; But they fought well. I have known
doubt, But they had not the right kind of stuff behind them: they were
Backed by Ohio troops and we were Backed by Sour Krout and lager Beer
from Missourie[29] or it is possible we would have lost our guns, seeing our
horses were shot down But the horses of some Batteryes had the traces
cut so you may judge for your self: Tom is writing to sarrah he will enclose
it in this envelop I am sure she must be happier than she used to Be: Tell
her from me to go and keep the new reading of the new leaf: and she will
gain in every respect Beauty of mind and Body; I am sorry for Poor Henry
Fraber[30] and hope he will soone be well:

There is no use of me making comments on the new aspect of afairs in
regard to our next movement as a part of this army for before you are likely
to get this letter you will see more than I can tell you: in the Papers: I cant
say a word at Present for I have heard none can say what they thought and
my own thoughts are not worth anything. the Pay master has not round yet
with the Bawbees: But he be here soon if he could only keep sobered so they
say. the water call has just blown and I must go and water my horses good
By of the Present your loving Brother,

William G. Christie[31]

ᕁ

27. Captain Allen C. Waterhouse, Battery E, First Illinois Light Artillery. Welcher,
Union Army, II:282.

28. Probably Captain Ezra Taylor, who commanded Battery B, First Illinois Light
Artillery. Welcher, *Union Army*, II:229.

29. This could have been the Eighteenth, Twenty-first, or Twenty-fifth Missouri, all
of which were in Prentiss's division at Shiloh. Welcher, *Union Army*, II:231.

30. The Febers were the Christies' neighbors in Wisconsin. Henry would have been
about twelve years old. U.S. Census (1860), Clyman Township, Dodge County, Wisconsin.

31. Thomas C. Christie and Family Papers, P1281, Box 2. Original at Louisiana State
University.

William Christie to James Christie[32]

CAMP NEAR CORINTH, JUNE 15TH 1862

Dear Father,

Here we lie idle and apparently useless, having done nothing except to move here close to Corinth since our bloodless victory sixteen (16) days ago. I have less hopes now than I had two weeks ago of seeing you this year. The great army that the rebel leaders had gathered here is now dispersed to the four winds,—that is, if we can trust the reports which we hear. Rumor says that 30,000 of them have gone to Charleston. It may be so. Our teams have just got back from the river, and bring the news that Memphis is ours. They say also that McClellan has been badly beaten near Richmond. I hope it is not so; but I fear that it is, for I have never thought that he is the right man for the place he is in. But if he has been defeated it will be good for us in the end; God will make it work so. It will cause less and less of clinging to slavery, that sum of all Villainies. Our rulers have kept back their hand from the plough; and what they reap must be full of cockle and tares. We soldiers are tired of seeing them handle slavery as tenderly and carefully as if it were eggs in danger of breakage. This has been the cause of more than anything else of prolonging the war, and of brining innumerable troubles upon us.

There is much to be learned in the army to take the gloss off from the thing called "Military Glory." If every thing that we know here, for example, were known at the North, I am sure our people would rise in their might to drive many of our surgeons out of the hospitals. Some of these men do us more harm than the enemy. They are careless in the operations they perform and in their attentions to the sick; and they feed themselves and their friends on the delicacies sent down for hospital use. It is too bad to think of such things; to think of the poor wounded fellows far from home and kind friends, to think of their throbbing fevered brows and their weary hearts; to think also of the generous people all over the land sending their loved ones everything to make them comfortable;—and then to think of these wicked selfish doctors taking all these good things for their own use, and actually selling what they cannot eat themselves! And then, what a farce! They have the audacity to get up meetings and pass votes of thanks to the Sanitary Commission! Is it always the case that Villainy is so much bolder than Virtue?

32. Transcribed in Thomas Christie reminiscence.

Our men are gaining in physical health every day. We have a daily drill, and twice have had battalion-drill, of the five batteries that belong to our Division. It is gratifying to us to know that we have done as well on these occasion as any of the five. The weather is so very dry that after one or two evolutions you cannot see the man on the next horse, so thick is the dust. So we go galloping over the great cotton-field from this side to that side; the mounted officers shouting their commands,—until after a couple of hours we come out very grimy-looking fellows.

The peaches in the orchards around Corinth will soon be ripe, and there is an abundance of them this seems to be an excellent climate for the peach. But the curse of war is everywhere visible, and so is the curse of Slavery. Under free institutions the resources of this country could be developed wonderfully. Although warm, this is a very healthful region; plenty of good water can be obtained by boring for it. Some of the springs taste of sulphur, and some of iron, but not to an unpleasant degree. Some parts of the country are covered by magnificent forests; but we have yet to see the first saw-mill of any kind. In the matter of education,—there are some large seminaries in Corinth, but no common schools. Education down here is for the aristocracy alone. Indeed, this whole country in every department of life needs the revising breath of freedom.

T. D. is out at present pitching quoits;[33] he is very expert at the game, and keeps in excellent health, although very thin. Some of our boys have left us for the hospital at St. Louis; among them is corporal Frye,[34] our gunner. He showed great courage at the battle of Shiloh; but during the advance on this place his horse fell upon him, and both horse and man, being very heavy, he was seriously ruptured; he will probably never come back to us: Others have left on account of general debility. Our present gunner, who is also acting Sergeant, is used up by rheumatism, so that he has to go on crutches. Still, on the whole, our men are improving in health . . .[35]

33. Horseshoes: apparently a popular game with the First Minnesota Battery. As artillerymen, they would have had no problem acquiring the necessary equipment.

34. Sylvester Frye, a native of Massachusetts, enlisted from Winona. Frye's injuries seem to have led to his eventual discharge for disability in October 1862. *Adjutant General's Report,* 783.

35. The Company Morning Report for this date shows thirty-two men and three officers sick, a drop from forty-five and three earlier in the month. One hundred thirty-three men were available for duty. First Battery Company Morning Reports, June 1862.

Thomas Christie to James Christie[36]

CORINTH, JUNE 20TH, 1862

My Dear Father,

You must think much of this letter, for it is written amid difficulties. I am sitting on the bare ground, with knees drawn up, and a rough board placed upon them. Bent over the board, I am scribbling away for dear life, so as to get through before drill-call. Please try this posture the next time you write. I think Napoleon wrote his war dispatches in some such fashion, for they are models of brevity and pith.

The best of our non-commissioned officers, Corporal Hanks,[37] died yesterday morning after a long illness. It seems to be a fatality with us that we are continually losing our very best men. Corporals Hoppin,[38] Davis,[39] and Hanks are all gone from among us; men whose personal character was above reproach, while their efficiency as officers makes their loss to the battery well-nigh irreparable. We all turned out last evening for the funeral. The body was placed in a rough coffin, and 12 men from his own platoon bore it to the grave. The rest of us following two by two. On arriving at the spot where the grave had been dug under a large white-oak, the coffin was set down, and the men with heads uncovered formed around it. Then the orderly Sergeant made a short but excellent address that brought tears to every eye. There was something so sad in our comrade's dying alone so far from home and loved ones, to be buried in these nameless woods,—while the mighty march of events passes on and over his forgotten grave. To a man without belief in immortality a fate like this seems to terrible to think about. But when we remember that Corporal Hanks gave up his life for the benefit of all future humanity, that he is even now entered into his reward, free from the toils and pains of a corruptible body,—all grief for *him* disappears; we simply feel a deep regret over the loss of his companionship. Farewell dear comrade! Thou art far happier now than we.

At the close of the address the coffin was carefully lowered into the grave; this was quickly filled up; and a simple board was placed at the head with

36. Transcribed in Thomas Christie reminiscence.

37. Norman K. Hanks, born in Vermont, enlisted in the battery from Minneapolis. *Adjutant General's Report*, 783; First Battery Company Morning Reports, June 1862.

38. Henry C. Hoppin, originally from Rhode Island, died at St. Louis on January 30, 1862. *Adjutant General's Report*, 783.

39. C. S. Davis died of wounds received at Shiloh, April 27, 1867. *Adjutant General's Report*, 783.

his name neatly printed upon it. Then we all marched around the grave and back to camp.

These deaths have had a good effect upon the men, making them feel kinder and more brotherly towards each other. We are no longer a mass of discordant elements thrown together and called a Company, with no fellow-feelings for any one outside of our own platoons—as was the case at Fort Snelling and the Arsenal—, but we are now bound together by common bereavements and common dangers into one body. The feeling of isolation here in the South, and of dependence upon each other strengthens the bond. As a consequence we are today stronger and more efficient as a Battery than when our Morning-Report gave a hundred and fifty-six (156) men as fit for duty; the number now is 80. When the orderly Sergeant addressed us last night as "Brothers" the word went straight to our hearts, for we felt that it represented the Truth.

The people of this region are now carrying on their pursuits as in the days of peace; they have found out that we came not to make war on civilians and women, as had been represented to them by their newspapers and political leaders. All whom I have heard talk express surprise at the good usage which they have received. They say that their own soldiers acted very differently, taking whatever they wanted without ever saying "by your leave." The restraint in this respect to which we are subjected[40] is very distasteful to some of the men; they sometimes run the risk of arrest to dig a few new potatoes at night. The most of us, however, disapprove of jayhawking as a means of putting down the Rebellion, and so we scrupulously refrain from touching anything belonging to a citizen. I have picked up several pieces of newspapers in the Secesh camp; the strange lies which they tell to the people in order to arouse their anger against us convince me more than ever that their cause is an unrighteous one; any cause that needs to be bolstered up in this way is a bad one. However, there must come a strong reaction when this people discover the falsity of the ideas that have been imposed upon them by the leaders of this causeless rebellion . . .

40. For example, see General Orders Number 33, issued by General Sherman to the Fifth Division, article seven of which states, "As a rule all private property of citizens must be respected, but if forage or feed be needed, and the parties are unwilling to sell at fair prices, the division or brigade quartermaster and commissaries may take and account for as though for purchase. They will give the owner a receipt for the amount taken." U.S. War Department, *War of the Rebellion*, Series I, 10.2:270.

Thomas Christie to James Christie[41]

CORINTH, JUNE 26, 1862

My Dear Father,

We had news this morning about our wounded. The Captain is recovering fast, and will rejoin us in a few weeks. Lieut. Peebles is at Kankakee Ind.,[42] at the home of Judge Wilcox, an old College friend; the Judge took him out of the hospital. The bullet, weighing over an ounce, has been extracted from the left side of his head, under the ear, having passed through the right cheek and the mouth, knocking out several teeth, and cutting his tongue. A newspapers states that he was very low, and great fears were entertained for his recovery.[43] The Lieut. and his section have received the highest praise from Ind. journals for their conduct bearing on the field of Shiloh. Sergeant Clayton has completely recovered from his wound, (a rifle-ball in the left thigh), and has gone to St. Paul to report for duty; so we may expect him soon. Joseph Johnston is in St. Louis, having returned from his home to the hospital there; he will not come back to us.[44] The ball that wounded him struck his right arm, and owing to his position at the time, went up lengthwise through the biseps, then over his shoulder under the skin, and ripped along way down his back. This ball had tremendous force because it was fired from a distance of only 20 yards. I saw the rifleman at the time; he was dressed in butternut, and stood partly behind a tree; if I had had my old rifle with me, I think there would have been an end to him and poor Johnston would have escaped. But there we were in an open road, with not a single skirmisher beside us—— and the rebel sharpshooters popping away at us from behind trees and logs!

Sergeant Connor[45] is in St. Louis slowly recovering, and will soon be able to go home on furlough. He received a dangerous wound in the side from

41. Transcribed in Thomas Christie reminiscence.

42. Thomas probably confused Indiana for Illinois here. On the enlistment record, Peebles listed Illinois as his place of birth. *Adjutant General's Report*, 783.

43. Peebles resigned his commission on August 18, 1862. He eventually recovered and gained a commission as a lieutenant colonel of the Forty-seventh U.S. Colored Infantry Regiment. *Adjutant General's Report*, 783. National Park Service, "Soldiers and Sailors System."

44. Johnson would be discharged for disability on October 15, 1862. *Adjutant General's Report*, 785.

45. Jesse Conner, born in New York, enlisted from Winona. He returned to the battery and served for the duration of the war. *Minnesota in the Civil and Indian Wars*, I:783.

a two-ounce ball. The ball was taken out from near his spine. He has been in bed for nearly three months and has barely escaped with his life.

George Lammers died in the hospital sometime ago;[46] his ancle having been broken by a heavy bullet; he was badly neglected by our surgeons. Another of our men has been lost to us by unskillful surgery. Corporal Davis[47] had his leg amputated twice for a wound in the ancle, and the second time killed him. Such bad work would not be tolerated in any other service; it has cost our country a large number of valuable lives. Many of the army surgeons are young men just out of the Medical Colleges; who not having any practice at home, are put in here by friends and political influence. They are not fit to take into their keeping the lives and health of our soldiers. We have not been accustomed to the life that we are now living, and so are liable to contract almost every variety of disease; these, and many kinds of wounds on the battle-field, require the very best medical knowledge and skill to be found in the whole country. In amputations especially these young doctors are unfortunate; and yet many of them are ready to cut off an arm or a leg even for slight wounds. We think some of them do it just for practice. In one case I know of a leg which was saved by its owner's threat to shoot the doctor as soon as he got well. These are some of the reasons why so many of our sick men prefer to stay in camp with us rather than go to the hated hospital—unless it is in St. Louis. Not only this; in many cases the comforts and luxuries furnished to the hospitals by the U. S. Sanitary Commission and private charity are taken for their own use by wicked doctors and nurses; particularly do the wines and jellies usually go in this way. This is true at least of our Division-hospital; it is reported to be the case also by soldiers of other Divisions, as respects their hospitals. May the Lord keep me from falling into the hands of these surgeons—if the half be true that our sick men report! I think however that there is no present danger of such a contingency. We have discovered that idleness and dirt are the two chief causes of sickness in our camps. So I have resolved not to let Esculapius get hold of me by any neglect in respect of those two things. All the washing and mending for William and myself is done by me; ask him if it is not done satisfactorily. As to exercise, quoits and base-ball fill up every leisure moment I have; for among so many men there is never any difficulty in finding partners for a game. Quoits is our favorite,

46. George C. Lammers was born in Germany and enlisted in the battery from Taylors Falls, MN. He died of his wounds on May 21, 1862. *Adjutant General's Report,* 785.

47. See Thomas to James, June 20, 1862 (page 53, note 39).

being excellent for developing the muscles of the arm and expanding the
chest. There is another young fellow and myself who have beaten our best
players again and again. I bathe Twice a week at least, thus avoiding the
danger of keeping "body-guards," as we call them; some of our men are
fairly covered with them;—reason, personal uncleanliness.

You guessed aright as to the work of our Division this summer; we are
to be here in Garrison. We are well enough satisfied with this, if they don't
keep us at the business too long. Strong fortifications are going up; this
place is evidently to be made a military post with a permanent garrison. I
hope we shall be excused from making a part of it. Please send us some
postage stamps . . .

∾

William Christie to Alexander Christie

CORINTH JULY 2ND 1862

Dear Brother.

I have been waiting for a letter from you or some one else up that way,
for the last three days; But no espistle has come yet, so I will [. . .] go on
and write to you, as Best I can, on the meagre news of camp life, In the
first Place I wil let you know how we are That is Tom . and I, we are Both
in excelent health at Present; always on hand for what may 'turn up' as
Micawber;[48] use to say; and let me tell you there was nearly a matter of great
Importance turning up since the last day of the past month, and it may
turn up yet for aught we know to the contrary. There has an order come
from Washinton, for tuentifive thousand troops, and we were ordered to be
in readiness to march to Pittsburgh landing, thence to Evansville by Boat;
thence to Pittsburgh, Penn: and so through to Virgina: the veritable Tom
says he heard that the reason we were not on our way by this time was own-
ing : to the Boats that was going to take us down the River had struck on a
sand bar; and that soon as they can get smaller boats to come up, to the
landing; we will have to get up and dust: I hope it is so, for I would like to
see the country; as we journeyed along and to tread the soil of the "mother
of Presidents," yes, I would like to see some of the F.F.V of Virginia; and
knock at the door of Richmond, paying my respect to Jeff Davis and company, through old rake em' down that, (Being the Poical [poetical?] name I

---

48. A character in Charles Dickens's novel *David Copperfield*.

gave our Piece before the Battle of Shiloh, Now it may be we will not leave this place, at all, but if we do you will be duly notified of the Important event, as soon as the slow mail will carry the news to you. We have very hot weather just now yesterday we had a very liberal amount of rain, which has a very good effect on the corn that is Planted here. A Butternut[49] of the name of Williams close by our camp says this is a very Poor season owing to the cold nights; he says that cotton is not the Principle crop here. (this is not his manner of expression) But when it is grown; it gives a right smart yeild of cotton; his Boys says that Corinth is a right smart of a business Place before the war Broke out. doing a heep of tradin there Dialect is a strange mixture of Bad grammer, and Poor English; Do not wonder at it for the school is not heard of for these People; and they talk just like the Negro, (Nigger I should here said) There are lots of Dogs just similar to Dragon— in the Build and nature— and it is very easy gussing what they were used for. Just think of it: aint it horrid to thin of it—Dogs for hunting men and women: and then we have men in our midst; yes in our mess; that would just like to have things just as they were They say they would not have listed if they thought they were going to fight for the, "Nigger," well they are Professed Christians; at that: and some of them are fairly Robbing Uncle Sam, for they have a great dread of doing duty and rather than do so Play off sick, all the time one I could name has been in the hospital, and in trying to get home on the sick list took a stick and walked lame with the rehumetis but he did not get the furlough, and after he got off the Boat, he threw his stick away and walked as well as any Body could: he has not done any duty since he came Bach to camp. but two or three days and since he has been in the Doctores hands but he don't take the medicine, and whines all the time you have one sample of a soldier; Now since I have got to gossipping I will give you a few of the incidents that have been transpiring since pay day some here spent every cent of there four months pay, and have saved nothing: others have saved there money, and one man of the name of Francis Fleming,[50] has lost $110, on the day we were out on muster, for our Pay he has not got it yet and never will. Our cook lost $45 while gambling, he took

49. A nickname for Missourians, noting the color of their homespun clothing dyed with the bark of the butternut tree, and also for Confederate soldiers or sympathizers. See Mathews, *Dictionary of Americanisms,* I:232.

50. Corporal Francis B. Flemming enlisted from Taylors Falls. The loss of his pay must have been disheartening, for he deserted on July 3, 1862. *Adjutant General's Report,* 783.

out his Purse to get some change and laid down his money, and the man he was Playing with got it, so it goes. I have every reason to Believe the money Tom and I have Posted has got home safe: seventyfive Dollars in all, after Paying up our mutual debts we have very little to spend. But we only need little seeing we are Pretty well fed by our Uncles Sam, and Abe if we only Pay for the cooking of it; Tis true we buy Butter sometimes, and cheese; also a fish at times, white fish, we Pick heeps of Berrys. There Being right smart of Bushes; in the woods of Miss: I drink no Cofee; I Bought some excelent Tea; I paid fifty cents for four ounces, and have some of it yet, after using it neer day for the last ten or twelve days, and twice sometimes, I have sold about sixty cents worth of coffee— so you see I will make one do for the other; The fourth will be here in a couple of days, and with you als, it is not very likely we will have anything different from the usual routine of the soldiers life, Now I want you to give us a very vivid discription of what you see on that day in the Place of which you Patronise with your Presence. In your letters To Tom and I lately you have never said a word about Sarah's school or how she gets along: Now I want you to give us your Idea: of her progress and abillity: General Pope I see has got the command over Fremont,[51] Now I don't think that the Present or the Past has been made very agreeable for Fremont in his cappacity as a commander of an army, there has been some reason for crippling him, in every respect and I believe he is as good as any they could get in the army of the Cabinet. Cornel Sill of Mitchels Division[52] or rather army; has been forced to retire from Jasper to Stevenson, and the Mobile and Ohio R. R. I find out that our Boys has got the worst of before Charleston South Carlina, and Miss camp Rumor say that we have got the worst of it before Richmond. Now this last I do not see in the Cincinatty Gazzette; I bought a Pair of them for a quarter rather than pay fifteen cents for one. I had to go over to the Infantry Camp to get them so I left one with the Boys. the other I Brought to camp. Papers are dear you see it is dated the [. . .] of June:

I was over at the seventeenth Wis last night and had Jim Dempsey play some tunes on the flute. the Whole Divison is going to move, if any of us

51. On June 26, 1862, General John Pope was given command of the newly formed "Army of Virginia," superseding both Generals Fremont and Banks. Welcher, *Union Army*, I:297–98.

52. Colonel Joshua W. Sill, commander of the Ninth Brigade, part of the Third Division under General Ormsby M. Mitchel. These units were part of General Don Carlos Buell's Army of the Ohio, which was operating in northern Alabama and Tennessee. Welcher, *Union Army*, II:200–201.

go so we will be along together: They are all in very good health except Robert Mac Annulty; he is troubled with Phitisis I beleive. I was telling him he should try hard to get a sick furlough home; and then he might be Better Now you must be sure to write a long letter to me or Tom, giving us your Batiocanstions of thought and your conclusions, in regard to every thing in connection with this war. I am happy to see your character Developing so well, and macking so much of the already; I hope David is keeping pace with you in the same Direction: and that you will Bothe be wise thirfty and industrious: acquiring knowledge at school or out of school books. also aquiring a thorough knowledge of yourselves, threreby getting the key to all human nature: Sandy you must not think I mean to lecture you; But I have learned by experience that the Best way is to learn to know yourself and then you can govern your Passional nature so easy Now I must not try to make you beleive I have got to that Point, not by any means; I only wish I had. but my want if that is the reason I have for urging you to acquire that Power of which I speak of Give my love to all and write soon Directing as usual. When you write let me know what is going on at Ennissons. A few ago I wrote a letter to Uncle David, Tom writing Part of it, I hope you are all in good health as we are. What are they doing at Uncle Williams and how does the crop look. all round the country give us all items of every kind: having no more to say I will close by signing myself your loving, Brother William G. Christie

∾

Thomas Christie to James Christie

CORINTH, JULY 4. 1862.

Dear Father,

I have put off writing to you for several days in hopes of recieving a letter from some of the family to answer. I do not understand the reason of your long silence: we have got nothing from home for 10 days and begin to think something is wrong in that quarter. However, we hope to get a letter tonight and I will keep this open untill that time.

We have had a celebration here today that has convinced the citizens at least that we have not forgotten the Birthday of our Nation. The Batteries of our Division fired a National Salute of 34 guns at noon amid the cheers of the assembled Infantry. After this, our piece which had a Hotchkiss shell in it, put in on the evening of the 7th April, was discharged at a white oak

30 inches through and distant 100 yrds. The shell passed into the heart of the tree and there burst, driving the forward half through and about 50 yrds beyond, and leaving the base in the tree, it was a most splendid shot and showed the tremendous force and precision of this kind of projectile. The Hotchkiss shell is used exclusively for rifled 6 p'd'rs and weighs 12 pounds, being cylindrical for half its length and conical the other half. A heavy charge of powder fills a tube running the whole length of its interior and at the upper end this tube is capped with a large percussion cap. The hole in the upper end of the Shell is stopped by a large screw whose lower end nearly touches the percussion cap, a small piece of paper only intervening. To prepare the shell for firing this paper is taken out and the screw screwed tightly down. It will then explode the moment its motion is checked, by the throwing forward of the tube on to the screw. It is crated with lead to prevent the rifles of the gun from being hurt by contact with the iron, there is also an arrangement by which the lead is forced into the grooves at the moment of explosion.[53]

JULY 5

Your letter to William of the 30th Ult. came to hand this evening, and on account of its excusable brevity we expect another soon. I am glad to hear of the Clover cutting, it reminds me more vividly and pleasingly of Home than any other thing you could have mentioned. Do you have as heavy a swath this year as we had last? I don't believe, you have, but hope there will be better success in curing it than attended our efforts last June. There must be a great demand for wool to run it up to such a good price. I expect that the vast manufactures of woolen goods for the army has something to do with it. "It is an ill wind that blows nobody good." you know

Clayton arrived here this afternoon looking fresh and ruddy as Minnesota winter faces, the ball has not been extracted from his leg but gives him no trouble. Gov. Ramsey came down with him to visit the Minnesota troops here. He is in Corinth now and will come up to see us in the morning. I will give the details of his visit in my next which will be in answer to the first epistle I get from Clyman. Clayton brings a great deal of news from our State which are interesting to us I assure you.

The weather here is extremely hot and dry compelling us to keep in the shade, (or take a Siesta) between the hours of 10 and 4 and to haul our

53. A good description of this projectile. For a more technical explanation with drawings, see Gibbon, *Artillerist's Manual,* 125.

water 2 miles in barrels. The ground is baked like marble and the roads are 10 inches deep in dust. The sky blazes through the day like red hot brass, but the nights are *beautiful*. the moon shines with a brilliancey and softness of lustre which I never saw equalled in the North. I see nothing of the Southern Cross yet though I expected to find it this far south. I begin now to think that this Constellation is seen only in the Tropics. I am detailed to take care of the sick in our hospital tonight and so must stop writing at present.

JULY 7

This letter has been delayed by one of those accidents peculiar to this war. We got orders yesterday morning at daylight to be ready to move out of camp at 6, prepared for Action. Accordingly each one of us took 1 days ration in haversack and a blanket, and at the time appointed we were led out to a position 4 miles southwest of camp commanding a long bridge over the Tuscuhmbia creek.

We now learned that a body of the enemy's Cavalry had been encountered at Ripley, about 5 miles out, and they were expected to advance by this road. Our Battery was masked with bushes and we lay in wait all day but no Butternuts appeared. Towards night an expedition, consisting of 5 companies of the Iowa 11th, 3 or 4 Co.'s of the 11th Ill's Cav. and the 2 howitzers of our Battery passed out to beat them up. Gen. Todd went out with it. Our 2 rifled pieces remained in position untill this morning when we were relieved by a section of the 5th Ohio and returned to Camp. We have since learned that the expedition went out 9 miles last night and bivouacked, having seen nothing of the enemy.

2 or our company deserted a few days ago taking with them 2 horses and saddles and about 50 dollars that did not belong to them.[54]

Hoping that this will find you in as good health as it leaves us with, I remain, Yours.

T. D. Christie

54. Probably Corporal Francis B. Flemming and Private Russell Pease. See *Adjutant General's Report*, 783, 784.

Thomas Christie to Alexander Christie

CORINTH MISS. JULY 10. 1862.

My Dear Brother.

Yours of the 2d Inst. I read with pleasure some days ago but postponed answering because I had written home the same day and William wrote to Sarah the next.

I am glad to see the improvement in your handwriting and composition and hope you will apply yourself diligently to the study and practice of the former accomplishment, for I have found out that it is a most important part of Education and more needed in practical life than many other branches to which more importance is attached in the Schools. My own development in this respect has been retarded by my present mode of life, which leaves no time or opportunity for practice and necessitates hurry in letter-writing, for it will not do to hang over a sheet of paper for 2 or 3 hours when my duties call me elswhere, and in the way I am living now my hands are full from morning till night. This is the reason why I have not, (to say the least) improved any in this respect since I joined the Army. However, I think you can read my scrawl well enough; and that will have to do untill the war is over.

I will expect a good description of your doings on the 4th by the next Mail and also of your adventures at the River when they take place. I should think that there would be more game up your way this Summer than usual, owing to the absence of the most of the hunting population and the consequent application of the rest to the work of the Community. The game is plenty enough down here, if we only had permission to hunt the Camp would never be out of meat of some kind. I have seen Possum, turkey and any quantity of Squirrel and Woodcock, quail and partridge. there are also plenty of deer and Raccoon in the neighborhood.

I am becoming quite savage and chivalrous in my appearance lately, having become the possessor of an excellent rifled pistol and regular Missuss. Bowie knife with edge like a razor and silver mounted horn hilt. This knife was found in a haversack lying in the woods near the Rail Road by one of our Mess of whom I purchased it for a quarter. On account of this ridiculously low price and my friendship for the man, I regard it more as a gift than a purchase. The pistol I paid 1.50 for and consider myself very lucky in getting it at that price, for while we were coming down the Mississippi there was considerable practice at floating wood and crows on the Sand bars, and I made some very good shots with this same pistol which is of Allen and Wheelocks make, and carries a ball about the size of Buckshot.[55] I hope to take these things home with me together with a beautiful little powder horn that I picked up at Shiloh from beside a dead Rebel Rifleman whose flintlock rifle[56] was grasped in his hand even in death, this horn had been used for priming with being entirely too small for loading purposes.

Our 2 howitzers returned from their Expedition day before yesterday after remaining at a small village named Kossuth about 10 miles out for a night and a day. Nothing was seen of the Rebel Cavalry although plenty of Rebels in Calico were met with who would reiterate vehemantly the Southern cry "We will never be conqured." Well, Well, we will see about that. I notice that they have no objection to our money however, never failing to ask the very highest price for anything we want to buy, such as potatoes or milk. The old man from whose well we get our drinking water is becoming softened a great deal by our good treatment of him. He is a type of a large class of Southern men. Men who have only become Rebels by the immense pressure of opinion around them and who only need good treatment and forbearance shown towards them to bring them back to their allegiance. The difference between the Southern soldiers and our men in moral character, Mr. Williams says, has convinced him of the righteousness of our Cause and our eventual triumph. We get along firstrate with him now and, seeing that we have almost worn out his Bucket and rope by continual hauling, we took up a subscription yesterday and raised money enough to buy a new rig for him. The well is of the kind generally seen around here, bored very deep and having a long tin bucket on a rope that runs over a pulley and from thence is wound round a windlass. The water is impregnated with sulphur and iron to a great extent as is the case with all the water in the vicinnity.

We are expecting the Governor here today and consequently have had a good deal of policeing to do round Camp to make things look smart. He has been to see the other Minn troops first as we were out of Camp. Let me hear again from you soon. T. D. Christie

55. Allen and Wheelock manufactured a single-action, forty-four-caliber percussion six-shooter. Relatively few of these were purchased by the Federal Army; Thomas's pistol may have been picked up at Shiloh. Edwards, *Civil War Guns*, 282.

56. Although the Confederate Ordnance Department eventually proved surprisingly effective at providing modern arms for its army, early in the war many units were supplied with outdated weapons from state arsenals or older firearms supplied by the men themselves. McPherson, *Battle Cry*, 318.

[margin note] Save some Buckwheat cakes hot till I come home and tell Father to buy another cow before the time. Oh, yes I'd be green beyond measure to think that they miss me at home.

❧

William Christie to Alexander Christie

CORINTH, JULY THE 11TH 1862

Dear Brother.

I have not got a letter from you for a long time, but I am going to write to you because I feel like it: For the last few days we have been having fine showers of rain to lay the mud, which was very deep and very dry: so dry that a man could not see a great ways ahead of him: when drilling. Our sergeant got Back to the Battery a few days ago he is now acting as orderly in Place of bogswell:[57] sick. We had quite a fine speach from governor Ramsey[58] this morning. he said he came this way by request of the Peoples of Min. to see after the wellfare of the troops from the state: he complimented us highly for our Bravery at the Battle of shiloh: and told us the Honor of the state of Minn. was in our hands: And he new we would keep it bright and unternished with many other fine things. he also informed us he had made arrangements for the carreige of sick and wounded soldiers from St. Louis, to St. Paul. clear of charge, which is a very good thing. he has been to all the rigments and companies: and will leave us for Washington soon; I have been having some talk with one of the residents here, about farming and stock raising: he admittes that the farming here is not as it should be, he says that one mule is used with a small place and that the average depth of plowing is three inches; There method is to Break the land after girdling the timber and cutting the brush: and then they plant the corn: next year to cotton next ditto: and so on for about five years, with light plowing: still lighter plowing is then done; and the lords of the soil sow wheat, and expect a crop: aint they foolish! There are several strong redoubts being built in this Nebourhood to be used in case of need, There has been several reports here in regard to McLellan and his army before Richmond; they say one day

57. No one by this name is listed in the muster rolls of the First Minnesota Battery.
58. Governor Alexander Ramsey had been visiting Minnesota troops in the western theater—men in hospitals as well as units in the field—since mid-June and sending back regular reports, often published in local papers. See, for example, *St. Paul Daily Press*, July 6, 1862.

that he is victorious: then the reverse is going the rounds Then we hear that we are going east, and then we are going to stay here. Miss rumor again says. that there is going to be a Battle here, But this is a fact Our commanding officer has been ; requested to make out a requisition for (Ponchos) for the company. (Blankets India rubberd is meant) by that word:) Also for clothing, and one of our Boys says, the Blacksmith told him that he heard the Doctor say that we were actualy going East, so it may be so, We had a thunder storm last night an today the sky is over cast: with great Black chunks of cloud, and the weather is cooler than it has been for the Past week. I just now thikn of it Govr Ramsey, told us he has every reason to think that the war will be actually ended in a month only it is likely we will have to keep an army of Occupation untill such times as Peace is fully restored; I hope it may be so: for I would not care, how soon I could shake hands; with the whole of the connction; not that we live so Poorly or anything of that kind but because there is know Place: like home and faces like home faces When we get your letter; giving us a discription of the fourth of July celebration in the city of Clyman, I will be much disapointed if the Prizes are not nearly all awarded to our boys, and sir if that Hunt is not Productive of something to Bake or to Boil; I shall cut your aquantance, for a whole week or more: so yu see you will wish you had been careful if you have not been.

In looking over What I have written I find I have not said a word about the stock that is raised here. Well sir you must; or will know; that hogs and Negres: are the Principle, kinds of stock raised here in this country; Mr Williams says he raised six thousand Pounds of Pork one year ago last fall. And he says there are some men that nearly treble that so you see that they must use an awfull amount of hog: and they look like it, I think, you must know by this time that the male Population is nearly all gone and there are any amount of grass widows, Black and white round here. and the young niggers are very numerous, I assure you Williams says that there has been a great many niggers raised here and sent or sold I should say, south. Tom tells me there is a very curious epetaph on a board at the head of a rebels grave, in this vicinity. It is cut out in the Board, Itruns or rymes in this fashion.

Condensed by Tom.

He was mortaly wounded defending this soil

At the Bloody Battle of Shiloh

And this grave the only reward of his toil

Will not be molested I know.

his Brother

so you have a sample of southern poetry and now while my hand is in I will give you the titles that are on the tents: that the 2nd Ill Battery Picked up, that used to belong to secesh: One Bears the emponeous name of the Tigers Den, another The Mississippi snags, one the Indicative and suges-tive title of Burgalers home: next comes the Lazy mans house of refuge. then Loafers retreat: one was named the Devils Den and had six of the chief names of Tophets Lords on the wall by the door But the whole has been Painted over. so they cannot be read, one is called the soldiers home, sev-eral more has had the names painted over. and they are all like the above or worse, if any thing, I wish you were here to tell me what to write, I am glad that Father has Paid up the Dutch store, And it is very likely we will able to send him some Baubees to Pay his harvest help so that he will not have to be in a hurry to sell his wheat this fall, unless he thinks it will Pay best to do so, he says it is all in the family; the Debt he is in, and beleive me I think it is best so I wish you would let us know if it is at all likely sarah will go up to fox lake this fall, and if there is likely to be any trouble with the district, in getting her Pay. have you heard anything of tom Reid[59] how is he getting along, I want you to be very minute in your next letter to me, giving every bit of news: you can scrape up and sir you must let us know the definite news about Richmond. I hope we are victoreous. I have been getting up and down all the time I have been writing this letter to see to some apple sauce; I have been cooking. give my love to all. and being afraid of encroaching on your good humor I will dry up By signing myself your loving Brother, William G. Christie

Write soon Let us know something about the Ennissons, And all the rest of the folks good by I expect a letter tonight;

Bully Bully Bully Bully Bully

ᕲ

Thomas Christie to Sarah Christie

CORINTH MISS, AUGUST 6TH 1862

My Dear Sister,

I am really glad to learn by your letter of the 30th Ult. recieved last night, of your continued good health and success in teaching. So you really have had no trouble during the term let me congratulate you on the finding of

59. A cousin from the family of William's stepmother, Eliza Reid. He served in the Third Wisconsin Infantry in the Army of the Potomac.

your Vocation and I hope you are determined to persevere in the pursuit of the Profession you have adopted, for you must realize that it is one of the highest and most important of Human pursuits.

If this part of the Republic had taken the measures for the education of her children that have been adopted in the North, we would never have seen this wretched War. You can have but an inadequate idea of the deplorable ignorance in which this people are steeped.

This renders them ready tools for the educated and ambitious few. Those people are unfit to be citizens of a Republic and if this Rebellion should succeed would soon sink to mere Serfs of the Slave Aristocracy. They are not educated like New England up to the standard of self government.

I went to Hamburg[60] with the teams last week and experienced the glory of battling the tremendous current of the Tennessee the water of which is almost luke warm. I have no fear of drowning now, having almost learned the whole art of swimming, During our four days stay waiting for hay we bathed almost 3 times a day and fished the rest of the time, catching enough Catfish to keep our 7 men supplied piscatorially at every meal.

But, Oh, the glory of driving Mule team with single line. I mount the wheel mule, gather up the line and, "yep," "yep," they start with a jerk. Mule NO.1 makes a bee line for the trees, "wha-a-a-a," a few smart raps on the back with the line and he hauls off again the other way with mouth wide open straining at the bit, like the picture of the Egyptian ox.

I finally succeeded in getting them into a clump of bushes on the side of the road from whence it required all the cursing and skill of the regular driver to extricate them, and if there is anyone who understands the whole dictionary of profanity, that one is the Mule driver,

As I write, the splendid brass band of the 15th Michigan is practicing about a quarter mile from here. The stirring notes of the "Red, White, and Blue" swell triumphantly through the still night air, but such things are so common here that the beautifull tune is but little attended to.

We have a perfect surfeit of music here. The drum and fief are seldom quiet and the brass Bands often practice during the whole night, while the Bugle calls of the five batteries and Regiment of Cavalry in our Division make the woods ring.

60. A small town or landing on the Tennessee River about twenty miles north of Corinth. It was a landing place for troops and an important supply depot during the Corinth campaign. See U.S. War Department, *War of the Rebellion*, Series I, 10.2:117, for example.

Our Bugler is considered by Major Hinkellooper[61] to be the best in the Battallion and he always gives us the post of honor—the right—in all drills and reviews on account of our superior discipline.

We hope to recruit enough this fall in Minn. to fill up to the Maximum and get 6 guns again, for this purpose Lieut. Pfaender is going home as soon as the Capt. comes down which will be within a week.

We think we will have work here pretty soon as the Guerrillas are marauding in the neighborhood pretty extensively. They have even had the impudence to enforce the Conscription law in the immediate vicinity of Shiloh church and quite an expedition left this Division last Monday to break up some bands west of here near Bolivar. It has not returned yet.

Mr. Williams' son has been put under arrest and will soon be tried by Court Martial for furnishing information to the enemy. I am convinced that if he is guilty the old man did not know of it, for I know that his sentiments are for the Union.

We have seen Amos Noble[62] here, he belongs to the hospital of the 16th, and was living within about 10 rods of our tent for the past month. They are now removed some distance from here. Joseph Ennison[63] is hospital Steward in the general hospital in Corinth. We are going down to see him today. Has Luther Noyes[64] returned yet to the 18th? How does the Harvest go on? tell Father that I will write to him in a day or two, I hope he does not work any in the field, for I would rather have him pay 3 dollars a day for a man than work to hurt himself. Uncle Tom and Aunt Jane I see have made a new call for Volunteers, congratulate them for me. My love to all

T. D. Christie

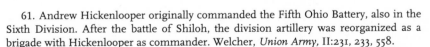

61. Andrew Hickenlooper originally commanded the Fifth Ohio Battery, also in the Sixth Division. After the battle of Shiloh, the division artillery was reorganized as a brigade with Hickenlooper as commander. Welcher, *Union Army*, II:231, 233, 558.

62. Amos Noble, a private in the Sixteenth Wisconsin. National Park Service, "Soldiers and Sailors System."

63. Joseph Ennison was a hospital steward in the Eighteenth Illinois. His connection to the Christies is not clear. National Park Service, "Soldiers and Sailors System."

64. Luther B. Noyes was a private in the Eighteenth Wisconsin and probably a cousin by marriage. National Park Service, "Soldiers and Sailors System."

Thomas Christie to James Christie[65]

CORINTH, AUG. 15. 1862.

My Dear Father,

We soldiers enjoy very much the letters we get from home. I have to thank you for so many and such good ones. I know that now you are busy with the harvest; still, I hope you will steal a half-hour occasionally for your soldier boys.

I returned from Hamburg Landing yesterday, where I had been with the teams for grain. Perhaps you wonder why I go so often on these Expeditions? One reason is, that life in camp is so dull. I am ready to do anything for a little variety, and in order to keep busy. I enjoy very much the freedom of life on the road. When I get tired of my horse I get into the wagon for an hour's ride. I wander through all the peach and apple orchards near the road; the fruit is now ripe and luscious. You may be sure all the boys share in what I get. When night comes, we stop beside a spring, build a big fire, and cook our suppers. These have, usually, a varied bill of fare, more varied than when we are in camp. We have fresh pork, vegetables, fruit, milk, roasting ears—and sometimes even a wild turkey, shot from the road. (Lately, I came suddenly upon a mother-turkey with her whole brood; they were enjoying themselves in the dust of the road; and fled at racehorse speed before I could get a shot at them.) So you see that some of us, at least, have no reason to fear an attack of scurvy.

Yesterday our four baggage wagons went out to forage, and came back with loads of good things for our hospitals. Farmers who had taken the oath of allegiance were paid for their property, at a good price too; others receive nothing. Such is War! But these foolish people brought these Evils on themselves, and many an Evil on us also. The soldiers are well pleased with this change of policy on the part of our Generals, for it shows that at last we are in earnest.

This is the last day of grace for absent men; but there are about twenty of ours scattered around in the north, from whom we hear nothing. A letter from the Captain came today, in which he says he hopes soon to join us; but he fears he will not be able to do duty for some time yet—his leg is still so weak. Of Lieut. Peebles we hear nothing. I heard Gov. Ramsey when he was here (I was his orderly) tell Lieut. Pfaender to recommend Clayton for

65. Transcribed in Thomas Christie reminiscence.

a commission, and he would issue it. (In Minnesota at least, the Governor commissions men on the recommendation of their commanding officers.) The men of his old Platoon are glad that Clayton's merits are at last recognized. We all felt that he was treated rather shabbily at Fort Snelling. But everything comes out right in the end. He is now acting as Orderly Sergeant, Coggswell having received his discharged. When the Company is filled up to the maximum this fall, there will be a good many promotions. We have scarcely an officer of whatever grade who is now acting in the place to which he was appointed last November; nearly all of them being either dead, [*note in 1904*—this is delicious Irish bull!] discharged, absent, or promoted.

How I wish I could join you for a day or two in the harvest-field! To swing my old cradle, and get a dish of bread and milk for supper! While I was gone to Hamburg, William sent you by express a copy of Byron which I picked up at Shiloh. It was lying beside the body of a young Rebel Lieutenant; evidently he was the owner, and the author of the verses that you see on the blank leaves. They prove he was a man of education, and no mean poet. Poor fellow, I pitied him; he lay there so handsome and so still! Please keep the book for me as a relic. I have sent for the "Independent" for the coming half-year; we get great good from it; indeed, cannot get along without it. It is almost time for me to go on guard, and I must close.

3

"Your Poor Soldier Correspondent"
September 21, 1862–April 8, 1863

Thomas Christie to Sarah Christie

CORINTH. SEPT. 21ST 1862.

My Dear Sister,

No doubt you have been forming all sorts of gloomy conjectures as to the cause of my long silence, but it is easily explained.

At 3 O'clock on the morning of the 17th we were roused by the notes of the Reville, and when our eyes were rubbed open fell into line. "Make ready to march Boys with 3 days rations in your haversacks and 2 in the Baggage wagons."

The "Boots and Saddles" was sounded immediately, and every man sprung to his duty,—the drivers to harness and hitch up, and the cannoners to do up the tarpaulins and fill the Sponge Buckets,[1] for it was well known to us that an action was imminent, as Price[2] had been threatening our left flank, having taken Iuka the day before.

In the ray of the drizzly morning we left Camp and passed down through Corinth, preceded by the 16th Wis. and followed by the rest of our Division with its five Batteries. Our handsome General, McArthur, led us out on the Iuka road, through the Rebel fortifications, and down into the great swamp that sweeps around the town on the North and East.

---

1. A bucket made of sheet iron carried under the axle of a field piece. The water in the bucket served to moisten the sponge used to clean out the barrel between firing rounds. Gibbon, *Artillerist's Manual*, 298–99.

2. Confederate general Sterling Price. On September 13 his forces advanced on Iuka, a small town twenty miles southeast of Corinth on the Memphis and Charleston railroad. Welcher, *Union Army*, II:620.

By this time it rained in torrents, the Infantry threw on their rubber ponchos and pressed bravely on through the mud, and we, having none, donned our overcoats and sat in silence on the ammunition chests, while the spattered horses plunged through the holes and over the rough corduroys of the narrow road.

After getting through the swamp we ascended to the level of the cotton and corn fields of *last* year, *now* a wilderness of weeds, with now and then a Cotton press or gin standing, solitary and dilapidated by the side of the road. At noon we stopped to eat dinner at an old church 9 miles out of town, the rain still continuing unabated.

The country we had passed through was alternate swamp and high pine land with here and there a clump of chestnut trees loaded with their green burs. Scarcely a house had we seen since leaving Corinth and those we did see were of the rudest construction, built of rough pine logs with the chimney running up the end *outside*.

We bivouacked that evening a few miles further on, our cannon frowning down on the little hamlet of Glendale, our horses picketed in the woods and ourselves wet to the skin, stretched around enormous fires of chestnut rails, that evaporated the water as fast as it fell on us. The morning dawned cold and rainy but by the time we resumed the march it cleared off and showed us the Sun once more.

Our progress this day was slow, the citizen guide, whether purposely or not, led us on the wrong road and had to counter march several miles to resume the right one. You never saw an army moving to Battle, "What a sight." thought I, "this would be to the quiet people of Clyman." as we would reach the summit of some hill and look back at the marching column of Cannons Caissons and Infantry, the dark blue of the latter contrasting finely with the crimson facings of the mounted artillery men, Anyone could see that an action was looked for, every Surgeon and ambulance was with us and marching in the ranks were men with white badges on their arms whose duty it would be to take care of the wounded.

We camped that night not far from the outposts of the enemy and in consequence the guards were doubled and the fires built in the hollows where they could not be seen from the front. By the neglect of our officers, our rations which were to have lasted 5 days were finished here and we had to depend on what we could get for the rest of the time till we got back to camp.

In the morning we pushed forward again, the outlying forces of the enemy flying before our skirmishers, untill about noon a high hill was reached that completely commanded the country in front for some distance the enemy was reported in force a short distance ahead. Our Right Section was ordered into battery here and we waited for some regiments of infantry to go in front and feel the way. Shortly afterwards *our* Section was marched down the hill and forward about quarter of a mile to another eminance.

"ACTION FRONT." is the command, and we come round into position like the crack of a whip, the guns are unlimbered, and brought to bear on the road ahead and the limbers and caissons take position in the rear. Axes are brought into requisition, and every tree and limb that would impede the sighting of the pieces is leveled to the ground. The cannoniers take their posts and we wait. Old Gen. Ord[3] rides by and looks with grim satisfaction at our bronze bulldogs. A half hour passes and no enemy. Not even a shot in front. Presently an orderly dashes up. "Limber to the front," and we pass ahead followed by our right Section which has come up. Another quarter mile, another hill, and again we take position. Here we stay untill evening hearing brisk cannonading to the right where Rosencrans[4] is pushing them in. Is there nothing for us to do? Tomorrow will tell.

We build our concealed fires and go to find something to eat, for we are absolutely starving. I set out with half dozen others, and soon return with a dressed calf and a sack of sweet potatoes. Don't ask where we got them. Men on the eve of battle are not apt to make nice distincitons of *Meum et Tuum* when they are famished, and tuum means, belonging to Secesh.

Another difficulty now presents itself, we have no cooking utensils with us, "Necessity is the mother of invention," The potatoes are rubbed clean on our pantaloons and nicely covered with ashes to roast, long forked sticks are cut on which we impale large slices of the raw meat and we all squat round the blaze *"a la' Indienne,"* just wishing, as Lieut Clayton remarks, that some of the dear folks at home could see us. Suddenly, something glides in between him and me, and, a young wild turkey stands inside the circle looking into the fire. We were so astonished that, for a moment, it was unmolested, but the desire of having a fine piece of roast soon overcame

3. General Edward O. C. Ord, commander of the forces at Corinth.

4. General William S. Rosecrans. Grant's plan was for Ord and Rosecrans to both advance on Iuka. Rosecrans's forces were to attack first, and Ord's corps, which included McArthur's division, was to advance when they heard the sound of Rosecrans's attack. The latter engaged Price's forces for most of the nineteenth in an inconclusive fight while Ord never moved. It's interesting that Thomas remarks that they heard the sounds of Rosecrans's attack, because both Ord and Grant claimed never to have heard the battle and so did not advance. Welcher, *Union Army*, II:620–23.

my surprise. Whack: went my roasting stick on the ground, close to the bird, who jumped clear over the fire and disappeared among the young pines. But what had become of my veal. I remembered once to have seen what we used to call a potatoe sling and concluded that its (the veal's) disappearance had been according to the same principle that gave us so much amusement when at school—Centrifugal force.

Next morning price was gone, "skedadled," as he always does, and we proceeded to Iuka without opposition, the road being strewn with clothing thrown away by the Rebels. We stopped at the town about an hour and then started back to Burnsville 9 miles this side. It was late in the afternoon when we got under motion and we travelled the last 5 miles in the dark. Never shall I forget that night march. The soldiers infuriated at the escape of Price fired every rebel house on the road that was unoccupied, which was the case with nearly all. They were mostly built of pitch pine and burned like so many matches.

The sight was sublime to one who, like me had never before seen any extensive conflagration. The immense red flames crackled and roared and threw their light far into the deep woods that surrounded them, the buildings fell with a crash sending up millions of sparks, and the heat was so intense that we had to drive by on the gallop on account of the caissons.

We bivouacked on a hill that night and the fires of our 2 Divisions—2nd and 6th—made the air lurid for miles.

Pushing on today, we arrived here this afternoon and found a stack of letters awaiting us among which were 2 from Clyman for William and 1 from you to myself.

I am happy to see by it that you are well and happy and my only fear for you is, that in attending to the development of the mind you will neglect the proper care of your physical system. Do not fall into this error, remember that the most splendid education will not renummerate you for the loss of bodily health, and that, while keeping one law you may be breaking a more important one.

I had almost forgotten to tell you that Clayton is acquainted in Fox Lake. He knows the Willards and a young man named Davis who attends College. Clayton's brother was wounded in the retreat from the Rapidan. Write soon and remember me as your affectionate Brother

T. D. Christie

[margin note] send to Clyman and save me writing at present

❧

Thomas Christie to James Christie

CAMP NEAR CORINTH, OCT. 18TH/62

Dear Father,

I begin to despair of ever getting another word from any of you, Since I came back from Iuka not a letter have I recieved, there must be a screw loose some where, for this long silence is unprecedented in the annals of our Correspondence.

I wrote you from Ripley acquainting you with our participation in the Battle of Corinth, but whether you have got the letter or not I could not say, for mail regulations here are in a very uncertain state![5] You probably have seen accounts of the great victory, and perhaps have seen our Battery mentioned, so you will know the share that we took in the first day's conflict.

Nearly all the correspondence that I have seen slights our Division most shamefully, and seems to give the impression that the first day's fighting did not amount to much. The number of troops engaged was not very great to be sure, But what there was, fought desperately, witness the losses of the 15th Michigan and 14th and 16th Wis. who supported the First Minn. Battery. As at Shiloh, our guns were the first to open on the advancing enemy, and unlike some batteries who have paid reporters and get praised accordingly we *never* limbered to the rear without the General's orders.

Let the Newspapers go, the official report will set us all right.[6] And now I suppose you would like to hear an account of my second battle.

My remembrance of it extends to these items, Country heavily wooded and intersected by chains of hills, every one of which we defended as long as possible and then fell back to the next, the booming of the guns and bursting of shell, the roar of the rifles and "spat," "spat," of the bullets around us, men limping to the rear or carried by comrades, with here and there a skulker hurrying out of the reach of the musical lead. All this I remember and also, that when our gun was heated it was mighty hard work

5. There is no letter dated from Ripley in the Christie papers.

6. Following the battle at Iuka, Confederate generals Price and Van Dorn combined their forces to attack Corinth. They initially outnumbered the Union forces and nearly succeeded in taking the town. The action described here took place along the Chewalla Road, where two brigades of Union troops resisted the initial Confederate advance. The First Minnesota Battery took a prominent part in this fight and, as Thomas assumed, received favorable mention in some official reports. See Welcher, *Union Army*, II:553–58; U.S. War Department, *War of the Rebellion*, Series I, 12.1, No. 89, *Report of Capt. Andrew Hickenlooper*, 341–43, and No. 95, *Report of Col. John M. Oliver*, 356.

to ram down the charge, which was my duty as I was No. 1. Nothing is so exciting as working a gun in real action. The sound of the discharge almost raises us off our feet with delight, Before the smoke lifts from the muzzle I dash in, dip the brush in the sponge bucket and brush out the bore using plenty of water, then seize the sponge staff and sponge it out dry. No 2 then inserts the cartridge which I ram home, then the shot, shell, or canister, whichever it may be, and it is sent home, then I spring out beside the wheel and fall flat, "Ready," shouts the Gunner, No. 3 (who has been serving vent[7] while I loaded) now pricks the cartridge, No 4 jumps in and inserts a friction primer,[8] to which his lanyard is attached, in the vent, springs outside the wheel and straightens his lanyard. The Gunner gives a turn or two to the elevating screw taps on the trail and has it carried round a little, and then, "Fire." "Take that,_____ you." says No 4 as the gun rushes back with the recoil. The other numbers run her forward at the command, "By hand to the front" while I load. While you have been reading this description we would fire 3 or 4 shots, so rapidly do we work.[9]

The sound of the gun is most exhilerating, it fills us with enthusiasm and we would die rather than desert her. However, you probably do not understand these feelings, and so think it all foolishness.

I saw James Dempsey[10] on the morning of the Battle, and we had quite a talk about the expected conflict. He was quite cheerfull and courageous. Little did I think when we passed the 17th drawn up in Battle line as we went out on the field, that it was the last time I should ever see him. As we passed over the Battlefield early on Sunday morning in pursuit of the

7. That is, "The . . . hole through which fire is communicated to the charge." By "serving vent," the number three man covers the vent hole with his thumb (protected by a padded leather cover called a thumb stall), thus preventing the premature combustion of the charge. Gibbon, *Artillerist's Manual*, 297. U.S. War Department, *Instructions for Field Artillery*, 110, 114. Taxdahl was "serving vent" when he was killed at Shiloh. See Thomas to James, Apr. 26, 1862 (pages 46–47).

8. Also called a friction tube; a small brass tube about two inches long and lined with friction powder, much like the material used on kitchen matches. The inside of the tube also included a serrated wire that ran through the top and ended in a loop where the firing lanyard was attached. When the lanyard was pulled, the wire ignited the powder in the tube, thus firing the charge in the gun. Gibbon, *Artillerist's Manual*, 323–26.

9. The mean rate of fire for a twelve-pound gun was one round per minute but "when close pressed and firing at objects not difficult to hit" could be as high as three rounds per minute. Gibbon, *Artillerist's Manual*, 250.

10. Dempsey was a neighbor and seems to have been a particular friend of the Christies. Letters from him to Sarah are archived in the Christie papers.

Rebels, I looked at all the bodies I could find but, although there was many a one of our brave fellows stretched out, I could see nothing of him.

Two of his comrades buried him that forenoon and put up a neat headboard.

The enclosed relick I picked up beside the grave of one of those who fell in the attack on the fort, they were in a bloody haversack that he had worn. This storming of the redoubt was the most desperate and murderous charge that has been made during the war. this is shown by the rebel graves that cover the space before the fort, Gen. Rogers is buried within 10 steps of the ditch, and his men lie in long trenches close by.

Hoping that ill health is not the cause of your long silence, I remain your affectionate Son, Tom.

⟡

Thomas Christie to Sarah Christie

CORINTH MISS. OCT. 28TH 1862

My Dear Sister,

Yours of the 39th Ult. came to hand day before yesterday, and I must offer several excuses for not answering it immediately. First: I was on guard, Second: wrote to Father yesterday, and one letter per day is as much as I have time for, and Third: I waited for another letter of later date.

I direct this to the lake in the hope that you have returned thither from Clyman. It will not pay, my dear sister, to leave your Mathematics every time you hear of a Battle that we are engaged in. According to my opinion we have work before us this fall and winter of no easy accomplishment, and you will have to bear with patience and fortitude the news of many a hard fought battle in this Department before the Mississippi is opened and Mobile garrisoned by National troops.

Our Major of Artillery[11] has gone to report at Bolivar to take a command under McClernand,[12] whose mission it is to take Vicksburg by a land assault, seeing that the Gunboats have made no impression on it with their shell. It is not at all improbable that we will fallow the Major as we all would like to serve under him.

11. Andrew Hickenlooper.

12. John Alexander McClernand commanded the Thirteenth Corps. A "political" general and constant source of irritation to Grant and Sherman, he was replaced in January 1863. Warner, *Generals in Blue*, 293.

By his absence Capt. Munch is brevetted major Commanding Artillery Battallion of the 6th Division, and this makes Clayton Lieut. commanding in the Battery. We held an election yesterday and appointed Orderly Sergt. J. M. Allen and Sergt. Munch, Second Lieutenants.

On account of want of men the 16th Wis. was consolidated today into 3 Companies and put in with the 14th and 18th to form one Regiment. The most of the men of Co. D (raised at Watertown) are coming into the Battery, which, with the recruits from other companies will give us our six guns again. John Shaller and Charley Visgar are coming in and if Amos Nobles was here he would join, but he is in the hospital taking care of the wounded.[13]

The boys are tired of the Infantry service and are glad of an opportunity to join the Artillery, which, as every Soldier knows, is the finest branch of the Service, and is to the army what the Old Guard was to Napoleon—the right arm.

We had some splendid long range practice on the third—the first time that we have had a chance to use our guns as they should be used, to play on heavy columns instead of scattered Skirmishers. At the very first shot from our rifle we had the range, and plumped a Hotchkiss percussion Shell right into the midst of the Greybacks, whom we could see plainly march-ing along, at a "Right Shoulder shift." The way they scattered was a caution to snakes, and wherever a bunch of them could be seen we would plant a Shell or Spherical case, till you could not see their backs for the dust. Some reckless scamps among them returned our fire with their muskets although they were a half mile distant, but I noticed that they sent no more men up *that* road.[14] I should like to get my revenge out of them in this way to com-pensate for the way we had to fight them at Shiloh—at short range—and compelled to use nothing but canister and short-timed shells. We may be in many a fight yet and see death and wounds enough, but I doubt if we ever see another such time as we had there.

Our troops here naturally look upon themselves as "Some Bumpkins" after giving Van Dorn the whipping that we did. They are inclined to look

13. These men actually transferred to another company in the Sixteenth Wisconsin and continued to be carried on that regiment's rolls. They do not appear on the rolls of the First Minnesota Battery. However, a number of men are listed in the latter as "veteran: served in 16th Wis. Infantry," and the battery's morning reports for November 19 state, "Fourteen men detailed from Infantry came to our rescue."

14. Thomas is again referring to the fight on the Chewalla Road on the first day of the Battle of Corinth.

down on the Army of the Potomac as inferior soldiers, but I think this is not warranted, as there they have had a far more difficult task to do than we have.

Did not the news of James Dempsey's death shock you Sarah? I am sure it did me and at first I could not believe it. He looked so full of life and so handsome, when I saw him on the morning of the Battle, that I could not bring myself to believe that he was killed. We have our consolation—that he died at his post with his face to the foe like a true Soldier as he was. I am sure that Clyman will morn his death more than the loss of any other one of those who have gone from among you.

Now Sarah I hope that you will not let your anxieties or your studies inpire your health, Keep a good heart and don't lose appetite.

And also remember me as your

Affectionate Brother

T.D. Christie

I wonder why Helen don't write to me

I must have offended her in that last letter of mine.

Thomas Christie to Sarah Christie

CAMP NEAR GRAND JUNCTION

NOV. 8TH 1862

My Dear Sister

Thinking you might be anxious to hear of our whereabouts I seize the first opportunity to drop you a few lines. We are in the Field at last and before we again establish a permanent camp the Confederacy will have been cut I two by the occupation of the line of the Mississippi.

At present we wait here a few days untill our communications are opened [. . .] with Memphis, Corinth and Columbus by the repair of the Rail Roads to those points. When this is accomplished we will push forward to Holly Springs and establish a new Base of Operations. At this latter place we will probably fight the decisive Battle of the South [. . .] for the Rebels are massing heavy forces there and fortifying industriously.

We left Corinth on the 2nd and arrived here (4 miles south of the Junction) on the 5th having marched through some beautiful country and seen hundreds of acres shinning with unpicked Cotton. A field of Cotton ready to pick is one of the most beautiful sights in this beautiful country. Far away, to the distance of a mile or more, stretches the billowy white, flecked with the brown of the short branchy plants.

The most of the country through which we passed is much superior to what we have hitherto seen of the South, consisting, (west of the Hatchie) of rolling, lightly timbered land in a pretty good state of cultivation.

We crossed the Hatchie at Matamora, where the Battle was fought on the fifth Ult. and by the same bridge that shook under the advancing columns of Hurlbut, when the Rebel shot were marking the trees on each side and, curiously enough, avoiding the bridge entirely. A Cousin of Jeff Davis resides in Matamora, whom we saw with his family sitting in the verandah looking at the passing of our troops. Some of the men, more jealous than merciful, proposed burning the house above his head, but this was not allowed, although some fellow set his Cotton gin and press on fire, and they were burning furiously when we left.

During the whole march the troops fired every gin and press along the road, and in many places the fences, so that it was sometimes dangerous for our Caissons to pass, and when we arrived at the top of some high hill the line of march for many miles ahead could be traced by the columns of ascending smoke.

Some of the troops, I am sorry to say, exhibited more the practices of Bandits than of disciplined Soldiers, going into houses and plundering and destroying, without the plea of necessity, and without even enquiring whether the weeping women were Unionist or Rebels. This has been put a stop to by Orders from the Commanding Gen. within the past few days, and when we again march every man will be kept in the ranks, and the "stragglers on the march and skulkers in Battle who commit these outrages" will be severely punished.

Our men are all in excellent health and desire nothing more than to be led against the enemy.

Our Baggage and Mail will be sent on before we move from here and then I expect a letter from you and will write you in return. When you write direct to *Macarthur's Division, Army of the Tenn. Via Cairo.* And also, I would like you to send a few stamps for we are out of them, and they cannot be obtained here in the field.

And above all my dear Sister, keep up your spirits, and do not yield to gloomy fancies or apprehensions on our account, for I assure you they are needless, as we are enjoying ourselves thoroughly, and "eating our bread," (hard crackers and sweet potatoes) "in joy and thankfulness." Begging you to dismiss from your mind all anxiety on our account, and to answer this soon, I remain your affectionate Soldado

Tomas,

Primero Minn Batterie, del Grande Armie del Tennessee.

[margin note] W. writes to Father today.

ᖌ

William Christie to James Christie[15]

NEAR GRAND JUNCTION FRIDAY, Nov.8, 1862

My Dear Father,

We are now in camp three miles south of the Junction, on the road to Holly Springs. Both of us are well and heartily enjoying ourselves. From Corinth to this place, we have passed mostly through forests, over low ridges running nearly north and south. The soil is a reddish loose clay; many of the valleys are swamps. Occasionally there are patches of loose sandy soil. The country is greatly cut up by crooked water courses. I say "water," but the fluid in them sometimes looks as black as ink. This however is only in appearance, for when the water is lifted in a dipper it is very clear, and good to drink.

I suppose we are going to Holly Springs. Our three Divisions left Corinth last Sunday morning, Nov.2, and came here in two days and a half. Now we are waiting for reinforcements. I hear that 25,000 men have left Bolivar, and that a large force is coming from Memphis. The troops from Bolivar passed through Grand Junction only an hour or two ahead of us. We are only 23 miles from Holly Springs; the rebels are abut 18 miles South of us in strong force. Three of our Cavalry Regiments went out this morning to feel the enemy. Last night some prisoners were brought in; they say the enemy are going farther south. I must warn you that all these statements about the enemy are only rumors that we hear in camp; still, they are probably not far from the truth.

We are out upon this trip without tents, except a few of the officers. When the reville sounds at half passed five there is noise enough from the bugles, the drums, the fifes, and the numerous bands to awaken the whole

15. Transcribed in Thomas Christie reminiscence.

neighborhood for miles around. Then you hear the busy clack of thousands of Tongues, where fifteen minutes before there was the stillness of death. All through the day you hear the sounds of happy laughter, the loud talking, of the braying mules, the sound of chopping, and the falling of trees; indeed, it is a tumult of Babel. But when night comes with its glories, then you have a wonderful scene. There are thousands of fires lighted in the forest. The splendid trees spread their branches over your head; you look up through them and catch glimpses of the stars. The camp fires are only three or four rods apart and they extend for more than a mile in almost every direction. In some places there are no fires; that is where the artillery is parked. but behind the guns and caissons, and the picket-rope with the horses, you see fires of the Battery boys; Here jokes are cracked, songs are sung, and the different qualities of all our comrades are displayed. In the conversation around the fires the characters of our officers high and low are freely discussed.

As you say, the death of James Dempsey in the late battle was a sore loss to his family, and his comrades here. We all liked him.

Address the "1st Minn. Battery, McArthur's Division, Left Wing of the Army of the Tennessee." . . .[16]

∾

William Christie to James Christie[17]

CAMP THREE MILES SOUTH OF GRAND JUNCTION

NOV. 23, 1862

My Dear Father,

We are still lying here waiting for orders, and it is wearisome business. The weather is beautiful; but day after day passes by without any move on our part. It is very difficult under these circumstances to have patience with our Generals. We hear that our advance has reached the Tallahatchie River about 12 miles beyond Holly Springs; Price is on the other side of the river. Our new Troops are moving in here very fast. It is said also that McClernand's expedition will soon be ready to move down the river towards Vicksburg. Almost every hour, among us, some new plan for our future

16. Thomas and Carmelite Christie Papers, M542.
17. Transcribed in Thomas Christie reminiscence.

operations is discussed. Some think that our big fight will be at Grenada; some at Jackson; some, at Vicksburg, etc. etc. It is agreed by all that at least one great battle must take place before Vicksburg is ours and the Mississippi opened. Our men say that they don't care if we have a big fight at every town from here to the Gulf,—if only we can move on and conquer. Every one of us is anxious to have this war finished as soon as possible.

It is very sad to see how full our newspapers are of the quarrels that go on in the Army of the Potomac. It is a good thing that this Army is free from such quarrels. But still we employ a great deal of time in disputing as to the merits of McClellan, Burnside, Hooker, and the others. We also have a great deal of disputing with our Irish soldiers on the negro question. They are very bitter against the black man; many of them even say that if he is made free it will lead to another war. But of course this is all nonsense.

I have just received a letter from Joe Johnson[18] formerly a member of the Battery. He was badly wounded at the battle of Shiloh, and got his discharge about two months ago. His letter is very interesting for he is a bright man.

Our Major has gone back to Corinth for our gun, some new horses, and other things that were needed for the batteries. He went away on Thursday and will be back tomorrow night. You will be glad to know that I am at last a cannoneer, I am No. 3, my duty is to thumb the vent while No. 1 sponges; then I prick the cartridge, and hold the friction–primer in place till No. 4 stretches his lanyard; I then step back, and No. 4 fires the gun at command. My place is on the right of the gun opposite the breech. We have a great deal of drill every day. Some of the men in the Battery are details from the infantry; five from the 1st Kansas, five from the 16th Wis., three from the 17th Wis.

(Monday the 24th) Last night our first Lieut. told me that 30,000 fresh troops have joined us here within the past three days. Probably this is an exaggeration. I have seen some of the new regiments. Each one is as large as one of our old Brigades. But it will not be long before the new men will begin to drop out. A very fine new regiment, the 95th Ill, has just been assigned to our Division; the regiment numbers a thousand and fifty men, all stout, good-looking fellows. Two men carry a small field tent, each one of them a half: the half is about as large as a blanket. These are called

18. Joseph Johnson of Olmsted County was discharged for disability on October 18, 1862. *Adjutant General's Report*, 785.

"shelter-tents," and are very easy to put up at the end of a day's march. Another name for them is "dog-tent"; but the fellows say they are so small that the proper name would be "puppy-tent."

We have received no pay for some time; so please send us some more postage-stamps; and we will pray that your shadow may never grow less . . .

○‿○

Thomas Christie to James Christie[19]

NEAR ABBEVILLE, MISS. DEC. 6, 1862.

My Dear Father,

Once more we are settled in camp, apparently for a few days at least. On the evening that William wrote we took up our march again, and encamped that night within a half-mile of the Tallahatchie. The next day we waited on the bank until dark for the bridge to be repaired, this was done under the supervision of Generals McPherson, Hamilton and Logan. That night we crossed, and Marched to Abbeville, where we bivouacked. On the next day we moved camp to this point, about half a mile east of the town. It is said that we are to remain here for some time, as the railroad must be repaired from the Junction.

The weather has at last taken on its Winter form. Day before yesterday it rained; we had sleet yesterday; this morning the ground is frozen hard. But probably tomorrow will be quite warm, and the next day we shall have rain; so it goes. These rapid changes of temperature and weather are not very pleasant. The soldiers invent many kinds of apparatus for warming themselves. In our tent (for we have tents now) there is a common camp-kettle with a hole punched in the side for draft: it is hung to the pole-chain in the center of the tent. When it is filled with wood and lighted it burns as merrily as any parlor-stove you ever saw; all the smoke passes up the pole and out at the top of the tent. Trust the American soldier for using his inventive powers! You remember, perhaps, what we read in the newspapers during the Crimean War, about the ways in which the French soldiers made themselves comfortable; and about the wretchedness of the English troops, these latter being unskilled in caring for themselves. Perhaps there is a good deal of resemblance in this respect between the French and American soldier. In both you find that ready wit that enables a man to adapt himself to

19. Transcribed in Thomas Christie reminiscence.

any circumstances, and to find a way by some expedient or other over any difficulty. This is allied with that feeling of independence and that spirit of self-reliance which make a man consider himself fully able to go any-where to do anything. It is plain from the story of the Crimean war that the English soldier is usually somewhat lacking in these respects. Here we con-sider ourselves to blame if we are not comfortable; we do not stop to look to our superiors in such matters. As I write I see our sergeant, Tom Gordon (formerly from Glasgow), at work making his bunk; there is another man manufacturing a splint-broom (for you must know that we allow no dust on the floor); others are carrying in corn-husks for their beds, many are read-ing or writing. Every one is for himself and his chum first; but always ready to help any one else who needs.

LATER, DEC. 7TH;

We hear this morning that we are to be the rear-guard of the Army, and repair the railroad as the Troops advance. It is an occupation not very well relished by our Division. The greetings of the Season to you all. This will be my third Christmas away from home; I trust there will not be a fourth . . .

⌒

William Christie to James Christie

ABBEYVILLE MISSISSIPPI DEC. 13TH/62

Dear Father,

Deeming it high time to punish you with the infliction of another dry and meagre epistle I with all dilligence sit down to let you know, that we have been looking very anxiously, for quite a number of days, Past for a letter or letters, from that frozen up regon you inhabit. But whether you are all so cold or the Post office is frize, tis hard for us to make out. for seeing we get no signs of your condition we are left in great doubts in regard to which cause we will be forced to lay the delinqunceys of the Epistolary items that in all justice we should have had before this time. Ah how do you do: very happy to see you. wont you walk into our tent and sit down, sir. don't be afraid, the wind wont Blow it down, although it shakes it so. ah yes those Boards, we have under the Beds; we got out about two miles from here at Pignes, where we got so many Books and papers. Yes they keep us off the damp ground, the books gives us ammusment, and that old Camp

Kettle, hanging on the chain form the Centre of the Tripod, keep us warm, for you see we have a fire in it every evening. and sir if you could only stay with us: you would hear some very good singing, and likely, some comments on the war. Perhaps you would hear, some, course jests. but taking every thing into consideration, we are not as rough, as you might suppose, from our looks. ah well so you cant stay, well wont you go round the camp with us and look at things well, away on our right (west) is where the 14th, 16th and 18th Wis: Vol: there Bands discourse very fine music, several times a day. the 14th's excelling. yes it looks as though they were rather in Broken order. But don't you see they take every advantage of the ridges and rising ground, down in that hollow, the night before last, don't stare so, there was, 700 and fifty Prisoners, besides enough more over in town to make up 13 or 14 hundred in all. well wat did they look like. well sir they looked very ragged, and used up, a great many of them were Irish and Dutch; many of them owned, that they were tired of fighting and all they wanted was to be Paroled; and go home. yesterday morning they were marched off. I don't know where, But I suppose, to memphis. well you want to know what Batteries those are off to our left. well the first next to us, is Company C. of the first Mo: rig: vol: then you see the 10th Ohio Battery, the Co. F of Sec. Ill: Vol: then there is the first Kansas rigment vol: Off to the right across the creek, furthur than we have yet been lies the Iowa Brigade composed of the 11th 15th 13th and 16th, the 95 Ill. is the first Brigade, along with 11th ditto. The fifteenth Mic. is at grand junction, so you have the Division just as it is. How do we get food. for man and Beast, well sir that we have been taking from the enemmy; Pork, corn meal, hay rye, corn fodder; and infact every thing that we needed, and some things we did not need. Now Before you leave, you want to know what kind of weather, we have had. Tis very Pleasant, just now. yes, and with the exception of a little rain last night, and some we had, a few days ago we have had the Best Kind of weather for soldiering. as to going furthur on south or staying here, we cannot tell you But, we can tell you we as a Battery, yes I may say as a Division Desire to so south: yea even to the Lands end. Good Bye. seeing you must go; call again, soon sir. and if we ever get any more flour: more than a fourth of a Barrel; since we left the junction: except what we Jayhawked; the fourth of a Barrel being all we would get owing to the rail road connection not being completed; we have been subsisting on corn Bredd, it Being Properly cooked: we have not asked any Pilet Bread: and although, our Batteries got a lot of it we have not used our share, so not wishing to have you eat meal in any shape, least it serve you as it has done our Infantry, (who eat it is shape of mush) give you the s___. I did not ash you to eat, so good By sir Now seeing you have got home, in fact have been there all this time, I will ask you a few questions, to which I hope you will return answers: that will be suitable, to me and let me tell you there is one question that only one answer will suit, that is an affirmative one, Now have you give Sarah the money she needs, if not, I will be very sorry to have you say so.[20] have you got any answer from George Stewart yet in regard to the money he is indebted to me. if so how soon he intends to Pay, or if he will trust you with the money, untill you send the Note. if not, try if will trust John Clarkson with the money if you will C. with the Note, and in that way I think Both of you would get the Business done, without much trouble and clear of expense.[21] Now the most important question comes last, are you all in good health, and going to have a good time at Christmass. Grand-mother[22] I hope is still able to give you an Occasional visit and let her know that I am rather inclined to think that the first time she ever saw me, thir-tytwo years ago (in five days ore from this date,) she little thought that I would ever be of so much use, or ever do as much good as I have here in being a soldier, fighting in such a great Army, and such a Glorious cause, as I am now fighting for. (that is when I can get an opportunity) Liberty, not only for four million of Poor downtrodden Black, But for the Liberties of twentisix millions Whites: and in fact of the World, so if she has never had reason to be glad, on my natal day before let her rejoice on this one my thirtiesecond, with great rejoicing. that I have been so fortunate and let her know, from me that she will yet have an opportunity; to shake my hand, or Box my ears or in fact, do what so ever she will either the one or the other, (That is God willing) Which I Beleve he is, sometime about the next fourth of July. Mother, I will expect you to have a jolly old Pudding and various other fixens on that day when we will trid in on your house floor with martial tred, and as we say to one another here, as Bold as a Mutton, Well perhaps we anticipate, But you know hope is one of the Prevailing ingredi-ants of my nature. I say, Sandy, has you frize, if so try and thaw out enough

20. Sarah's attendance at Fox Lake Seminary seems to have been somewhat contro-versial within the family. The older brothers supported her continued education, while James was somewhat skeptical about its worth. Christie papers, box 2.

21. This passage may refer to the debts William had accumulated during his attempt at farming in Olmsted County just prior to the war.

22. Janet Bertie, James's mother, also lived in Dodge County, Wisconsin.

to let us have a slight rill of [. . .] chat; Dave I hope you are doing a good stroke of Business at school in the way of getting a Penny's worth of learning for your Penny with compound interest addd ther too, and hoping By this time that you have go so as you can write a letter I would give much to see a line or two from yerself at the airlist opportunity that would [. . .] most convaniat te ye: Now mind I am not near tired writing to you, But being rather afraid you will be tired reading, and seeing the mail will leave soon, I must close, By requesting you all to think this my Birthday letter. that is if don't write another one on that day, and hoping you are all well old and young. I sign myself your loving son

William G. Christie

∽

William Christie to James Christie[23]

HOLLY SPRINGS DEC. 28, 1862

My Dear Father,

For some reason our batteries have been brigaded; so captain Munch has resigned,[24] and started yesterday morning for home *Via,* Memphis. His brother[25] also has resigned and gone with him. So we are again under the sole command of Lieut. Clayton; for Lieut. Peebles is on the Staff, and report says that he also has resigned. Lieut Pfaender will not come back to us.[26] So Clayton will be Capt. If Lieut Allen's resignation is accepted (as is likely) there will be some promotions in the Battery. It is likely that T. D. will then have a chance. We have 95 members of the old Battery now on the rolls; and a dozen or more detailed men. But six (6) of the old members are likely to be discharged; their papers are now on the way, but there is much red tape about such matters, causing troublesome delays.

23. Transcribed in Thomas Christie reminiscence.

24. Emil Munch resigned on December 25, 1862. The following year he was commissioned as a brigadier general of the Minnesota state militia in charge of frontier defenses against the Indians. In early 1864 he joined the Veterans Reserve Corps (Invalid Corps). He ended the war as a major with the First Regiment of Heavy Artillery, Minnesota Volunteers. Munch papers.

25. Second Lieutenant Paul Munch.

26. Peebles had, in fact, resigned, and Pfaender resigned to accept a commission as lieutenant colonel of the Minnesota Mounted Rangers. *Minnesota in the Civil and Indian Wars,* I:525, 650.

After two days of rain and cloudy weather we have now bright sunshine, and the nights are resplendent with stars. Soft breezes blow continually from the south.

(29th) I have just received a letter from S. He says that I will no doubt answer him from Vicksburg or Montgomery. Alas! this letter will show you that we are on the back-track; he must wait awhile before getting a letter from those cities. Grant and Co. are evidently not going to give us an opportunity very soon of dating our letters from Vicksburg. Within the past month I have been reading the poems of Burns, Moore, and Campbell, also Sterne's works; I have marched and countermarched; I have listened to camp-rumors without end; and have done my share in abusing McClellan, Grant, and the rest. So you see I am not idle. I am now deep in the history of Columbus by Washington Irving. Tell us all about your Christmas; here it was just like any other day of the year.

Holly Springs was lighted with gas, and was a fine-looking town before Van Dorn made his raid into it. But he and his men did a great deal of damage to the place, and our boys did more when they returned; so that its beauty has been sadly marred. Oxford is in the same case; it was a more wealthy place than this.

We have found here a large number of letters which a rebel in the Virginia Army sent to his friends in Holly Springs, they are very interesting. Poor fellow, I fear he will be greatly disappointed, for he evidently thinks that the South is going to beat us!

(Jan. 1, 1863) A happy New-Year to you all! Since writing the above we have marched from Holly Springs to this place, Moscow, on the Memphis railroad. We came in one day and a half, and have lain still yesterday and to day. We are likely to stay here sometime, for we are guarding a bridge across Wolf River. Our Division is pretty well strung out on the railroad. But after a while, I suppose we shall follow the other troops to Memphis. It seems an age since we saw a newspaper . . .

Thomas Christie to Sarah Christie

MOSCOW TENN. JAN.4TH *1863*

My Dear Sister:

No mail has come to us since we left Holly Springs and so I cannot chide you for not writing, as there may be a dozen of your letters lying at

Memphis waiting for communications to open. Our Division is scattered all along this R. R., a Brigade here, a Regiment there, at every little station or bridge between this and Memphis. This is the reason probably, why our mail is delayed, and we must just be patient until things get settled down again in the old shape. I am expecting with the first mail a letter from you giving an account of how you passed the Holidays.

We are both in good health although the weather has been very rainy of late and our tent leaks badly; two or three of our boys are down already from the effects of the marching we have done lately, and the poor weather, but I have no fears for either William or me, as we practice the rules of health better than any others, I think, in the company. Moderate diet, drinking neither tea nor coffee nor eating much meat: Exercise, taking a ride once in a while, and being busy *all* the time at some thing. Cleanliness, changing clothes once a week, and bathing regularly when I have opportunity. These are the means by which *my* health has been preserved so well up to this time, and I think that a continuance of my employment of them will insure future health *and* happiness. I hope that you are as careful of yourself in the same way.

Your wishes in regard to my promotion have at last been gratified: a vacancy arising in our Platoon by the promotion of Corporal Everts[27] to Quartermaster Sergt. I was appointed, in accordance with the vote of the men of the Squad, to fill it. So now I wear the chevrons of Second Corporal or Chief of Caisson. That is, rather, I am entitled to wear them, for there is scarcely a Non Commissioned Officer in the Battery that sports the stripes now. To use the classical and appropriate language of our Boys, stripes are "played out." I am the youngest man that has ever held office in the Company, and the smallest. Another curious fact is that our Sergt. Gordon,[28] Gunner Rogers,[29] and myself are the three shortest ones in the Platoon of 21 men. From this you can infer that we believe in Napoleon's axiom, that the smallest men or men of medium hight, make the best soldiers. I know they are the toughest and most enduring, not so apt to give up in the face of little difficulties as the Lengthies.

Probably you have heard, through Father, of our marches from Abbeville, through Oxford to the Yokima Creek, from thence back to Holly Springs,

27. Rezin Everts, a native of Ohio, enlisted from Winona. *Adjutant General's Report*, 784.

28. Thomas Gordon, a New York native, also enlisted from Winona. *Adjutant General's Report*, 785.

29. Albert T. Rogers, also a New York native who enlisted from Winona. *Adjutant General's Report*, 783.

and after a short stay there, up to this point. I have written regularly to Clyman, and without answer too, but this I blame the P. O. Department for, and not our folks, who I believe answer regularly. I always take it for granted in any letters that you have maps handy and so don't take pains to give distances and locations, as these you can ascertain for yourself.

We are camped now near the banks of Wolf river which you know runs into the Mississippi at Memphis. Down below us in the cypress swamp through which the river runs the 5th Ohio Cavalry are camped and up near the little town lie the camps of one of our Brigades. Our Battery is posted to defend the bridge over the river. I must give W. a chance, so no more at present. Yours fraternally, T.D. Christie.

∽

William Christie to Sarah Christie[30]

MEMPHIS, JANUARY 14, 1863.

My Dear Sister,

Both T. C. and I are in excellent health. We had very pleasant weather during our march to this place from Moscow. But today it is raining in torrents. The ground is like a soaked sponge, and almost everything else, is dripping with water. What is worse, the weather is likely to continue bad for some time.

On the 10th we left Moscow about noon. That night we stopped at Lafayette, a march of 10 miles. The day was sunshiny and pleasant. The country was beautiful, resembling the best parts of Wisconsin. There are no marshes down here, and only an occasional swamp. At dawn of the 11th we marched from Lafayette and camped that night at Germantown. The country that day was still more beautiful. The land is well cultivated; there were many fine dwellings on both sides of the road, each with a yard filled with evergreens and flowers. The finest tree we saw was the Magnolia; they say it carries flowers as large as a saucer and very fragrant; the leaf resembles that of the laurel. Our road is called "The State-line road," and it runs close to the rail-road nearly all the way. We passed several regiments guarding the road; and saw several trains heavily loaded with troops, cotton, and materials of war. We feared that at Germantown we also would have to remain to protect the rail-road. But greatly to our joy, on the morning or the

---

30. Transcribed in Thomas Christie reminiscence.

12th at sunrise, we marched for this place. We made the 17 miles before
3 O'clock. Our camp is 1 mile east of Memphis. We are thankful that the
weather was so good during those three days; men were ploughing in the
fields. Near our camp are several large gardens, with hot-beds for starting
early vegetables for the city market. The buildings here in the suburbs are
better than any we have yet seen. Just before we arrived we passed in review
before Gen. MacArthur. Yesterday we policed the camp; today we are signing the Pay-roll for two month's pay, only one third of what the Government is owing us. We learned yesterday that Gen. Grant has given orders
to let us and one or two other batteries have clothing in place of what
we lost at Shiloh. This will be quite a help to a good many of us, for we
lost $25 worth of clothes, each. My bill for clothing from the time of enlist-
ment to this date amounts to $74 ; this is an excess of $32 over my yearly
allowance from the Government.[31] I hope that next year my expenses on
that head will be less. The paper and the music that you sent came yesterday. T. D. and the other boys are already trying the new War-songs. There
are many good singers in the battery; if they were in Fox Lake they could
help your choir wonderfully. I think our Tenor and Bass would be welcome
to you. But it is altogether likely that our *cannon* will have to sing Bass a
good many times at Vicksburg before *we* can sing anywhere in the North.
It has rained a steady stream since midnight. Worst of all, out tents are
leaking. So you see we are not as comfortable as you are at College! . . .

∽

Thomas Christie to Sarah Christie

ON BOARD TRANSPORT "JEANNIE DEANS,"[32] MOUTH OF THE YAZOO,[33]
JAN. 24/63

Dear Sister,

Your favor of the 12th inst was recieved at Memphis in the hurry and
bustle of embarkation, I was officer of the guard too, at the same time, and

31. Civil War artillery men received an allowance of $36 per year for clothing, mak-
ing the loss of personal items at Shiloh quite significant for William and Thomas. Any
difference between the clothing allowance and that actually issued would be subtracted
from a soldier's pay at the end of the year. Todd, *American Military Equipage*, 1:38.

32. A side-wheel packet built in Madison, Indiana, and completed in St. Louis in
1860, she often ran the St. Louis–New Orleans route. *Way's Packet Directory*, 243.

33. The Yazoo River enters the Mississippi from the northeast a few miles above
Vicksburg.

so had too much to occupy me without writing. This must be my excuse for not answering sooner.

Here we are at last, after a voyage of 3 days, tied up on the sacred soil of Louisianna, and a very poor looking soil it is. I shall not attempt a description of the greenery of the lower Mississippi, you can find that in many a book of travel, enough to say, it was just as I expected to see it. I may sometime, if GOD spares us both, interest you by descriptions and incidents which I have no time or inclination to write, and untill then you must be satisfied with bare statements of facts, satisfied that nothing of interest is forgotten by me, and that I only await an opportunity to satisfy your curiosity. "Good time coming" you know.

There is no immediate prospect of fighting here; troops are rapidly concentrating, Division after Division is sweeping down, and when we *do* attack again it will be with force sufficient to overcome all opposition and carry the key of the Mississippi by a *Coup de main.*

The Kansas First is on board with us and a wild set of fellows they are.[34] I have discovered in their ranks an old schoolmate no less a personage than Martin Croover.[35] I knew him at once and had quite a talk with him in which he told me that when he ran away from Billy Welch's he went to Milwaukie, from there to the Missouri River, and when the war broke out went to Leavenworth and enlisted. He was in the Battle of Wilson's Creek and in many skirmishes, and looks just as he used to in every particular.

Before leaving Memphis we got two month's pay, 26 Doll's and between small debts contracted during the moneyless summer, and necessary purchases, such as shirts, boots etc. my pile is extremely small, as is William's, and I must advise you to apply to Father on our account for the money you need. You should not conceal your debts from him, tell him frankly all about it and it will be the best way. I will write to him in your behalf, and I am sure that, as your requests are reasonable they will be acceded to.

I send a specimen of Southern moss as found on shore. You can not imagine the beauty of the scene that presents itself in these woods, the trees are all covered with this moss which hangs in thick clusters or bunches on every part of the branches, draping them in silver tassels. You can imagine

34. Indeed: "Unmilitary men, often in trouble for robbing henroosts, yet grim in their hatred of the slave power they had been fighting since 1854." Monaghan, *Civil War on the Western Border,* 146.

35. Croover does not appear in the muster rolls of the First Kansas. He may have enlisted under another name.

the effect when I tell you that the bunch from which your small specimen was taken was three feet long and large enough to make an armful.

Write soon, and remember me as Your affectionate Brother T. D. Christie.

[margin note] Lieut. Clayton sends his respects to you and desires you to assure his friend of his regards.

[margin note] forward immediately to Clyman and let them hear from us. I write soon to them and then you can again hear from me

[margin note] I received this, this afternoon you may get another letter from me on Saturday, Sarah

∽

Thomas Christie to James Christie[36]

OPPOSITE THE MOUTH OF THE YAZOO, JAN. 26, 1863

My Dear Father,

Here we are at last, only a few miles from Vicksburg, and waiting for something to do. We arrived at this point day before yesterday, after a voyage of 4 days. On account of guerrillas, our steamers tied up at the shore every night. Twice we were fired into, but no damage was done. Twelve steamers brought our whole Division down; now they have gone up the river for more troops. In the mouth of the Yazoo opposite we can see a part of our fleet of gunboats; the guns of the others we can hear from down the river, in their fighting with the batteries. Work is going on at the canal, a short distance below us. This canal will enable us to get our gunboats and transports past the batteries.[37]

This voyage was much pleasanter than the one we made last year up the Tennessee. A part of the First Kansas were on the ship with us. I am sorry to say that some of them and some of our own men were drunk a good part of the time, and there was much quarrelling and fighting. some drunken men fell overboard and were drowned. Drunkenness is one of the worst things in the world.

36. Transcribed in Thomas Christie reminiscence.
37. This undertaking was the first of Grant's "experiments" to find a way past the Vicksburg batteries. The idea was to dig a canal through the relatively narrow neck of land in the river bend opposite the city, but a very high river and flooded lowlands foiled this plan. See Foote, *Civil War*, II:191–94.

The scenery of the lower Mississippi is very monotonous: cut out a mile of it anywhere, and it represents a thousand miles of the river. Swamps on one side, young cottonwoods on the other; that is all. South of the White and the Arkansas rivers the country is protected from inundation by levees; these are usually about 20 feet high, and as many wide at the base, rounding off at the top and covered with tough grass sod. This embankment is very convenient for us; we use it as a road, for the country on each side is very low and muddy. Down near the canal the levee is used for breastworks, on which the Artillery is planted which protects our men at work.

The weather now is exceedingly pleasant, a great contrast with what we had last week.

The campaign promises to be a short one. Men enough are being brought down to take Vicksburg by storm. When the battle takes place I think you will hear from "Mac's" old Division: All the men ware eager to get their share of the fighting. I send a small specimen of Spanish Moss: the trees in this neighborhood are draped with it. Your Ever,

T.D.C.

∽

William Christie to Alexander Christie

LOUISIANA MISS. RIVER FEBRUARY 5TH 1863

Dear Brother, tis a long time since I wrote a letter to you, or any one of the family. But let me tell you if you were here, and I where you are, you would not be more likely to write any more than I do: and I would be more apt to write, to you. Now let me tell you we don't feel very much encouraged down here. for there is not that energetic support of the govermnet in the north, that there should be. and the effect of the letters that come to the men in various camps, are very bad, in there consequences; causing much dissatisfaction and grumbling. The Niger, my Dear Brother is in the fence and casts his shadow over the whole land, or rather his past condition. There are thousands of men now in this army that think the President has gone to far in doing as he has done, in giving the slaves there freedom and the worst of it is the officers are quite free in showing there minds: and generally speaking they are against, the Proclomation. I cant tell much about the outside world, for we get no papers and very little mail of any kind so we fluctuate between Hope and fear, discussing the Probable results of the Battle of Vicks—h, and the majority of the men I have heard talk we will have the worst of it. There is diverse reports about the canal, you have heard, so much about. I beleive we have had one of the messenger Boats through it. But as for the truth of the matter I cant say, on the second, of this month, one of our rams ran past Vicks—h, and there was a very Brisk cannoade kept up as she went By on her way down she ran intoo and destroyed one or two Boats of the Rebs; she had one or two shots strike her, we learn that the Eastren Army has gone intoo winter quarters and that the Rebels has been strongly reinforced, By troops from there army there. Bregg we hear has got a great accession to his army, and so has Lee; and johnson, here. Banks we learn has been cut up Badly, and Repulsed at Port Hudson so if these things are all true and so much opposition north to the vigorous Proscecution of the war also, is true I ask you have we not reason: to feel as though all our sufferings were in vain, for we are surely suffering in many ways, not for want of food, or clothing But there is a lack of good moral influences round us, the want of total home enjoyments, and so from day to day the men grow weary of waitting. the slow movements, of our semisecesh generals, men dwarfed in morals, men that would do anything that would Prolong this war or cause it to end in favor of secesh: It realy is no wonder that we do not succeed in our cause any better than we do, when the employes of the goverment, are so full of sympathy for the traitors It looks to me that the Nation is fast tending to the condition you spoke of in one of your letters to me, our Capt'n says there is a milk and water Party rising in the north that will make the war futile in it[s] results, But some how I think it will rather be as you speak off, and that as trying as the ordeal may be we will come out of the fire as gold seven times tried, Truth and Justice, and Liberty triumphant over all the Devilish machinations of the Present day. Now I am not dumpish neither is Tom, allthough the weather is none of the finest, being rather moust, at times. the River is Rising and the drift wood looks very like the wreck of many vessels in a storm Boats keep gliding up and down the River But it is wonderfull how soon we get used to everything we dont trouble ourselves to learn anything, or if we dont is very seldom we can learn the truth, so we wait and if we can get up a report, just for the fun of it.

Now you must know or if you dont I will tell you that Tom and I are bond to do our whole duty By the goverment, and if it is so that we fail, in gaining what we enlisted for, I at Least, think if the goverment is subverted, will just walk over to ther Britannic majesties side of the line and stay there. But there is no use in thinking the Goverment will be swamped, for just before day it is darkest at least let us hope so, and so let us cheer up. Beleving in the mercy as well as the Justice of God, For I think he is just serving this nation as He would an Individual that had been Debaching himself as we as a Nation have done.

If it is the case that Banks has been repulsed at Port Hudson,[38] we in our company at least have come to the conclusion that Eastren troops are as good as the westren troops. There is a rummor in camp that it was the intention to run this Division Past Vic—h only the captains would not run there craft, it was to be done in a fog, I think the Plan is quite feasable as there are very heavy fogs on the river at times as heavy as the famous London fogs, I guess. I for one would be willing to stand my chance among the company in doing the run, if they could not hit the ram any more than twice in Broad daylight, I think it is quite likely they would do But little damage to us in a fog. A Brigade of this Division has gone up stream to do guard duty, and keep the guerilles from fireing on our Boats, The twentininth, rigment Wis Vol. are down stream from us about five miles, But we cant get down to see them and I suppose, they cant get up to see us, so we might as well be five times five miles apart. Our Company as a general thing are in good health, and full of the Devil: or something else so having nothing more to write or rather being unable to write as you or Tom, I will quit By requesting you to write to me a very long and interesting letter, give my love to all.

and beleive me ever your loving Brother

William G. Christie

[postscript] I have not had a letter from Sarah or any of you in a long time, and I am getting very anxious to hear from you all. the last letter we had was from sarah, Tom got it at Memphis

༄

William Christie to Alexander Christie

FEBRUARY 6TH, 1863, CAMP ON YOUNGS POINT OF THE MISS RV.

Dear Brother, I received your very welcom. letter last night, containing your handsome Present, of Pen, and Holder, allso Mother's Present came to

---

38. Port Hudson was a second, heavily fortified Confederate position 255 miles downstream from Vicksburg. Although General Banks was assigned the task of taking this post, he did not attempt an outright assault until May.

hand, And let me tell you that money, could not buy, either of the rigs, we were the envied of all the gazeing crowd, when your gift was openned to there sight. The letter I sent to yesterday was written in a way that might make you think I was in the Blues, I admit I was a little so, But in the after-noon we got some Papers, of the third ult: and although it cost a 25 cents to get a Paper yet we felt well Paid: on account of the cheering news we received, in my last letter I stated to you that the 29th Wis: was down here, But I am mistaken. Tom is to Blame, for that he would insist they were here But I was as certain that they were up the River at Hellenna. They were down at the takeing of Arkansas Post,[39] and I hope Tom Reid got through safe, we have no way of having a correspondence, with him or I would write to him. They have Projected a new Cannal, and they say it will be dug wide enough to allow a River Boat to Pass through and tis said that it could be dug in four days. you speak of Camping out, in such weather. Now I will give you a few extracts from my Journal to show what is what. On the 13th had to give up our tent to the quartermaster, and take the guncovers. fire under each, wind in the south and dreary Black clouds in the sky, 14th commenced raining at midnight and has been raining incessenly ever since on guard to day and find it very disagreeable, wind S E. by E. spongy ground and dripping sky makes mud very fast, the horses are standing up to there fettocks in mud, and are shivering with cold, wind changed to the N. W. about noon, 15th very cold weather, and a heavy fall of snow being layed down Passed a very uncomfortable night on guard, on account hav-ing a Poor Place to sleep in, so you may [see] that soldiering at times is not very nice. the snow fell to the depth of 9 or 10 inches and frost set in so having wet and cold to contend with we looked for a Place to sleep. I will now resumed my journal that you may see another Phase of our life. 15th moved about a mile from camp tonight, and slept in a Deserted house, the under Part was used for horses, the men slept up stairs, wind north fine snow falling. The house was an elegent Building when we first saw it you may suppose, what it looked like when we left it after the horses being in the various rooms for three days. 18th Roused out of Bed this morning By our sergent, Before daylight telling us to hurry for orders had come for us to be on Board of the Boat By eight oclock, then commeced the Bustle and excitement of moving, I was detailed as one of those who should stay to

39. A fortified Confederate base on the Arkansas River from which rebel gunboats could threaten the federal supply lines, it was taken by Sherman and McClernand's troops on January 11. Foote, *Civil War*, II:134–36.

load the teams, every one worked lively, and our Battery, with all the traps was quickly ready to move there was a regular time of jesting among us, on account of the officer in command of the 1st Mo. Battery the Brigade commandant that he could not move until his gun carraiges and harness, were thawed out, we made our own fun out of it and our Battery was the first one ready to move, we had every thing down to town By ten oclock all the cassions aboard and Baggage, shortly after we all came from camp, and got the guns aboard, and the teams went off after forrage Jennie Deans, is our Boat, the Kansas first Infantry are on the same Boat, and we are crowded. made our Beds on the Bow of the Boat, others slept on the upper deck some under the Boilers, and some on the cabin deck, early in the night it began to rain and all or most of us who were not under cover lay while we were throughly soaked, Drunken men numerous, fighting frequent, and Black eyes common, Wind south west, 19th Slush in the streets slush on Board, slush everywhere, where soldiers are allowed. the muddy River Rolls on to the sea, the soaking rain falls incessently and steamers whistle and Puff from Place to Place on the levee, the Black gunboat lies midstream terrible to look at, and the few houses, on the Arkansas side of the stream look like specks of snow, Ice and logs, drift down the stream in great, and everything shows that there has been a great extents of Country under the stormcloud, that is dripping on us here, Drunkness, is on the increase, And the officers and them are using there fists quite freely. I think the officers are more to Blame than the men. Being very abusive and drawing there side arms, threatening to use them, and in some instances using them. Jim Macpheeters got foul of two Infantry officers, that was abusing one of there men, and he getting his scotch up walloped them Pretty well, our own officers use us well, and the Infantry officers trying to ride over us, found it would not Pay, so they give it up. We are lieing in camp and our guns are facing out to the woods having cut embrasures in the dyke for that purpose, I have not much more to say, only that your letter and Present together [. . .] very deep down intoo our Hearts, Mothers gloves keeps, and will keep our hearts warmer than our fingers and hoping you have as fine a day, as we have, I will Close, By giving my love to all and closing on account of the mail, by signing. you Loving Brother

William G. Christie

P.S. I will start Staury [story?] with this letter.

Thomas Christie to Sarah Christie

NEAR LAKE PROVIDENCE LA. FEBRUARY 13TH, 1863

My Dear Sister,

Your sermon is read with much interest: it being your first effort in that line I was anxious, and rather doubtful of your abilities in exhorting. But now I am astonished that you do not turn your talents for the pulpit to account by turning itinerant preacher, or even army chaplain, and thus edifying hundreds as you have me. Seriously: my Dear Sarah, I am distressed at your anxiety for my moral welfare, I did not think you considered me such a sinner as I appear to be by your homily; always congratulating myself on being rather a good fellow, who stood a pretty good chance of promotion in the ascending ranks of moral progression, *Now* I know this to have been all self righteousness, in itself a deadly sin.

No, No, sister mine, when I am converted it will be through sound and philosophical reasoning, and not by vage appeals to my affectionate propensities; that is, I must be reached through the intellect, and not the heart. Whenever I can be convinced by good logical arguments of the truth of the christian plan of Redemption, I stand ready to adopt the christian life, knowing as I do, the happiness that there is in it, and the advantage there is in having a sure and consistent guide to conduct through the phisical existince.

To tell the truth, our mode of life is not favorable to moral development, and there is a decided antagonism between the feelings that prompt us to direct our shot and shell where they tear off the most heads and limbs, and those teachings that tell us all men are brothers, and should be treated with christian charity and Kindness. I am very much pleased that you are living religiously, for after all, I believe you are right, although I can't see through some things in your system.

Our Division has moved camp from the Yazoo to this point, where we are in position on the shore of this beautiful lake, and about 4 miles back from the little French town of Lake Providence where our men are opening an old channel connecting the river and the lake, which will allow our boats to pass down the Red River by way of the lake and bayous of the interior. Camp here is very pleasant, overlooking a fine sheet of water, with opportunities to boat, fish, and bathe, and the men enjoy themselves firstrate.

All are in good health except our Lieut. Allen,[40] poor fellow, who is not expected to live long. He was a private 6 months ago, then a corporal, and during the battle of Corinth directed his piece with skill and effect untill severely wounded through the shoulder. For bravery there we made him Orderly Sergeant, and afterwards 2nd Lieutenant, but a chronic Diarrhea has afflicted him all the campaign and now he is lying very low in the hospitalboat.

I am in reciept of a letter from Helen tonight that delighted me. She is a good writer, and her style is easy and pleasant, but she is second to you in affectionate gossip. To speak fairly, I prize your epistles for gossip mostly, and the more piquant the better, Tattoo has blown and I must to bed, Tom.

[margin note] Now that you have determined on German put it through study it thoroughly. A good knowledge of it will aid you in studying your own language.

[margin note] I have bought a watch from a comrade and so you can use my other one. I am compelled to have a time-keeper to post the reliefe by when on guard.

∽

Thomas Christie to Alexander Christie

LAKE PROVIDENCE LA. FEB. 26TH, 1863

Dear Brother,

Yours of the 14th is received and with great pleasure! you are improving in your handwriting fast, and no less in composition, as your letter shows. I think you must be studying well this winter, if you do not go to school, as your letters evince considerable improvement.

The thermometrical record is very interesting and I am glad to see that you still continue the observations. Here we have just passed through the greatest rain storm that I ever saw, lasting since yesterday noon to nearly noon today, and, as a consequence, our tents were flooded with water this forenoon to the depth of some 6 inches or more.

40. Joseph Allen was born in Ohio in 1840 and was a resident of Taylors Falls when he enlisted in the battery. *Adjutant General's Report*. He died on March 3, 1863.

We are all in usual good health, notwithstanding the weather, and expect to continue so at least as long as the sweet potatoes and other fixtures require our attention! When we lose appetite it is a dangerous sign, and a mans fitness of Duty is guaged by the extent of his achievements at the Mess table. You will observe that we have now reversed the old rule that prevailed while before Corinth where it was expected that a sick man would eat two rations and a well man, one.

It would amuse you to see us eat our dinner in camp, it is so different from the civilized meal of that name, both in material and adjuncts. As a preliminary observation, I must tell you that the company is divided into four squads, each of which messess by itself, having a cook and cooking utensils. Each of the cooks has a particular call to meals so that the men know by it whose dinner is ready. One has a small bell, another blows a bugle, a third has a kind of gong, and ours contents himself with shouting, Grub pile. When this good sound is heard among the tents, there is a general rush from them to the cook tent in the rear, every man with tin plate and cup, knife, fork, and spoon brandishing in the air. At the cook fire we find a black mess Kettle full of as black coffee, another mess Kettle of sweet potatoes, (splendid.) a bake kettle of fried meat, and two messpans, full of sliced bread, and sugar for the coffee. Some times, when we have been out foraging successfully, our diet is varied with chicken soup or roast, and great is the rejoicing on such an occasion. Having got what we think we can dispose of safely, we return to the tent with the "grub" in our hands, and sitting down on our rolled up blankets, teeter the plate on our knees, set the coffee or water on the floor, and fall to with a will, generally, (as is the case with me an my bedmate) two eating out of the same plate, on account of the scarcity of that article of aliment supports. When the meal is over the plate is scraped clean with a knife, and both are laid at the head of the bunk in readiness for next meal. I would have been quite destitute of anything to eat off if I had not picked up a battered plate on the march between Holly Springs and Moscow,

[. . .] (to . . . the greasy paper.) On the whole we are not badly off for food, although its want of variety sometimes makes it distastefull.

We would have had inspection today if it had not rained so hard, and will probably have it tomorrow. The inspection will be of everything, men, horses, guns ammunition and tents, and is the first we have had since we were at Corinth. Gen. Logan's Division has come down the river lately from Memphis, and is now camped near us.

Work is going on at all the canals briskly, and it is likely that we stay here for some time. Hoping to hear from you soon, I subscribe myself T.D. Christie.

∾

Thomas Christie to Sarah Christie

LAKE PROVIDENCE FEB. 27TH 1863

My Dear Sister:

Yours of the 14th was recieved a short time ago, and I would have answered sooner but for a tremendous rain storm that has raged almost two days, and precluded either reading or writing, on account of the leaky character of the tent! To keep dry ourselves was a hard enough matter as we had to keep our rubbers on all the time to defend us from the wet. It would have made you laugh yesterday, to see us all standing upon our bunks, which are raised some 6 inches from the ground, to avoid the water that dashed about in the center of the tent like a miniature lake, washing it little waves up against the stove and the saber bayonet stuck in the ground for a candlestick. Thinking some obstruction had got into the ditch outside, and that this was the cause of our deluge, I seized a spade, donned my cap cover, opened the tent door, and dashed out into the storm—only to find myself boot deep in a tremendous lake, that filled the whole of our camp! the drains being utterly unable to carry off the vast volume of water that dashed by buckets full from the clouds. you may imagine that this prospect soon damped my ardor, and I was only too happy to make my retreat to the canvass in as quick time as possible, while the storm, raging with redoubled fury outside, seemed to laugh at my temerity. Fortunately, this was its last effort, and it soon after subsided, or we would have been swamped. We thought of the old adage, and comforted our hearts with the assurance, that if it was our fate to be hung, we should at least escape a watery grave, as we stepped forth to "view the face of nature" after the rain.

We are having some good times now vocally, and all we lack to complete the harmony of our notes is a female voice or two to vary our too masculine base. "Kingdom Coming"[41] is a great favorite with us, having learned it from the sheets you sent us, and all the singers wish me to request you to

41. Part of a popular series by Henry Clay Work known as "Songs of the Negro," this song poked fun at southern slave owners abandoning their plantations. Heaps, *Singing Sixties*, 268–70.

send down anything more of the Kind you may have: if you can not send the originals, let us have copies, of anything, Sacred, or mirthful, for our singing is about equally divided between the two, with a specimen of the Sentimental thrown in once in a while. Send the notes for "Our Captains last words," if you have them, and anything else in the patriotic or martial vein. If you can find them, send the lines "Annie Lisle," for which we have the tune but have forgotten the words since we used to sing them at the arsenal last winter: it is a beautiful tune, and you should learn it if you can find it.

I am afraid that I am giving you too many commissions to execute, and will ruin you in postage stamps, but we have so much time to dispose of here in camp that a new song is a perfect Godsend, it is sung in full chorus by a dozen deep base voices at a time, and is whistle and hummed in solo at all times of the day. Among our favorites I can commend to your notice a few choice tunes, such as "Oh! Sing to me of Heaven." "Coronation," and another hymn beginning "Forever with the Lord, Amen, so let it be, Life o'er the Dead, is in that word, Tis immortality." The tune is splendid, and if you are not acquainted with it, I will take down the notes, and send them to you. I assure you it will repay you for learning it.

Among the Sentimentals in favor with us, may be counted "My Willie's on the Dark blue Sea," "Lilly Dale," and some others whose names I forget, These with "Gay and happy," "Kingdom coming," "John Brown," and the old patriotic songs, "Red, White and Blue," and "The Star Spangle Banner," comprise our list of favorites.

So you see, anything at all will be acceptable, and if you have any air that you like *especially*, be sure and let me have it. I will send any of the tunes I have mentioned, that you are not acquainted with, if I have to jot the notes down from the voices of the singers.

Oh; I was about to forget telling you to forward "Rally round the flag boys"[42] words and music, if you can. I heard the 52d Ill's sing it one night on the march from Grand Junction to Holly Springs, as our Division waited for theirs to pass by; and I thought it sounded grand. Part of the chorus has rung in my ears sometimes since then, and I could fancy I heard again the swelling notes, as the whole Regiment joined in, and kept-step to their

42. Although there was a song with this title by James T. Fields and William Bradbury, Thomas is more likely referring to the very popular "The Battle Cry of Freedom" by George F. Root. The chorus of the latter includes the words, "Yes, we'll rally 'round the flag boys, we'll rally once again, shouting the battle cry of freedom!" Heaps, *Singing Sixties*, 71–72.

song. "Rally round the flag boys, Rally once again . . ." These words sound all the more inspiring to me, after hearing them shouted amid the din and smoke of a terrible battle, as at Shiloh where I saw a boy of about 16 grasping the colors of the 19th Wisconsin (I think) and shouting, as the tide of panic struck men swept by him, "They will never get *this* while there's life in *my* body." And again at Corinth after we had fallen back from the hills by the Rail Road, where the 14th Wisconsin was cut up so dreadfully, I saw a mounted officer of that Regt. with their colors in his hand, dashing about and calling on the men to rally again to support our two guns which were blazing away again in the road.

The 14th responded nobly, and falling in in the rear of the guns they supported us well untill the arrival of reinforcements. Of all the Regiments in the 2d Brigade, we would rather be backed by the little 14th, for they are men whom we have seen tried. They are camped close by us, and many of the boys are known to us, coming from Minnesota, as many of them do.[43]

The 17th is camped close on the other side of us, so you see we have plenty of company. Lieut. Jackson of the 18th comes occasionally to see one of our squad, and then we have glorious singing, for he has a beautiful voice and understands the science well.

I have just read over your letter again with much pleasure! I can see almost the life you lead, and its routine, just by these letters of yours: continue to write naturally, and you will write well.

Tell your Professor that I *would* like to join your dinner party *sometimes*, especially when we are on the march, and have to dine off an adamantine cracker, with perhaps a little sugar for seasoning. But when in camp, just after a successful foraging of the country by our baggage teams, I would not exchange one of our dinners for an average one of yours. *Then* we will have sweet potatoes, chicken roast, vegetable soup, bread, molasses, and honey. I must confess though that these lucky days are (like angels visits) few and far between, and if the choice were left to me, I think I should be

---

43. It is difficult to sustain this statement from the published muster rolls. No one in the Fourteenth seems to have given Minnesota as a "residence," but their reply may have been convenience or formality. It is worth noting that many men in the Fourteenth seem to have enlisted from La Crosse, Wisconsin, and others from strange places like "Pittsburg Landing, Tenn." See *Roster of Wisconsin Volunteers*, 770–803. The Fourteenth did take heavy casualties at Corinth, thirty killed and forty-eight wounded, and was praised by the brigade commander for its role in the fight on the Chewalla Road. Quiner, *Military History of Wisconsin*, 602–60; U.S. War Department, *War of the Rebellion*, Series I, 17.1:355.

greatly tempted, to say the least, to give your eating accommodations the preference.

I cannot make out what you mean by saying in your letter, that I would doubtless rather get a letter from some one else, for I am sure I value your letters as much as I do anybody's, and have never signified anything else: you must not think, because I sometimes scold you for some things, that my affection for you is diminished or that I do not care to hear from you. It is true, I have found fault with you on some accounts, but not through any loss of regard for you, and if I have hurt your feelings in this way, I am sorry for it, and beg your forgiveness.

Perhaps Father has been telling you of my correspondent in Connecticut, Miss Minnie R. Southwick, the young sister of my friend and comrade, Charley Southwick. I informed Father of the correspondence (which has now continued some 6 months) a long time ago, and desired him not to let you or Helen know of it, but I suppose he has blabbed on me, so you shall know all about it. In the camp at Corinth I had often had an opportunity of reading her letters to Charley, and finally got him to introduce me to her by letter, since which time we have corresponded regularly. She is a splendid writer, and her letters are well composed and entertaining. As a specimen of her style sometimes I may mention her description in a late letter of the hard times in Connecticut, she says,— "Times are so hard here, and money is so scarce, that the people have to use jack knives, pocket combs etc. for small change, and a flourishing wooden nutmeg manufactory has had to suspend operations, as the people are too poor to indulge in such luxuries." I have seen her portrait that she sent to Charley, and she is a regular Puritan, high forehead, and well chiselled face.

Having now written you quite a respectable book, on a *variety* of subjects, I will close by assuring you of my unchanged affection,

T. D. C.

～

Thomas Christie to Sarah Christie

LAKE PROVIDENCE LA. MARCH IITH/63,

My Dear Sister,

Yours of the 26th Feb. is just received by me, and I am charmed with it, indignation, example, poetry and all. I am truly thankful that my ears were not at hand when you so amiably thought of pulling them, for, heaven knows; they are long enough now in all conscience. Henceforth we will drop religious discussion in our letters, and then we can agree, and this is not the first quarrel produced by that cause, you know.

Apropos of Religion, you must know that I attended a prayer meeting a few evenings ago, in the camp of the 18th Wisconsin, conducted by their Chaplain, Rev. Mr. Crane of Oshkosh, I think.[44] We sat on boards, outdoors, in the moonlight, and while the Evening Star sunk brilliantly to its rest behind the moss-hung woods in the west, our hymns filled the mellow air with harmony, and prayer and exhortation arose when the singing ceased. It was so romantic and heart-softening, this meeting of Christians in the Louisiana swamp, far, far, from all the advantages of the home worship, that I really enjoyed it much, and will go again tomorrow evening.

Mr. Crane officiated a few days ago on a mournful occasion to us—the funeral of our late Lieut. Allen. We all attended, mounted, and dressed in full Artillery uniform and escorted the chaplain from camp down to town, where there is an old French graveyard, all full of old, crumbling, unique headstones: and in this old graveyard poor Allen was buried with military honors, the minister making a short prayer and address appropriate to the occasion.[45]

Would you not like to take a peep at us just at this time? Let me see if I cannot give you an idea of how we pass an evening here in camp, and you can compare it with your life in College. In the first place then, you must know, that we are now living in tents of the wedge pattern, each made to hold four men, and the name will give you a very good idea of their appearance. Imagine a canvas wedge whose sides incline to each other at an angle of about 80 Degrees set on its head. Expand its proportions till it will measure about 7 feet across the base, the sides 7 feet wide and 7½ high. To support it, imagine a perpendicular pole at the middle of each end, connected at top by a horizontal, over which the canvas is stretched, and secured at the bottom by pegs driven in to the ground through rope loops fastened to the cloth. At the middle of one end the canvas is slit vertically for a door, and strings are fastened to each side that it may be tied up at night or in bad weather.

44. It seems no chaplain in any Wisconsin regiment went by this name. The chaplain of the Eighteenth Wisconsin at this time was George Stokes, from Oshkosh. *Roster of Wisconsin Volunteers,* II:83.

45. Lieutenant Allen's body was later moved and reburied near his family's home in Ohio. Joseph M. Allen Letters, MHS.

Now that you see my habitation and understand how it is built, I will ask you to step inside while I introduce you to my tentmates and the internal arrangements. The tent, as I said before, is intended to accommodate four, but we have only three in ours, which gives us more room and comfort. I feel tempted to give you an elaborate description of my two comrades, as they sit now visa vis on opposite bunks, a knapsack between them, and all their faculties engaged in an exciting game of euchre. But this would weary you I know, and so, without giving you a lot of talk about complexions, hair, style of nose, color of eyes, shape of mouth, and the facial angle[?] ; *a la* approved novelists: I will merely say that they are both good fellows, conscientious, affectionate, young, and good singers, with their share of good looks, and hearty love of that soldier's consoler, Fun.

You look up as you enter, and see, hanging from the ridgepole, in threatening symetry, our three sabres, and my revolver and spur, They hang over the back end of the tent so as not to be in the way, and immediately under them is a shelf supported at each end by a stake driven into the ground, and in this shelf are a dozen books, a foraging cap, a razor case, a soldiers pocket looking glass, and a burning candle stuck in a round match box for candlestick.

Among the books you may notice, Bishop Hornes[46] works, Brewster's Legendres Geometry,[47] The Household of Bouverie, a Southern Romance,[48] two music books, a hymn book, or two, and my Diary. Under this shelf there is another one, near the ground, on which are our tin plates and cups, and our knapsacks, you will understand that these shelves occupy the whole width of the tent at the back end, opposite the door.

Looking down to the right and left of you as you stand in the entrance, you see two bunks stretching along the sides of the tent, the foot towards the door, and leaving between them a narrow passage way. One of these bunks, which are built of boards laid on blocks to keep them from the ground, is wide enough for two, and the other for one. On them are the blankets, made down ready for bed time, with the rubbers on top to guard against the rain, which may come at any time of the night and which pours through

46. Anglican theologian George Horne, Bishop of Norwich, 1790–92.

47. *Elements of Geometry: On the Basis of Dr. Brewster's Legendre* by James Thomson, published in 1855.

48. *The Household of Boverie, or the Elixer of Gold: A Romance* by Catherine Ann Warfield, "Southern Lady," published in 1860.

our tent very badly, the canvas being of an inferior quality, about the same texture as cotton sheeting at home.

I should have told you before, that you could see before entering, the name of the tent done in black paint on the front, at one side of the Door, "WINONA." Almost every tent in the Company has its name, invented and put on by its inmates, and some of them are characteristic and amusing. Thus, William's tent has painted on it, "The Three Kings," which assumption of superiority is due to the fact of the there being three William's resident in it. "St. Paul," "St. Croix Rangers," "Lady Ward," "Tigers Den," such are some of the names. The German platoon from New Ulm, have some unique ones, "Beatus Hohle," named after a famous Robber of the Schwartz Wold, "Wasserdictes Lach," Water tight-hole, etc.

After this digression, let us return to "Winona," and see what its inmates are doing this evening, you find us sitting on our beds, Kelly,[49] my bunk mate, and O'Hara[50] turning over the leaves of a music book, and singing sacred hymns to well known tunes, while I am busy writing to you my Dear Sister, using my Diary for a portfolio, and my spread knees for a desk. Ah! sister mine, when you sit down at your Desk to answer this poor epistle, when you unkey your portfolio with its stores of everything needed to make a well finished letter; when you lean your arm on the Desk, and indite at your ease the words that are so precious to me; think, think, of the difficulties that surround the Literary and espistolary duties of your poor soldier correspondent. Without desk; setting his ink on the ground, and his sheet on his knee; the blanket his seat, and the noisy mirth or songs of comrades his prompters; you must acknowledge that the adjuncts of my literary labors are not as favorable as yours. However, I still make out to laugh instead of crying, at vexations and I still preserve my appetite and sound sleep by living up to my motto "Begone melancholy," "Care avaunt:"

When it is time to go to bed, we take all the books from the upper shelf, and put them below, covering them and the knapsacks with an old rubber that I picked up on the Corinth battlefield. With our pantaloons for pillows, and the soft side of a cypress board for feathers, we sleep sound and dreamless, fatigued by our exertions at Base Ball through the Day.

49. Private Murray Kelly, originally from New York and a resident of St. Anthony when he enlisted.
50. Private Joseph O'Hara, originally from Ohio, enlisted as a resident of Winona.

I received some time ago the Sentinel[51] and Temperance Advocates[52] you sent, and you cannot imagine how much please we were by the little piece of music in one of the latter. Continue to send them, especially if there is music in any of them.

There are some things in your letter, which I have not noticed, as I know you did not mean what you wrote, so all that nonsense about not writing any more is not believed by your affectionate Brother T. D. Christie

∾

Thomas Christie to James Christie[53]

PROVIDENCE, LA., MARCH 21. 1863.

Dear Father:

We are glad to hear of Sarah's return from College; glad also to receive the two copies of the St. Paul "Press" that you sent. Above all, we are glad to hear from you once more, as our mail has failed us of late, and we feared a steamer had been taken by the guerillas. Our canal here is a complete success;[54] the water rushing through it with tremendous force, and twelve feet deep. The lake has, in consequence, risen about six feet, and in forty-eight hours will overflow our camp; for it is up to within 18 inches of the bank already. But we expect to leave camp today or tomorrow, to go aboard a steamer for an expedition somewhere. Logan's Division went aboard some time ago; all but one Brigade, and that is passing now. It is said they went some 25 miles up the river, to a higher camping ground. The water has begun to run into the mouths of the ditches that drain our camp, and we have had to fill them up. You should see the old Mississippi now, he is grand! You get such an idea of *power* from the immense and swiftly-flowing stream. I look upon him, and take courage. The strength of the North-west, in men and munitions, is rushing down with him to the Gulf; they

51. Possibly the Beaver Dam *Sentinel*, which began publication in 1852 and would have been a hometown newspaper for the Christies.

52. A number of contemporary publications appeared with this title, most out of New England or New York.

53. Transcribed in Thomas Christie reminiscence.

54. The plan behind the Lake Providence canal was to create a link with several small bayous to the Red River and thence to the Mississippi below Vicksburg, a route of almost four hundred miles. The work was finally completed at the end of March 1863, but by then Grant had decided to move overland from Milliken's Bend, and the Lake Providence route was never used. Welcher, *Union Army*, II:861.

will sweep away every enemy of the Flag from all these lands, that our noble River may flow unobstructed to the sea.

We sometimes get letters suggesting that our Army here must be losing heart, we are meeting so many difficulties. This is a great mistake. Never were we in better spirits, never more sure of conquering in the end our deluded enemies. For myself I will say that not for a moment have I ever wavered from this belief; and my comrades are like me. All we need for the final triumph is the cordial support of our people at home. We will fight this thing out, if it takes ten years.—But as I write I hear the men say we are to move up the river to a new camp; this letter must be finished there.—

Six miles north of Providence,
    march 22.

Sure enough, my last sentence yesterday was broken into by the sharp staccato tones of the bugle sounding the "Boots, and Saddles." Orders had come to change camp. Portfolios were closed instantly; books were hastily thrust into knapsacks, with clothing and such odds and ends as we could carry; blankets were rolled up; the tents were leveled with the ground,—all this was the work of the cannoneers. The drivers in the meanwhile were taking down the picket-rope, and harnessing their teams. The change in our quiet camp was great; all was now bustle and activity. But the activity was not confusion; all was regular and orderly; our men have gone through work like this so often that everyone knows first what to do, and how to do it in shortest time. Occasionally, in the midst of the work you might hear a driver swearing over the temporary loss of a bridle or a legging; or a cannoneer grumbling because the game of cricket was interrupted just when he was about to have his innings. But the non-coms kept everybody too busy for complaints. For there is much emulation among us; every sergeant and corporal tries hard to have his men ready to move before the others. It was marvellous, the brief time required to put the Battery all ready to move. Then in quick succession—"stand to horse," "Cannoneers to your posts," "Drivers Mount," and "Limber to the front"! Every lunette-eye was over the pintle-hook[55] before you could say "Jack Robinson,"—and away we went in column toward the river. No steamer was ready for us; so, with the other batteries of our Division, we bivouacked last night on the

55. A ring-and-hook system by which the guns were linked to the gun-carriage and the carriage to the caisson. Gibbon, *Artillerist's Manual,* 169.

broad top of the levee—it was the only dry and safe spot to be found. I slept under my caisson, with clothes and boots on; a horse at each wheel munching corn all night for my lullaby. We were roused by the bugle at dawn, ate a hard cracker or two; and began at once to put our guns, horses, and wagons aboard the "Iatan."[56] In an hour the work was finished. The "Assembly" was blown to recall stragglers; and our big steamer pushed out into the stream. Then upstream we went, very slowly, past the fleet lying at the levee, past the mouth of the newly-opened canal, through which the water was rushing like a torrent, past the half submerged town and the forests behind it,—and so up to our new camp on this higher ground. On the way up I had time to look over the "Iatan." She saw service at Island No. Ten last year, and bears the marks of it. There are many holes through the smoke-stacks, made by canister-shot; on the sides of the "texas" I counted over thirty bullet-marks, (the pilots must have been plucky men); even on the bell there are two indentations made by canister, in one of them the crease stamped by the slight ridge that the iron shot gets from the mould.— The shores as we passed looked fresh and green; the young cottonwoods and willows in full leaf. and the peach and quince trees showing their pink and white blooms. I was reminded of the banks of the Tennessee and our expedition to Eastport a year ago. How incongruous seems the thought of war amid such scenes of beauty! But the war is not of our seeking; we are here simply to restore peace and security to these lovely shores.

In an hour we were again tied up to the Louisiana bank; and two hours more saw our tents up, our guns parked, and the streets of our new camp nicely swept. Part of Logan's Division is here. But the whole Division is ordered down the river to near Vicksburg; they are embarking as I write. The stirring times for which we have been waiting are evidently close ahead. In a month it will be decided, probably, who owns the Mississippi. We have great confidence in our generals. Our cause is the best that ever was fought for; God is with us! When the time comes, after all this weary waiting, for this Western Army to *act*, we shall move forward as sure of success as men can be. Don't heed the croakers there in the rear. We feel that the Nation as a whole is in hearty sympathy with Grant and this host of his. When Vicksburg is ours, those noisy Copperheads near you will have to change their tune!

56. A side-wheel, wooden packet built at Cincinnati in 1858, measuring 221 by 33 feet. *Way's Packet Directory*, 220.

We were paid lately; but I have now only two dollars in my pocket. However, the comrades is my platoon owe me five or six more. Do not fear for us; we are lively as crickets . . .

⌒⌣

Thomas Christie to Sarah Christie

NEAR LAKE PROVIDENCE LA. MARCH 24TH 1863

My Dear Sister

Yours of the 14th with the Sentinel and music came to hand an hour ago, with two Independents, and after reading the letter, looking at the likeness, (which I must say in the best one I have yet seen of your) trying the music; and lending the Sentinel and Independents to eager claimants, after doing all this I say, it occurred to me to remember my debt to you for your favor.

Your promise to furnish us with music sets us wild with delight, and if you could see how quickly we have mastered the two pieces you sent and what pleasure they afford us, you would allow that the musical talent of the Battery is not to be despised. We have "Rosalie the Prairie flower,"[57] but you can send the others you spoke of and they will be welcome I will note down the hymn "Forever wit the Lord," and send it in this and I am made disappointed if you do not consider it a gem.

MARCH 25TH

Your likeness is firstrate much better I think that the one sent to William, and my tentmate, Kelly, says that you should be called Tommy instead of Johnny. All who look at you say "Ah; that is Tom's sister'"

This is the worst hole we have been in yet, the water is a foot deep where our guns are parked, and the whole camp is better suited for the abode of reptiles than any species of the Mammalia, let alone civilized men, used to the high prairies of the Minnesota. This country is not worth fighting for, unless for a place to breed frogs in for a French market. Low cotton and corn fields, the furrows between the rows lying full of stagnant water, and cypress swamp, with here and there a belt of cottonwood; this is the general appearance of the face of the country. To be sure, there are many fine houses to be seen here also, and some beautiful gardens, but *now,* the

---

57. A popular song by George F. Root written under the pseudonym Wurzel and published in the early 1850s. Ewen, *American Popular Music,* 76.

houses are deserted, perhaps burned, and the gardens are trampled into mud by the horses picketed in them all the rare and beautiful shrubs and flowers broken down and destroyed. The sight of this desolation always makes me melancholy, although I know that it is nothing more than a just punishment on these wealthy people, who, in their insolent pride, set Justice at defiance, and in their supposed strength thought to substitute *their* will for the Right and equity. Thus they have called down upon themselves the merited vengeance of the soldiers of the North, soldiers of a people who read and think, and *work,* and whom they in their fancied superiority, despised. The retribution is well deserved.

I am glad that you have left college, and I attribute the superiority of your last letter to the fact that your mind is not so much occupied and oppressed now by your studies as when at school. I forewarn you that I shall now expect more lively letters than you have been in the habit of sending to me, and when you open your school, you will surely have material for correspondence, such as I used to get last Summer.

Your insinuations in regard to my correspondent in Connecticut are unfounded: I take no more pains with my letters to Minni[58] than with those to you, indeed I take pains with none of my letters, but just rattle them out of my brains in the shortest time possible, and sent them off without revising, as Pope would try to make us believe was the way he wrote his poetry.

The weather is pretty hot just now, and the drying up of so much water as is on the ground from late rains, will not be the best thing for the health of the troops. I do not fear anything for myself, but there are constitutions in the company that will be affected by the malaria sure to be generated, and I hope we will leave (as is rumor) to go to the other side of the river before long.

We have rumors from Vicksburg of heavy cannonading by the gunboats of the advance of our Infantry towards the enemy works, and of the failure of an attempt to land some of our Field Artillery, on account of the water.[59] It is said that our branch of the service will have no chance to do anything there on this account, and that cavalry is as useless. The Generals have to go afoot with the rest.

58. Minnie Southwick, sister to Sergeant Charles Southwick: see Thomas to Sarah, Feb. 27, 1863 (page 108).

59. This passage probably refers to the unsuccessful attempts to approach Vicksburg via the Yazoo River in mid-March. Welcher, *Union Army,* II:863.

Mr. Allen, the brother of our late Lieutenant has been down here a day or two. He came too late though to see pour Joe, and goes home today.

Awaiting your next installment of music, I remain your affectionate Brother,

T. D. Christie

∽

William Christie to James Christie

LAKE PROVIDENCE LA: MARCH 19TH 1863

Dear Father, I write to you to give my hands and mind something to do and at the same time gratify you with the knowledge that we are Both in excellent health. The Levee at this Point was oppenned two days ago and the work of drowning an area of 25 × 200 miles in extent that is from this one oppening alone. there is another oppening some thirtyfive miles up river, on this same side, that will help augment the waters in several Bayous and over flow a great portion of the country, this oppening would not have had any effect on, on account of the Washitah hills that come to within twelve miles of this Town, to give you a slight idea of the quantity of water coming in here, just think of the River Mourne[60] on a slight Bender and you see the stream that is running past our camp, and within six or eight rods of us. The weather we are having is very warm, and the trees are fast Putting forth there foliage, and every thing looks Beautiful. MARCH 20TH Father you see By the Heading of this Letter I was going to punish you with one of dull scriblings, But my besetting sin Laizeness Phisically and every other way such a term may be applied to a man stopped me, just where you read the last word; Beautiful. Before you stumble on too the New date, your letter came today: so love or a sense of duty, has overcome the evil, and here goes: wether you will or no, to Punish you By a letter or mess of scribbling that will make you cry Peccave,[61] for a long time. Now I will give you a sketch of our camping ground and then you will see I have reason to think with me Beautiful to the south and East of our camp we see away down the River some twelve or fourteen miles, the distant timber looking diminutive and hazy. While the River looks like a Broad Ribbon of silver: as far as it can be

60. The River Mourne, located in County Tyrone in the province of Ulster in Northern Ireland, flows through the town of Sion Mills, where James Christie worked as a millwright and William spent part of his childhood before emigrating to America.

61. Probably the Latin word *peccavi*, "I have sinned."

traced with the eye: right in our front is a large: Cotton field with the old crop ungathered, and our camp occupying the east edge of it: the west side of it being skirted with timber. Our guns as well as the other two of our Division Batteries, are exactly in a line unlimbered on the extreme front, next comes the limbers of the guns, at a distance of three or four yards, next come the caissons, then the horses then the tents of the men, then on the flanks of the battery are our fires for cooking: two on each flank, in the rear are officers tents, and the commissary tent. I must go drill. C. Tom is going on hunting out the men. Drill over I resume my writing, and a number of our squad are going to have a game of cricket as soon as they can find the ball. the once quiet lake is in our rear: now turned into a River of surging roaring water, on our right the second Brigade is camped, and on the opposite side of the lake the third, or as it is called the Iowa Brigade is camped, on our left is the town and the tents of the first Brigade and one of our Batteries are glistening in the Bright sunlight, the boats are lieing at the landing, and some of there great chimnes are pouring our vast lines of black smoke. the merry shoat of the men voices are heard, and the heavy smooth chug. click: of the workings of the [. . .] on the Iorn axles are heard as a Battery is out drilling the horses and drivers. There are a great number of white fleecy clouds in the sky, and the murmur of the rushing water in its new channel through the levee falls on our ear just like the sound of the Mourne over the carrie at the zion, and we look over the field : and the trees in blossom and the first green of there years dress, and there is the songs of Birds and everything is bathed in a fine blue summer hazeiness, dreaming and quiet like, and I Bleive it is Beautiful. Now to business you ask me if I have sent home my money. No neither have I spent it. To give a clear look, I will just give the account, of everything and be very glad to think you are interested to know so much about. For I am but a Boy yet, to my cost, in many ways.[62] In the first Place I was indebted to the government eighty Dollars and 95 cents for clothing.

so it stands like this.

government allowance of one year $42

Total amount drawn 80. .95.

after deducting some for wear, I was

allowed amount lost at Shiloh————————5. .50.

leaving 55. .45.

---

62. William was more than thirty years old at this time.

bringing me twelve Dollars and ten cents after paying fourteen months clothing which is as follows.

one rubber Blkte $2.55.

" pair Drawers. . 80.

. . . . *socks 32*

Total $3. .67

So if you deduct a fraction of a month or I should say add a fraction you can make change, All I am Indebted to government now for clothing is What I got on the 2nd of Feb. and if there is no accidents takes place I think I will not need a great deal of Clothing before next fall. For I Bought at Memphis shirts, Boots, Hat, to the amount. shirts $6.00

Hat 2.50

Boots 5.00

for the likeness sent to Sarah 3.00

Bread 1.00

17.00

paid an old debt 2.00

Express on same 1.00

these should be socks in the[. . .]account 1.50

Butter, onions, papers 2.00

Total 24.50

lent two dollars to one of our boys.

The reason that I Bought these things was this. There was no clothing in our quartemasters hands and we had snow and it looked like winter

After all debts were paid and I had what was due me. I had $15. on hand I was going to send home to you. But our sergant, Thomas Gorden[63] had great need of some monies so our Tom, and myself talked the matter over and we came to the conclusion I should let him have twenty Dollars, for six months, Tom giving me a lend of five Dollars. so you have the reason, I have sent you any money. I have 65 cents on hand, and am 150 cents in Debt. Tom and I have sent a Box of Books to your address, Watertown. But it had not left this landing last night before dark. so you may even get this letter before the Express agent charged us two Dollars for the Box and the Provo marshal a Permit so it is likely you will get it Before a great deal of time Passes Bye. The Books are well Bound and are worth twentyfive Dollars.

---

63. Thomas Gordon, originally from New York, enlisted in the battery from Winona County. *Adjutant General's Report*, 785.

I am very glad sarah has got home and I hope she is well. Tell her to write soon for I have not had a letter from her in a great while. There is none of you forgotten anyway: and there is not one of the family I don't think about more or less every day, so now you have a long letter and yet how little of the inner life, there is displayed in any of the Epistles we write to each other: your letters to me are full of much that is cheering but at the same time old, and although you are loyal yet I can see you are weary; of this protracted struggle, and if I am not much mistaken more discouraged than I have ever Been.

I for one have never been fearful on my own account, But it really would grieve me to see the country ruined. I suppose I weary, so I will close. your son

W. G. C.

◦∿◦

Thomas Christie to James Christie[64]

LAKE PROVIDENCE, APRIL 8. 1863

My Dear Father,

Lieut. Clayton left us today for the North on leave of absence. He carries with him about $3,000 that the boys have asked him to take to their families. He will give you $66 on Williams account, and $57 on mine. This means, as you see, that we received, last night, our pay for four months. Uncle Sam keeps all his promises!

APRIL 10

On the day before yesterday at an early hour we were ordered to march to the Headquarters of our Second Brigade, to let Adjutant General Thomas see how we looked. He has come from Washington to arrange for the enlistment of negro soldiers.[65] Our Division presented a very fine appearance. All the men were in their best clothes. The Division was in one solid mass in front of headquarters, drawn up by regiments, battalions, and batteries. (I noticed that the 17th Wisconsin had been put away back in the rear;

64. Transcribed in Thomas Christie reminiscence.

65. Brigadier General Lorenzo Thomas was authorized to recruit black regiments in the western theater and to appoint white officers to them. His recruiting tour was very successful: by the end of April 1863, ten new regiments of black soldiers had been created. Trudeau, *Like Men of War*, 47–48.

there are many men in that regiment who do not believe in arming the black man.)—Gen. McPherson introduced Gen. Thomas to the troops, and described the plan. The new regiments are to be officered by white men promoted from our army; and are to garrison our captured towns, thus permitting all White troops to go to the front.—When Gen. Thomas stepped forward to speak he was greeted with Enthusiastic cheering. There could be no doubt as to the reception the new plan will meet with in our Western Army. He seemed greatly pleased. He said he brought us the salutations of President Lincoln, who being himself a Western man had followed us in our victorious campaigns with the greatest interest and pleasure. The new measure is very near the President's heart. "I shall be glad to tell him," said the General, "of the enthusiasm with which you have heard of it. I am authorized to officer two negro regiments from this Division. I shall commission all men recommended by Gen. McArthur—whether they be now officers or privates. These new troops will be of very great service to us in putting down the rebellion."

McArthur was then called out, amid vociferous cheering, for our "Scotch Mac" is very popular with his men. He told it was not his forte to "mak" speeches. But he was "gled" to hear of the purpose to arm the negroes. He would recommend only the best men for commissions, without reference to their present rank.—Excellent speeches followed, by Col. Chambers of the 15th Iowa,[66] Capt. Klink,[67] and others. The Captain's speech was very humorous. He said he would be most thankful to any man, white or black, who would kindly take his place when the bullets were "zipping" thick and fast; he would not stop to ask what his color was! After some more such funny remarks, he told us he thought he would like to be Colonel of one of the new regiments himself, asking us what we thought of it. Of course he was answered with a mighty cheer. Gen. Thomas then told us he would have to commission him, and there was much laughter as the Generals congratulated "Colonel" Klink. Gen. Thomas stepped forward again. "Men of the Sixth Division," he said, "I want to be able to tell the President just how you feel on the subject. let every man who favors the new policy take off his cap." The next moment there were not a dozen covered heads in the Division. Thousands of caps went twenty feet up into the air; I know

66. Colonel Alexander Chambers.
67. No captain by this name was listed in any Iowa, Missouri, Minnesota, Ohio, or Wisconsin regiment; however, Sergeant Peter Klink served in Company D of the Seventeenth Wisconsin.

mine did. Three rousing cheers were given for the new measure, Gen. Mac swinging his Glengarry cap as he led them. Then the President, and Gen. Thomas, and Gen. McPherson, and Gen. McArthur were all hurrahed for, one by one; and we marched back to camp. We all felt that we had taken part in a scene that will belong to the history of our Country. Many applications have already been made for commissions in the new regiments. Our officers want me to apply. But it would break my heart to separate from the old Battery. Our Lieut. Peebles is to be a Lieut. Colonel in one of the two regiments. We shall be sorry to lose him. No man at Shiloh was braver then he; he got a fearful wound there . . .

4

"No Glory in It"
April 11–October 2, 1863

Thomas Christie to Sarah Christie

NEAR LAKE PROVIDENCE LA. APRIL IITH 1863

My Dear Sister,

In penitent mood I take up my pen to answer your last letter received some time ago. I do not think I ever passed so long a period before in which I felt so disinclined to all literary pursuits as during the past fortnight, and I cant write a thing that will satisfy myself when I don't feel like thinking steadily. My last poor attempt that I sent to Helen is self evident proof of this axiom, and I don't think I can do any better this time. My habits of playing cricket, quoits, and base ball, and the fine weather we are enjoying, which tempts one to be in the open air as much as possible in preference to the hot close tents, must be my apology.

Your music is all received, and the whole singing population of the company is greatly obliged to you for the fine new songs, especially, "Rally round the Flag Boys," with which we have serious thought of serenading Gen. McArthur when we get it all learned. I have copied some of the music at the request of comrades who wished to send it north to singing friends, and everybody unites with me in asking you to continue favors of the kind.

I made my tentmates laugh when I read to them your inquiry as to their religion, and I have to inform you that they are as sound "Protestants" as any of the Christies. Still more, we have now for a fourth inmate of the tent, a man with as Irish a name as the others, and who is also free from suspicion of Catholicism. I refer to Sergt. Conner[1] who was dreadfully wounded

---

1. Jesse Conner. See page 55, note 45, Thomas to James, June 26, 1862.

at Shiloh, and has just returned to the Battery from the hospitals where he has lain during an entire year. Now, don't you begin to distrust the power of your faculty for discovering nationality and religion by names.

I have been greatly tempted, and so has William, to apply for a commission in one of the negro Regiments organizing here, but *my* reasons for not doing so are these: In the first place, I do not like the Infantry branch of the Service, secondly, there were so many applicants from Infantry Regts. (about ten for each office,) that I thought an artillery man who knew only the rudiments of Infantry tactics would stand very little chance, Lastly, I do not approve of the way they are doing, in commissioning men who are, and always have been, *enemies* to the negro and to his just rights, and who now take command of him solely for the sake of the high pay and office.

Here we have one of our privates selected for an officer in the 9th Louisiana, Col. Klink. He has been in the Regular service, in the Dragoons, and probably knows something of drill but morally, he is a worthless scamp, and has always been a bitter opposer of the abolitionists, as most of the Regulars are. This disgusts me with the plan, for there are any amount of good men in the Division who would have their hearts in the work, and these are the ones who should get the offices, even if they are not so proficient in drill as these other unprincipled men. It may be different in other Divisions however, and I hope so, for this plan of enlisting the blacks is excellent, and by it we could raise one hundred Regiments on the banks of this grand River, and they would be very serviceable in holding the country conquered by us. The negros who were swarming in our camps a week ago, are enlisting now with the greatest alacrity, and soon they will pour in from the country by hundreds when they hear of the chance we offer, to fight for their own Liberty. If they would only authorize here the raising of Artillery or Cavalry, I would apply at once for a commission, and I would get it too.

I received some time ago a letter from cousin Robert[2] at Fernandina, Florida. He wants me to tell you to write to him, as he says you have not answered the last on he sent. Lieut. Clayton started for Minnesota on the 8th, and W. and I sent 123 Dollars home by him, to be expressed to Watertown.

No more until you write. Tom

Give my love to Grandmothers Reid and Bertie.

2. Robert K. Reid, son of Robert Reid, Elizabeth Christie's brother, who served in the Seventh Connecticut Infantry.

William Christie to Alexander and Sarah Christie

ON THE MARCH, APRIL 29TH 1863

Dear Brother and Sister, not forgetting the other loved ones, I take this opportunity as we are camped on Smith's Plantation On Round about Bayou[3]
lieing over to rest after traveling two days and a half to get hear. Our teams
and men being Pretty well tired out on account of the roughness of the
road. we had as many as four of our teams fast in the mud at one, and we
had to lift and Pull a great Deal, we getting daubed all over with the sticky
mud, and for a full half day Pelted, with a heavy rain storm. Jokes and songs,
kept us marry and hunger made us enjoy our hard tack, with great gusto.
so if you could see us now you would find us rough healthy, and dirty.
There is as near as I can learn some five Divisions ahead of us between
here and the Mississippi River, some 8 miles distant south and East, of this
Point. We are about twentifive miles from Millikins Bend, and twenifive
west of Vicks-g, and when we get to Carthage we will Be some twenty or
thirty miles below, Vicks-g, and rumor says we will have to contend for the
Passage of the River with the Rebs, we have Received St. Louis Papers up
to the twentifourth today, and we cannot see or hear much that is going
on, I Believe Tom sent a letter to some of you Before we left the Bend, and
all I have to speake of since is that through mud thick and thin we are here,
in the mud, waitting for our turn to cross the River. I suppose it will take us
another day to get through so you see we do not move very fast, for the roads
are just as Bad as any you ever saw in Wisconsin. The most of the road
has been thrown up By our engineer Corp, and they have fairly striped the
fields of fenceing, and we have been following, a Bayou called round about,
and I think it is very well named, A Boat followed us up the Bayou, and I
Believe that this is the same Bayou I spoke of in one of my letters, to Father.

The twentithird Wis. Vol. hospital is hear, and we will have a good opportunity to see the twentininth, so we may soon see Tom Reid,[4] But we may
not see him allthough so near for we cant go just where we Please, as you
folks up there can do when you wish to see a Friend that is neare you. Tom
sent a letter to Father's address, with ten Dollars enclosed to sarah, he sent

---

3. Also known as "Roundaway Bayou," Smith's Plantation is about halfway through
the route past Vicksburg. See endpaper maps in Foote, *Civil War,* II.

4. A cousin of the Christies, Thomas D. Reid served in Company H of the Twenty-
ninth Wisconsin.

it to Watertown so I hope you will get it. I cant write as I would like too for the very Reason, I do not know what to say, so you may think it will Be easily said, But that is just the worst Posable fix to Be in you can think of. you just sit down to write a letter, and you having nothing to say, and you will soon see I am stating a fact, If I were writing such letters as my last to Father and Sandy, why you would have every reason to think I was a fool, or an Ass, or Both. It surprises me very much you have not got the Books yet, all the rest of the Boys that sent home Boxes, have heard from them, But you don't say the Box is in town, In your next letter to us we expect to hear from the monies we sent north with Clayton, I enclosed 66 Dollars, and Tom over fifty, Father must make good use of it. The five I sent with Toms to Sarrah, I Borrowed from W. H. Wiltse [one] of the Kings,[5] the other King is an Irish man from County Derry,[6] from Killrea; on the Dann, We have had, an accession of another King, John Torry,[7] an American, from Michigan to Minnesota. he got along very well, and have no trouble and there is more good feeling among such a mixed up set of men, than you would Possably think there could be. Don't you have a mixed up mess of a letter to read every time I write. you would think a regular hop O my thumb had written it, I am very happy to think Sarah Passed her examination so well, and I am very happy to think D [?] Benson, has not for gotten us, Remember us to him when you see him, and Really Sarah I would like you to be kind enough to write another letter to Janet Clarkson, and learn the News from that quarter, When you write give the Clarksons our Best respects and ask them when they last heard from James Streachan Tis a very long time since we heard from him.

Now a word to you all Before I stop this letter of many nothings. Do not be in the least uneasy about either of us, if you should not hear from us for a long time, There may be a great Battle before a great many days or weeks, Pass Bye, But if you all trust as much in the goodness of God, as I do you have nothing to Fear for either of us, and if anything should happen to us, There is a way Father or Mother will hear of it quicker than By letter. Tis growing dark I will have to stop. there is word of us moving on tomorrow, Tom rides on the march; so he gets along, easily, The nearest I have come

5. William H. Wiltse, one of three Williams who shared William Christie's tent, known collectively as "The Kings." See Thomas to Sarah, Mar. 11, 1863 (page 111).

6. Possibly William McGuinness.

7. John W. Torrey, like the other "Kings," enlisted from Winona. *Adjutant General's Report*, 786.

to seeing an Alligator was the skin of one, about eight feet long, snakes are numerous, and they havent hurt any one yet that I have heard of. Tom is going to write a little so I will stop,

your loving Brother Wm. G. Christie

∾

Thomas Christie to James Christie[8]

SMITH'S PLANTATION, MAY 4, 1863

My Dear Father,

I wrote you that we were likely to see a battle soon; but probably I was wrong. All the rest of the Army has gone ahead and the fighting has begun; while we lie here guarding the road. Our men have gained a great victory, of which you have doubtless read in the papers.[9] To lie in the rear in this way is not very pleasant; but somebody has to do this work, and it is a soldier's duty to obey orders. We have *heard* all the fighting (at least the cannonading), if we could not *see* it.

Four hundred and fifty of the prisoners taken at Port Gibson passed our camp this evening under guard; they have stopped for the night at only a short distance. Most of them belong to the rebel Sixth Mo. Infantry, and are know by men in the Second Ill. Battery, which was raised at Cape Girardeau. One of the battery-men found among them his old school-teacher, several schoolmates, and 2 of his cousins. I must say they are a fine-looking lot of men, and are quite cheerful, seeming to be satisfied very well with their present circumstances. As they marched past, all the men of our Division lined the road on both sides. Both the prisoners and we were in great good humor; many a joke flew back and forth between us. It is due to our men to say that not an insulting word was spoken. One well-dressed Texan in conversation with one of our boy inadvertently used the word "Yankees" in speaking of us. He instantly corrected himself, and with a graceful bow begged our pardon. "We do not consider you Western gentlemen to be Yankees." One of our fellows replied laughingly, "I think you will find that although we are Western men we have Yankee principles!" "Boys," said one of them. "we are going North. but you will have to stay here with the

8. Transcribed in Thomas Christie reminiscence.

9. On April 30, five divisions of Grant's army, 23,000 men, crossed the Mississippi at Bruinsburg, just downstream from Grand Gulf. There was heavy fighting at Port Gibson on May 1. Foote, *Civil War*, II:344–45.

alligators!" Indeed no one would have thought in hearing the talk that we were enemies.

I saw several alligators today both dead and alive, while I was scouting along the bayou. They are ugly-looking brutes, just like the pictures in the Geography.

I sent a bit of a letter to the Saint Paul Press: and they now forward me the tri-weekly. The boys beg me to write again; which I may possible do at no distant date.

Yours Ever,

T. D. C.

∾

William Christie to Alexander Christie

VICKSBURGH MISS. MAY 26TH 1863

Dear Brother, I Received your letter yesterday, and am very happy to learn you are all well. So I now take my Pen in hand, (as some say, just as though it was customary to take a Pen in foot, to write a letter). to let you know what we have been doing, and where we have Been doing it for the last sixteen days. On Sunday the 10th ult. our Brigade of MacArthur's Division consisting of five rigment, under Bregadier Gen. Ransome, left Smith's Plantation for Grand Gulf, some 40 miles down the River, we followed the Bank of the Mississippi, traveling on the Levee, the whole distance. making the place of embarkation on the 5th day. where we got on board the Boats and were ferried over the River. to the forts that had been but a few days before in the hands of the enemmy. While on the Louisiana side of the River we traveled over a flat Rich soil, abounding in Bayous and lakes, these Being litterally full of fish, and Aligators; numerous, we did not see any of these gentry alive, But there were numbers of dead ones lieing along the route of travel. They had been killed By the troops that had Passed before us, and the sight and stench together, was far from Pleasant. I assure you, they are ugly looking Brutes dead or alive, and do a great deal to take from the Beauties of the Country. The difference between the Miss: and La. sides of the River are decidedly striking and look as though you might have crossed a sea instead of a River. We staid one night at Grand gulf, next morning starting a five oclock, for to join our Army corp. ahead of us as we heard at a Plase called Bolton, our road lay over a very Broken Bluffy, country, covered with a very good crop of thrifty corn where it was under cultivation, and various kinds of hard wood, where the forest coverd the ground, There was very little of note took Place on the road, until we reached Raymond, a small town about eight miles from Edward's Depot, where we heard cannonading, and we went of in that Direction to help if necessary, we were Pushed up to the front and got within hearing of the musketry, But we did not need to come into action, we had Busy times of it from that time untill such times as we drove the Rebs over Black River on a grand Skedaddle, leaving behind them a great number of field pieces, and a large number of Prisoners, the Papers will give you all the Particulars, if not I will tell you a great deal more when I see you, than I can Possably write, after waiting to Build Bridges, to get the stuff for which we Pulled down some Buildings, we crossed the Big Black River and Reached this Point, meeting But very little resistance, and stopped for the very reason that we cant go any further at Present, not so much on account of Secesh, But because the natural protections of Vicksburgh are very efficent to Bring a large army to a stop. even if there was no oppoising force, to keep us in check. To give you some Idea of the country just think of all the odds and ends of such ridges as the HogBack thrown together in a jumble with deep gulches Between, and the Bottoms of them cut up intoo great gulleys By the heavy rains of Winter. now the earth works of the secesh are Built on the crest of a ridge that skirts the Bluffs on the opposite side from us, the ravines . are full of felled trees. and the sides of them the same, so it makes it imposable to take the Place By storm, for our men has tried it twice, and failed, on account of utter exhaustion, when the[y] got only over half the intervening space. Our guns are in Position and has done good execution among the Rebs, we have been very Busy, and Played on the enemmys works, for three days. in a regular steady manner, But for the last two or three days we have been very quiet. The sound of Bullets frome secesh, as they Passed over us or By us, made us feel rather uncomfortable. But we lie By our guns and listen to the fire of the skirmishers on Both sides, with indifference and there is nothing in the world to hinder you from think- ing as the report of the muskets reach your ears that there is a large force of men in the woods clearing up timber, the occasonal Boom of a thirtitwo, or ten or six pounder, and the like sound of a twelve Pound Howitzer, mixed up with the sullen roar from the mortar Boats on the River, help to keep secesh aware of our Presence, while the sharp whistle of a Bullet as it Passes over our heads or Past us, gives us notice that we are watched by sharp eyes, But we have them fast, and they cant get away, so it is merely a

question of time, about Vicksburgh being ours, we are under minieing
some of there forts, it would not do to say which, there has been some con-
versations between our Boys and the secesh, for instance one of the rascals
asked our Boys if they were Blue Bellies. the answer went Back we were
Blue Bellies enough for you. The estimates of how long secesh can hold out
is simply amusing. some say they can live six months on what food they
have. others have it as many weeks. some so many days, But there is not
a man on our side yet, that I have seen Dont says it will come, and so we
are hopfull, and confident yesterday a flag of truce came out to the Breast
works; and hostilities ceased for four hours and a half, the dead were burried, and the union Boys had a good look at secesh. that is what showed
themselves, our men appeared in great numbers, and looked well in comparison to the rebs.

Major Gen: Logan,[10] was a little sprung, so he told a secesh officer, that
when they saw a man on a white horse with a mustache ridding along the
line they must not shoot him for he was a Damned good man, meaning
himself, for he has been in the habit of ridding along the lines the Mustache Being on him and not on the horse. In all the fights outside vicks-b,
we got 72 pieces of Artillery.

[rough sketch of lines at Vicksburg showing location of 1st Minnesota Battery]

a Poor sketch,
William G. Christie.

∽

William Christie to James Christie

MAY 31ST [1863] CAMP CLOSE BY VICKSBURGH

Dear Father,

I will try in this letter, to describe one of the Grandest sights, I ever saw.
This morning at three o'clock, the Batteries of Gen. Grants Army at his
Place, oppenned at once on the doommed city of Vicksburgh, And the
effects of such a sight allmost defies description. The line extends some
eight miles round the Beseiged town. There is Artillery enough on this line

10. Major General John "Black Jack" Logan commanded the Third Division of
McPherson's Seventeenth Corps. He later received the Congressional Medal of Honor
for his services at the siege of Vicksburg. Warner, *Generals in Blue,* 282.

to shoot from one to the other. Now just stand with me on the Point where our Battery is Placed, and see the vivid flashes of the Guns, like lightining, and the showers of shell, as they made there quick curves through the air, hissing and hurtling, and finnally explodding with a report almost as loud as the Gun. The air waved like the sea, and vibratted with a horse murmuring sound, while the valleys were filled with the loud thundering sound of the detonation of the firing of the mortor Boats, on the River and the flash of there shots, were seen on the Backgroun exactly like lightening, But still there is one phase of the scene I have not spoken of and that is the Burning of the fuse, in each shell, while they are going through the air. The fuse burns, with a blue light, and looks to say the least very Devilish. and I have no doubt the secesh thought so, we kept up the Cannonading for over an hour, and made some ecellent shots. Tom and I worked on the gun together he as four, and I as three, so you see when there is anything going on we are generally close together and we were volunteers at that. There was not much danger in the dark from the Rebel sharp shooters, But we have to stand our ground in the daytime, and then we have to dodge the Bullets frequently, I have been doing the duties of Driver no. 3, ditto also on the gun, and I don't see as there is much danger at the gun as there is driving. Now you must think me a coward But I will try to give you and the Boys an insight, in my feelinks, on the occasion of my first ride full in sight of the Rebel fortifacations, within rifle range. On the first day of the seige, we were ordered to a Point on the left of the main Road, from Jackson to Vicksburgh, and in front of the largest fort on the works Now I had stood my ground on the oppen field, and did not feel very shakey on the legs, But to be mounted on the back of a horse and know that there was not only hundreds of men that would shoot at you, like they were shooting at a Turkey, with a cool deliberate aim, but at the same time just such a thing as you were drawing after you, only larger, if anything, made me feel very nervous, I assure you. But still there was not a man near me would have thought that. I really would have liked to have run away, I drove my own team with Precission, and even d[i]rected the other drivers, how I thought we could get along over some parts of the ground, (it being very rough) to the Best advantage. We had got our guns in position and got our horses and limbers under shelter of the hill, and beginning to feel that we had not so much to fear, when we found out that our officers in command had not got our Howitzers in the right Place, so we had to take the same ride over again, and ride up to within five or six hundred yards of the enemy works, in the oppen range of his Batteries and sharpshooters Father, I was desperate, Desperately afraid (But Thank God,) only of myself. you know my Bump of Firmness, is large and it is well for the Christies, it is so, or I really am sure I would have run away, could you have seen my inner self, you would have seen a very strange trial of strength. How I reasoned with myself, about my duties as a soldier. how a deep trust in the goodness and mercy of God would speak up in me to keep me true to myself and Country. I can only give you a faint idea, of what I felt, and really suffered in that ride, But the Battle was fought, and Praise be to God he gained the victory, over me and I am considered good coin anywhere, as far as soldiers is concerned, and really now I do not think I will ever feel so again. So now you see the confessions not of a great man, but of a Poor weak fellow that scarsely knows how to live after trieing it now for nearly thirtithree years. In my letter to A. D. Christie, I gave you an account of the appearance of the country, and so I have nothing new to say about that, Therefore I will have to fill up the Balance of this sheet the Best way I know how. lately I have been in the habit of digging away down intoo myself, to see what I was, what I thought and how or why I generally thought just as I did. I often ask myself, are all men like me, in any one respect as far as thinking is concerned or the methods of thinking, is every one as erratic in there modes, not that [I] am in the least excentric that is, to be noticeable, But at the same time, I am so well aware of my weakneses; and yet it seems I do so little in the way of mastering them. There must be some thing Fundamentally wrong in a character such as mine or at least in my surroundings, when I was more easily impressed with greater or lesser good, than I am now. Not that I can say anyone is to Blame. for me being just as I am. so much as I am myself, For in looking over the Past, I see nothing But a great many shortcomings, in every Respect on my own part, in all circumstances, and a wonderfull forbearance on the Part of all with whom I have come in contact. Tis true I have been often Missjudged, through mistakes of others, and my own. And it must be that there must have been some reason on account of my own action or they would not have not judged just as they did and acting accordingly. Now about that money[11] I am really sorry that I have caused you to feel just as it seems to me you must have done when you wrote that Letter to Tom in which you abuse me so unmercifully, and talked so

11. William seems to have had an ongoing financial dispute with his father. See William to James, Dec. 13, 1862 (page 89), and Mar. 19, 1863 (pages 118–19).

foolishly about me and Poor Cousin Jessie,[12] It surely cant be Mother saw that letter before you mailed it. Now you may not relish this little bit of advice much, but still it is about all the scolding I will give you. Whenever you feele again, (which I hope wont be very soon, for our own sake) just as you did when you wrote that letter, just ask Mother what she thinks you had Best do, and I'll be bound you will do well to take her advice. Do with the money just as seems Best to you don't loose a cent on your wheat if you can help it on my account, and if you do make yourself whole out of my funds, I regretted having asked you the question about David Bertie,[13] in connection with anything of mine before the sunset on the day it was written Not that I thought of the Past, or what he has been to Both of us, But I saw the folly of it in annother way alltogether, Now when you write to me give me Bread, even if you have to think to do it for I am very hungry, I will certainly write to Mother soon. Father give me some clue to my self if you can for as sure as you live, I am at fault, or wont give way to the solution. write soon give my love to all and believe me you Affectionate son Wm G. Christie.

∽

Thomas Christie to Alexander Christie

BEFORE VICKSBURG JUNE 5TH 1863.

My Dear Brother,

A mail, which had been chasing us, and following us around for the past 3 weeks, gone to Grand Gulf, come to McArthur at Warrenton and went out with him and the Third Brigade nearly to Yazoo city: finally ceased its wanderings yesterday by falling into the hands of the Orderly Sergeant, from whence you may well believe, it was quickly distributed. I could not well complain of being slighted, for 6 St. Paul Pressess, the Independent, and a letter from you of the 3rd May containing a sheet of postage stamps almost large enough to make a blanket, fell to my lot, besides 2 letters for William which I read of course, and Harpers monthly and weekly and New York and Chicago Tribune which came to the club of which I am honored member, (note: parse this last sentence if you can, if not, give it to the School marm, whom you may remind at the same time, that she is

12. Probably Jesse Aimer, daughter of James Christie's half sister, Jessie Bertie. After the war, William married Jesse's sister, Mary Aimer.

13. Jesse and David Bertie were the children of Janet Smith Christie's second marriage, following the death of James's father.

neglecting her espistolary duties, and may be convicted by Gen. Pope of
aiding and abetting traitors by refusing to enliven the hearts of the Defenders of the Republic with cheerful, or any other kind of, letters).

You shall have the full benefit of the stamps, and when they are gone, I
shall know to whom an appeal will be most affective. It is odd is it not, that
while I am penning these lines, which you will soon be reading in your
quiet Wisconsin home, the balls of the Rebel sharpshooters are hissing
by me and crashing through the green bushes in our rear: and now I am
watching two or our fellows who are leisurely walking over the crown of
the hill behind us, where they are just as sure of being shot at as they are
of anything in the world. There's the crack of the rifle: *"ping:" "whack."* that
was a close shot, struck the ground within a rod of them, raising a cloud of
dust. Not in the least disconcerted, our chaps turn round to look at where
the ball hit, and while one shakes his fist at the rebel breastworks, and gives
vent to his outraged feelings in epithets not choice enough to be copied
here, the other coolly goes up to the bullet-hole in the hill, big enough to
stick your hand into, and digging a while soon exhibits the Minnie to this
wrathy companion, and the two pass on over the hill. There is no fancy in
this description; it is sober fact, and its parallel may be seen here every hour
in the day. Our boys seem to derive as much pleasure in seeing how near
the balls will come without hitting, as the Rebels do in trying to hit them.
I shall not risk securing a reputation for "gasconade" by telling you how
often I have been shot at, or how near to me the messengers have struck,
but I will tell you there *is* a certain exciting pleasure in being made a target
of, and also, that they have not yet succeeded in their oft expressed design
of making a pepper box of my posterior, To be serious; the Rebs with all
their practice have as yet succeeded in wounding only one of us, and in
killing some half dozen horses. But when they get *too* audacious we throw
over a few shells behind the works, and then you should see them make
tracks, the cowardly bushwhackers.

We are still in the works that we occupied when I wrote to Father, but
there is a new position being made within spitting distance almost of the
enemy, and we expect to occupy it: *then* we can rake the scamps lengthwise,
and they will have to abandon their rifle pits.

Do not despond of our success here: Grant and his Boys are determined
to go into Vicksburg if we have to stay before it all Summer; Every morning
sees our rifle pits and batteries nearer to the Rebels, and we have artillery
enough to knock them to smash when we get ready to open the whole line

and keep up a continual fire. Our partial cannonades have already done them a great deal of damage, and it would not take long to destroy them altogether when we can cover all the ground they occupy, with bursting shell and case.

Speaking of Grant reminds me that he and Gov. Saloman of Wisconsin came to see our fort a day or two ago with Gen. Ransom, commanding the 2d Brigade As they came into the work, the guard who was on the guns at the time, belonging to the 12th Wis. Battery, who are with us, advanced to the gents, and said sharply, "*no smoking* allowed in the Battery," Grant, who had two thirds of a Havannah stuck between his teeth, instantly flung it through an embrasure, to the great delight of a crowd of high privates who, like myself, witnessed the incident. When the General went away the guard went and got the cigar, and said he should send it home in a letter, and tell the folks that he ordered it out of General Grants mouth.

That is one thing we like our Generals for, they are as plain as farmers with us, and indeed: to see old Grant as we see him almost every day around among us, without staff or shoulder straps, and wearing an old hat that looks as if he had slept on it all night, you would take him to be no more than a Lieutenant at most, and McPherson, although the most refined look-ing of gentlemen, is just as unassuming in manner.

I can give you a very good idea of how McClernand looks. He is as like what Uncle Samuel Noyes used to be as you can imagine, and his voice put me in mind of Mother's brother very forcibly. You get no good likenesses of our generals in the pictorials. Grant's portrait in the Harper which we got yesterday is not worth a cent. I like the mathematical part of your letter very much and I would have give you something of the sort in this, but that I have crowded myself out of room

There is some fatigue duty to do and I must close.

T. D. Christie

William Christie to Alexander Christie

BEFORE VICKSBURGH, JUNE THE 6TH 1863.

Dear Brother,

I have not any letter from you to answer, But nevertheless, I will een write to you just as the spirit moves, me; By the way what do you think of my Punctuation marks. seeing I cannot Propound such wise Problems as the sage Thomas, can I will just ask you to criticise my method, (which I fear consists of a total lack of method) of writing. But Be that as it may, Pens must be kept scribbling or there is no telling how many chaotic thoughts would be left just where they ought to Be in oblivion. So you think that there is not as much Prospects of the war closeing as there might Be. that is just my fix But still I do not feel in the least discouraged or dismayed, for it is allmost impossable that the thing should be finished so soon after we as a Nation have been nurseing the cause of this eruption so long. Tis Curious aint: it to see the People of these states doing just now, what John Brown done a few years ago Banding with the Negro to do away with his Bondage hundreds of thousands that helped to strangle the old man, for lighting the torch of Freedom for the oppressed thoughout the land are this day Praying God to give us the victory. they were so much afraid John Brown would get in fiftiseven. When down at the yazoo the other day, after hard tack for the Rebs: There were a great many curious thoughts Presented themselves to me. when I saw a son: or sons: of the Emereld Isle: and the damned Nagurs: sweltering together under a Broiling sun, and the weight of Amunition Boxes: of shot and shell, and laying all Prejudice aside, the Nagurs were the Best looking Part of the gang. so up north the People at large let the serpent grow grow and petted it. other looked on with indifference, and did not care. Untill the thing grew untill it thought it could swallow up the nation just for a snack before Breakfast like. The Devil as usual thought everything was ready for a Break, and spoke as of old through the serpant and Liberty doing a little Better than Eve, wouldn't take the apple and Commenced to scotch the Brute. thinking to Put him down a with a rap or two over the Candle [cranial?] appendage. But it was no go. so we are getting up towards the Head and it may be we will crush the life our of the Pesky varmint in a year or so, The law of compensation, and you might say of dispensation make things about even in the long run. The Negro worked and the master reapped, Building fine houses, and laying out Beautiful gardens, making graneries, ridding round in fine carreges; and in short enjoying themselves in every sensual way you can possably think of untill they waxed Proud, and fat and so they Brought on there own Punishment, and tis full I assure you. there are large numbers of there fine houses gone up in smoke, there fields are lieing Idle or are in the hands of the goverment. worked By and for the Negro. there fine carraiges are used for ambulances: and there People are slain. sons and Brother: Fathers and children are mangled on the same field of Death. and now since we have invested this city, even there women and children are slain, for let me tell you spherical case, and shell don't discriminate between combatants and those that are not. Let every one of you be thankful you are not in a Besieged city night and Day, night and day there is that loud roar from the morter Boats, on the River up goes sixty or a hundred Pounds of Iorn into the air. some seven hundred feet, making what a man of science would call a Parabolic curve, But I think if you could see it you would say Diabolic: Down, Down, it falls, and finnally bursts, and scatters Death to all, we hear some that don't Burst go creshing through a house, or with a chug, in the ground, the Batteries on the land side are never Idle, all at once some of them are shooting, night and day so you see that there is But little rest for the wicked. There are a number of new Forts being Built within one hundred and fifty yards of seceshes lines: there is some talk of us going intoo one of them. it would just suit us. there are large numbers of new Rifle Pits being dug allso, within a few Rods, of the enemmies' works, and it looks as though we were getting very close round them. There has been some men trying to get intoo Vicksburgh with caps[14] for secesh. one of them that was taken had three thousand of them sewed into his clothes, there were ten taken in all I believe and one got away, The Pickets keep talking to each other at times. this incident is told as occurring last night. some of our Boys: and secesh got a talking, when there was a Proposition they should meet each other and have a talk. so they met, talked and our man gave him a late Paper he was one of the seventeenth Wis: however secesh went Back and as he got ontoo the top of his own works, he called out all right, and he fell shot By some of our Pickets, soon after another secesh told our Pickets that man they shot was severly wounded, that is all in a Peice with [the] seventeenth. Now while there is room I must ask if sarah got that letter with the money we sent to her. five Dollars from each of us, we want her to let us know some thing about it. We would like her to make a fixen for us to hold needles: thread and Pins and sent it along. Father has been very rash with his accusations on me all for asking a foolish question. But I suppose he has repented, before this time. if he has not, I Pitty him. and feel all right myself give my love to all enquireing Friends I saw Tom Reid[15] a few days ago he said he had a letter from you and Sarah, he looked hardy, and dirty he stayed with seventeenth all night. Now let me tell you you do

14. Percussion caps.
15. Thomas D. Reid, a cousin. *Roster of Wisconsin Volunteers*, II:410.

not write as often as you should. none of you. we should have a letter once a week at least. and now we don't get more than once a month. We are very much obliged to you for sending the stamps and so after telling you so much will have to quit for tis so infernal hot I can hardly sit up.

good By. write soon Believe me you loving Brother

William G. Christie

❧

Thomas Christie to Sarah Christie

BEFORE BICKSBURG, JUNE 7TH 1863.

My Dear Sister:

In my letter to Sandy I gave vent to feelings of impatience at your long silence, which I would now gladly recall since receiving your doubly addressed letter of the 27th, Ult.

The description of the wedding and your feelings on that occasion are very interesting, and I hope you will continue to employ your descriptive talent in writing to us, for heretofore you have given us but few specimens of you skill in that line.

I wish I could present to your mind's eye a picture of our situation here, for I think it would be interesting to you although so commonplace with us, but the most I have room for is a rough draught, which you can fill up from imagination. First, as to position; Our fort is built on the crest of a hill, and between it and the rebel breastworks, which are in plain view— a long line of yellow earth with white cotton bales and sandbags on top— is a very rough succession of narrow steep ridges, with ravines to match, and all covered with a tremendous abbattis, which you must know, is made by felling forest trees in such manner as to make an advance over the ground extremely difficult. To accomplish this, the trees are felled with the tops toward the enemy, and a very formidable obstruction it makes. Our fort is built of earth, faced on the inside with fascines, or bundles of canes 15 feet long and a foot through, and tied around with wire from the rebel telegraph line, These fascines are laid, one on top of the other, and each one is fastened down securely with stakes drive through it and through the ones below into the ground. The fascines are to prevent the earth from falling down into the fort, which the concussion of the guns would soon make it do if unsupported.

The embrasures, through which we fire, are made by setting up gabions on each side of the space left for the embrasure, where they are staked down and filled with earth, A gabion is made of stakes, with grapevines, young cane or flexible brushes woven through them, so as to form a hollow cylinder something like a large willow basket without the bottom, only much longer. The stakes are left projecting at one end some distance beyond the wicker work, and when the gabion is put in its place these projecting ends are driven into the ground and the gabion is filled with dirt. When we first came into the work the embrasures were not lined with gabions, and the consequence was that in one day's firing we blew out the embrasures so wide that a two horse wagon could have been drive through one of them.

When I tell you that the fort has 8 guns in it, (4 of them 2nd Ills, 2 of 12th Wis, and 2 of ours), and that we have a deep ditch running from it to the magazine behind the hill, by which the ammunition is carried to the guns without exposure; you will be able to form a very good idea of its appearance. If you could be in our fort during action and could command composure enough, amid the continual explosion of the guns on each side of you, the sulpherous smell of the burnt powder, and the fierce "whiz," "whiz" of the enemy bullets, to observe the working of our howitzer, you would see something interesting. There is No. 1: his hands face, and clothes blackened with the wet powder from the sponge, on his knees ramming home the charge, (if he stood up opposite the embrasure he would get a ball in an instant) There is No. 3, (William) with his thumb on the vent to prevent a premature explosion when the piece is hot, Now the gun is loaded and no. 1, and 3 step back, the latter to the trail handspike to traverse the trail at the Gunners biding, "By hand to the front" and the piece is run up close to the embrasure, the Gunner sets his pendulum hausse on its seat, sight carefully and gives the right elevation, perhaps 2 degrees, then, "Ready," "Fire," now, if you are standing to one side where you can see, you will observe the shell flying through the air like a great black bird, make a gradual curve, and fall behind the Rebel works; then you see a white smoke where it fell, and pretty soon comes the report of its bursting Through all the din and tummult and smoke, No. 6. sits coolly cutting the fuses to the proper time and the proper Nos, of the Detachment carry the shells from him to the gun. According to tactics, I have nothing to do at the guns, but I have been there ever since we first opened: sometimes acting as gunner, and sometimes changing with one of the cannoneers. We are to move into a fort tonight much further to the front, within 200 yards of the enemy, and then we may expect some warm work.

I saw Tom Reid some time ago, and found him in good health but horribly dirty. The Regiment left all their clothes at Helena except what the men are wearing, and you may imagine to what a condition their late rough campaigning has reduced them. Nevertheless; the boys are all in good spirits and tough as bears. I will go down on the left again soon and see them.

I want you Sarah, to make a fixing to carry our needles, thread etc in I forget the name of it but as Mrs. Mon[. . .] says "you know what I mean," your loving Brother

T. D. Christie

[postscript] My St. Paul Press gives an account of the rejoicings on account of the capture of Vicksburg, and it makes me mad, to think that people should make such fools of themselves, and of *us* too. They have *no business* to expect the fall of this stronghold so soon, and we don't want this town to get the reputation that Richmond has got for being taken. Just keep cool and we will work the surer if not the cheaper for not being hurried.

[margin note] Send a supply of good Black thread in the whatdoyoucallit and some *assorted needles*. Don't bother with fancy work, something *stout* and durable and to carry in breast pocket.

[margin note] Remember I write no private letter, that is, to be concealed from any one of the family.

[margin note] I send a piece of Secesh flag captured by our Battery in a hotel at Richmond La. It is pretty well faded but you can see where the red was.

[margin note] Be very sure to give my love to mother, and my 2 Grandmothers.

[margin note] Got a letter from Strachean lately, He is in the hospital at Paducah, we keep up regular correspondence.

William Christie to Alexander Christie

VICKSBURGH BLUFFS IN REAR WHERE OUR TROOPS ARE STILL IN
POSITION

JUNE 23RD 1863,

Hillo [Hello?] Brother O Mine, have you got so immersed in the solution
of Problems in Euclid, or Algreba, that you have forgotten to answer the
sage question I asked you in regard to my method of Punctuation, or are
you so hard at work on that Patch of Praties, that you cant find time to give
us a few lines from your Pen, or a few Idees of your own. I have another
question to ask you in this letter, and I Believe I will have many more to
ask even if there is a great likelyhood of them remaining unanswered, for
a long time. have you ever thought whether man is most a creature of
Immitation, or an Independent actor on the stage of Life. I have come to
the conclusion that Immitation and habit are the motive powers in the
Present age, of the world, if it were not so we would have a different class
of men at the Head of affairs: or more properly speaking a Representitive
man; that would get us out of the various difficulties that the Nation; and
this world at large, is at Present Plunged intoo. We assuredly need such an
one, But it looks as though we had not got him or if we have the time has
not yet come for us to recognise him even allthough he may be at work, for
us every day. You may see every day that there is a Pulling of ropes By the
various leadders: of the government, and the Officers, of the Large force
that has been called into the field for the Purpose of putting down this
Rebellion. Seward and Blair Pulls against Lincoln and Stanton. Halleck,
and Hooker: jerk and snap different ways, and Banks, and Schofield; undoo
all, or nearly all that Butler, and Curtis has done, in the way of Keeping the
treacherous and accursed Rebels in Proper Bounds in the different Dis-
tricts of New Orleans, and St. Louis, Now if these things could only be done
away with By having more sameness of oppinion among these different
Individuell's how much sooner we would have this villianous condition
of things supperessed, and the War Brought, to a speaddy and triumphant
close, But here I must stop this Plaver and get ontoo another track, Spades
are trumps here, and are likely to Be for a long time yet. I Believe if the
unsuccessful charge of the 22nd of last month had not Been made, at all
we would have had Vicksburgh Before this time, for now there are good
roads made up to within a few rods of the works, and in fact there are our

rifle pits, in where the Rebs had theres about eight days ago, there is two of
our Pieces going intoo a new fort or rather entrenchments that are actually
within 50 or sixty feet of the Reb's lines. there are great sheilds of rope
being made to put on the guns, to keep the gunner and nos. three and four
from the secesh sharpshooters, (the whites of there eyes can be seen,) there
are three thicknesses of inch and half rope, agains which a Ball strikes
flat and drop harmless to the ground, We have Been amuseing ourselves
for the two Past evenings, in throwing shell over intoo the enemmys lines,
mortar fashion, we prepare the shells By taking out the Baurman fuze or
(Barman),[16] we then take and make wooden Plugs, screw them into the
shell, fasten in a long time fuze, and elevate the Piece by diging a hole for
the trail, giving her elevation according to the length of the fuze, and charge
of Powder. We have fired forty of them in all taking about four hours time
to fire them, and that would keep us up pretty late at night, Tonight we will
likely Build another fort for our Piece, so that we can have a new range, as
well as the one we have at Present, the Rebs has a gun Planted so that they
can shoot at us without us returnning the compliment, and we don't like
no such one sided affairs. Tis true they have not meddled with us before
this morning, only as far as shooting over us was concerned, we Being in
the exact range of that gun of theres; and some half Dozen of our own, that
over us and Behind us. secesh shell Burst Prematurely sometimes as well
as ours, and Between the two we run very narrow escapes. But these things
don't trouble us, But not more than an hour ago the Rebes had the coolness
to Deliberately throw a shell, at us, taking our a huge chunk of dirt on the
left side of our fort, about two feet over our head, the shell went on a little
further and Burried itself in the ground without Bursting. We will dig it up
tonight, and fix it up so we can fire it out of our gun, to do so we will have
to put in a fruit can, it being a long shell out of a twenty Pound Parrot (the
gun that was taken the first day of the fight at Corinth last fall, from the
first Missouri Battery The Lady Richardson, so called;) the reason we have
to fix them so is to make it fit our Piece, and keep the rifled flang on the
Base of the shell from injuring the gun.[17] we are going to make the new fort
about sixteen or twenty yards in rear of our Present Pesition. the Captain of
the 2nd Ill: Co. F. made the one we now occuppie, and if he had not been

16. The Bormann Fuse was, according to Gibbon, "the best and most regular of any
now in use." *Artillerists Manual*, 257.

17. They probably used one of the battery's twelve-pound howitzers for this purpose
rather than the smaller-bore James rifles.

an Ass he would have Put the fort where we are now compelled to have it. we will be in fine Position to throw shell into the Rebs fort, and not in any worse fix to get them from him. The Rumor in camp this morning is to the effect that Port Hudson is taken, and Farragut's fleet is Bombarding the City of Vicksburgh, Whether Port Hudson is taken or not tis more then I can tell, But sure enough Farragut or some other down on the river is giving and has been giving them in the city great quantites of Iorn, ever since last night. After we got through our Bombarding last night, and got about ready to sleep we heard a good Deal of heavy fireing on the left of the line, it lasted for an hour or so, and was finished By a couple of very heavey volleys, we have not heard yet what the fuss was about, But suppose that our left line was getting a Position nearer to the Rebs works, There are a few Deaths from secesh Bullets every week, and occasonally one from the Premature Bursting of a shell, from our own guns, we are so near the Rebs we cant hurt any of our own men, But one of the eleventh Ill. infantry was I fear mortally wounded yesterday By a fraction of shell from the first Missour's Battery Co. C: his Bowels were torn and both of his lungs visable We find the most of the St. Louis shell spherical case, are not trustworthy,, I Believe there are numbers of secesh workmen in that Arsenal, that Deliberately make a Bad job of there work, so that there Southern brethern may not Be hurt, Tom I suppose has given Father a sketch of our Position, and the lines of works. I would if I only thought I could, But I am afraid I would spoil a great many horns before I would make a spoon, give my love to all and let me hear something about mother in your next, and all the rest of folks, how is our new Cousin, making it as a southerner would say, we had some rain last night But it will soon clear up again, I have not had a letter from Father in a long time, this will have to be a family concern although I have Posted it to you. I am not tired writing But I have not the least doubt you will be tired reading and you can see I am in a hurry. Now let me tell you a secret, I am generally in a hurry about this time of day, for it is near dinner time. so you may be able to judge By that I am more in favor of the Baker, than the Doctor, Long may I wave, Long may we all wave. and be right side up now and forever. so mote it Be,

Yours affectionately Wm G Christie

HEALING

[postscript] We had Baked Peas for Breakfast and some fine Bread and coffee, we are all happy and generally speaking

∾

William Christie to Alexander Christie

Mistake
WALNUT HILLS, IN REAR OF VICKSBURGH,

right
FORT HILL VICKSBURGH, JUNE 27TH 1863,

My very Erudite Brother, I have made a slight mistake in Localiseing of the date of this Letter So hear I make the ammend honnorable, By informing you that Walnut hills are on our extreme right, and only Partially occuppied By a small Part of our forces, the Balance Being in the Possesion of the Rebs, or more Properly speaking tateredemallions. You speak of heat. I have not the least doubt, But you have cause to complain, But you have just to go through the following way of speaking about the differnece between you and us: so fashion, hott hoter hotest, with all the other est esterest, etc, things you can think off, or as the Preacher said it is damned hot, and if he were here, I would Be very happy to say, you are right, old Fellow; and no mistak. ONE DAY LATER. I would have Proceeded with the writing of this letter, But there was two men from the 36th Mass. Infantry mannnaged to come this way, and so we had to listten to there Plaver, they came in from the Army in our rear, They are a Part of Burnsides forces,[18] They say that all the troops under Burnside have great confidince in him, They say there are 90,000 men in our rear, so we have nothing to fear from fire in our rear. For if there was any need of it we could spare as many as 5,000 men, from the force here.

On the 26th ult. at five O Clock in the evening, The large Fort on our left, about four hundred yards distant was blown up a heavy firing was Immediately oppened up along our line in which we joinned; at the Instant the Fort was blown up, a Portion of Logan's Division rushed in and took Possesion with a very small loss of men, but I beleive severe on the officer. We raised the Devil with secesh: after we fired about 30 rounds, we stopped fireing and looked at the fight. all the Artillery on the right ceased: The Bravery displayed on both sides was not, or could not be beatten by any troops in the world, hand grenades were freely used on both sides, and our men barely held there ground shovelld dirt put up sand bags and timbers

18. General Ambrose Burnside took command of the Ninth Army Corps and the Department of Ohio in March 1863. Originally assigned the task of occupying east Tennessee, this force was diverted to reinforce Grant's army at Vicksburg. Welcher, *Union Army*, II:207.

to protect the sharpshooters, it was the 46 Indiana, and the 20 Ill, supported by the seventeenth Wis; in reserve, that did the work. night of the
25th Brigader Ransome[19] came to our gun and requested us to drive out a
nest of Rebs. that were throwing handgranades intoo our entrenchments,
he gave us the word where the Rebs were, and we Plumpt the shell and case
right among them, and dried them up, for that night, and pleased Ransom
very much. in the time of the fight there was one or two narrow escapes on
our gun: one bullet split and spoiled the spare hand spike, on the night of
25th there was some very narrow escapes from secesh bullets, But owing to
our being under cross fire from Both sides we are in danger often from the
Premature explosions of shell, But there has been none of us hurt, yet. on
the evening of the twenty seventh, the secesh gun oppened on the Fort
we have Partially taken, and we with a half dozzen round or so dried it up,
and there was Peace, for a short time, that gun has not oppenned in that
place since. There is mining going on in two different Places: But there is
no use in knowing too much, we have had some good times even if we are
under fire all the time, There are regular Artillery duels going on very
nearly all the time, our sergeant, has just come from our 84 Pounders, a
secesh oppened on them, ours made reply, But some how secesh don't
work there guns near so well as we do ours, at 1,000 yards our twenty four
pdrs. will Put there shells through the rebs Portholes, three shots out of
five, we know this to be so, for we can see being right in the line of travel,
the 84 pouders at the first shot in this mornings duel, sent the first shot
over the Rebs works, the other three went into the Portholes and that Port
hole is about ¾ or a mile from our large guns, we can hear lots of funny
thing[s] but they are to coarse to tell generally very Profane, so tis Best to
keep them out of circulation.

The Left of our line has made very close advances to the Rebel lines, and
are digging trenches up to the various forts on there front. In all likelyhood
we soon have Vicksburgh and without much loss of life. Our Army as a
general thing is healthy, and there is not a word of complaint as far as I can
learn; and every one is hopfule of the way this seige will end. I think it will
not be a great while before we have another rowe, and there will [be] as hard
a time for secesh as the Past one. There has been as many as five hundred
men carried off on litters at that one Place, our loss didn't amount to three

19. General Thomas E. G. Ransom commanded the Second Brigade of McArthur's
division, and the First Minnesota Battery was attached to Ransom's brigade. Welcher,
Union Army, II:303.

hundred in all. The Rebs are getting Desperate, and the country between here and the City is very much honey combed, with rifle Pits, and trenches. I have not the least doubt But Porter speaks truth when he says that Vicksburgh is stronger than satastopol[20] for Sandy if the forts that our guns Play on were of stone instead of King Cotton and dirt, we would have had them knocked to Pieces long ago. But we do not despair, for if it were needed our Boys could go in. But it is not needfull for them to storm the Place, General Starvation—will soon be in full command inside the Place. Gen. U.S. Grant, was all round the central line of the camp yesterday, he was in our gun room, and from his manner you would have thought him a very unpretending Private, he was very thoughtfull, and I think he is working our some Plan to raise the Devil with secesh, for a few words exchanged between him and one of his staff hinted as much. The flock round him are very social also, But more carefull, of themselves than Grant, he smoked and smokes very much.

I am very glad Father did not take the job Cotton has got,[21] And if there is any trouble to be antisipatted, I know on what side you will Be, shoot as you would shoot at a dog carrying off one of Fathers lambs, I am sorry for the Poor fellow in Labenon, I do not think any such thing would have happened, to Father, But it would hardly vex me a bit if Cotton got a little of the same sauce; I am looking for a letter from Father eney day. What is Mother Doing it is very seldom, we hear of her is she a nonenity: give my love to all. is Davey daft or dumb, that he has quit writing I am afraid I mearly write trash so I will quit. Good bye for the Present,

Believe me your affectionate Brother
William G. Christie.

20. Commodore David Porter was commander of naval forces at Vicksburg. William refers to the Russian city Sevastopol, the heavily fortified Black Sea port on which the siege by British and French forces was the central event of the Crimean War, 1854–55.

21. Probably George G. Cotton, a local merchant. U.S. Census (1860), Clyman Township, Dodge County, Wisconsin.

Thomas Christie to James Christie[22]

VICKSBURG, JULY 4, 1863

My Dear Father,

We have celebrated the Fourth today by walking into Vicksburg! I do not know all the particulars; but at least it is certain that we have taken *everything*, the Rebel Army, their Artillery, ammunition, small arms &c, &c.[23] Logan's Division is marching into town as I write. We were supported by them during most of the siege. Read the newspapers for particulars, and rejoice! The Army of the Tennessee has made the glorious Fourth doubly worthy of commemoration. I suppose there will be great firing of cannon and anvils when the North hears this news.

I think now that we shall move immediately to cut off Johnston.

Yours Ever,

T. D. C.

Thomas Christie to Sarah Christie

VICKSBURG JULY 6TH 1863

My Dear Sister;

The bustle and work attending the removal from our position outside to our present one in the suburbs of the Town being about over, I take advantage of the first spare minute to answer your favor of the—. (By George; there is no date to it I find on referring to it, except the rather general one of "A.D. 1863")

It is said that our Army Corps, in consideration of the harder work it did in the Siege than any other, is to garrison this post during the Summer, while the rest of the army goes into active service; One thing is certain, Sherman and Ord are both gone with their commands, and we are here in permanent camp.[24]

22. Transcribed in Thomas Christie reminiscence.

23. With men starving and with no hope of relief, the Confederate commander, General John C. Pemberton, asked General Grant for terms on July 3. Breaking with his usual "unconditional surrender" policy, Grant allowed Pemberton's troops to put down their arms and accept parole rather than remaining prisoners until formally exchanged. Some of the troops eventually returned to service, but many simply went home. McPherson, *Battle Cry*, 636.

24. On July 4, William T. Sherman's expedition against Jackson, Mississippi, began. His troops included the Ninth Army Corps under General Parke and two additional

Here is one of the strangest sights to be seen; our Regiments and Batteries camped side by side with the Rebel troops; and the men fraternizing and joining in friendly arguments as if there had never been any gunpowder invented. Riding along the road, you will see many a group of grey or butternut coated soldiers in social conversation with our Blue Jackets, and perhaps you will hear as you pass (as I did this evening) the following snatches of colloquy. Blue: "What Regiment do you belong to"? Butternut.— "Wards Battalion Smith's Division." "What State?" "Missouri, Benton County," "Ah; I come from there." "What is your name." It is told him, and the pair discover that at home they had met often, and then ensues inquirys about mutual friends in each army.

We are camped close alongside a Mississippi Battallion of artillery, and we get along firstrate with the men, but the officers are less approachable, conceited, bigoted men the most of them. Their mental callibre is small. I had a long conversation with a Second Lieutenant yesterday, and just think of an artillery officer talking about "32 Pdr. Parrotts," "cap shell" etc. and not knowing the difference between Horse Artillery and Mounted artillery. You must know that there are no 32 pdr. Parrotts and that what he meant by cap shell was Percussion Shell, and also that there is a great difference between Horse, or Flying artillery and Mounted, or Light artillery. These fellows were at the Battle of Corinth, and were in the advance the first day. They were much interested when we told them that our Left Howitzer is the gun they found spiked in the creek that forenoon. They tell us that the "Lady Richardson," a 20 pdr Parrott captured by them on the hill by the R. R. close to us, is here, having done good service during the Siege.[25]

I cannot give you any particulars of the amount of our captures here, as there is nothing reliable to be heard, but you can read the Newspapers and they will tell you all bout it. Enough for us to know that it is the greatest achievement of the War, and an irremediable loss to the Confederacy, for this place can *never* again be captured.

The health of our men is excellent, and if I alarmed you about *my* condition by the tone of my last letter, I have now to assure you that your fears

---

divisions. On July 6, he was reinforced with General Edward O. C. Ord's Thirteenth Corps. Welcher, *Union Army,* II:624.

25. Technically speaking, the horse artillery was a branch of the field artillery used primarily to support cavalry operations. The major difference between the two branches was that all of the personnel in horse artillery units were mounted, while some field artillery troops walked or rode on the limbers. *Field Artillery Manual,* 1.

were groundless as I am now in my usual vigarous health, although I have lost considerable flesh since the siege began. William is well and hearty but chafing and grumbling at our present inaction while the rest of the army is on the march. But the boys generally, and myself among them are not displeased at the prospect of a rest after our toil.

I was up to the heights this afternoon, and saw the monster guns that tried to impede the navigation of the old River. From them, (the heights) there is a most splendid view of the river as it winds around the low peninsula opposite; the green swampy woods of Louisiana, the smoke of the steamers at Youngs Point and the mouth of the Yazoo; the town, with its riddled roofs and bushy trees; and the fleet of gunboats, mortar boats, and transports sailing about or tied up at the levee. Looking at all these and meditating on many things occupied me a full 2 hours, and when I aroused myself it was almost time for Roll Call.

In answer to your inquiry I will tell you that I got a letter from Southwick[26] a few days ago, and he was still at Memphis and his wounds doing well. I think though, that you will see him before long, if he is not already at Clyman, as he promises me that he will visit you on his way to Minnesota.

Yours contentedly T. D. Christie

[margin note] I got a rebel paper a day or two ago by exchanging my last Independent for it, and sent it to Father Yesterday Have you got it?

[margin note] Got a letter from Strachen: He is at Murfreesboro and had just been in quite a skirmish. I will answer Helen's letter soon.

[margin note] Has Robert McNulty got home yet?[27] We are camped close to Gen. Greens grave. Green you know started the Helper controversy in Congress.[28]

26. Charles W. Southwick was hit by a Confederate sharpshooter's bullet on June 21 "while eating his supper. The ball passed through his upper arm, entered his right breast, followed on the ribs and lodged about the middle of the breast, right under the skin." Minnesota Adjutant General, Official Communications, First Battery, Light Artillery.

27. Robert McNulty served in Company D, Seventeenth Wisconsin Infantry.

28. While Thomas probably refers to Confederate general Martin E. Green, killed at Vicksburg, he conflates him with Democratic senator James Green of Missouri. The "Helper controversy" probably relates to the antislavery book *The Impending Crisis* by Hinton Rowan Helper, which stirred extreme reactions from southern politicians when the Republican Party used it in the 1860 campaign.

William Christie to James Christie[29]

VICKSBURG, JULY 8, 1863.

My Dear Father,

Here we are again within hearing of the whistle and puffing of the steamers! It sounds good. Already there is a mile of steamers tied up to the bank. The Rebels are perfectly astonished. They had been told that the river was completely closed by their batteries and sharpshooters. But this is only one instance of the way in which they have been deceived from the beginning.

We are encamped in the midst of the prisoners, while they are being paroled. The men of one of their batteries are close to us; we have our roll calls, orders read &c., and they have the same on the same ground immediately afterwards. A great deal of friendly talk goes on between us. Usually the subject is the Negro. As I write one of their Irishmen is holding forth in a loud voice on the beauties of Slavery. He is quoting the Old Testament and the New, and especially St. Paul. It is most amusing to listen to him. But the majority of their men are heartily tired of the War. One of their common expressions is, "this is the poor man's fight, and the rich man's war." They say that many of the rich planters come out and make speeches, and even go so far as to put down their names to be soldiers. They will drill with the men until the Co. is full; then they buy a substitute, and stay at home themselves. These rich men leave the families of the poor soldiers in great want, notwithstanding the promises that were made when the men enlisted. "The tender mercies of the wicked are cruel!"[30]

Another thing plainly to be seen is this: the soldiers from the different States are very bitter against each other. If they should succeed in this war, it would not be long before their States were at war with each other. We of the North always think first of the Union, and put our State into the second place; with the Southerner it is just the reverse. This will always be a source of weakness in them.

There are about 35,000 prisoners; but they will not all be paroled. Hundreds are getting away to their homes; some by crossing the river, some by dodging through our lines. Our guards are very kind to them: "I want to go through," says the poor fellow. "You can't get through here, its contrary

29. Transcribed in Thomas Christie reminiscence.
30. Proverbs, Chapter 12, verse 10: "A righteous man regardeth the life of his beast: but the tender mercies of the wicked are cruel."

to orders. But you may go up over the hill by that path there, you will meet no opposition." They say they have lived for seven weeks on 17 days' rations; and they look like it. They had plenty of powder and ball on hand when they surrendered, but were short of caps. We can well believe it, for there are simply cords of boxes in their magazines, each box holding a thousand rounds. It is nearly all of English make. In the trenches, each man had two guns by him, one a reserve to meet our charges. But we had so many trenches made close up to their works that they could not have hit many of our men before the thing would have been finished. That Irishman is getting so violent with his Biblical argument that I cannot write!

Yors Aff'ly

W. G. C.

∼

William Christie to Sarah Christie

VICKSBURGH, JULY 11TH, 1863

Dear Sister, Received a letter from you two or three days ago, (I am so warm it fatigues me to think up to a day,) and was glad to learn by it that all the nummerous connections of the Christies were in good health, "yous all know up thar." By this time that "we all" got intoo Vicksburgh on the fourth of July, And you may be sure it will ever be a mermorable fourth; to the ever victorious Army of the Tennessee: think of it on that Day the Brightest in American History: The Army of the Lord, added a new luster to the glorious Remmembrance of the Heart of every true and Loyal cittezen. By Breaking the Back of one of the most accursed Rebellions ever got up in this World or I Beleive in any other, I need not go intoo any of the high fallutin Rhetorical styles or get intoo [?] and all such like things about it. But let me tell you it will [be] as a new era; for me to count from, and I have not the least doubt with many others. In your letter to me you complain about the Corporal: giving you a drubbing over Helens Back for the want of something in your letters. Him and I have often talked abut your letters. I have really tried to find excuses for your. But the sage Corporal, the Pragmatical Corporal; yes the stubborn Corporal; The infallable Corporal; has no excuses for such shallow People as you and I unfortunately happen to be. I suppose if you were corrosponding with a sister or a very Dear Friend such as Helen should be, instead of the Pair of soldier Brothers: we would see a little more under the surface, and the Imovable Corporal, the unbeleiving Corporal, would see a great Deep sea of thought that he now scarcely Dreams of. I Beleive so at least, now mind I do not mean to flatter either you, or myself. For I know that flattery is bread and meat to you, But I am speaking what I think is the truth: Now do for once give the wise Corporal, a feast of Intelect, in one of your epistles: and as for me Poor weak fellow, I will een be content with the old gossipping sort of things you have disgusted the Profound Corporal with.[31]

Sarah I am really sorry to hear you say you are almost Discoraged in regard to your Penwomanship; Persevere, for I really think you are improving in your Cheriography, and if at first you dont succeed try, try again, I am rather too old or I would enter the lists with you: and see who would gain the day, if you say so I will as it is and allthough I have all the inconveniences of a camp against me I will try for the Palm of Victory.[32] Sandy's X's Ply y's and A B's equal to F. F' or some other such fixxens in answer to the Mathematical Corporal, muddles my poor weak Brains and this confounded Country is so warm I am sure allmost that some very wise folks we know of will get such exotic growths of knowledge into there heads that I am beginning to think that we will hear an awful complosion! Equal in sound to the oppening of a fine thrifty cabbage head at a certain stage of its growth, one of these mornings.

Be that as it may I will for one take great care of the fragments and forward some of them to the most Learned friends of said folk and the Balance to P. T. Barnum, or some other man of Notority, and fame. You ask a great Deal about C.W. Southwick I have nothing to say for or against. We are antagonists allways have been, and so we dont hitch. Tom will gratify you in all likelihood: about him, and let you know the Particular traits of his most excellent Character; Bah, The Clover and grass sprigs Hellen sent to Tom gave me a glimpse of the old old home, just as it was many years ago when I used to stand at the old well, and look down the ridge side and dream of it covered with green waveing wheat. I have always been a Dreammer: and so I suppose that's the reason I am so much of a sleepy head today, and it gave me a look at it now. Then the whole ridge was covered with brush, through which I one fine spring morning sent a devouring fire; I was so very ambitious to Burn Brush heaps; I disobeyed orders: and

31. The "corporal" referred to is undoubtedly Thomas. "Helen" is probably their cousin, Helen Reid.

32. Like his spelling and grammar, William's handwriting was untutored and very difficult to read.

a great conflagration was the consequence. Beautiful Country then, more Beautiful now; when my Dream is a reality; although I cant be there to see it.[33]

Sarah oblige me as soon as you can By getting me some news about J Blair, through Janet Clarckson: November will crawl on before we are fully aware of it, and I would like to learn something about Blairs concerns, for you know I am Pennuriarily interested.

Since we came in here, we have had any ammount of talk with the Rebs as a general thing they are a very poor unintellegent whiskey drinking people; and much in need of the schoolmaster among them. He would Be highly esteemed if he was armmed with the Whiskey Bottle instead of the Book. There Dialect is a miserable Negro jargon; and they really look worse than that nigger "over thar!" The Bluff, are Pretty well cut intoo for places to get out of the way of the yanks cannonading the cells are made straight in for about four feet, wide enough for a man or woman single file, then they are dug to the right or left, some Both ways; and made so that several can sit or stand: or lay down;[34] there are But few houses in town that has escapped being hit, several has been very Badly torn by bursting shell; houses are standing with the ends torn off, some with the roof smashed in and the floor torn out, the effects of war is seen every where. Great patches of ground are litterally trenched with graves, thousands of Bodies must have been Buried since we locked up this army in vicksburgh, the wounded were Brought in here, of the other Battles, But there has nevertheless been a great destruction of life By the bombardments and seige: Let us hope that these things will soon cease, and that war will end, and we soon return home. Tell Sandy I will write to him soon if the heat dont make me too lazy; and give my respects to Miss Mary and Maggie Amiers; and let them know they are very great strangers indeed. Tell Aunt Jessie and William Enisson that I hope to see the Laddy rosey cheeked and strong, when I return from the wars: a bould sojer Boy, My love to all the old Ladies; and hem: hem; he-m my Respect to all the young ones; good By for the present.

P.S. you must not take nothing herein written, as being said in malice pretense.

33. William probably refers to his experiences in clearing the land around the Clyman farm, a job he had as a teenager, when Sarah and Thomas were quite young.

34. Vicksburg's civilians created an extensive system of caves, some of them quite elaborate, to shelter themselves from the federal army's bombardment. See Foote, *Civil War*, II:412.

Your Loving Brother Big fool,
William G. Christie
what a Delic-a-te De-li-ca-te Ladies h-a-nd this i-s.
Say where do you learn geography, vick-g is in Mississippi

∽

William Christie to Alexander Christie

VICKSBURGH MISSISSIPPI JULY 16TH, 1863

Brother, I lay aside my lazy fit as I would a load, and I will try and write you a letter. But here I have to come to a dead halt for want of something to say.

JULY 19TH Dear Brother I once more resume my pen, to scrible a few lines to you. We are much Pleased here with the Prospects in Tenn: and Penn, and are well satisfied with our own acheivements, Rummor has it the greater Portion of the garrison at Port hudson gave Banks, and fleet, the slip crossing the River to La. side and cutting some very smart yankee tricks, let these things Be as they may. The Mississippi River is oppen and the Southern Confedracy is cut in twain, it will be out of the question to think that the Pesky critter can live with our the tail, and if Meade only gives the Head a scrunch with his heel we will soon make away with the Body.

This city is very nicely sittuated, and has been very handsome Before the war. I have been over the whole Place and I have changed my mind in regard to its appearance. Tis very filthy and although large gangs of Negroes have been employed in cleaning the streets, there has been But little, apparently, (comparitivly speaking) done. the Rebels have been very filthy, and it has just been here as every where else. We have been driven to a great Deal of work for healths sake. There are waggon loads of old rags of clothing, full of vermin and disgusting to Behold, there are one or two Rebel hospitals in town, and you can tell long before you come near them By the odorous stench, where they are, and let me assure you that they as a general thing have a Peculiar odor, belong[ing] to their camps and hospitals, and you can tell when Passing through a country, where troops of Both sides have been camped. the difference, between each camp By the smell even before you see a scrap of clothing or anything else to tell the difference by.

A Report is current in camp today that Joe Johnson has got out of Sherman's net and is running away as fast as he can. We do not hear much about what is going on in our rear, But we do not trouble ourselves much. We have any amount of confidence in U. S. Grant and feel sure of everything coming out right.

I have picked up an old Grammar, Kirkham's; first published in 1830, and I study it with great Profit and Pleasure. getting some very good assistance from the Corporal, I will say nothing further at Present, about my Proficeniancy in the rules or application of them, for I have not the least doubt, you can see no improvement, in the grammatical construction, of my sentences, and there is none in the sense either.

You complain of having nothing to write abut, what do you suppose we Poor Devils have to write about, nothing only drumming here: and drumming there, drumming everywhere, and fiffing for the same. Dixie Played on one side of you Yankee doodle Behind you. The Praire flower in front, and girl I left behind me on the other side; accompanied By the Devil's Dream, by another Band close bye. the whole makes a very curious mixture of sound like one grand Devil's Dream, or some such other villanious compersion of music. Next we might tell of transport hot weather, then of the daily arrivals of Contraband, from the cane brakes, where they have been hid away by there masters, untill so near dead with exposure and want, poisoned by vines of various kinds, and in such horrid Plight, that numbers drop Dead in the streets, or lie down in some unoccupied house, and die. Is this war too much for the Nation, that has had such a system in it that bears such fruits. No, and untill this accursed thing is Put from among us there will be no end to the war. I might also tell you a large quantity of Provisions, have been found under the house of a citizen of vicksburgh, while he was drawing Rations from our commissary, fifteen barrels of flour, several of sugar and a great quantity of melossas. he was taken in Custody and the goods seized. I might also tell you of the departure of Ransome's Brigade for Natches, how the 13th Ill, releived the 11th, and so you see you might learn a great deal if I was only disposed to tell you. The 11th I might say followed the Balance of the Brigade. I might also let you know there is two of the collord rigments camped in vicksburgh, and it is said in camp that a numer of our troops down the River near Natches captured five thousand head of stock, two thousand heard being Beef Cattle and the Balalance mules and horses. I might also tell you about an Election of officers in the first Minnesota Battery and how near like a Political thing of the same kind, in Clyman it looked, But Being like [Gruncio?] : I do not feel disposed to do so, and so you may die of curriosity, or Ignorance.

But I hear the Ringing of the church bell, making music in the air: and they Bring many many Pleasant memories before my minds eye, not that I have ever been a church going Individual, no sir. But I can go away Back to the sunny sabbaths when I used to Be in Dundee, making music with my fingers on the railing round St. Davids Church, or stand near the Catholic Church at the foot of Tys Street and listen to the Organ as it helped to swell the chorruses of the peiceses played in the service. Then I used to go and see the tide come roaring over the Banks, as it came in, and Now I go and see the Mississippi, Pouring to the sea its water Beaten white By the Paddle wheels of the transports, and thrown up in spurts by the propellers of the messenger Boats, as they glid up and down from one Place to another Keeping up communication between the gun Boats. One of these goes Past at times grim and Black to look at, and there Port holes, thereateningly oppen.

My letters are wearisome, I know. But there is only one excuse for me writing and that is it lets you know I am well, I am also light in weight, (not to say or imply anything else) Being, only 140 *lbs*. By the scales. so you see I am But a bunch of Bones: But lively and well. I am glad we left Lake Providence, for we learn it is very sickly there. The sixteenth Wisconsin and 120th Ill. has a great number on the sick list, there does not seem to be much increase of sickness among our troops at this point and the old contraband inhabitants say "dat, Dis will not be a yaller feve yar, dis yere: thank de lod:" Poor things they may be mistaken, but they are it seems quite confident, then they go on and tell of faithfull watching over thankless masters, and mistrisses and how they would be taken with it themselves: and left to die or get well as they Best might. The Christian Episcopal Methodist Church about a year or so ago gathered up a subscription for the erection of a church; for the use of the collored people, would have nothing But gold or silver. got eight hundred Dollars in hard cash, never built the church, nor returned the money, and so the mater is in "status quo" or some other such fix, Be Patient in all things, is my advice to you and if I had only written so at the head of this letter you would have been profittably warned and spared you self the trouble of reading such a jumble of nonsense, Read and forgive, and Remember me to all,

Believe me your affecttionate Brother
Wm G. Christie,

PS. we had lots drawn in the Battery yesterday for furloughs of those that drew three detailed men from the [. . .] got Prizes; and are going home, I did not

draw neither did T.D. it would cost 2 cents mile each way. James fischer is one
of the men going home. he will call at Uncle Davids. Fischer resides in Portlan
enclosed Myrtle Blooms.

ᔓ

William Christie to Alexander Christie

VICKSBURGH, MISSISSIPPI AUGUST 2ND 1863,

This is decididly a Beautiful morning, fresh and cool the sky of that dreamy
Blue, in fact everything looks as though they had on there Sunday Braurs.
I individualy feel first Best and am as you might say fully awake to life and
its enjoyments, so I will just victimise you this Blessed morning take you
By the Button and have you listen to me. So there is no use in you trying
to get away. Now you needent try to listen to that Band up on the ridge discovering sweet music, never mind that fellow out there on the road swearing, But just talk to me hear what ever I may say. Morgan the Horse theif
is trapped and taken at last and sure Pop this time. Bragg still keeps up
his Big skeddadle, with old Rosey after him. Johnson has taken a Big run
and Sherman after him, and we (that is the seventeenth Army Corps,) are
to take care of Vicksburgh and vicinity and I assure you we can do it even
if there was more danger than there is at Present.[35] Our corps had the sever-
est Part of the job in investing, I might say infesting also, the Graybacks,
(Body lice) are very Plenty among our Infantry, the City so we are to have
the honor of keeping it safe untoo the fall of the year. then [. . .] I suppose
we will have an opportunity to confiscate Chickens, and such truck. don't
think we steal as we march through a new country, no sir however like
stealing it may look, we never never never do such a thing By the By Father
once made a remark in one of his letters about those Books we sent home
looking or smelling to him as though they had Been stole. Poor Innocent
soul, does he think the little Corporal would steal or I either for that matter
or Better still Perhaps he meant that they were stole from the darkies, By
the men that has there names written on them Before we got them, any way

35. Confederate general John Hunt Morgan led a bold but unsuccessful cavalry raid
into southern Ohio, while Union general William S. Rosecrans, Army of the Cumberland, maneuvered Confederate Braxton Bragg's Army of the Tennessee out of east Tennessee, forcing him to abandon Chattanooga. As noted earlier (pages 147–48), Sherman's
reinforced corps had driven Johnston's forces out of Jackson, Mississippi.

he must never be so vulgar again while we are in the army to talk the word steal to us. he should say Confiscate, then we will know what he means.

There is much excitement here among us, in connection with the Chaleston news,[36] and every Paper is closely scanned, by us to learn the finale. If I was wise I might write or say something that would be very learnned, or interesting But no matter you must just take me, as you find me, and if you can see anything that is not sapient, and so forth, well never mind, The health of the Battery, is not as good as it could Be, neither Phisically, or morraly, yet there is nothing serious by the matter, as far as the Doctor is needed, But I am half inclined to think that there is much need of a spiritual cure, of our many derelictions from the narrow Path of well doing for we are truly guilty of innumerable sins in that way. Gambling is one of the curses that follow after us, and when those that are so taken up with it cant Play any where else the cemetery is a quiet Place and a marable tombstone a very nice table. So on such games as Chuckluck,[37] and Honest John, twenty one, and other such things, money changes hands very quick, and of course the men that shake the dice or handle the cards make the most of it, Love of Whisky is another sin that sticks to some, so that they willingly pay four Dollars, for about three Pints (a canteen full) it is sold on some of the Boats on the sly, at the above rates. I need not enumerate more of the weaknesses that we as a Body of Men are liable too But be glad you are exempt from draft even if you were of age, for if I can read the law aright Tom and I are all Father's family would have to furnish.

Whatever is the Reason of it we are not getting any mail from the North, that is the Battery not near as much as we should seeing we send so much out. There has been no letter from Clyman in a dog's age, dog's age. If I were to judge By my own feeling and set them up against time. I would say, that time for at least two Methusla's had gone Past, intoo Eternity, since we had a letter from home. There is half a dozzan of you and you cant get up as much as one letter a week, for us starving Divels down here. I tell you I verily Believe you are every one of you committing the unpardonable sin. I am almost sure of it. But you know there is room for repentance so had

36. Union forces began an assault on Charleston, South Carolina, via Morris Island on July 10, 1863. Foote, *Civil War*, II:696–97.

37. Chuck-a-luck is a dice game; it's not clear what sort of gambling "Honest John" might be, but "twenty one" is another name for the card game blackjack. Mathews, *Dictionary of Americanisms*, 1:129, 323. The types of tombstones William describes are flat slabs that cover the tomb itself, rather than upright markers.

Better Pent, right off, or I will be under the necessitty of excomunicating
the whole set of ye so hurry up there institute a new era, or some such a
thing Before it is too late.

Did you ever read Pollok's course of time,[38] if not, read, and be careful it
don't make you a ridged old school Presbyterian, there is much in it that is
very good indeed But after all I cant say I like it. it is too full of the wrath of
God, He is Portrayed here only at the avenger of sin, to an infinate degree,
Read Bailey's Faust[39] either Before or after, Pollok's Poem. Perhaps Father
would say read neither, and he may be right But I don't regret Having read
both productions.

Yesterday our section Built an oven of Brick, so we have three such in
the Battery, the Bread that is Baked in them is more like Baker's Bread,
than when it is baked in a dutch oven. Captain Clayton is ailing, he is at the
hospital, Dumb ague, or ague of some kind; there are a number of the Boys
troubled in the same way. The Corporal is not in tip top health, he is not
Bedfast, he enjoys a laugh and a joke, and as sure as shooting, or I should
say Preaching he will Be well as usual in day or two, he has been living
on rather low diet, and is now under my hands for care. I have ordered
Cold water Baths every morning, and Three small quantities of wine each
day, and Beef soup. he will write in a day or two and speak for himself. I
know he is only low on account of the time we had in the trenches, and his
ever lasting cold water and Bread, now mind dont get up and Fret yourselves any of you for I assure you he is not even seriously ill, and is as able
to do all his own duty as ever. I am going to Prevent anything serious By
my method of treatment. the other chaps are in the Doctors hands and are
swallowing Quinine and of course don't get Better fast.

Have you read that Letter of Horace's to Heanegin[40] I think is the name,
of the [R]everend he writes to on the evil spirits of the Bible, Old Horace is
about as near right in his opinion as any man can be, on such a subject and
I haven the least doubt he is right in his conjectures.

---

38. Robert Pollok (1799–1827), Scottish poet and theologian, published his epic, ten-
volume poem *The Course of Time*, a Milton-like history of human religion, in 1827.
He died in the same year from consumption. See www.electricscotland.com/history/
other/pollok_robert.htm (accessed June 2010).

39. William probably refers to the poem "Festus" by Philip James Bailey, a romantic
retelling of the Faust legend first published in 1839. See http://diglib.princeton.edu/ead/
getEad?eadid=Co148 (accessed July 2010).

40. William could be referring to the published letters of Horace Walpole.

lies is the cash current among the secesh in regard to our movements and seeing we don't know anything about it we are evacuating Vicksburgh, that is if getting rid of the filth of the Place and the Burying of dead rebs and the sending of Prisoners off in various Directions, is evacuating vicksburgh, then sir we are evacuating it with a vengance. Lord a massay what a lot of niggers are in town Whew, how they do smell, By the Powers of mud rancid Butter is actualey as a sweet smelling savor in comparison to a Batch of sweaty Negro mule drivers,

do let me know all the news when you write an answer to this, and do Be spry with your answer too, That is if you are not so much taken up with the harvest that [you] don't have time. Is David dead, that we never hear from him either directly or indirectly. I am actually run ashore for something to say just now so I will wait a little while before I finish. [. . .] so there may be something to tell. Nix come arouse, there is nothing to say, only dinner is ready, and I must pay attention to the Bell, Call, and have some vittles and drink. dinner and roll call Both over for the day, I sweltering in heat and sweat, unable to write more than just as I feel, so I will vahe[41] to leave so much of this sheet unwritten that it will seem like waste What did you have for dinner. I had Bread, Butter, Apple sauce, coffee with sugar, and condensed milk in it, so you see we don't starve. But lord man woulden't I make one of Mother's Pans of milk: non est. if I could only get my hands on it. But after all man don't live By Bread alone, even if he has all the other fixens added, for I really would like to get hold of some good work, or another. I should Be either sorry or ashamed to say that the Bible is not interesting to me. That is others may think I should Be Both But let me tell you quietly that I think for meself, about that very thing, and I am not troubled about feeling just as I do. But Lord a mercy I will have the Page so full I shant have room to sign my name. if I don't stop soon and then you might die guessing who this letter was from. Then I would Be liable to be tuk up for a shewiside, or some other arwful

Ass'n n a tor,

William G. Christie

P.S. is that last word before the writer's name latin Please answer.

41. This could be the Latin word *vale*, "farewell."

William Christie to James Christie[42]

VICKSBURG, AUG. 6. 1863.

My Dear Father,

We are all thinking a good deal now about the French in Mexico. Now that the Mississippi is open, and Lee has been so thoroughly whipped, it will not be long till this snake gets his quietus. We soldiers think it will then be our duty to attend to the Man of December. If *we* do not prevent France from subjugating Mexico, who *will*?[43] I am sure that in this we shall have the sympathy of England; but neither they nor any other Power of the Old World will do the work of themselves. Whatever be the result of all these wars and upheavals, I feel sure that God will take care of His own Kingdom. Nations may die, and others arise; but on the whole, the movement is ever forward. Progress is the law of the universe. Men like Napoleon are strong, but they are not so strong as He who inhabits eternity. When the right time comes, God will snuff him out as one snuffs out a candle.

Father, I am sick of reading in the papers of "the glory" of war. The truth is, there is no glory in it; Everything about it is simply horrible. Were it not that we are fighting in a good cause, for the destruction of slavery— that sum of all villanies —, and for the preservation of the Union, were it not for this, no money could hire me to stay in the army. Is there glory in the shrieks of men torn by bullet or shell? Is there glory in the cry of the mother as she sees her child's head swept off by a cannonball? Is there glory in the weeping of widows and orphans? Is there glory in the burning cities and the desolated homes that War leaves behind him? Is there glory in the undying hatreds that war creates and nourishes? It seems to me that it is only a fiend who can rejoice in such things, or praise them. Let these news-paper men come down here and see for themselves war in its terrible real-ity. Let them paint it as it is—the fearfulest scourge that God sends for the punishment of a sinful race!

T. D. is better again, and takes his regular turn of guard-duty today. A good dose of quinine seems to have broken the fever. It is good to see him around again . . .

❧

42. Transcribed in Thomas Christie reminiscence.

43. In 1863 Emperor Louis Napoleon sent a French army to Mexico to overthrow the government and establish a monarchy under Hapsburg Archduke Ferdinand Maximillian,

William Christie to Alexander Christie

VICKSBURGH AGUST 14TH 1863.

Brother Alexander. So you think I am a surveyor, or a Topographical Engineer, That you ask me to give you a full Description of Vicksburgh and
vicinity. in every detail and point of view. Now I have not the least doubt of
it you are what might be called damned Hot, as you toil in the Harvest field,
But let me tell you we are a damned sight Hotter, as we lye round here in
the shade, or our tents, with Nix Bantaloons, or anything else But our shirts
But after all I will try and give you a look at this city, and surroundings Provided you do not hurry me this remarkably warm day and just let me get a
few minutes to wipe the sweat off of my noble Brow Ahem . . .

Well sir let me inform you in the first Place that this Part of Mississippi
is very rough so that vicksburgh might Be set down as the City of many
hills, it contains one courthouse, which is as near the centre of the City limits as you can think for, on this Court house there is a town clock with four
faces that showes the time of Day to all that can read the signs, of the times
and this clock has a Bell which strikes the hours so that all may hear that
are not deaf. the Courthouse and all its appurtenances are set on an hill,
so that it may not be hid, and for the easy travel of the citzens of this City
the streets are graded down so that there are high Banks of red clay on each
side of you as you go on your way rejoicing Past the Provost guard in the
vicinity of said courthouse, in the sides of these Banks the die in the last
ditch folks of the south made many small caves to hide in so that they
might Be out of the way of the wrath that had come, and let me inform you
that since they have come out of these Burrows, there are great numbers of
them going to Better and happier homes, at least we hope so, seeing there
mortal remains are Being hid away in the Bosom of Old Mother Earth, at a
very fast rate The Principl streets of this city run Paralell with the River
Being interceted at right angles By cross streets, so that the whole city is a
Paralelogram or some such thing. every kind of Buildings are to Be found
in this Place according to the taste and means of the Builders. nearly every
home has a garden, and evergreeens, adorn the yard, among with are the
myrtle and the Pine mullbery trees are very common, and Black and yellow

---

who styled himself "Emperor of Mexico" in true Napoleonic fashion. The Confederacy,
which relied heavily on Mexico as a source of commerce, supported Maximillian.
McPherson, *Battle Cry*, 683–84.

locust are also very Plenty, But the serene or China tree[44] is the most con-
spicuous tree in the lot just mentioned The dark green of its leaves are
refreshing to look on and its wide spreading Branches make a splendid
shade, in June it is litterally covered wit ha beautifull Blossom of a lilac
color, and it has a very delicious smell, the sweet gun is a very good shade
tree allso. there are four churches in town that I know of, But I can say very
little about them for I have never been in one of them, there are two has
steeples on, and one looks like an old gothic tower, But let us get at the
River Batteries and as we look at them we cannot see how it ever was that
a Boat got Past these terrible looking guns, let me tell you if the first Minnesota Battery had manned these guns there is only one way I can think
of, that Boats would have got Past us, and that would have Been Because
they would have come faster than we could have fired. The river sweeps
round a great Bend, and with the Batteries where they are they command
as sweep of the River just like the Bend of and S. and as the River was high
at the time the Boats ran the Batteries they had allmost straght lines to
shoot in so that they could very easily have hit every transport that tried to
Pass the Banks of the River had rifle Pits along its front and these large
guns has a sweep of some three or four miles, how grim they look Behind
there works as they sit there night and day with there Black throats oppen
ready to speak in thunder tones, at any time.

Trenches are not much to look at nor very much use apperantly unless
filled with armed men. Trenches are not unlike the great ditches that we
made through the marches, only wider and about the same depth the dirt
trown out making Part of the defence, and a few feet of loose earth is more
to save men form Death By Projectiles of war than a civillian would Believe
Possible.

So now just think that the Giants of the Fable had there Battle with the
Gods, in this vicinity and that getting out of rocks to throw at them, they
immediately got about two thousand ridges like that one [known] up your
way, as the Hog Back, these they cut off in great chunks and throwed about
in all Directions (at there immortal foes, of course) and these falling here
made this country look as it does, now you have just as adequate an Idea
of the land as you can get short of seeing it, and at some future day we may
have a look over the ground in company. Now just think of these great

44. *Sapindus saponaria,* the Chinaberry, a favorite shade tree in the South. Mathews,
Dictionary of Americanisms, 1: 313.

heeps of dirt being covered with felled timber, and cane Brakes, then the Rebs made trenches along the crests and across the Ravines of a number of them hills and you have the Defences of vicksburgh. . Bah, how wearisome this will Be for you to read, and it is like Paddies Epistle just as Clare as mud, Bedad, mine letters are all just so, and I have no doubt they are very interesting as Puzzles, or enigmas:

Evening has come we can hear the Clear hum of the many insect on the wing, the great Bright stars are looking down on us: While quick and vivid flashes of shivery lightening quiver over the deep Blue sky, an occasional whistle is heard as a Boat at the landing backs of or Back out intoo the River. But let us listen to the Band on that Bluff a little to the right of our camp. Hear how the first cornopean[45] rises over all the other instruments and in the full vigor of his Power makes a number of somersaults, while the Bass strives in a Bewilldered way to follow after him only making out in long awkward strides [?] but in perfect harmony, to keep in sight of Active 1st hear him how he exalts in glee, and making all kinds of twistings in his flight stops short with a suddeness of move as would make you think he had Broke down But no sir again, seeing the second and third and so on down, to the deep sounding trombone thinks they have got the Better of him, alass they find out there mistake up By degrees he comes and with a sudden spring he over does his last exertion and comes out conqueror: yes tis very nice to sit and listen to the Band, and think each note Represents the movements of an Acrobat as they Pound out into the night air.

Well I am getting almost in the Notion of having a furlough sometime this fall, if things will Permit, and there is not any liklyness of me Being away from the Battery when there might Be a fracas with secesh. I am trying to Persuade the Corporal to take one now if he can get it. he is as well as ever But still I think it would Be for his good to have the trip round costing about 30 Dollars, I Believe, Now mind don't strain your eyes looking for either of us, for there is not the very sure sign of either of us succeeding in getting away.

The health of the members of the Battery improves, only our Capt. is troubled with ague. a man of the 17th Wis: who has Been in our Battery all Winter and this summer died a few days ago, drunkeness the cause, he is Buried in the Buried in the cemetery, close By, and I Believe would not

45. William probably refers to the cornet, an instrument common in military bands.

have had a Better a Buriel if he had Been in Janesville where he Belonged, his name was James Bray.

By the By did sarah get a letter from me containing a dollar so that she could send me stamps. Perhaps the letter containing the stamps was Burnned on the steam Boat Ruth,[46] on the Mississippi about a week ago. I have to tell you you need not send any more stamps while we stay at this Place as we can Purchase Plenty of them at the Post office there has not a single trap come from sarah yet, in the shape of needle case of anything else her papers came to hand let her keep sending on such things for we enjoy the music very much. I do not sing or Practice a great deal for tis troublesome, on account of my eyes, and Besides I have no voice that can do any thing But holler and scream like sixty I would really like to hear what davy has to say for himself, and how you are all getting along with the summer work, has the horses been forth coming, for the sixtyfive Dollary should be home By this time and the greenBacks are either going to fetch the work or the horses:

The sixteenth wisconsin are here now But they are very Badly off, much sickness Prevails among them But the long stay at lake Providence has hurt them and they will not Be able to do much here. Amos Noble is here and in tolerable good health, he sends his respects to sarah, and the rest of you John Schaller is allso in a fair way of gaining his ordiary condittion of health, the 17th are down at Natches and so is the 29th, so I cant say any thing about them, or the Boys in them. I cant learn anything about the 20th Wis: nether can John Schaller. But John thinks if there was anything the matter with John Frank his Capt. would write, and in fact I know he would, if the Franks have not heard from John since you were Bid ask, (I should say sarah) tell them to write to Capt. Koosle it's a german name they will know how to spell it, and he will tell them all bout John. They should have the number of the Division and General's name, allso the no. of the Army Corps, and then they could learn about the Boy at any time. Herron I Believe is the Division Commander that the twentieth is in they should allso know the no. [of] the Brigade if not the commanders name, if those who have friends in the army only now these things they would hardly ever Be at a lose to here from the absent, By writting to the rigment or company commander,

46. A new paddle-wheel steamboat, the *Ruth* was carrying a cargo of military stores, including $2.6 million in cash, when she burned on August 4, 1863. The fire was later attributed to Confederate arsonists. *Way's Packet Directory*, 405.

Write as soon as you can I will write to sarah in a few days,
good By
William G. Christie

[postscript] how do you like a Reb envelope

∽

William Christie to Alexander Christie

VICKSBURGH MISSISSIPPI, AGUST 20TH 1863

Dear Brother. This morning is Rainy. Raw and disagreeable, So you see
by every letter I write to you there is always something wrong with the
weather. Tis either too hot or its opposite, or too wet or too dry, and in fact
there is no Pleasing of humanity or at least this small portion of it that
addresses you I Believe I would growl if I were going to be hanged, no matter how soft the Rope, or accommodating the hangman. So you will have
the little Corporal among you and one or two others of the Bould soger
Boys, use them well, and see that they will Be well used by the Infernal
Copperheads that slip and crawl round among you. within the past two
weeks we have lost two members of our Battery By Death. one of them a
detailed man from the 17th Wis. his name was James Bray, he enlisted at
Janesville, Whiskey I Believe was the Reason he had to Pay dame Nature
the debt due her. the other died on the evening of the 17th. he was a
german a very good man, and succumbed to Dysentry and Ague.[47] so there
are great numbers going off with one ailment and another, which might be
expected among so many men, where so few know or understand But little
about the laws of health, or any of the phisical laws of Nature. But the Death
of a fellow soldier, is a thing that is not calculated to shock us very much as
long as it is in the field or Hospital. But when the lives of a number of men
and some women is taken unexpectedly, and in the shocking manner that
a number Perished yesterday; it makes even the most thoughtless of us feel
afraid, or something akin to fear, at least it does me, yesterday morning I
was detailed with some others of the Battery to go to the Levee for hay. we
had slayed quite a while Before we got our hay, and about noon as we were
leaving the Levee, I saw a great cloud of smoke flame and steam, and a loud

47. Company day books show that Henry Schuler died on August 17. According to
the *Adjutant General's Report*, 786, he was born in Germany and listed Taylors Falls as
his place of residence at the time of his enlistment.

prolonged roar as if a great gun had Burst. But we soon learned that it was
the City of Madison, a goverment transport, that had nearly completed her
load of Ammuntion.[48] I left the waggons and hasttend in the Direction of
the scene of Disaster, having about sixty rods to run. What a sight when I
got to the Boat, or where she had Been, there she lay or what was left of her.
a small portion of upper deck and the stern besides the right hand Wheel-
house, she was, at the time of the horrible accident, getting up steam so
that she might Procceed to Natchez. But as her load was not complete there
was a large Detail of as many as eighty men at work getting aboard the
boxes of fixed ammunition, when unfortunately some careless or thoughtless Person let a box of Percussion shell fall, and it fell points down and
then men, and boat went up in one great cloud of smoke and flame. Men
mangled, were thrown as much as one hundred yards from the boat, and
ceased to breath, Boxes of ammunittion were thrown up to a great hight
and fell among Piles of the same that were on the Levee. Tis said the captains family were on Board, Besides the deck hands, one hundred Negroes
were in the hold, stowing away the loading, and in fact I suppose there are
over a hundred lives lost, I may learn more Particulars today, if so I will forward them to you But the papers will give all the different stories, afloat,
about it. after what I seen I cannot write about it with any other feelings
than those of horror. The Ewd; Walsh a very large Boat lying outside the
City of Madison is a total wreck as far as her upper works are concernned,
there were a number of people hurt on her, also.[49] There is a great amount
of all kinds of Millitary Business done here. large quantities of amunition
is Being shipped down the River and it would seem By the kind that it was
for siege Purposes; Tom's furlough and those for the other invalids are
Being made out just now; and it is very likely he will be there with you, as
soon as this letter. Now you will all Be troubling him about how Big Willie
looks, so I will just tell you that he looks about as when you last saw him
only not so many Pounds, Avoirdupois, in whight as he was then. Not any
wiser But Probably tother way. so give the lad rest and me too, for I may
Be up to see you and speak for myself, for I am going to try for a regular
furlough,

48. A side-wheel, paddle steamer built in 1860, the *City of Madison* was used as an
army supply vessel on the Tennessee and Mississippi rivers. Official reports listed 156
killed in this incident. *Way's Packet Directory,* 93.
    49. According to *Way's Packet Directory,* 142, the *Edward Walsh* survived this accident
and continued to work on the Mississippi until 1867.

O gory what am I to fill up this long sheet with. Horses is the talk
Between me and the Corporal, we have come to the conclusion that one
span of Horses are as easy kept as two yoke of oxen and seeing that Father's
Place is all under the Plow we, or rather I have come to the conclusion he
should have a Beautiful span of Brood mares: and seeing there is another
year for me to Be in the service of my Country: (don't that sound Big!) and
if it is God's will that I should get Back to the "old old home," I will want to
rusticate as much as another year, and look round to see what will turn up,
I think Father could not do much Better than just use what ever We may
send him to get things in shape on the Place, and he would have time to
Refund the green Backs, at his lessure. There is one thing vexes me very
much and that is I have not anything to send you. . I have not money
enough on hand to have my [photograph?] taken. But you can just think
you see me looking at you, with a Broad grin on, and my Ivories displayed
to great advantage. Don't trouble the Corporal with your trines, and signs
of X Plus y, and all such very valuable things let his Brain rest. jaunt him
round and let him see as Be seen you have not any need to Be ashamed of
him, I assure you. If he begins with any of his learned Book truck and wont
stop when you tell him too, and that would Be Before he was well begun you
up and knock him down, then have sarah maul him with the Broom stick
untoo he says he wont say a work about Algebra or any other A. of the kind.
So now you know how I would have the thing done. Amos Nobles and John
Schaller will Be likely to pay you a visit, and they are Both good and useful
soldiers, so do the Best to make them feel happy, and Pleased among you,
Bear with some of John Schallers modes of Expression and Be considerat,
you will find Amos a very quiet fellow, and able to give a very good account
of the Battle of Shiloh, also a Pretty good Idea of Hospital life, he having been
a waiter or nurse in these Places at different Points, he wont exagarate, John
may draw the long Bow a little, Now I said all I can say about these things,
and then you see I will have to dry up, and leave all this Paper unused; down
come the rain in coppocous showers and old mamy Earth Bleaz through
the rain haye, give my Respects to everyone that is not snakey, and Be you
write soon, Love to Mother; Grandmother and all the rest of the Women
gear, good By for the Present and Believe me your loving Brother
    William G. Christie
    I don't mean to slight the men folks in the least.
    Good By

                                ∾

William Christie to Alexander Christie

VICKSBURGH MISS: OCTOBER 2ND 1863

Dear Brother I Receieved yours: of 20th of the past month the ninth day from date. I of course should have answered it Before this, But I never having much to say even [when?] at High tide or full flood: could not Be expected to do anything when at Low water Brought on By excess of drought. But seeing old Mother Earth is smilling once more after having her face washed, and that the sky looks Bright likewise: and I feel after yesterdays Review that I might Possably, write a few lines that you might think Readable, Being Partial to said writer of these lines. Yesterday morning after a Blustering Northwester which had [squeezed] out all the mosture out of the rain clouds that had come in on us from the East, finnaly rolled them up like a scrol and last night everything looked outside of the camps: as though we had a new Heaven and a new Earth. the sky was so Blue, the stars so Bright, and the air so Bracing if cold: at eight o'clock in the morning we went out on Review, not only the Batteries But all of the Division that was here. The Iowa Brigade three Rigments (the fourth on Being up in the city doing Provo duty:) did not come.) four companies of the first Kansas infantry, mounted. The Batteries three, making in all about 2000: men, the sixteenth Wis: Vol: has gone out to do guard duty on the Road Between this Point and Black River, where some guerillas had the audacity to capture some trains, going out to our extreme front on Black River, and the second Brigade entire is in or about Natchez, Besides some of the first Birgade, so you see that the first Division is Pretty well scattered

There are twelve Rigments of Black troops here in the way of Being filled up. some are already full up to the maximum and have Been in service quite a while. the old rigments are about one thousand strong, the new ones are to Be two thousand strong. I hear they are going to Receive there first pay today ten dollars Per month, some of them will get five months. how Proud they must feel.[50]

Well what do you think of C. [D ?]. and is he still with you to such times as Tom leaves. I am happy to hear that Father's crop has Paid him so well for your labor, and that he still continues to take the Best yeild off of the same amount of ground. taking the Beef intoo account you have not Paid

---

50. Black recruits earned three dollars less per month than white soldiers, a discrepancy that caused much resentment. See Trudeau, *Like Men of War*, 91–93.

over much for the ox that you Bought, of Connor, and now since you have got the Horses, or is going to get them, you will Be able to make thing[s] hum on the old farm, But it is too Bad that Father has to Pay a Premium to get anything like his rights, even from his own Brother, But even if these things are so and I Believe they are, Father seems to get along Better than those that grip him so hard. so never mind his eighty acres of land, horses and Reeper with what he has got Before will thrive with him. so he will get along full as well as [Ramsey ?] Rogue No. one or Rogue No.'s two. so mote it Be. But I am not so sure But Uncle William may Back out of the offer as it stood when you wrote to me, it would only be in accordance with his Past Plans and Proceedings so if he thinks he is not making enough he will squeeze Father a little more, Provided he thinks or finds he cant come it on Ramsey.[51]

We have Received no Papers from the North of a very late date, But the Rummor is Prevalent in camp that Rosecranz and Burnside has whipt Brags forces, at or near Pigeon Mt. in Georgia: close By Chatanooga: if this Report Proves true I think the war is nearly over, and we likely Be on our way home By next summer, afternoon I have waited for a Letter But waitting has Been in vain. no letters and only one Paper the Chicago Weekly Tribune of the twentysecond in which we learn about Rosecranz falling Back to his stronghold, Chattanooga.[52] I see the very wise People up North has come to the conclusion about the Army of Virginia, that the stupid soldiers down here has had for the Past year, that is that it seems to make it its Business to lye still untill our western armies has time to fight and even if loosing ground whip the Army of Jeff Davis and Co: that should have Been knocked out of exsistense by them long ago: well I need not say any more about this, But I am serious. cant the People & government see these things and try to hinder them from happing again. OCT. 3RD This morning and last night there is a Rummor in camp that a colored Rigment has Been taken By surprise at a Point on the River opposite Natchez, and Badly cut up by a Body of Rebel Cavalry, mind it is only a Rummor. The limbers has Been taken out Behind the horses to the flat By the River, so

51. Alexander Ramsey was a near neighbor of James and William Christie (Uncle William). Although the Christies boarded with Ramsey when they first came to Wisconsin, they had long-standing disputes with him. See U.S. Census (1860), Dodge County, Wisconsin; Christie papers.

52. William probably refers to the Union defeat at Chickamauga, Georgia, on September 22, 1863.

that the men and horses may drill. We expect a set of new guns carriages, and fixens complete, in a few days. the Rodman Gun, is the kind made of wrought Iorn and Borred out, they are very long range guns and effective.[53] The pieces we have now are Bronze, called the James Rifle, the Howitzers are Bronze also But no Particular make from other field Pieces of the same Calibre, twelve Pdrs: all the Batteries are on drill or will be. I am on detail to go with the quarter master after clothing and ordinance stores: light truck for a sadler and Black smith. Health is Returning, or rather we are returning to Health:

give my Love to all and Belive me your
affectionate Brother
William G. Christie

53. "Rodman" guns were officially known as three-inch ordnance rifles. Although they resembled the cast-iron heavy artillery manufactured by the Rodman process, they were made by a different method.

5

"This Dull, Idle Existence"
October 20, 1863–March 19, 1864

Thomas Christie to Alexander Christie

VICKSBURG, OCT. 20, (1863.)

My Dear Brother,

I sent off a letter to Father this afternoon, but, as it was but a short one I must write again to tell some of the incidents of our journey.

At Cairo we embarked on the stern-wheel steamer Emma,[1] bound for Memphis, taking with us some bread, butter, and bologna, for grub. The latter article was declared to be fresh by the storekeeper—"yes," said Sam, "I know it must be fresh, for I heard the dog howl when you threw it down on the counter just now," This hit at the supposed composition of the sausage was received by the crowd of soldiers standing around with an appreciating laugh, and by the injured vender with a look of disgust and indignation.

The boat was crowded below, so we went up to the hurricane deck and picked out a place to sleep aft of the smoke stacks. But when the boat started the coals from said smoke-stacks fell in showers all over the deck,— some of them as large as walnuts, We were in a fix, the coals burned our blankets, our clothes, out hats, (I would like to send you a photograph of the crown of Dave's white felt, it has about 20 black holes in it.) Suddenly, while we were wondering what to do about it, a happy idea struck us so hard as to knock us endwise; we went to the steamer's life boat, which was turned bottom up on the deck, tipped it up on one edge and propped it with

---

1. Probably the side-wheel, wooden-hull packet *Emma* built in Cincinnati in 1856, which became a U.S. transport in 1861 and was lost in action on the Red River in 1864. *Way's Packet Directory,* 148.

a board, and then crawled under, bidding defiance to the fire. Here we slept during the voyage, (nights I mean; not all the time,) and the large boat gave us good protection against coals, wind, and rain. Sam's rubber was ruined however, it being in much the same condition as my hat.

We stopped at Columbus the first night, (you must know that the river is navigated only in the day time on account of the sand bars and guer-rillas, the boats anchoring at night in the stream,) At Island No. Ten we stopped some time to discharge freight, and I took a look at the old Rebel fortifications, and the old spiked guns in some of them; they are truly for-midable. Stopped at New Madrid also, to take on live hogs for the Memphis market, and here we saw some fun. About 200 citizens, deckhands, and young darkeys were engaged in driving the crowds of frightened porkers down the steep bank and over the gangway on to the lower deck of the vessel. They would drive them very well untill the planks were reached, and then they would scatter, and break through the heterogeneous crowd that surrounded them, tripping up long haired citizens, active youths of African descent, and swearing Roustabouts. Each man would try to secure a pig as they broke through, but abrased shins were all the could generally get, although some fellows would hang on to legs or ears and be dragged for rods before assistance would arrive and the vanquished resistant be hauled aboard grunting and squealing. One of the hogs being cornered at the river edge actually took to the water and swam halfway to the opposite shore when he was overtaken by a boat, and compelled to relinquish the idea of leaving the State. One of our fellows shouted to the owner of the hogs that he never could get them aboard so long as they saw so many soldiers on the hurricane deck: "Those hogs," he says, ["]are not to be fooled, they *know* the blue coats," You must not suppose that these animals resembled your sober, fat, Suffolks, No, they were fine active characters, lean and light-footed such as you would pick out to run a race and win, in fact some of them would need a knot—tied on their tails to keep them from going through a fence. When the last protesting victim had been remorselessly dragged over the planks, the line that held us to the shore was let go from the stump, the gangway was hauled in, and we proceeded down the green-banked river, the monotony of the voyage broken only by the passing of a steamboat upward bound, or the shout of a "butternut"[2] in his canoe as he approached the steamer: "Throw me a newspaper overboard, please."

2. See earlier note on this term (page 58).

A paper would be folded up and thrown into the water, and he would raise it on his paddle with a care that showed how much dependent he was on this precarious mail for all knowledge of what was going on in the civilized world. You would be surprised to see the dexterity with which he would manage his canoe among the fierce waves that followed our paddle wheels when a single false stroke of his paddle would capsize him into the water. After a tedious voyage of 3 days we arrived in Memphis, and our progress from there is it not to be chronicled in the letter that I shall write soon to Sarah.

My last dispatches from the Big Black, brought by Co. "C" 1st Mo. artillery, which came in tonight, is that our fellows are on the march to this place, Good night.

T. D. Christie

[margin note] When you answer this tell me how the horses get along, and everything about the farm, Plowing, husking, hunting, etc.

∽

Thomas Christie to Sarah Christie

VICKSBURG, MISS, OCT 21ST (1863)

My Dear sister.

As I have a little leisure today I must let you have the rest of our voyage as promised in Sandy's letter yesterday.

As we turned a bend in the river we saw Memphis, seven miles away, an irregular looking mass of red brick and green trees surmounted by the cupola of the Overton House and half a dozen church spires. In three quarters of an hour we were landed, and picking our way through the crown of men, women and children crying their wares, "Apples, four for a dime," "Here's the late Chicago, St. Louis, and Cincinnati papers of the 10th" " 'Eres the Memphis Bulletin and Argus, all about the fight at Colliersville," we took refuge in the New Orleans eating house where the first man we met was Corporal Jo Colman[3] of our Company, who had started from Cairo a day later than we did and arrived before us. Jo was alone and consequently very glad to see us which was evidenced by the kicks, slaps,

3. Originally from Maine, Joseph Coleman enlisted in the battery from St. Anthony. *Adjutant General's Report.*

and handshaking that he bestowed liberally upon us. Jo is a good fellow, but very rough, having been educated in the woods and on the "drive" as a Lumberman. Joe's delight at seeing us was so great that, *nolens, volens,* we *must* have dinner at his expense. So, in partaking of a good dinner, served up by Monsieur Choteau in his best style, and in telling our several adventures and home pleasures the time passed pleasantly enough till five O'clock when we again took our luggage under our arms and went on board the Steamer Westmoreland,[4] advertised to start at five, But when we went aboard we were told that she would not start till the next morning, as there was some Government freight to take on, (hay, and beef cattle, for the troops at Helena,) So we picked out a good place, and slept on board that night, the boys, except myself, going to the theatre.

We clubbed together and bought 12 loaves of bread, 2 pounds butter, a canteen of syrup, and some cheese and dried beef, and were therefore very well provided for as far as Helena, Besides this we bought a teapot, and I furnished the tea from what I had to take to William. Sam[5] was duly elected "chief cook and bottle washer," and in this position gave universal satisfaction, although we remonstrated once with him, when he was drinking some cold tea from the teapot, on stirring up the leaves with his nose.

Before leaving Memphis, the soldier passengers, of whom there were about 300, were mustered on deck, their names and rank taken down and then divided into Companies with a Captain and Orderly Sergeant to each, and a Lieut, Colonel in command of all. This was on account of the danger from guerrillas and incendiaries, and it was announced to us that there would be a regular guard kept up during the voyage. Sure enough the first one detailed was myself, and I mounted guard that morning as corporal of the first relief. The Guard detail consisted of a Captain, as Officer of the Day, a Lieutenant as Officer of the Guard, a Sergeant: 3 Corporals and 18 men,—6 on a relief. Receiving my instructions from the Officer of the Guard I at once posted my relief, 2 men at the forward gangway to keep the men aboard, 2 at the cabin doors to allow none but cabin passengers inside, and 2 aft of the engines below, to look out against fire. My men were

4. A side-wheel, paddle steamer built in 1861 that worked the Cincinnati–New Orleans trade. *Way's Packet Directory,* 484.

5. Thomas's traveling companion mentioned in this and previous letters was Private Sam Wooley, who, like Thomas and William, enlisted from Winona. Originally from New York, he seems to have accompanied Thomas to Clyman or visited him there before returning to the battery. *Adjutant General's Report;* First Battery Company Morning Reports, Oct. 1863.

all strangers to me, so, to enable me to find them when I would have to put them on again, I took down their names and *also* the place where they slept. This latter precaution was not adopted by the other corporals so that when they were looking up their men at night they would wake up almost everybody to find them. "Ho, Second Relief, does Bellville sleep here, or Murphy." Then you would hear the man wakened by mistake cursing the corporal, Bellville, Murphy, and all the rest for breaking his sleep, and wishing the whole guard in the hot place.

My post was with the sentries at the gangway planks as it was the most important place—men showing passes to go ashore, or those who did not have passes trying to get by the guards without them continually. (You see I have not got away form Memphis yet.) As I stood there examining passes I remembered that when we went down the river last spring I was doing the same thing, and then I thought of the changes that had taken place and of all I had seen since that time. I thought that if I had been told, when I stood on the bow of the Jeannie Deans last January, of all the things that would happen to me, I would not have believed the tale.[6] But soon the whistle of the boat gave signal of our approaching departure, a crowd rushed aboard, the line was let go, the planks hauled in, the 2 guards changed their posts to the hatchways, and the great vessel backed out into the current. Soon we swept down by Ft. Pickering with its black guns trained down on the city, so that if an insurrection broke out the town could be knocked to pieces in an hour; down by the high bluff where tradition says Jeff Thompson[7] stood and watched the battle between our gunboats and the rebel fleet, till the only surviving vessel turned bow down stream and fled by him, when he turned, and as he mounted his horse for flight exclaimed, "curse those Yankee mud turtles," Poor fellow; those Yankee mud turtles now guard the river from St. Louis to the Gulf, and there is not a chance for a Rebel skiff to cross even.

I will have to write again I see, to finish the voyage so I will now turn to other things. I found both Kelly and Bill Wiltse[8] sick when I came but they tell me that William is still untouched, and is as well as ever. I expect to see him today, as they are coming in from the Big Black. I heard yesterday that Ransom's Brigade is in town and I will go and see the 17th soon if

6. See Thomas to Sarah, Jan. 24, 1863 (pages 94–95).

7. Possibly the Confederate guerrilla leader. McPherson, *Battle Cry,* 353.

8. William's tentmates, the "Three Kings." See William to Sarah, Apr. 29, 1863 (page 126).

it is so, I also heard that the 17th has been dismounted again, but I cannot tell much about anything till I see them.

You must write as soon as you get this and tell me all about your search for a school. Give everybody my love, and tell Grandmother Reid that I must find the address of the 29th at Head Quarters before I write to Tom Reid, this I will do as soon as I can get to town, which is almost 2 miles north of us now. Tell Grandmother Bertie that the apple she sent to William is so mellow now that I dare not touch it for fear of its falling to pieces. The boys tell me that W. was not very well pleased at receiving so few letters while I was gone,

your loving Brother, T. D. Christie

[margin note] Remember; this is no private letter, but for all the family to read, *and appreciate.*

∾

William Christie to Alexander Christie

VICKSBURGH MISS. NOVEMBER, 4TH 1863

Dear Brother,

Tis two years ago today since I first entered the service of our Country, and I having But little to do feel like giving you a few thoughts of mine in connection with the life of a soldier now in contra distinction to my Ideas about it this time two years ago, and previous to that time. My impressions when I first saw great masses of men at Fortsnelling going through the first steps of Initiation in there duties as soldiers: looked like mere childs Play to see Bodies of men marching hither and thither, without arms in there hands and apparently without object, there was such holiday appearance about the whole thing, if fact it looked like a huge Joke. People were so full of ammal spirits and good nature, it was hard to realize that they had gathered to save the life of a Nation at the risk of there own. But after a short stay among the vast throng you would observe a growing earnestness among them, not seen at first sight, But made apparent By the strong desire to assume the garb and the arms of a soldier, the desire also to reach the nearest Point of contact with the enemmy: Being the wish of nearly everyone of the throng, Then in our green state we thought we would Be always on the move, and that there would scarcely Be a day or at least a week without a fight, But how different the realittes of the Past two years from all our supposittions about them while yet in the future. How few our actual conflicts with the enemy has Been, only three Battles in two years, and yet how much has been gained By these fights, to the cause of Liberty, and God. Pittsburgh landing, (or Shiloh) was not a victory, that seems to Be much spoken of at Present and I have even seen it mentioned By some writter as a fight that Brought us nothing, But a mass of dead and wounded men, But it was [more ?] than the mere Possesion of the Battle ground of our forces after the second days fight, it was the keeping of all the victories Previous to that time in the south west and was acctually an acceleration of the gaining of Island No. 10, and gan [gain?] us Corinth without a Battle, in as you know a short time after, of our long rest at Corinth after it became ours, our drillings, and marchings for short distances hither and thither, our cleaning [?] up of allmost everything fit to eat, every man becoming theives as you might say, as well as murderers, according to the Copperhead creed, But in reality (as things were then and are now,) true Patriots: serving there goverment, not any too well, But often Better than the officers of said government wished them to do, Of hopes and fears, of mournings over Legions of men carried of By sickness, and wounds. and laid in hastily made graves with there Blankets as a coffin and a winding sheet, to Be looked for in vain By friends in the North and Perhaps forgotten among men, in a few Passing years, how indifferent you would think soldiers are to life, and I Beleiv as a general thing we are, for as a general thing, we might Be considered gamblers with the chances increased By two hundred fold against us, over and above what they would Be in civil life, so if the drum and file [fife ?] Precede the Earthly remains of a Brother soldier to the grave with Dolorous; note and low muffled sound, do they not as soon as dirt is heapped over the Body, lead Back to camp giving out the heart inspiring notes of a march or quick step So mirth jostles greif, and life and Death Pushes along through the world, Jolly Rolicking Life a few steps ahead of old Death, and thereby gaining, on the old BareBones in spite of all he can do. We you know after Being at Corinth all summer came nigh smelling Blood at Iuka, missing it By only an hours march or rather By Rosenzrances Precipitating matters a little quick, and Bringing on a row that was the means of Price getting away from that Place, At Corinth we did have our second row and By repulsing Van Doran Price Villepeige and Co; Broke up one string of Jeff Davis' Plan of driving Back the vandal Hordes; of the north I wonder if he ever read History, if so, did he think the lieing vermen whipping cutthroats of slavedom, could do, what the Legionaries of the old

Roman Empire failled to accomplish; Poor withold [?] if he did, how foolish he must feel, just now at the Poor success of his Plans, after the Battle
of Corinth a winter of marches, and counter marches: interspersed with the
excitments incident to Passing through a Portion of country abounding
with corn, Beef, Pork, Chickens; and too many good things, to mention,
Cotton Gins and other out Buildings, giving out huge volumes of smoke
By day, and vast Pillars of fire By night, long lines of Burning fences marking the road the army had traveled; and occasionally a dwelling house
adding its lustre to the Blaze; then our trip down to Youngs Point, thence
up to Lake Providence, hence to Millikins Bend, The march of three Army
Corps; from that Point to Grand Gulf, through a land abounding to the
first Passers; with meat; milk: and honey, corn and cotton abundant for all
commers. The Glorious victories of Port Gibson, Raymond: Champion
hills Blackriver Bridge and finnally the capture of Vicksburgh; Why Sandy
I do think sometimes, I have not lived in vain, from the fact of my merly
having been a unit of such an army, that drove a force half as large again as
itself,[9] fought three or four Battles with it, and kept the communication
oppen of an ever lengthing line, untill it caused them to yeild up a Portion
of there Fortifications, giving us a Base of supplies only 8 miles from our
Place of opperations; instead of over 100 miles as at first, and then crown-
ing feat of all, Putting them intoo what the Rebels themselves called the
Bull Pen, and litterally starving them out; Surely Brother of mine "The Lord
hath Been on our side." or we could never have done these things, Is it, or
is [it] not Profanenation, to use such language as the above at the end of
such a tale of horror, and Horrable things as this letter speaks of, in
such an apparently easy and flippant way, under all that I have said, there
remains, shattered limbs and mangled Bodies of men, By the missles of
war, there arises Before me now the looks of horrible Hatred Pain and
agony fixed By death on the face of the slain, through the hum of camp life
there comes up the cry of Pain from the wounded, and over all there comes
the solemn sound, of mourning from nearly every family north and south
for those that are dead, to them and this life forever, But Let us not be
cast down, for these things had to be, We as a Nation, have gone astray: and
now through Blood and tears, we are Returning to the Path [of] Rectitude,
and Purity, God willing, and we working, we shall By His help gain our

9. Reality was actually the reverse of William's assessment: Grant had about 40,000
men under his command as opposed to Pemberton's force of 30,000 Confederates.
McPherson, *Battle Cry*, 629.

Salvation, as a People, and within our Borders, shall Be worked out the highest Destinies of our Race,

I have been troubled with a slight attack of Acute Rheumatism,[10] it has gone and I am now getting the upper hand of a severe cold. Tom is well and as a Battery are coming out, in new Paint, as well as a new year, the Health of the co. in the main is good; give my Love to all, write soon, and often, for I am very hungry for letters: do send us a letter each week, so many of you might with great ease

Good Bye, William G. Christie

∾

Thomas Christie to Sarah Christie

VICKSBURG MISS. NOV. 28TH 1863.

My Dear Sister;

At length I received a letter from home after waiting for it so long,— Yours of the 6th came to hand this noon, and I answer without delay, William also got one from Sandy, and one from————.

The continuation of the "tale" of my adventures comming down from Memphis you will have to wait for till I come home, as there did not enough of interest occur on the journey to make it worth recording. William and I are both in good health as you will readily believe when I tell you that my weight today is 150 pounds, without overcoat. I am very comfortably situated at present in the Orderly Sergeants tent, but still mess in the Squad, and do duty there, Southwick is well and hearty, and he and I mess together, that is, we buy and use butter, cheese, etc. in common. Romer[11] is not any better, to say the least, than he was when you saw him, as his diarrhea still continues bad, and the change of climate and mode of life has done him no good, Sam is stout as ever and in a fair way of getting rich fast, as he buys apples by the barrel in town and sells them out in the Company in such a manner as to gain about five dollars per

10. This incident may have been the beginning of a chronic problem that afflicted William the remainder of his life. His pension applications mention "disease of the heart result of rheumatism" as a major disability. See Civil War Pension Applications, William Christie, No. 255203, National Archives, Record Group 15, Washington, DC.

11. Possibly Roemer Reimers, a private in the battery from New Ulm. *Adjutant General's Report*, 786.

barrel, (out of pocket,) This extraordinary result may be attributed to the fact that like Cotton[12] in his grocery, he is his own best customer,

We have a way here of what we call "saddling the horse," for the apples; The modus operandi is this,—Suppose there are 5 of us who go into it; a slip of paper is marked on one side with the numbers 1, 2, 3, 4. 5, and on the opposite side is marked, in secret, *one* of those figures, the paper is then handed to each one and he selects of the five figures by crossing it with his pencil. Whoever crosses the figure which is also put down on the other side has to pay for the apples for the crowd, This mode of making a man stand treat is much in vogue in our squad, and as Sam comes around pretty often with his pailful of apples to peddle, we generally manage to inveigh him into it, and, as he has miserable luck in marking, he almost invariably has to come down with the fruit, Yesterday evening Sam came around, as usual, to Southwicks tent where I was and I, being the prime mover of mischief of this kind; immediately proposed to "saddle the horse" for a quarters worth, This they all agreed to, Sam included, and we all marked our figure, throwing the treat on the luckless Woolley. This did not suit him, and he proposed to try it again when we had eaten the first treat, His object was to get it on to me, as I had been having a good many apples at his expense, and had not been saddled yet,—So we went through the operation twice more, and, singularly enough, he marked the fatal figure each time, so that he must away with an empty pail and minus the yainay [?] greenbacks which he should have realized by the sale of his apples,

We have got a society in town called the Vicksburg Union Literary Association, and W and I are members of it, I joined only last Tuesday evening, and have not taken any part in the proceedings as yet, but Wm has taken an active part in two debates, and is the leader in the one to come off next Tuesday. The proceedings of the weekly meetings are, Debate, Reading of the magazine published by us, and delivery of an Essay by one of the members, the meeting opening with prayer and singing. If we stay here all winter we will have a good time, for besides what I have mentioned, we attend Divine Service every Sunday and I have heard some of the best Sermons here that I ever heard in my life, There is a young fellow in the 10th Ohio Battery, Sergt Gage,[13] who visits us sometimes and I like him very much,

12. Probably another reference to Clyman neighbor George Cotton. See William to Alexander, June 27, 1863 (page 146).
13. Joseph B. Gage of the Tenth Ohio Battery.

as he is well educated, a good conversationalist, a good singer, and can draw first rate. He was in our tent last night, and we were all enjoying ourselves very much, when one of our boys came to the door and looked into the tent for a long time, then, to excuse his standing listening to us, he suddenly asked if so and so was in, Gage very soberly looked under the bunks, pulled out a drawer in the Orderly's desk and peeked into it, and lifted up the large Roster book and looked under it, then turning gravely to the eaves dropper said he thought so and so could not be in, as he could not find him anywhere, The chap turned off, perfectly satisfied that the man he wanted was not in *our* tent at least.

We made a chessboard and men a short time ago, and I have learned to play quite well. We have some good players in the Company and I will have a chance to become a pretty good player. It is a much deeper game than checkers, and we sometimes are 2 hours at one game.

William and I sent home 65 Dollars a few days ago with a request to Father to pay your debts at Lowell and Watertown, and he will probably do it. You must give me a description of your new school and the people of the neighborhood in your next, and give my respects to our old schoolmates, the Foxes.

The Bugle Call[14] which you sent down is much appreciated among the singers here, and "the Gun boat Song" and "Gone to the War" are special favorites. We sometimes have great old sings in our tent, when half the company will come to hear us. My new tentmate, Sergt. Heywood[15] is an excellent singer, and a good fellow altogether. Kelley[16] is now in the hospital, sick with the fever and ague and he has not been well since he and I were taken sick together last Summer. We had a note from John Schaller yesterday, telling us that he is with his Regiment[17] at Red Bone some 12 miles south of here, and wishing us to come out and see him, we will go out on Wednesday,

I am on Guard tonight, and it is awful cold, we have had some rain lately and may now expect a cold spell, but last week the weather was just like Indian Summer.

14. Thomas likely refers to a publication of the Sanitary Commission, which probably included sheet music.

15. F. L. Haywood, originally from Vermont, was a resident of Taylors Falls when he enlisted in the battery. *Adjutant General's Report,* 783.

16. Tentmate Murray Kelly.

17. Sixteenth Wisconsin.

Write promptly in answer to this and then you may expect a like virtue in me

No more, Your loving Brother T.D. Christie

[small drawing of a razor-back boar chasing a sow]

William Christie to Alexander Christie

VICKSBURGH MISSISSIPPI NOVEMBER 29TH 1863

Dear Brother I received a letter from you at last, and have Occult Proof that you were yet an Inhabitant of this mundane sphear, at the time of dating and inditing said epistle I hope you yet continue to walk the Earth in the full enjoyment of all its blessings and maintaining with your usual vim that E. Pluribus Uning is the life of this govermunt now henceforth and for ever and that old Uncle Abe, shall Be the man to Uncule Samuels Business, for the term of another four years, after he has done with his Present term. I say Mister what do you think of thingamy Blairs Speech in daddy Prices Mary Land: as "Blast" would say, if that Individual had heard it "well heres a go," but I think it was rather a sell, on Blair and Co: when old Abe, said so very Plainly Blair you lie, I never told you that I would conduct the affairs of the Nation in that manner, tis true Abe did not speak these words But he might have done so. But I suppose it would not have done to Be so vulgar.[18]

I see the weather changes up your way. Well sir it changes down here also and is as fickle as the wind or a weather cock, not to say anything to the disparagment of the female sects of our own speices, By comparing them to anything so easily moved as the article last mentioned, fortieight hours ago we had summer weather, accompanied by a genuine thunder storm with all the compounent Parts of such an Article thrown in, with great abundance with the storm round went the wind and for the thirtisix hours we have had a Blustering Jolly Rolicking Northwester, clearing the Atmosphere of all supperabundant vapors and making the sky look so Beautifully blue, (ditto with our noses, last Item not by any means desirable, and not

18. William refers to a speech by postmaster general Montgomery Blair delivered on October 3 in Rockville, Maryland, in which he attacked the reconstruction plans of radical Republicans. It was widely believed Blair spoke for President Lincoln on this issue, although Lincoln carefully avoided the controversy. See Donald, *Lincoln*, 470–71.

in the least Particle conductive to comfort.) and the ground frize, under foot quite firm.

The dirtifications, Progress rappily towards completion round this ever famous City of Vicksburgh. I need not tell you they are hard things to look at if they are made of dirt, and the Poor Deludid brethern of the south that remain here in durance vile, or in hospital say that the yankees are the greatest hands to gopher they ever saw or hearn tell on, they think we throw up dirt right smart, and swearing they wouldn't do it, while there was so many Niggers to do it. Item. our government is conscripting all citizens in town that are able to Bear arms; making that a condittion of there right to our Protection and food for themselves and famillies, that they shall serve in our armies.

We are not dead here, no siree, we have a Lyceum in the City, I am a member of the society It is styled the Vicksburgh Union Litterary association there is quite a number of the soldiers interested in the Proper management of the concern. we are going to Issue five hundred Circulars to the Proper Parties so that we may have a Libbrary and in about a few days I will likely send you one or Perhaps two so that sarah may forward one at least to Fox lake College. I Believe the Circulars will Be Distributed to us next Teusday evening, that Being the regular night of meeting on Monday evening (that is tomorrow) we are going to have a Business meetting for the Purpose of Revising the Constitution of the Society, and Perfecting arrangements for a social to Be held By the members on the first Monday in December: for the Purpose of making the members Better aquainted with each other, I am sorry to tell you the machine was running four weeks before I knew anything about it, and so I missed much that was Both instructive and amusing. The question up for disscussion on Tuesday evening is, Resolved that soldiers ought to vote out of there states. I am chief on the affirmative and of course the subject will be conducted in a very "hem," able manner. There is also a weekly Paper in connex with the society and there has been some able articles contributed By the members of the Club, I will appear next evening myself, that is not me, But an article of mine entitled Our Country, Tom thinks some of coming out too in a descriptive humorous sketch of some kind. Mine is historical Being a compliation, and is to Be continued if you will agree not to throw the Ms: in the fire I will send it along to you to laugh over, or Perhaps cry over seeing it is so worthless, ah I really wish I could have you at our social, at Which accordding to the Resolution of the ninth as it was drawn up by the chairman of the committee; that every man has to be as social as he can, the first evening of my membership I with the other members of the society Received a comfort Bag all the way from the state of Maine. The Bag is very neatly made of strong cloth and contained the following items, one infusion of the Best green Tea, sugar to sweeten the same Tay, a small Package of aspic one of carraway seeds, some ground Ginger, a little Black pepper ground, a small quantity of Blue woollen yarn, and darning needle, also a small quantity of Black linnen thread, a few Buttons, half of a Black lead Pencil and last but not least a letter also some extracts, or rather clippings from some newspapers; I will enclose the letter and extracts in this, and I wish they may be kept safly for me espeically the Letter,

T. D. is faster for reenlisting than I am. I Believe when there is an opportunity to do so, he will do it wether I will or not, so it is very likly we will Both reenlist and Perhaps offend Father very much, But why should any of you object to us going in again we would not Be at rest at home if the war still continued after our three years were out. and Besides we would Be liable to Be drafted after we had been at home But a short time, if the government needed men, if we were out you would then Be liable to come intoo the service, and I am well satisfied you would not stand a southern climate But a very short time, I Believe they cannot draft out of a family, if there are two in the service of that family already.

I wonder what sin the Christies have committed in times Past, to be set down in such a hellhole as Clyman, Copperheadism, Romanism and every ism but Progressive Ism and Patriotism seems to thrive around you in full Power making a great Blotch of moral darkness on the face of the Earth. I am or rather I should say we are Glad to learn you have done so well with the farm work Putting much of it past. I really feel happy you are so Pleased with the horses, and if the stable is warm [?] cost you so very much to keep them growing and in good condition remember a horse grows untoo it is seven years old if not over worked in any way, after that age they gain in weight and fill up all muscular Parts to there greatest capasity, work Dolly with a shorter line than Charley, and use a whip on him untill he learns to do his duty if he is a heavy slow horse and stronger than the mare, give her a little the advantage on the evener As for the Wheat, I am very glad father got such a good Price, and how nice you have got the corn husked and has such a great number of Bushels of "Lugs"

We desire to hear from you offtener than we have been doings, As for the Batch of curses you speak off round Clyman I say to the Devil with the whole of them, it would make a dog vomit to Put them on a comparison if he was cappable of feeling the insult. such Beings ought to Be compelled to live among the Hottentots or New Zelanders, Poor things they may yet Repent and Be saved, But I do not envy them the position they occupy, no sir,

In your next letter to me send me a list of the names of the Presidents of the United States, there Places [of] birth and all such. you will find the information on one of those maps or charts in Hellens room at Uncle Williams. I need it on account of the articles I am getting up for the Paper, and if you respond to my request as quickly as Possible it will reach me in time to be of service. In this letter, you say nothing whatever about the recept of a Hair chain I sent you I Posted it on the 26 of Sept: it was for a watch guard I had it Braided by one of our Boys, it was of Black and white horse hair, a ring of each alternately, if you see any such thing round Clyman, you may guess where it came from, it must Be you have not got it or you would have spoke of it, Well nix difference, let it go. I have to dry up for want of something to Plaver about, Who teaches school in Clyman this winter, or has the old devil Persuaded his Imps to do without a school this winter. I guess Father will live through the Praise or Blame of such a set as the Cottons.

Write soon, Good Bye

I am your affectionate Brother William G. Christie

⁓

Thomas Christie to Alexander Christie

VICKSBURG MISS, DEC. 6TH 1863

Dear Sandy:

Your algebraical letter was recd. last night,—along with 3 others to William from you, Father, and the Lowell girls.[19] All your arguments to W. against reenlisting are of no avail now—he and I are into it so far that we could not back out now, if we wished to, without disgracing ourselves, and, you know, death should be preferred to dishonor. But we do not wish to retreat, and I know you would not wish us to, if you could see the glorious enthusiasm pervading all branches of he Service now, caused by the recent Orders of the War Dept. relating to the Veteran Volunteers. There is

19. Bertie cousins living in Lowell, Massachusetts.

a perfect furore for reenlistment, and the troops who have seen the most Service, hardship and ill usage, and lost the most men in battle are the most unanimous in going again, and seeing the thing out, "In at the Death," you know.

You must not think that W. and I go into it because of the influence of example, for we were "veterans" when not more than 10 men in the company thought of enlisting, and, 2 days ago, we were the first of 21 to step to the front as volunteers. Now, we have 45 names on the list of men pledged to reenlist, and before this time tomorrow over 60 will be pledged. This great increase from the original number is due to the publication of a recent Order, allowing Veterans the privilege, where three fourths of a company or Regiment reenlist, of going home en masse to recruit.[20] There is also a flag promised by McPherson to the Battery which shall enlist again the most men is proportion to its numbers, and we have strong hopes of getting it, But no matter whether we can go home in a body or not, the Veterans still have the privilege of a 30 days furlough inside their state, equivalent here to a 50 days furlough, and all transportation furnished to and from their homes. So you may soon expect to see William at least, and perhaps myself, but I think considerably of going east to Boston and Connecticut if I get a furlough, but I don't believe in castles in the air, or *chateau in Espagne,* so we will drop the subject, and take up something more to the purpose and that is the Union Literary Society of Vicksburg. I tell you it is a fine institution, and it is wonderful how much talent it has brought to light among the Soldiers of this Corps. I have formed some most pleasant acquaintanceships through my connection with the Association, and expect to make more tomorrow evening, when we hold a grand Social Gathering in the Presbyterian Church here. The Association did me the honor, 2 weeks ago of electing me to the office of Secretary, and my duties in that position are, to keep minutes of each meeting, and read them and any other reading matter to be read, to the Association, and to take charge of the books of the Association. William was on a committee appointed by us to visit Gen. McArthur with an invitation to attend our Social Gathering, and they were received by old Mac with great courtesy, and we have the

20. In July 1863 the War Department issued General Order 191, primarily concerning the reenlistment of veteran volunteers. In addition to the furlough, an immediate bonus of $402 dollars was promised. Local commanders, like General McPherson, offered their own incentives. See U.S. War Department, *War of the Rebellion,* Series III, 3:414–16.

promise of his attendance. In order to get a good address and letter of invitation to present to the General, the committee agreed that each member of it should write one, and that they should then be presented to the association for their choice. I wrote one for William, and when they were submitted to the association last Tuesday evening, mine was selected almost unanimously. I have not written anything for our magazine yet, as we have been so busy the past week putting up a stable for our horses, and, in the double capacity of Corporal and [?] carpenter I have been kept pretty busy with hammer, saw and square.

In any work of this kind, the Corporals are expected to take the lead, and direct the men of their respective squads. Of course they will work in emulation to see which Squad will do the most work and the best. We have good reason to be proud of the 4th Platoon, for at the first call for veteran volunteers, before we knew anything about the furloughing or the flag, 13 of our men stepped to the front, while the other 3 platoons furnished 8 altogether, and the most of them belonged to the Winona Boys.

Connor is in, Southwick, Rogers, O'Hara and Wiltse all in, besides many other good fellows whom you do not know. Sam Woolly won't join us, for fear of consumption and we tell him the only specimen of that disease we need be afraid of is the consumption of bread and beef and apples. We will have the three fourths of the Company in tomorrow, and then those who do not reenlist will be mustered into some other organization to serve out the remainder of there terms of service, and we will get $175 in our hands and a chance to ruralize in Minnesota.[21]

I need not justify my conduct to you or Father for you will at once see and appreciate the motives which prompted my course and you must approve of it if you have any Patriotism in you. This thing is so near finished now that I must see the end of it before settling down in Life.

That was a confounded story your Clyman Copperheads got up about Father. I am much interested in your account of the horses, you need not write to us untill you have heard from us again, as we may walk in on you some fine day within a month.

Your Loving Veteran, Thos. Christie
Secretary

---

21. He likely refers to lands offered veterans under the Homestead Act of 1862.

Thomas Christie to Sarah Christie

VICKSBURG, DEC, 9TH 1863.

My Dear Sister,

Your long and interesting letter of the 20th Nov. came to hand yesterday, when it should have been answered, but I had so much writing to do which I could not put off,—such as the minutes of the Social Gathering that our Association held on Monday evening,—that I could not find time to write up my Journal even, So you will have to accept this excuse with the schoolboy's promise from me that "I'll never do it again Sir."

Speaking of that Social Gathering reminds me that I must tell you of all the good things we enjoyed at it, but first for preliminary explanations. Our Literary Association, which meets every Tuesday evening in the rooms of the Christian Commission, consists of about 50 members, the most of whom were strangers to each other. For the purpose of getting acquainted with each other we determined to have a Sociable. Now, I need not tell you, who have moved in the first circles of Fox Lake Society, what a Sociable is, for doubtless you have attended many a one, but this was a *Soldiers* Sociable so the description of it will probably be interesting It would weary you to tell of all the steps we took to ensure success in our entertainment, (for we had determined to admit everybody, and ladies especially,) of all the committees we appointed the Ushers we elected, (Southwick was one of them,) of how we appointed this one to read an Essay, and that one to lecture, so and so to be master of ceremonies, and Sergt. thing um bob Leader of the choir. The long expected evening came, and although it looked like rain, the large Presbyterian church was filled to overflowing with a splendid audience, officers, men, and citizens not to forget all the front seats full of ladies, some of them from the North, and many from this city. The Brass Band of the 1st Brigade, 3rd Div. was in attendance, and a full choir sat in the gallery, besides the "Quartette club," who were on the floor.

Gen. McArthur arrived about 7 O'clock and the exercises commenced with singing and prayer. As I was Secretary of the meeting I had a good position to hear and see from,—immediately in rear of the Chairman. After the prayer, we had a stirring tune from the Band, and then the essays and reading of our magazine came next, interrupted by frequent applause from the audience. I could not tell you half of the good things in the magazine; it is enough to say, that I have never seen a Harper so interesting, and then it was all original matter, Poetry, Editorials, Stories etc, *all* good enough to be printed. Then we had the Song, "Dreaming the happy hours away," by the Quartette club, and I think, in fact I know, that I never heard such beautiful singing, and never expect to hear better.

After this came the intermission for sociable purposes, when introductions were made, conversation carried on, and "a good time generally" enjoyed by the members and the audience. By the remarks I heard from the audience, it seemed that nobody expected to find such a high order of literary talent among the common soldiers of this army, it being generally though that we are a rough set, with but little principle, and still less intellectual tastes or capacities. They who think so make a great mistake, if they could see the eagerness with which anything good to read is sought after by us, how many dear daily papers are bought in the camps, and if they could hear the animated and profound discussions of abstruse subjects in our debates, they would alter their opinion. Indeed, what is our army composed of, if not of the youth of the land, trained in the common schools and colleges of the free North, whose wits are sharpened, and ideas expanded, by the rough experiences of arduous campaigns.

But I digress. After the intermission we had more singing and more music, and then the second part of the magazine was read, and an essay delivered by Sergt. Rawlings of the 95th Ills. of whom I will tell you more at some other time. A thanksgiving Anthem from the soldier choir succeeded, and the audience dispersed at a late hour after singing the Doxology. A collection amounting to 40 Dollars was taken up for the benefit of the Soldiers Library during the evening, making the total amount subscribed for that purpose during the fortnight something over 85 dollars. You and Father must circulate the circular I sent you Tuesday in the neighborhood, and try and send us some books. Put those volumes of Douglass Jerrold[22] into the box. I sent a copy of the Circular to the St. Paul Press with a few words of comment, and you may see it printed, if so, sent it down to us.

I saw Bill Deverough[23] in town today looking well. He came down in 9 days. I had an offer of a clerkship at Headquarters of the Post last night, but declined with many thanks. I don't want to leave the boys. We are not reenlisted yet, but before this reaches you we will be in for another 3 years,

22. Douglas William Jerrold, an English humorist and playwright, was best known for his contributions to *Punch* magazine.

23. William Devereaux, first sergeant in Company D, Seventeenth Wisconsin Infantry, was from Watertown, Wisconsin, not far from Clyman. *Roster of Wisconsin Volunteers*, II:60.

and perhaps on the way home to recruit, so don't write till you hear from us difinitely about it I send a letter from T. R. by this post. He seems to be well. No more tonight

Your loving Brother T. D. Christie

[margin note] W is well, Southwick and Konner[24] do [ditto]. Sam is gone to the Theatre tonight I prefer to stay at home and have a talk with you. I have a great mind to go to the theatre once just to see what the thing amounts to. Write me when you do write another such letter as the one I answer T. D. C.

[margin note] Love to all the family, Grand mothers included, many thanks for the compliment on my handwriting

❧

William Christie to Alexander Christie

VICKSBURGH MISSISSIPPI DECEMBER 9TH 1863.

Dear Brother, your welcome Letter came to hand a few days ago, and I am happy to Perceive By its contents that you mean to keep us Better writed if I might coin a Phrase, than you have been doing. Now you must not expect anything very nice, or writing, for I have written no less that four different Epistles today already One to Proffessor Goldthwait, and one to John Ford of Watertown one to [Rosine?] Bertie and also one to Jessie Armeirs, and having got the mill running I am bound to keep it going wether there is grist or not.

On last Monday evening we had our social, and it was a complete success: everything went as merry as a "Marriage Bell," and as social as it was intended to Be, for Particulars see Letter to Cousin Jesssie. or you may listen to the Raphosides [Rhapsodies?] of Brother Tom, and if he may happen to use highfalutin Language, you may be sure every word of it is as true as Preaching By the By, I do not know if he has written or intends to write a Letter about the social; But if he has not or does not then sir, I will Put you in all things concerning said social; for you know my memory is tough, if my wit is dull. Now on what theme shall I spread myself at the expense of a bit of indigestion seeing that my stomach is full of Beef and gravy and Bread and Coffee as accompaniments Shall I Blow you up for loving me

---

24. Jesse Conner was wounded at Shiloh and promoted to sergeant. *Adjutant General's Report*, 783.

Better than your Country, and advising me to Bring my worthless carcass out of the way of rebel Bullets, God willing in a year from now. No that would not be fair for the latter Part of your appeal to me does away with the first. But let me ask you and not only you, But Father if I would be doing my duty to either God or man if I failed to see this war to a close, if I am fortunately spared, for another year's soldiering, and through it, without the work being done. Now just think of it Probably before these lines reaches you I will have seen my thirtiethird, or as Father would say my thrisecond Birthday, and when I look Back through the past and see how much better off in every respect I have been through God's Providence seeing I might say with the Psalmist "truly my lines have been cast in Pleasant Places;"[25] Tis as little as I can do to stand firmly by the reglorified Flag of my Country, Trusting ever in the mercy of him who hath so Blessed me in the Past, Now God forbid I should speak these things in a canting manner, or being void of the sence of there full meaning. What hath my Part been how have I used its many Priviliges, what have I ever done to make me worthy of a Place in the Great human family. nothing I have mearly vegitated, or done but little good, generally been found wanting in any contest with my lower Passions: Never Being strongly tempted, I may not have done as much evil as others, But I have failled to do good, when I might and thereby I have transgressed, so let me do what I can in this way, to cover the many sins of ommission in the Past. For I Believe Dear Brother that if a man fall on the Battlefield or dies on a sick couch, in consequence of this strugle, Between Gods right And Mans' wrong, and falling with his thoughts and works on the side of Liberty and Justice, that many of his sins shall be forgiven him, and if it is God's will I should Pass through safly, and why should I doubt his Grace, or Mercy Being extend through the coming years of my soldiering, seeing he has not forsaken me in the Past. I will have learned much that may enable [me] to be a Better man in the duties of the life here [. . .] And there is another thing, we must Bear, in mind, "Wether we live or wether we die." we are none the less surrounded By his Love,[26] you will all Be aware of the fact Before this letter reaches you that T. D. and I are Pledged to renlist, and if we can pass the mustering office and there is but little doubt we will we will be soldiers for two years more than the one of the term we are now serving Provided the goverment

25. Psalm 16:6: "The lines have fallen to me in pleasant places."
26. For a discussion of religious motivation among Civil War soldiers, see McPherson, *For Cause and Comrades*, 62–76.

needs us so long so it is likly I will be among you some time this winter or next spring,

Our Litterary society is a complete success in every respect, and etlics much thought among the soldiers. Which finds expression in the Pages of the weekly magezine and the debates, everything is conducted in a most excellent manner, and there is as much decorum in our meetings as if we had the Presence of the most moral Weman among us, and there is never the face of one of them of any kind in our conclaves. There are numerous schools in town for colored Children, and adults, and the reports concerning them say much to the honnor of Both Pupils and teachers.

We have had change of weather since I wrote to Father and Dave, wet and cold, now cold and cloudy. Cousin Jessie informs me of Uncle's Dave[27] being drafted, and at the same time assures me he will not serve, Now I really wish he had no way of getting rid of shouldering a musket unless it was by Being a Light Artillery man. it would do such a dog in the manger, as he is good, to Be a soldier for a year or two. To I verily Believe he is one of the kind that would send his Father to the Poor house, or to the devil, if the first was not avalable, if the old man was likely to Be troublesome. Oh his Patriotism must have been greatly taxed when he dedicted a copy of the Bugle call to the first Minnesota Battery. Well he will have to Pay three hundred Dollars to get rid of the draft, But Lord have mercy on his customers afterward: for he wont, until he gets Back the Dollars cent Per cents interest. don't do any more trading there for at least two years; thereby making great savin.

Well you see I began like a fool with this letter and end like a slandering rogue. But I realy think Truth is sometimes very like slander, that is when you [serve?] some folk's just as they should Be. I may be uncharitable,

Least you should all die of disappointment, and curiosity. I will tell you why I wrote to Messrs Ford, Goldwaith. I enclosed a Printed circular to each, stating why I done so, I will send one or two more off next week, and you will get one in the family's Perhaps T. D. has sent one already, Give my love to all to Father and mother especially. and say to them that if I was at home on the eighteenth day of this month I would make them a Birthday Present. Grand mother Bertie, also, Love to all and Belelive as ever your most affectionat Brother

William G. Christie

27. David S. Bertie, James Christie's half brother.

Thomas Christie to James Christie[28]

VICKSBURG, DEC. 12, 1863.

My Dear Father,

The only fault of your last letter is that it is too short. No other letters please me so much as yours. You have doubtless heard of our intention to reenlist; I am glad you think of it as you do. It means great sacrifice for all of us, but so did our first enlistment; the need of the country for men is as urgent now as it was then. Our hand is on the plough, and we must not look back now till the good work is accomplished. That day, if all goes well, is not far off. I am very busy, with others, making out all the papers; we hope to be mustered in tomorrow. It is probable that we shall get enough men to entitle us to a furlough, but this is not yet the case. There are some who are still undecided; you may fancy the earnest discussions that take place every day.

I like our life here better than I did at any other camp since we came South; we have many privileges. Every Sunday, those of us who are not on duty can attend church. In this way I have heard Chaplain Porter several times, and like his sermons exceedingly. Besides this, we have the Literary Ass'n. to attend; this gives us good exercise for the mind. Our Meetings are held every Tuesday evening; I wish you could be with us on these occasions: By the way, can you not send us some books? They will find many readers.

We had an inspection yesterday, of clothing and equipments. Sufficient time was not given to the men to prepare for it; we have not had an inspection for a long time. It is not to be wondered at, therefore, that Capt. Hogan[29] criticised our appearance with some severity. We were drawn up in single line, each man having his knapsack or valise at his feet. The inspecting officer was on the ground while we were falling in, and expressed himself as much dissatisfied with the performance; he said we made too much noise, and took too little pains in "dressing" the line. Corporal Rogers came upon the ground eating an apple. "Put that apple in your pocket sir, and button up your jacket!" When we had got into line, and the knapsacks were opened, he began at the right and passed slowly down, scrutinising closely the men and their clothing; if he found the latter deficient, he

28. Transcribed in Thomas Christie reminiscence.
29. This inspection is mentioned in the battery morning reports. Hogan is identified as the inspector general for the First Division.

ordered more to be drawn. One of the fellows was standing in a careless attitude, his arms akimbo; "Is that the way to come out on inspections sir? Stand at attention, why don't you?" To another, "Take your pants out of your boots, and button up your blouse!" thus he came along the line, here finding fault with a man because his boots were not polished; and there reproving another for having his best clothes in his knapsack and his worst on. Our excellent commander, Lieut. Hurter,[30] was greatly chagrined. He told the Captain that the men had had only 10 minutes in which to prepare; and that they had come out, in consequence, in their fatigue suits. But his words seemed to have no effect on our stern inspector. When he came to me, he stopped as usual and looked carefully into my knapsack; with this he could find no fault, my spare clothing was all clean and well packed. The he glanced at me, when of course his eye was caught by bro. D's white hat. "Out of uniform sir! Is that the only hat you have?" "It is sir," I answered, "but I have applied for a cap, and have not yet received it." "See to it then that hereafter you do not allow your wardrobe to become deficient; you are a corporal I see," pointing to the chevrons on my new blouse, "and you are expected to show a good example to the men." "I beg pardon Captain, I have just returned from furlough. My younger brother came with me to the train, and at the last moment snatched off my cap and put his hat on my head." The Captain laughed and passed on to his next victim. I escaped very easily. He told one of our Sergeants that if a Sergeant in *his* company came out on inspection so badly dressed, he would be reduced to the ranks in just the time it would take to pull off his stripes!

But when Captain Hogan inspected our camp, guns, stables, and horses, he gave us very high praise; saying that we had the best-looking and best-kept horses in the Division. This is encouraging. We are determined that when the next inspection comes off, he will be able to praise the clothing of the men as well; we drew new things today, and will be able now to make as good an appearance as we used to in the Arsenal.

Lieut. Koethe's falling from his horse and dislocating his wrist puts more work in writing upon me. So good by.

30. Lieutenant Henry Hurter was in command of the battery while Captain Clayton was on recruiting duty in Minnesota. First Battery Company Morning Reports, Nov.–Dec 1863.

Thomas Christie to Alexander Christie

VICKSBURG MISS. JAN. 14TH 1864

My Dear Brother;

I thought today that I would sit down and send you a few "sums" that have been of much interest to me. If they are too difficult for you, you might let Mr. Benson see what he could do with them.

[one geometry problem, one mathematics problem follow]

I will send the solutions of these problems with this but not to be opened untill you and the School maam have tried the sums yourselves. They are two that were given me by Sergt. Gage of the 10th Ohio Battery, and in return I proposed some to him. He is a good Mathematician, and before he came into the army taught school in Southern Illinois. I worked some time on both of them, as I made a good many mistakes at first.

We hear through the papers of the awful cold weather and snow you have been favored with up there.[31] We were not passed by ourselves, for we had a cold snap here, beginning on the night of the 31st December, and lasting about 10 days that made us wish ourselves still further South. All the clothes we could get on would not keep out the searching wind, and even the fireplaces in our tents were not sufficient to keep us from shivering. The River here is full of running ice which phenomenon, the citizens say, has not bee seen here before for 12 years. I thought something must be up when we could get no mail or Newspapers for so long.

Lieut. Hurter has reappointed all the old Noncoms, but one and that is not me. He made a slight mistake in my commission by dating it 1803 instead of 63, so I took it back to him and told him that was making rather too much of a Veteran of me, to make out that I had been 60 years in the Service. He made it right and returned it to me. Nothing more yet about our going home. W. and I were talking about it last night, and we thought it would be a good thing for us to select our Quarter Sec. while in Minnesota I wish it could be that you could go up there with us and see the country, perhaps buy land beside ours, see what Father says about it.

Your Loving Brother T.D. Christie

31. According to Minnesota newspapers, a severe cold snap with accompanying blizzard struck the region on New Year's Eve; Rochester reported −40F on New Year's Day. *St. Paul Pioneer*, Jan. 9, 1864.

Thomas Christie to Sarah Christie

VICKSBURG, MISS. FEB. 7TH 1864

My Dear Sister:

I can not blame you for not writing after the foolish advice I gave you not to write, but it is a dreadful long time since we got anything from you, and you will not wonder if we *do* feel a little disappointed as mail after mail comes in and nothing comes for us. Our anxiety to hear from home is very great, for we want to know how you get along with your school, and how things genirally are prospering.

Here, we are in the best of health, and enjoying the most lovely weather that could be desired, just like June up north. The buds are bursting on the trees, the grass is starting to green everywhere, and all the birds that denizen your woods in the Summer are beginning to show themselves among us. It was only yesterday, that, as we went out to the piece to drill, a little Blue Bird flew out of the black, sulphur-stained bore of the howitzer, where it had been, poor thing, to see about building its nest. It reminded me of when we were camped at Shiloh church before the Battle, I there observed a little bird, with straw in its bill reconnoitering attentively the muzzle of our Rifle, and probably thinking that such a nice bright, clean cavity would be an excellent place to bring up a family in. Our guns at that time had never been fired, and were so shinning inside that the bottom of the bore could be plainly seen, but in about a week from that time they were black enough. How suggestive would such as incident be to one who possessed "the poetic fire," and many good poems have been written on subjects far beneath it in interest. The innocent little bird, in the boldness of a guiltlessness that knows no fear, confidingly rearing its nest in the very jaws of Death. For it those deadly, shining tubes possessed no terrors, it only saw in them beautiful abodes, where could be reared in peaceful security the coming brood. If I were a poet I would favor you with a sonnet on the subject, or, "lines on seeing a bird building its nest in the mouth of a Cannon," or if I was even good at moralizing I would give you a whole string of reflections on the insecurity of life, ("In the midst of life, we are in Death") the courage of innocence, and the strength there sometimes is in utter helplessness, all drawn from the same subject.

I send enclosed the photograph, and an excellent likeness it is, of one of my comrades of whom you have often heard me speak, Joseph O'Hara.[32]

---

32. Joseph O'Hara was also among those who reenlisted in 1864. See page 111, note 50, Thomas to Sarah, Mar. 11, 1863.

He is one of the best fellows I ever was acquainted with, and it is said of him in the squad that if any one of the 4th Platoon goes to Heaven it will be "Old Harry," as we call him. He got half a dozen photographs yesterday, and I coaxed this one from him, for your album. Perhaps you may have my phiz[33] to put beside it sometime. J'o is always good natured, I never saw him angry in my life, and he is always ready for a joke, practical or other wise. To hear him talk about the women you would think him a perfect woman hater, but this is only on the surface, he was jilted, handsome as he is, some time ago, by a woman whom he devotedly loved, (his nature is capable of *deep* and *noble* passion) and this has soured him somewhat, in respect to the gentle sex, his otherwise frank, loving disposition.

He and I get along together like two schoolboys, (he is about 28,) Sometimes, when we are tired reading or talking, Jo will challenge me out to jump with him, then, when he beats me at that, I will challenge him to go out to the piece and see if I can't "stall" him on the Nomenclature, that is, the names of the different parts of the gun and carriage. Then you will see him puzzling his brain to remember the names of "trunnions," "rimbases," "chaser," "reinforcer," cascable" etc. and when I finally stall him, and flap imaginary wings and crow in consequence, he will dare me to a game of quoits; Beaten in that also, he has resort to the dictionary (we have an abridged Webster,) and will try to beat me in spelling and definition, at which he is an adept, having an excellent knowledge of words.

The 16th Wis. has come inside the lines from where they were camped at Redbone church, some 10 miles south of this, and I went over to see Shaller today. I found him not very well, having had recently a shake of the ague. His folks do not seem to like his reenlistment, by the letters he let me read, but John does not care for that, he knows he is doing his duty, and if the folks at home do not feel willing to make their part of the sacrifice, it only shows their lack of Patriotism.

I wish I could tell you whether to write to us or not. I think you had better, as we will not be likely to leave now untill the expedition which left last week is returned, and that may not be for a month. I wrote to the P.M. at Cairo recently to send down all letter awaiting W. or me there, and I think you had better continue writing the same as before. I wrote to father 2 days ago, directing the letter to Watertown, and enclosing Drafts to the amount of $310. I hope he has got it. When he does, let him write immediately. We are expecting Clayton with 80 Recruits down on every boat.

33. Slang abbreviation of "physiognomy," meaning face or portrait.

The Tattoo sounds, and out must go the light in two minutes. Good
Night, My Love to Mother Father, Grand mother's Reid and Bertie and the
boys, not forgetting a large slice for yourself.

Your loving Brother,

Thos. D. Christie

[margin note] I break open my letter to put in Small's[34] likeness.

ᘐ

Thomas Christie to James Christie[35]

V. , FEB.23, 1864.

My Dear Father,

I have sad news for you. William was taken down with fever and went
to the hospital;[36] he will be there perhaps for a month. Our Veterans go
home tomorrow; I must not go and leave him alone, but I hope that he and
I will come together before long. Another reason for my staying is that the
Capt. wishes me to do so. He wants me to drill the recruits, and help our
acting orderly Sergeant. I have command of the 4th Platoon, and do all
the writing for the O.S. For 14 weeks I have lived in the Orderly's tent, and
so have learned all the routine. As soon as the Veterans are gone we shall
begin to work the recruits still harder, for they have a great deal to learn—
foot-drill, cannoneer's drill, and driver's drill. Although they are good learn-
ers they will have all they can do until the old men come back about the
10th of April. With but three exceptions all the 74 are native-born Americans; they are very bright intelligent fellows. To drill them as I do twice a
day, 2 hours each day, is a great pleasure; they also seem to enjoy it. As
the assistant of the O.S. my duty will be to keep the Roster, make out all
details for duty, write six Reports for the Asst. Adjt. Gen. of the Division
each month, besides a Morning Report for the Company-Book every day.

34. Probably John Small, a native of Ireland who enlisted at Winona. *Adjutant General's Report.*

35. Transcribed in Thomas Christie reminiscence.

36. This detail is not noted in the morning reports. According to William's pension
application, he made it "a policy to keep *out* of the hospitals, remaining with his battery
even when taken down sick, being then nursed by his brother and his comrades." U.S.
Pension Department file 452.949, Affidavit of William G. Christie, Winona County District Court, June 5, 1882.

This work with that of Sergeant and the care of my horse will keep me very busy. I think that perhaps when the men come back and we get six guns, there will possibly be another stripe added to my Chevrons.

Yesterday we celebrated the Birth-Day of Washington, by command of Gen. McArthur, in charge of the Post. We fired a national salute, marched through the principal streets of the town, and heard plenty of good speaking and singing. The only part I took in the affair was to have charge of the firing of the salute at daylight in the morning. This was done at the Courthouse in the city; we used 30 Pdr. Parrotts. with 4-pound charges. You should have seen the glass fly from the windows of the Courthouse! The detachment was made up of the best drilled men in the Company, 4 of them Corporals; they did splendidly. Major Maurice, the Chief of Artillery, was present, and complimented us; he also gave a dram each to those who wished to drink. The thunder of the guns must have reminded the citizens of the terrible Siege. As I was on guard-duty yesterday I could take no part in the other exercises.

Our Literary Association is still doing good work, although the expedition has taken away most of our working members. We held a sociable last night in honor of the day; I was on the Committee of arrangements; everything went off well. There were singing, speeches, essays and much conversation. Quite a number of ladies from the North were present, the widow of Governor Harvey of Wis. among them; you remember he was drowned in the Tennessee just after the battle of Shiloh.[37] I had a good long talk with her. She has charge of all the work of the Sanitary Commission here. The ladies distributed 150 comfort-bags, needle-cases &c. to the soldiers present. I was so lucky as to get a fine needle-case containing needles, pins, thread, buttons, &c. &c.; and last but not least, several good tracts. Some of us received letters in the cases, to which we are asked to reply; thus many new friendships are begun.

Please hurry up that box of books for the Association Library. We have more than 500 volumes now, and every week brings more. No news for two

---

37. Governor Louis Powell Harvey traveled to Tennessee following the Battle of Shiloh to visit wounded Wisconsin soldiers and see to their welfare. While boarding a steamboat at Savannah, Tennessee, on the Tennessee River, he lost his footing, fell into the river, was swept away by the current, and drowned. His widow, Cordelia Perrine Harvey, continued his efforts to aid Wisconsin soldiers by acting as the state's agent to federal hospitals and establishing other hospitals in Wisconsin. Quiner, *Military History of Wisconsin*, 118–99, 236–37.

weeks from Gen. McPherson. It is rumored that he has been killed, but no
one believes it.[38]

Yours ever,

T. D. C.

❧

Thomas Christie to Alexander Christie

VICKSBURG, MARCH 5TH 1864

My Dear Brother;

We were delighted this afternoon with an enormous mail, among which
were 3 letter for me from you, Father, and the School ma'am. They were
the first we have seen for something like 6 weeks, and so you may be sure
they were welcome. That was an awful accident that Father met with, and
I cannot understand yet how it could have occurred. The loss of his teeth
is dreadfull: I can't imagine how he will look, but he must get the loss
repaired by a dentist if it should cost a hundred dollars or two. Your letter
is full of interesting news, as might have been expected after so long a
silence, and William and I laughed till our sides ached over your description of the hay larceny. I think you must have thought as we do about the
Rebs, that all is fair in a war of the enemys making; that's the reason why
we soldiers can confiscate with such a good conscience.[39]

Father writes me that you are very earnest sometimes in your desire to
enlist, and give him a great deal of trouble and anxiety on that account. I
am sorry to hear of this Sandy, for several reasons; 1st, you are needed at
home; 2nd, you are too young to come into the Army; 3rd the family is not
in a condition to allow any more of its members to leave the Homestead,
nor is it needed, as more has been done by us now than could have been
expected of us. You see my reasons bear on two points: your duty towards
Father and the rest of us, and, your duty to yourself individually. I know
you have thought upon this subject enough that you will readily concur
with me when I say that should you leave home, the old Homestead, which

38. McPherson was away from Vicksburg at this time, commanding part of Sherman's
Meridian expedition.

39. In Alexander's farm diary from 1860 to 1864, most of the entries relate to crops,
weather, and work on the farm. There are some hints regarding the "hay larceny" but
nothing about James Christie's accident. Christie papers, box 45, vol. 20.

it has ever been our pride to say, has always been managed better than any other in the neighborhood, would have to pass into strange hands, for you well know that Father and Dave never could carry it on, and you should recognise, and be proud of the fact, that on *your* shoulders rests the responsibility of advancing the welfare of the family at home, while we sustain its honor in the field, and of the two duties, yours is the more really difficult, and *therefore the more honorable.* For, Sandy: we must work together, and I hope never to see the day when your interests and mine will be separated: I know you are eager to be doing something for the cause of the Country: but rest assured; that you are serving it far better on the farm than could you in the camp. Let Father give up to you the whole management of the farm, I know you are competent to it, and I think he would be fully willing. Here would be full scope for your ambitious desires to be doing something on your own hook, and you would at the same time be acquiring as much knowledge of men, and the ways of the world as you could have in the Army.

Again: on your own personal account I would strongly advise you to stay quietly at home for a year or two yet, untill you are older, before thinking of pushing your own way through the strange world: I tell you Sandy, I came away from home at an early enough age, and I have never told you how many times I would have given up every thing willingly, only to catch a glimpse of the old home with its *dear, dear,* faces, only to enjoy for a short time the society, and many other blessings, which you now esteem so lightly. You must not think that the soldier's life is all bright and sunshiny: I know the romance of the thing weighs with you greatly: But did you ever reflect that what appears so romantic when viewed at a distance may prove, on a close acquaintance, the most dull and prosaic life that ever man lived: I tell you it is so, and it would be unbearable were it not for the cause for which we endure these things. Even as it is, my heart some times sinks within me at the thought that 3 long years are to elapse before I can again enjoy the privileges of the home life. Take my word for it, *this is one of the most miserable of existences,* and it is only by the constant exercise of my faculty of Hopefulness that I am kept from absolute despair. Ah! Sandy, you know nothing, really about it. Everybody in describing our life in uniform, (and I acknowledge myself to be of the number,) always takes pains to show only the bright side, for why should we pain the hearts of our friends by telling the whole truth, and besides, we ourselves have to think the most of it is sunshine, or we would soon die of downheartedness. I shudder when I think of you coming into the Army, for I remember how many young faces I have seen in our hospitals, faces that should have been shining over a desk at school, but doomed *never* to see dear ones again, doomed, when a few short weeks of wasting sickness should be over, to rest in the grave.

The novelty of this kind of life would make you bear its inconveniences and disagreables for a short time, but that would soon wear off, and, as I said before, the major part of a soldiers existence, is so dull and "tedious" that we (I mean the most of us,) don't know what to do to relieve this terrible monotony. You know we have got a lot of Recruits and a more homesick lot than the most of them are now, you could not imagine. I was making out the Morning Report this forenoon, as is my duty, and a chap who is considerable of a tough nut, who has been in the Rebel service and twice, in ours, this chap was looking on.[40] When I came to enter in the appropriate column, 2 "sick" he laughed and said "2 sick, and how many sorry?" I told him that was not a usual item in the Report, but I would put the number at about 50.

And a very dangerous and painful disease is the Homesickness, I hope you may never have it. I am glad to hear from Fathers letter of the safe arrival of our money I did think it was gone the way of my other 20 dollars. I will answer his letter just as soon as I can find time, and would have done so this morning but for the fact that William is using his letter at the hospital, and is answering it. W. is much better is able to be up, and out doors, and will soon join us again in the Company. We are sorry to disappoint you but we can not come home till summer, say July, when will also be the best time to change climates.

I am getting along firstrate and about 20 men are all wanting to get into my squad but I have too many in it already, although a better set of men to get along with I never saw. You ought to see the improvements we have made in things since the Veterans went off, But I must reserve what I have to say for Sarah's letter, which I intend to write tomorrow, so I will bid you

---

40. The enlistment records for the First Battery do not indicate who this individual is. Often referred to as "galvanized Yankees," such men were Confederate prisoners of war offered release from prison on condition of service with the Union Army. Their motives ranged from a simple desire to escape the misery of POW camps to a genuine change of allegiance. What is unusual about this individual is that he was still in the South. The standard terms of service for these men stipulated that they would fight Indians, not their former comrades. See Brown, *Galvanized Yankees*, 1–10.

Good Night for I must turn in. Remember me to Mother, Love to all, write soon. Thos. D. Christie

> [inverted postscript] Beautiful weather here now, I am busy all the time in making out our Pay Rolls worked till 11 Oclock last night, Expect our pay soon, but in no hurry. must take out patent for this style of letter It has at least the recommendation of novelty.[41]

∾

William Christie to James Christie[42]

VICKSBURG, MARCH 10, 1864

My Dear Father,

Your letters do us a great deal of good. We have splendid weather just now. The rough hillsides, where the tents of the soldiers are not pitched, are covered with grass; rose-bushes are out in full leaf; daffodils and all the early flowers are abundant; peachtrees are full of blossoms.

Another expedition is now being fitted up, this time for the Red River. I fear we shall lose one of our best regiments, 14th Wisconsin; it is said they are to go.[43] Many of the other regiments have gone home on furlough. Our condition just now prevents our taking part in this expedition also. But now again we have six guns, having turned over our old James rifles and obtained 4 Rodman guns, new, neat and handy. They are better than the others, especially at long distances, doing good shooting at 6,500 yards.[44]

The expedition to Meridian did immense damage to the enemy. Cattle, mules, horses and many negroes were brought in. At Canton 21 locomotives were destroyed. The soldiers tell us that they saw Generals Sherman and Leggett, with coats off, and sledge-hammer in hand, working like the

41. Last page of letter written inverted, between the lines previously written in a different color of ink.

42. Transcribed in Thomas Christie reminiscence.

43. A "provisional division" of troops from the Seventeenth Army Corps, including the Fourteenth Wisconsin, was assigned to this campaign. See Quiner, *Military History of Wisconsin*, 607; Welcher, *Union Army*, II:749.

44. Although commonly referred to as "Rodman guns" because of their resemblance to the large, costal artillery guns manufactured by the Rodman casting process (see note 53, page 171), these were actually the three-inch ordnance rifles made in an entirely different manner. The ordnance rifle was a favorite of Union artillerists and one of the most effective field guns used in the war. See Morgan, "Green Ones and Black Ones."

privates; and laughing heartily when they succeeded in punching a hole through a boiler or smashing the flange off from a wheel!

Your loving son,

W.G.C.

⌒

Thomas Christie to James Christie[45]

v. MARCH 11, 1864

My Dear Father,

I am busier than ever before, but keep in excellent health. My platoon has the reputation of being the best drilled in the Battery. The Capt. and the men often come to watch us, and we receive praises from everybody. I am so concerned in the training of the men that I dream about it at night! I ought to have been quietly sleeping last night, but according to my tent-mate this was what I was saying: "By detail, *load;* two, three, four! *Sponge;* two, three, four! *Ram;* two, three,! *Ready; fire!* Malison, bend that knee a little more; hold your shoulders square to the front: back of the right hand up, that of the left down! Number five, bring your cartridge! Number three, serve vent better, elbow raised so that the gunner can sight over your thumb, right hand on the tube-pouch!" Some of these men are old enough to be my father, but they obey as if they were little boys, so anxious are they to learn. Today they learned to dismount and mount the piece like Veterans, with crowds looking on; and when they broke ranks it was with a cheer "for our little Corporal!" Do pardon all this egotism.[46]

I have had a talk today with a Union refugee from Winston county, who came in with Sherman. The stories he told of his numerous escapes from the conscripting officers were interesting enough to publish. He says the Rebels hunt down men with bloodhounds, he knows many who have been captured in that way; some of his neighbors have lain hidden in the swamps for months at a time, their food brought to them by their families, as in the days of the Covenanters. He says that this rebellion is the work of

45. Transcribed in Thomas Christie reminiscence.

46. According to the final roster of the First Battery, those recruited between December 1863 and March 1864 ranged in age from eighteen to forty-four. Although most of the men were in their twenties, a substantial number (approximately twenty) were over thirty years old and five of these men were in their early forties. *Adjutant General's Report,* 787–90.

the aristocrats, the slaveholders of the South; the poor whites were dragged into it against their will, or in their ignorance bamboozled by bombastic oratory. But now their eyes are opened! They see that slavery is the real cause of the war, and they have become as earnest abolitionists as any of us. I should like some of our northern apologists for slavery to have a talk with this man and his friends. For myself, I feel more determined than ever to do all I can to put and end to this iniquity.[47]

17TH)

It takes about a month for a letter and its answer to make the journey from us to you and back. There are many interruptions in the mails, due to guerillas and other causes. We are half-choked with smoke and bad colds, the high winds making our chimneys smoke badly. We thought a week ago that Spring had come; but now again it is miserably wet and cold. Drill, drill, drill ! I am putting all that I have learned in over two years into these willing and hard-working men. Even when off duty, they discuss fine points with the veterans. A good many of the recruits are earnest christians. They have organized prayer meetings, that are held twice a week. At the last meeting I rose for prayers, and said I wanted to be a christian. Yes, Father, I have resolved to try what reality there is in religion, and I want you to pray for me. I have begun to pray daily for all of you, as well as for myself; for I believe that the very thought that those you love are coming to God in your behalf is a powerful means of good. I do wish that you would begin the service of daily prayers in the home; you will find it easy, if you only make a start. And why should you not hitch up the horses every Sunday and go to meeting, at Watertown or at the Grove?

Yours Ever

T.D.C

❧

Thomas Christie to Sarah Christie

VICKSBURG MARCH 13TH 1864

My Dear Sister:

I only wish you could see the number of waste sheets of paper on my shelf, all beginning, "My Dear Sister," and dated all the way from Feb. 28th

47. Military defeats and economic troubles combined to create a growing war-weariness in the South. Conscription had never been popular in the Confederacy. See McPherson, *Battle Cry*, 432, 691.

to the present time, some of them are half written, some with one page
scribbled over, and 3 or 4 have just the date and address. Sometimes I
would flatter myself, as I do now, with the expectation that I could finish
them without interruption, but when just in the midst of some interesting
(to you) sentence, the Orderly Sergeant perhaps would poke his head into
the tent with, "Christie the Captain wants you at Hed. Qrs." What the duce
is that for? "Oh; something about that Ordnance Report that is to be made
out." So, down would go your letter into the cigar box which serves me for
desk and portfolio, with a mental promise to finish it "tonight," on would
go my best cap, and that would be the last my tent would see of me till perhaps 10 O'clock at night, for the Captain always had plenty of other work
for me when the Report would be finished, and I would have to stay and eat
dinner and supper with him, while his waiter would be sent down to the
company to feed my horse, and excuse me from Roll call; Or, perhaps the
interruption would arise from the cry of "come Sergeant," (they all call me
Sergeant now, although I am only acting,) "divide the bread," or, "divide the
sugar," or, "get your squad out to the piece for drill." Then; next day, when
I could spare time to sit down to write again, I would not be satisfied with
what had been written, and would start another sheet only to be thrown
aside again like its predecessors.

I have not much news to write that would be interesting to you: if it were
to one of my comrades I were writing, I could tell him a great deal that
would be interesting to him, but by you, such items as, Dick and Sandy,
(the 2 negroes,) died of Pneumonia last week,"[48] "James Cheatham,[49] the
brother of him who died of Small Pox, is very sick with the same disease
that carried off his brother," such items are not appreciated ~~by you~~ The only
thing I can tell you of special interest is that William left the hospital today,
and is again with the Squad, but can not be put on Duty yet.

A little incident occurred this evening that I must tell you of; We were
out in the park playing Quoits, Dave Duryee and I being playing against
Dan Wright and his partner, all of us were deeply engrossed in the game
and were "playing," as the boys say, "for all in sight." Dave had just thrown
a "good shoe," and it was now the turn of Dan's partner: all our heads were

48. In the morning reports, they were listed as Dick Lune and Sandy Turnbull, both
on the battery's roster as cooks.

49. James and Nelson Cheatham were among the new recruits enlisted in December
1863. Both were from Plainview Township, Winona County. Nelson died on February
27. *Adjutant General's Report*, 787.

bent down over the "hub," to see the effect of the throw, when down came the shoe, square on to the peg,—a "Ringer." On seeing this, Dan, sent up a shout of exultation at the success of his partner, and unfortunately, at the same instant, Gen. Chambers, the commander of the 3rd Brigade,[50] was riding swiftly by, coming from town, and, as our officers generally are after being in town, he was about 3 sheets in the wind as Mother says. On hearing the shout, he was fool enough to think some one was making fun of him, as he is very unpopular in his own Brigade, and immediately he reined in his horse, rode up to where we were standing and dismounting with difficulty, walked up to *me,* and took me by the shoulder, saying, "I'll learn you to holler at me, come along sir." I saw at once the mistake he had made in first supposing that the shout was intended for him, and secondly, in thinking that *I* did it. So pointing to the "ringer" still lying on the hub, I said, "General, you are mistaken, there is the cause of the shout you heard," one of the boys spoke up and said that I was not the one who had made the noise, whereupon he turned to me and asked me if such was the case, saying that he saw me "holler." I told him then, that it was not I who shouted, and reiterated the assurance that no disrespect was intended by it. This he would not believe, and asked me who was the offender, which I refused to answer, and he was threatening punishment if I still continued obstinate, when Dan stepped up and owned to the act, giving the reason for it. I had got my "dander" up, and would not have told who was the supposed culprit, if he had put me in the Guard house for a month. "Come along you, sir" the drunken fool, (it is hard to use such language about so high an officer, but it would be perfectly applicable if he had been a private,) said to Dan, whereupon, Dan demanded to be taken before the Captain, which, Chambers acceding to, away they went, and I run my head in the lion's mouth by going too, to bear testimony in Dan's favor. It was needed, too, for after the General had preferred his charges, in which he implicated me pretty deeply for aiding and abetting, the Captain turned to me and sternly demanded our reason for the insult, He believed our explanation, and told the General that it was customary for our boys to make a noise when playing,

---

50. Career army officer Alexander Chambers (West Point class of 1853) commanded the Third Brigade of the First Division. Earlier in the war he had commanded the Sixteenth Iowa and was wounded at Shiloh and Iuka. Promoted to brigadier in August 1863, he lost his command soon after the incident described here (April 1864) by order of the U.S. Senate, as he was not a resident of Iowa. Given the details Thomas shares, however, there may have been other, unstated reasons for the change.

but Chambers would not believe but what it was intended for him, and after abusing the artillery generally, and us in particular, threatening Clayton with punishment if Dan were not punished, and swearing he would shoot the next man who should shout at him, he went off. Isn't it melancholy to think of this drunken bully having command of thousands of men, the meanest of whom is more of a gentleman than him. All our starred officers however, are not like him.

No more now as my paper is out and so are my ideas.

Love to all, and believe me Yours. Thos. D. Christie

[margin note] I have heard nothing of Tom Reid since that letter I sent you Tell me *all* about Helen when you write I judge by what is in one of your letters, that she is not living with the Malcombs.

[margin note] While writing, the candle has twice tipped over and dripped on the sheet, but I suppose you can read it anyhow.

ᝌ

Thomas Christie to Alexander Christie

VICKSBURG, MARCH 19TH 1864

My Dear Brother Sandy:

"The cry is still they come," I had just posted a letter to Father this morning, (dated 17th) when the report came into camp that there was a mail for us at Division Hd, Qrs. The Co. P.M. (acting artificer Scott) went for it, and sure enough, there was something like a peck of it, (these Recruits have increased our mail amazingly,) and in it were yours of the 9th to me, and Father's, same date to W. It was the first notice we have had of the arrival of the V.V.s [Veteran Volunteers] in the realms of civilization, and I am very sorry that Father did not know what august Company he was in when he rode out of town with them, and sorry also, that he saw such a poor specimen of the Battery, as that drunken fellon, Charley Norton, I suppose it must have been.[51] Be on the lookout for them when they come down, and see our Lieutenant. By the time this reaches you though, I hope

51. Charles Norton, one of the new recruits (December 1863), listed his place of birth as Wisconsin; from this context, he may have been a former neighbor of the Christies. Alexander noted in his farm diary that his father "took the cars" to Watertown and realized later he had been traveling with veterans from his sons' battery. *Adjutant General's Report,* 789; Christie papers.

you will have seen some of them at home, and perhaps, among them, Connor, O'Hara, and Bill Wiltse.[52] We hear that there are 7 men enlisted for the Company at Winona, and more at other points, if they come down, we will have an eight Gun Battery. We have six now in the park, and will have more men than we need when the Veterans come Back! I suppose you must have seen that rumor in the Newspaper about sending the 11th, 12th, 16th and 17th Army Corps to the Army of the Potomac. It comes in the Washington Correspondence of the N. Y. Herald, which besides this, says that Grant is to concentrate 200,000 men on Richmond, and is to take the field in person, to command them.

It will be as good a thing as we want, to go either East, South, or West, if we can only be in active service; This lying in Garrison is enough to kill anybody: waiting, waiting: the same thing every day, dull Routine of eating, drinking, sleeping, Roll call, feeding horses, cleaning horses, watering horses, drill, guard duty, details for wood and water hauling, and attending to our personal comforts; these constitute our daily life, varied once in a while by Inspection, drawing of Rations, Musters &c. Now, you see, this would not be very bad to undergo for a month or even two, but when it is the only mode of existence for 6 months or a year, it becomes tedious and monotonous. In my position, there is not much chance for *ennui*, for I always have enough to do to keep me busy, but that is not the case with one man in fifty in the army, and the most you hear our Recruits complain of, is the sudden transition from their busy farmer's life, to this dull, idle existence, the more sensible of them, entering with might and main into the Base Ball, Quoits, and Cricket of the Camp, to replace the home work, while others will soon die of diseases engendered by inaction, for there are some men who would not get out of their bunks all day if they were not compelled to.

I send you in this a Valentine that was sent by some fair Minnesotian to one of the Recruits in my squad. Its dilapidated condition testifies to the fact that it has been in the hands of about every man in the Co, a sure sign that it is appreciated by the Boys. Its laughable significance is more readily appreciated by we old hands, after the thousand and one absurd questions that are daily asked us about the duties and arms of artillery men, and after hearing them call the Gun carriage a "Wagon," and the Breech and cascable,

---

52. Sergeant Jesse Conner, Private Joseph O'Hara, and Private William Wiltse were all from Winona. *Adjutant General's Report.*

the "but" of the Gun, not to speak of the question asked by one of the new boys of me, when I was showing them the ammunition, (which is you know, fixed for howitzers, that is, the cartridge is attached to the shell by; a wooden sabot,) he asked me which "ball" we inserted first in the gun. The same one who sent this caricature sent also one representing "A Recruiting Officer" to Tom Gordon, who was up with the captain. It was the same character as this, only "a little more so," and Gordon had the laugh turned against him awfully when he opened his supposed letter in a crowd of men, and found this terriffic caricature staring him in the face;

What hay bargain was that, that Father made with Lutton? If Osgood Noyes is with his Regt. on Black River we will have a chance to see him, but I heard some time ago, that the 8th was home on furlough, and we did not know where to find the camp of the Recruits, All of the 4 Regts comprising the 3rd Brigade of our Division, (11th, 13th, 15th and 16th Iowa) are gone home in a body as Veterans, and you can see nothing where their tents stood so thickly a few days ago but a forest of chimneys dotting the bare side hill. W. and I conclude to go home as soon as we can after the boys get back, but our going home at all will depend on circumstances; if we went into active service this spring we could not leave, nor indeed would we ask to, but the general impression is that we are to stay here during the summer, unless the Corps is ordered East.

Give my love to all, and especially to Grand mother Bertie: From your affectionate Brother, T. D. Chrisitie.

6

"Enough Fighting to Satisfy Us"
March 25–September 9, 1864

Thomas Christie to James Christie[1]

BIG BLACK RIVER BRIDGE, MCH 25, 1864

My Dear Father,

We came out here on the 23rd, and are camped on the bank of the river, close to the ruins of the railroad bridge; my gun is trained on the pontoon bridge. The cavalry of the enemy are within four miles of us; our own videttes are in plain sight. I think our generals expect a fight very soon at this point. New works have been thrown up; large reinforcements have come in quite lately; shots are often heard out in front; and every precaution is taken against surprise.

The three new companies of the 16th Wis. came out with us, and fully sustained the Regiment's reputation for marching; the road was rough and muddy; but they came the 18 miles between 11 and 5 o'clock. We left two caissons behind, in the machine shop; and the two howitzers in the care of a lieutenant of another battery; so we have here only the four Rodmans. They say we shall not see the old guns again, but will draw two more Rodmans in their place. We shall be sorry to lose the "Pumpkin-slingers," that have done such good service in all our battles.

Our camp is in a pleasant spot, handy to wood and water. The latter is not very nice to look at, for the heavy rains have given such a color to the river that we call it not the Big Black, but the Big Yellow. Yesterday the rebels launched into the river above us a lot of beams fastened together crosswise, trees, and rubbish, in order to carry away our pontoon bridge. The water is high and the current strong. The great mass came down like

1. Transcribed in Thomas Christie reminiscence.

a raft, lodged against the anchor-ropes and the boats; they sank almost
under the water. Our pioneers were not strong enough to clear the bridge,
and disaster seemed sure. Capt Bedford, the Adjutant General of our Division called on the Captain for a detail of men to help; and some fifty of us
ran down. It is hard work to save the bridge; but by dint of much chopping,
and prying, and hauling, and rather vigorous talk, we finally set all the trees
&c afloat below the pontoons. Then we got buckets, and emptied the boats
of water; they had been nearly swamped. The rebels are very active, doing
all they can to annoy us. Our fellows only wish they would come across and
give us a chance at them; or that we might be ordered to go and drive them
off! But I tell the new men not to be too anxious to get into a fight; that
before Shiloh we used to talk as they do, but never after! Still, I feel that
these new fellows are men to be relied on, when the time comes.

You should have a longer letter, but for the work of getting the camp into
order. In this matter also the recruits have everything to learn. "How do
you want his ditch dug?" "Show us how to stretch this picket-rope, will
you?" "What space shall we leave between the tents, and where shall I put
up mine?" "Which is best for a bunk, shakes or cane?" And so it goes for
hours. But everything will come right in time. And now to clean up our
dirty cannon and carriages! No more till that is done, from Yours Ever,
        T.D.C.

∾

Thomas Christie to James Christie[2]

BIG BLACK RIVER BRIDGE, APRIL 2, 1864.

My Dear Father,

I have just had another attack of chills and fever; it lasted three days. This
shows that the malaria is very hard to get out of the system. It is rumored
that we are to go to the Army of the Potomac; we look daily for orders. Part
of the Corps has already gone up the river, accompanied by the Corps train.
Our officers say that we will surely be in Cairo within two weeks. There we
shall meet the Veterans, and be reorganized: then, ho for the Potomac, the
Rapidan, or the James! Capt. Clayton is ordered not to draw any horses
here, but to take them all in Cairo. So probably there is a lively campaign
before us. There is every indication that the coming summer is to be one of
fiercer, harder fighting than any that has yet passed; if our armies are led

2. Transcribed in Thomas Christie reminiscence.

as they ought to be, this campaign will be the last. Never before were our troops in better spirit, health, and discipline than they are at present. They see that the end of their labors is fast approaching; and will fight with a sure confidence of success. All that we require is, that those who have the command of us shall move upon the enemy's works without delay. It is likely that all of us will get enough fighting to satisfy us thoroughly.

You can send books to our Library by expressing them to the Christian Commission at Cincinnatti; send at the same time a letter to the agent there telling them that they are for Vicksburg. There are nearly 1,000 volumes now in the Library.

God be with you all, and with His cause is the daily prayer of yours ever, T.D.C.

P.S. Every Sunday, Wednesday, and Friday evening we attend the prayer-meeting in the 124th Ill. I am going there tomorrow for the sermon. The have the best chaplain that I have met in the Army.[3]

Thomas Christie to James Christie[4]

VICKSBURG, APRIL 6, 1864

My Dear Father,

Here we are again, bivouacked in an open space near the Courthouse, waiting for a boat to take us to Cairo. When you read this we shall be either there or in Mound City, 6 miles above, on the Ohio. We are now in the 3rd Division, having been transferred from the 1st. This is Gen. Logan's old Division, now commanded by Gen. Leggett.[5]

We marched from the Bridge to this place yesterday forenoon. Shall write again from Cairo. We are all well, and in the best of spirits over the prospect of going to the Potomac.

Yours ever,

T.D.C.

3. According to the National Parks Service, "Soldiers and Sailors System," Horace B. Foskett was chaplain of the 124th Illinois.

4. Transcribed in Thomas Christie reminiscences.

5. In March 1864, many of the regiments of the Third and Fourth Divisions of the Seventeenth Army Corps were on veteran's furlough and were ordered to rendezvous at Cairo, Illinois. In April, the First Minnesota Battery was assigned to the Fourth Division under General Marcellus Crocker. Welcher, *Union Army*, II:308–9.

Thomas Christie to Alexander Christie

CAIRO ILLS, APRIL 18TH 1864

My Dear Brother:

Here we are once more, in the outer edge of civilization, in this swampy, watery copperhead town: camped in a spot where we have to look up to see the steamers on the Ohio ten ft. above the level of the town, whose streets still are encumbered with the skiffs and boats used by the inhabitants in former inundations, and which, I think will be required again pretty soon, if the River continues to rise. I feel very jubilant at the idea of again being so near home, where it will not take a month to get an answer to a letter, and I hope I have seen the last of Vicksburg and the banks of the Mississippi. Although the weather was good, after leaving Vicksburg, we had rather a tedious voyage, being crowded like sheep in a pen, as the boat we were on was from New Orleans, and had aboard the 4th Wis. Cavalry, and the 8th Indiana, all Veterans from Texas going home on furlough, who, of course had all the best places selected before we came on board, and so we had to shift as we could below stairs. I and my bed mate slept under the traveling forges of the Battery, where we bumped our heads on the Assembling bolts at every motion, and had to eat our meals (very temperate ones I assure you,) lying full length on our blankets, the very circumscribed limits of our dormitory making it impossible to sit up, unless we stuck our feet through a wheel, for a hundred men to stumble over in the gang way. To give you all the dates &c of our movements, I will transcribe a page or two of my little pocket Diary, kept in pencil, and which I find far more convenient than the cumbersome pen-&-ink Journal that I used to keep.

VICKSBURG, SATURDAY, APRIL 8TH /64

Fine weather: Troops going on board transports all day, Our boys impatient to be off. William, Dave (my bunkmate) and I now sleep in the Orderly's tent, Resigned my position of Trustee of the Union Library, on account of leaving the Post. SUNDAY, 10TH, Had orders to go on board the "Iatan," this afternoon, countermanded, & given out by the officers that we would not leave till tomorrow morning. Then at 5 P.M. orders came again, and we had to tumble aboard the "J.C. Snow,"[6] in an awful hurry. Everything

---

6. A side-wheel packet built in 1856. *Way's Packet Directory*, 230.

in confusion, and everybody, especially the new boys, in a terrible "stew." William left behind. Left the wharf at dark, and steamed up river. MONDAY: 11TH Passed Providence this forenoon: 4th Wis. are the greatest gamblers I ever saw, and seem to be very flush of money; TUESDAY, 12TH Made very good progress today, and stopped seldom. Passed Napoleon at 11 A.M. Desolate looking town, Saw 12 Gunboats during the day, mostly at anchor. WEDNESDAY, 13TH, Passed Helena before daylight, Made Memphis at dusk, Great excitement about Ft. Pillow being captured by Forrest,[7] 10th Ohio Battery on the "Hope," fired into yesterday, Guerrillas infect the River, TUESDAY, 14TH Disembarked this morning, marched through town, and camped in the suburbs, about 2 miles from the River. Put up tents, and made ourselves comfortable All troops, passing either way, are stopped to garrison the city till Forrest's intentions in regard to it are discovered. The fort has been abandoned by him, and boats run by in safety. FRIDAY, 15TH Made preparations to stay in camp for some time, but orders came about noon, and we broke up camp, and went aboard the same boat as before. Found William on the levee, he having come up on the Iatan, Left Memphis this evening.

SATURDAY, 16TH Passed Fort Pillow at daylight, Gunboat at anchor there, Bank of the river at the fort, high and bluffy. Passed several boats by racing. Stopped a long time to wood up about noon. River very high. SUNDAY, 17TH Stopped at Columbus at daylight for a short time. Arrived in Cairo at 9 A.M. Steamed up the Ohio about a mile above town, disembarked, and went into camp north of the city, in the midst of a cold, drizzling rain, camping ground low and muddy.

That was yesterday, and today we are as comfortable as could be expected, the rain having stopped, and enough lumber for bunks having been jayhawked during the night: Speaking of jayhawking: I noticed several cups of milk at breakfast this morning, which, considering the price of that commodity in town, (20cts per Qt.) and the "strapped" condition of all our boys, looks rather suspicious, especially as several female specimens of the Genus Bos were to be seen about daylight tied with halter straps to some of our Gun carriages.

I got your letter, post marked 28th March, before leaving Vicksburg, and also a letter from Father of the 30th, which I will answer soon if we find that we cannot go on furlough from here, for which we will try as soon as things

7. Confederate cavalry under Nathan Bedford Forrest captured the Mississippi River post on April 12, 1864. A considerable number of U.S. colored troops were massacred when they tried to surrender. See Trudeau, *Like Men of War*, 166–67.

are more settled here. The most of our Army Corps is here in camp, and the rumor is that we are not to leave for a month, but this can hardly be, and I think all we wait for before going to Huntsville, is the arrival of some more troops. I wish it could be managed so that Father could come down and see us, for I am afraid that it will be impossible to obtain furloughs. The fare to Chicago from here is about 12 dollars, and 4 ½ from there to Clyman so his trip would not need to cost more than 35 dollars, which he could use from William's and my money, and be welcome to it. It would be worth 2 month's pay, to see him down here, and it would be of great benefit to him, I know. The Spring labor could spare him for a few days.

I fully agree with the ideas of emigration advanced by you, and shall do my best to further your plan, as I am convinced it is by far the best thing the family could do. More of this in my next.

Wm. got your letter to him at Memphis, where I also found a letter from Dave, which smelled villainously of ducks, and Marshes, and wet feet, and burnt powder, besides a slight scent of the horse stable On the whole it was a good letter, which is more than can be said of this from

Yours aff'tly, Thos. D. Christie

⌒

Thomas Christie to James Christie[8]

CLIFTON, TENN., MAY 1, 1864

(Stuck in the mud!)

My Dear Father,

Here we are in the field again, in good earnest. I wrote you from Cairo just before starting. We were two days coming here, up the Ohio and the Tennessee, just like two years ago. Our boat stopped here yesterday afternoon. We disembarked during the night, in the midst of a pelting rainstorm, hauling our guns up a steep slippery bank in the most profound darkness. By midnight everything was off, and we were all wet to the skin. After that, we had to hunt for dry places in which to sleep. However, the boys took everything in good humor, and worked with a will: only ejaculating sometimes, when the rain poured in worse torrents than usual, "who wouldn't sell his farm to be a soldier!"

8. Transcribed in Thomas Christie reminiscence.

Today is warm and pleasant. We hear that tomorrow morning the march must begin for Huntsville, 125 miles distant; by looking at the map you will see that we shall thus cut off the great bend in the Tennessee Clifton is on the east side of the river, 25 miles below Savannah, that we knew so well in '62.[9] We find here no troops except part of the Second Tenn. Cavalry;[10] they march with us tomorrow. Huntsville is about 8 days distant. My health is excellent; so is W.'s, and that of all the men. This life, with all its hardships, always suits us far better than does that of the camp. I would not have written this scrawl were it not that there will be no other opportunity for some time to send you a letter. The boats of the expedition, on their return will carry this. We are the Advance-Guard of the Corps, 4,000 infantry and our Battery; Gen. Gresham[11] is in command.

Your jubilantly, but busier than a

Wet hen,

T. D. C.

∽

Thomas Christie to Sarah Christie

ATHENS, ALA. MAY 13TH 1864

My Dear Sister:

It is so long since I have got any news from you, (something over 2 months,) that I begin to think you do not intend to let us have the benefit of your correspondence any longer. Father and Sandy write regularly, and sometimes Dave sends us a few lines but either you have too much to do, or you are regardless of the claims we have on you, for it is a long time since either of us has heard from you. I hope you will sit down, after reading this, and write me a good long letter in answer, containing all the news, a bit of Gossip and something of your own thoughts, prospects, duties &c.

9. Savannah, Tennessee, an important landing on the Tennessee River, figured prominently in the Shiloh campaign.

10. This federal unit was organized at Murfreesboro, Tennessee, in July 1862. Most of its operations were in west Tennessee. Dyer, *Compendium*, 230.

11. A native of Indiana and a member of the state legislature with no formal military training, Walter Q. Gresham raised a company of men in 1862 and rose to command of the Fifty-third Indiana. He proved himself an able officer and was advanced to the rank of brigadier in August 1863. In April 1864 he organized a detachment of troops from the Third and Fourth Divisions of the Seventeenth Corps to intercept Confederate raider Nathan Bedford Forrest. Not finding Forrest, they were ordered to Clifton, where they rejoined the Seventeenth and proceeded to Huntsville, Alabama. Warner, *Generals in Blue*, 188; Welcher, *Union Army*, II:309.

For myself personally, I have only to say that my health is good, in fact better than ever before since I had the ague, which I think has left me for good my spirits buoyant, (for I have enough to do to keep me busy and prevent melancholy thought,) and my hope strong in anticipation of a short, successful campaign and a return *home* soon.

You know how it is about getting a furlough, when at Cairo we could, perhaps, have got leave to go home on furlough, if we had tried for it, but in view of the prospect of active service, I thought it would not do for us to leave the Company just as it was ordered to the front. So you and we will have to wait till the Summer Campaign is finished, which, judging from past experience, will be in July sometime, before you will see us.

William wanted a furlough worse than I, for very good reasons, for he has been gone from home now nearly three years, and naturally, is more anxious to see you than I am. I think, by the likeness that Schaller brought us at Cairo, that you must have had a hard time of it last winter, for you look dreadfully thin and care-worn, and I trust it does not represent you in your usual condition of health, for if so, you make that school teaching too hard work, as I suppose it is anyhow.

I have enough to do to keep me busy at something all the time, but no hard work. As acting Sergeant I have charge and command of 25 men, whom I must drill and see that they all do their duty as Drivers, Cannoneers, and Supernumeraries. Then, there are 12 horses, besides my own riding horse, over whose feeding, grooming, watering and working I must exercise a superintendence, and am answerable to the Capt. for their condition at all times; If a Driver neglects to attend to his team in my platoon it is my business to compel him to, or give the horses to another man. Besides this, there are my Gun and Caissons, with 222 Rounds of Ammunition to take care of. the ammunition to be aired frequently, and the carriages to be kept clean and bright.

So, what with these, and miscellaneous duties my time is pretty well occupied, and pleasantly occupied too. Since we left Clifton, the Bugle has roused us at three every morning, either to march or to form in Line of Battle in anticipation of an attack by Roddy[12] Every morning since coming here we have had to be ready for action before daylight, with horses harnessed and hitched up, a days Rations of hard tack and raw pork in our haversacks, and the infantry under arms on each flack of the Battery.

12. Confederate general Philip Dale Roddey commanded the district of north Alabama at the head of a cavalry division. Wakelyn, *Biographical Dictionary*, 371–72.

We are without tents here, having left all the camp Equipage at Cairo, and so we are domiciled under tarpaulins, and in empty houses in the vicinity. William and I are under tarpaulins, and so are Southwick, and Connor. Perhaps you did not hear before that Southwick was married while up in Minnesota, and so was Joe O'Hara who got the prettiest girl in Winona County. And this after all his vows of eternal bachelorhood. In the re-organization of the Company our old Squad was all divided up, and there is only Southwick left in my Platoon. However, the Captain seems to think a good deal of us, for many of the boys of the "old Fourth" have been pro-moted, Southwick, O' Hara, and Wiltse are acting Corporals, with every probability of receiving their Warrants soon. Jesse Connor is now in com-mand of the 4th Squad so that his Platoon and mine form the centre sec-tion, commanded by Orderly Sergt Heywood who is to put on the shoulder straps of a 2nd Lieut. soon. Sam Woolly is detailed in a Field Hospital as Cook, and we left him in Cairo enjoying himself firstrate. Schaller's Regt., was left there also, but we expect it up soon. So, you now know how all your acquaintances are getting along, and if there is anything you want to know that I can tell you, about anything here, you can ask it in your next and I will answer to the best of my ability. As Shakespeare has it, "Since Brevity is the soul of Wit. And tediousness the limbs and outward flourishes, I will be brief." So give my love to all, and remember me as

Your Loving Brother

T. D. Christie

[margin note] In your letter tell me all you hear from Helen, I am going to send her a letter soon

[top margin—first page] PS The last of this is written on Sunday, the 15th All is well Roddy has left for parts unknown & we can now sleep till daylight without fear of molestation. No mail yet Cheering news from the East Have dispatches to day from Washington yesterday, so are kept well posted.

⁓

William Christie to James Christie

ATHENS ALABAMA MAY 13TH 1864

Dear Father, I would have written, and should have written to you sooner, of course but Tom stole a march on me, so I did not feel, as if you would be in any trouble about us, and so I waited. I have not much to tell you only

we made very fast marching over a very rough hilly country, driving with
us some seven or eight hundred head of beef cattle. The hills were covered
with a heavy growth of timber, oak being the most plentifull however their
was a number of flowering shrubs in the woods and the ground is most
beautifully enammelled with various species of phlox. our road for the day's
travel was over a very nicely made road, and all along it[s] sides, there was
large piles of Pig Iron, lying as though they had been brought out of the
wood, and corded up. We Passed a large foundry or rather smelting furnace
on the afternoon of the first days travel, but the second night out, we only
move from camp in Clifton five miles on the evening of the 5th our journey
was through a poorly settled country, and their was not much to jayhawk,
but our Battery mannaged to have a little more than Uncle's Sams grub
for supper and Breakfast. large Piles of fence went up in smoke for we had
to have something to keep us warm, and cook with. we made an average of
some twenty miles a day, by the sections, but we must have done more by
the actual travel over a road that turnned to every Point on the compass, in
its windings among the hills of Tenn: We Passed through the County seat
of Waynesborough, and on the same day Passed through Lawrenceburg,
County seat of Lawrence County our road on this day (Sunday) was in many
place over the solid rock, for as much a mile at a time, and late at night we
drove intoo a large flat at or near Pulaski, on the Bank of Richland Creek
we stayed at this place over night and at or near noon we started for Athens,
on the Nashville and Huntsville turnpike, and after four miles travel on it
we turned to our right for Elkton, on Elk river, our road was good through
a very good farming country, and we go intoo camp before sundown, making a march of 15miles, next morning a[s] day dawned it began to rain, and
it ceasing at eleven o clock we started for this Point, crossing the River on
a Bridge of Boats covered over with Plank. our Infantry and Battery got over
all safe, but those who had the Cattle in charge let to many of them on the
Bridge, and it Parted in the middle, let a large number of them intoo the
water, But there were none drowned. We got along very well on the road
climbing some very high hills, and having but a very little trouble to get
along. about four oclock, we had got through climbing a very high ridge,
and shortly after a heavy rain storm commenced falling accompanied with
a high wind, vivid lightening, and loud crashing thunder. the scene, who
can describe it, I cant, but I will try. Just think you see four thousand men,
with their waggon trains, and seven or eight hundred head of cattle, winding through country covered with a heavy growth of young timber. the road

was litteraly like a river, and the men and horses slushing through it, faugh! I cant Paint it no sir, but we had a very disagreeable night of it I assure you, but our men are all in good health T. D. and I ditto, and we have had quite a nice rest here on a very nice flat West of Athens a few rods. This Country could be made the Paridise of the south, the formation of it gives A Pleas-ing variety of line to the eye. the soil is very fertile, and water very plenty for digging thirty feet.

Now for the People, they are rather a sorry looking set, and have the most filthy habits of any People I have ever heard tell of. Tipping is one of the bad practices I speak of not table tipping, nor tumbler tipping, but Tobbacco tipping just thing of it old women and young, Black and White, Yellow and Brown, Massa and Missis tips, and so sambo and [?] tips, and steal young Massa's and misses snuff for the sake of the Plasure now for the method of tipping so you may enjoy the new use of Tobbacco it will give you. get some snuff, and a small reed hollow out said reed fill the hollow with the snuff, then put one end between your teeth and gently raising one end, if not in a hurry get the snuff intoo your mouth, which must be full of saliva. then commece squirting the Back and forth through your teeth keep the lips shut, you will have the first Process. next take a small stick and commence rubbing your teeth and gums. if the stick ain't handy use your knuckles, and so on. when tired [of] that chew when tired of chewing smoke and then with your Back brain on fire be ready for the first develtry that comes in your way, if none come seek some, and you will be sure to find it. Life in the south, is not Life in the North, you have little Idea of what has been under the surface through the Past years of the every day life of this People. Olmsted's Book of travel in the south[13] don't give you any Idea of Life as it has been here, no matter how high in Position, Politically, or morraly, in the eyes of the world, well no matter. So the sun shone, Roses bloommed, Birds sang, men and women dressed fine and fared sumptuously. The whip cracked on the Backs of the toilers and the chains clanked on their limbs, and when it suitted their Masters, _____ , so we needed this war, and God sent it, and surely it will end Right, for he will assuredly not cease untill it is well done.

We are having Glorious news from Lieut. Gen. Grant's opperations in the East. I hope that we are having no wrong impression in our minds, in

13. Frederick Law Olmsted wrote a number of travel books describing the South: *A Journey Through the Seaboard Slave States* (1856), *A Journey Through Texas* (1857), and *A Journey in the Back Country* (1861).

regard to these things. Many brave men are falling but through these trials
we will yet be made free. There are slight rummors in camp here that our
advance at Tunnel hill in Georgia, has fallin Back on Ringgold, we have no
Particulers.[14] Banks; what is he: I did not like his actions in his adminis-
tration of affairs last fall and summer. This spring he had too much to do
with the making of the Governor of Louisianna. I really hope that things
are not as bad as the Papers say they are, in the district. I expect a letter
from you every day now. But there is not any telling when we will get mail,
tis said that on the evening of the fifth of this month, after we left Clifton
Their was fifteen thousand men and 1800 head of cattle landed there, and
it is likely we will get mail when they come they should be here tomorrow,
or the next day. there is a report that there are 10,000 men under some
Rebel general within a few miles I don't believe it allthough we have to get
up each before day light and boots and saddles being sounded, we harness
and hitch up, the Infantry also fall into line. this road is guard[ed] at many
Places by colored troops, raised in this state and the Borders of Tenn. three
regiments in all. we are with some troops we were never with before, the
30th Ill. and 32nd Ohio, are among them, also the 14th Ill.[15] they all think
we are as good if not better than any Battery then have ben with, and think
we done well in getting so well a long in the storm. the gen.[16] in well
Pleased with us to I hear, we are the only Battery in this force,

  my love and respect to all and Believe me ever your affectionate son
  William G. Christie

P. S. send along Post stamps a dollars worth, at least Love to mother and
grand mother good by for the present.

Thomas Christie to James Christie

DECATUR, ALA. MAY 27TH / 64

Dear Father:

  We left Huntsville day before yesterday in the forenoon, the whole corps,
four Divisions, being in column on the same road, extending six miles along

---

14. These rumors were probably related to the opening maneuvers in Sherman's
Atlanta Campaign. See: Foote, *Civil War*, 3:322–25.

15. These regiments were from the Third and Fourth Divisions of the Seventeenth
Corps. See Welcher, *Union Army*, II:308; Dyer, *Compendium*.

16. Probably General Walter Gresham, who was in charge of the detachment. Welcher,
Union Army, II:309.

it. Before we left the Baggage of the command was reduced, and everything left in town except a change of underclothing, one Woolen Blanket and one Rubber do.[ditto] for each man, so that we are in light Marching Order, which always means work. This was done the day before we started and our Knapsacks were all turned over to the charge of an officer appointed to receive them, to be forwarded to us by R. R. when the campaign is finished. Our camp equipage and stores that we left at Cairo came up to us in time to be turned over with the rest. Everything is made as light as possible, as we have a long hard March before us, our destination being well known to be Rome, Ga. for which we start as soon as Rations can be furnished us here. The Corps is 20,000 strong, and it is not anticipated that we will have any difficulty in pushing through, although the road is new to our Army, and very mountainous. If you hear anything in the Newspapers of Blair's[17] column you may see where we are and what we are doing, and when you read this you may imagine our guns in position somewhere at the front, (which is fast going South, till it pushes the Rebels into the Last Ditch at Mobile.) We made about 16 Miles day before yesterday, and yesterday pushed on to this town, crossing the Tennessee on a pontoon bridge three fourths of a mile long. Here we rest today till something to eat can be provided for we are on two third Rations, which is our only trouble. If we march for Rome ten days grub will have to be carried. The country between this and Huntsville beats anything we have yet seen for beauty and cultivation. You will think us extravagant in praising Northern Alabama so much as we do but it is actually the loveliest Land in America. Abundance of the best water, springs gushing our everywhere, gently rolling land, a cool climate, for this hill country is so elevated that a cool breeze blows continually. I do not see what is to prevent this from being one of the richest, as it is the healthiest of regions in North America. Any of our fellows would take a Qr. Section here without grumbling.

The Capt. left us at Huntsville[18] and I sent a letter to Sarah by him to be mailed on the train. I hope you get all of our letters for we write often

17. Prior to the Atlanta Campaign there was a major reshuffling of command in the western armies: William T. Sherman replaced Grant as theater commander, James McPherson, Seventeenth Corps commander, took over the Army of the Tennessee, and Frank P. Blair, commander of the Fifteenth Corps, took McPherson's place. Welcher, *Union Army*, II:308–9.

18. According to the First Battery Company Morning Reports, Captain Clayton left for fifteen days furlough on May 22.

enough. I am sure Our permanent address now will be—"1st Minn. Battery. 4th Div. 17th A. C." Genl. Crocker is in command of the Division,[19] the man who led the famous bayonet charge at the first capture of Jackson, Miss. and the Division is the old one of Hurlbut's the "fighting Fourth," that checked the Rebels at Shiloh and stopped the retreating army of Price on the Hatchie at Matamoras. All of our old 1st Division Regts. are in it, so you see we are in a good command. It is cheering to see the old veteran Regts. which last year at this time, before Vicksburg, could, some of them, scarce raise 200 men for duty, now mustering their 800 and 900 Bayonets.

On the day before we left Huntsville the position of Ordnance Srgt. for the Division was offered to me, but I declined it as I did not wish to leave the Company although it would have been a good promotion, as the Ordnance Sergt. has charge of all the ammunition of the Division, Infantry and Artillery. When Lieut. Hurter, who is in command of the Company, was ordered by Capt. Spear, Chief of Artillery, to recommend a Non Commissioned Officer for the position of Ordnance Sergt he came at once to me and said he would give me the first refusal of it. I thanked him for his good opinion of me, but told him I would rather stay with the Boys as I wished to be identified with the Battery in all that I did. My friends say I should have taken it but I still hold to my first decision. Am I not right? Yours truly,
    T. D. Christie

[postscript in margin] All your letters are recd. and I must thank you for that one of the 25th April to me which I got at Hville. So you are more unlucky than usual this Spring in getting in the crop although having the long wished for horse team. you see the impossibility of our asking for furlough at this time. It will be August before we can be at home, But let us each in our sphere of action do our whole duty, you with the Reaper and me with our Rodmans and when we *do* meet it will be more of a pleasure the longer we wait till that time I wish the war could be over before we go, and that I could take home my wheel team on the gun. You would see the best farm horses that ever have been in that region. T. D. C.

[postscript interlined on third page] Tell Sandy I am so weak with knawing only 8 ounces of hard tack per day that I have to lean on a caisson wheel to

19. At Huntsville, General Blair organized the Seventeenth Corps into two divisions: the Third under Mortimer Leggett and the Fourth under Walter Gresham. Welcher, *Union Army*, II:310.

spit. You may judge from the shortening of our Rations, that it just takes[?] us to get enough to eat. This morning I dealt out to the men of the Mess 4 little crackers apiece to last 2 days. The boys say that Blair has been superseded, and that the General who [replaced?] him is Genrl. Starvation. Tell Sandy also to send down in his next letter complaining about not being allowed to enlist, a few pds of that Mutton you Killed a few days ago, some of Mother's Biscuits, with a cake of that sweet Butter (what is [left] over we can sell for a dollar a pd.) Also some potatoes, and a few garden vegetables, all of which will be thankfully received by this starving community T.D.C.

∾

Thomas Christie to James Christie

ROME, GEORGIA, JUNE 5TH / 64

My Dear Father;

We came through here from Decatur, by way of Somerville, Warrenton, Cedar Bluff and a dozen other little towns in the Mountains since the 27th May, having marched every day but one, arriving in this town this afternoon. I can not enter into details in describing the march, interesting as they would be to you, for we push on tomorrow for the Front, beyond Kingston, and I am writing this *only* to let you know that we are all right yet, well and hearty, only a little worn by the severe march. The Corps, 2 Divisions of it rather, has got through without the loss of a single wagon or caisson, although we crossed some awful Mountains and forded a few pretty deep rivers and creeks. I had no idea of Mountains till this march. Our horses have stood the trip far better than I expected; owing to the care that is taken of them by the men.

One of the worst hardships with us has been the want of sleep, many nights we would not get into the blankets till past midnight, once it was after One, and then routed out at half past two, or three in the morning. William has driven his team all the way through and so has ridden the most of the journey, as I have also, so we are neither of us foot-sore, as many a poor fellow n the Infantry is tonight. All that ails Bill, is, the caisson wheel run over his toes today, making him limp a little, but nothing serious. One of our boys shot himself accidentally through the foot yesterday, which is the only casualty we have to report in the Battery. Perhaps you may have heard of the brisk little fight our Cavalry had with Roddy near Moulton, in which our Left Section was engaged It occurred on Sunday, the

29th and the Rebels were nicely cleaned out, Our section, the Centre, was not engaged.[20]

When we got here we found a very large mail awaiting us, and Wm and I got yours and Sandy's to both of us, dated the 16th, 17th & 21st of May. They were read with a relish I can assure you, and I regret not having time to answer them as they should be answered, but I am stealing time to write this that should be devoted to sleep, and the most you can expect for some time from us will be the *shortest kind of letters.* "Duty before Pleasures" you Know, and we have plenty of the former to Keep us busy all the time. Just rest assured that we are *doing well,* performing every thing pertaining to our share of the work here, and that is considerable.

I hear tonight that the Corps is ordered forward tomorrow so we will not get the day of rest we thought we would, there is a train of 3000 wagons waiting at Kingston for us to conduct through. The Front is about 40 Miles south of this and there is where you will next hear from us. W. would write only *he* is too tired tonight It has been pretty tough on us[21] "but what this bods so long as you be appy"

Love to all, T.D. Christie

[margin note] I could fill a dozen sheets, but have no time. I keep notes regularly however and you shall have the benefit of them sometime.

⌒

Thomas Christie to James Christie[22]

THE FRONT, GEORGIA, JUNE 14,1864[23]

My Dear Father:

Vicksburg over again! Here we are in position, our guns looking through their embrasures at the enemy, the rifle-pits full of infantry on our right

20. The morning reports for May and June 1864 note the detachment of the left section on May 27, the day the rest of the battery left Decatur, Alabama. They also report marches of fourteen to eighteen miles each day. The wounded man was John D. Ross, one of the recruits who joined the battery in January 1864.

21. In pension applications filed in the 1880s, William described a number of ailments, some of which he attributed to the extreme exertions of this march. U.S. Pension Department file 452.949, Affidavit of William G. Christie, Winona County District Court, June 5, 1882.

22. Transcribed in Thomas Christie reminiscence.

23. The Union Army was at Big Shanty. Having maneuvered Johnston out of his lines near Allatoona, they now faced his army dug in between there and Marietta, near

and left, "*crack*," "*crack*," "*crack*" going on from the line of skirmishers and pickets, the balls from the enemy whistling over our heads. In this part of the line the rebels are in the edge of an irregular-shaped plateau covered with timber. Our zig-zag line of works runs through the middle of a some-what hilly but open field. You see the Johnnies have the better position. Our Battery is in a fort in an apple-orchard, the horses and limbers in the rear, ready to move on the instant. These are screened by a little shrubbery from the view, but not from the bullets, of the enemy. There is a difference as compared with Vicksburg—we are kept in readiness to move at any time; the horses stand day and night hitched up to the limbers, the drivers lying by them. The cannoneers wear their equipments at all times, and remain within easy call. Last evening we did some firing, mainly to test our new guns; the test was satisfactory; the infantry said they never saw better practice. As soon as the weather permits we must either flank the rebels out, or charge them in front. It is necessary to press them before they receive reinforcements, for which they seem to be waiting. They do every-thing possible to avoid a general engagement.

For a week the weather has been very bad; we are drenched with rain by day and by night. You can fancy the condition of the red-clay fields! On Saturday night we were busy till dawn, making gabions in the dark, and lining the embrasures with them; it was tedious work, for we had nothing to split the oak saplings with but our sabres and jack knives. Today has been cloudy, no rain; a few cannon-shots have been fired by us, but none by the enemy. Their sharpshooters, however, are pretty active; most of their bullets fly rather close to us. The blankets hung up to dry have many a hole in them. One fellow paid his complements to my breeches and boots this forenoon, in a way not the most agreable in these days when both tailors and shoemakers are hard to find. I was cleaning my revolver; the Captain was near me doing the same for his sabre; quite a crowd of men were standing around. Two rifles cracked in the edge of the wood, about 300 yards away. One heavy ball went close over my shoulder, the other slapped right through the gunner's haversack, riddling his tin cup and pepperbox; next it took me close to the ancle with tremendous force, mak-ing me spin around like a top. Luckily, it did me no harm beyond making two holes in my pantaloons 2 inches apart, and one in my boot-leg where

---

Pine Mountain. This date is also when Confederate general Leonidas Polk was killed by Union artillery. Foote, *Civil War*, III:352–57.

the crinkle is at the ancle. If it had gone an inch to the left, it would have ended my soldiering; for I never yet saw a broken ancle that did not cause amputation of the foot. It is a bad place for a wound. However, a miss is as good as a mile, and I am thankful. I remember that the limb of a tree fell just in front of me once, when I was about twelve years old. You saw my narrow escape, and said you felt sure I was spared for a purpose. Now that I have had so many "close calls" in battle, and am still unhurt, I begin to think the same—that God is keeping me for some future work. Somehow, there is within me all the time a feeling of perfect security and confidence. Even when the danger is greatest, when men are struck down all around me, when no one knows whose turn it will be next—I have the assurance within me that I shall come out all right.

On Saturday we came up into position a little to the right of where we are now. We unlimbered in an open space without the slightest shelter, within 400 yards of the rifle-pits fairly swarming with Rebels. They were in plain view, looking earnestly at us while we shoved our guns forward and got ready to open fire. It is a marvel to me yet that they did not annihilate us with their rifles. Many of our men were almost beside themselves with fear or excitement—lying down or crouching about in the funniest attitudes. I hope you will not think I am boasting when I tell you the plain truth, I was "as cool as a cucumber" all through the affair. Of course, we very soon threw up a defence of earth and fence-rails. I tell you all this to induce you also to share this confidence that I feel. The balls are "zipping" by me as I write; there goes one now through a tarpaulin near by! The leaves and small branches of the apple-trees are constantly falling. But I feel absolutely no fear. It is strange; but it is true.

What you write of S. in remarkable—his being able to tell you always when to expect a letter from us. I never have any premonitions of that kind. The mail is about to go to Big Shanty; I must close. Your two letters have done me more good that an extra ration. We are as near to starving as we can be and live. Nothing but hardtack, and very little of that.[24] But nobody complains. Your penniless and hungry Son. *T. D. C.*

෴

24. Sherman's maneuvers to force Johnston's army out of its strong positions at Resaca and Allatoona had required the Union army to move away from its railroad sup-ply line. By this date, rail communication had been restored but resupply still lagged. See Foote, *Civil War*, III:353.

William Christie to James Christie[25]

IN LINE OF BATTLE NEAR BIG SHANTY, GEORGIA,

JUNE 14, 1864.

My Dear Father;

   T. D. has had a very narrow escape. He was down at one of the flies by our gun-limber, cleaning his revolver, when a heavy ball passed through a haversack on the ground near him, and cut a hole in his boot, just in line with his ancle. We are glad it was no worse. I am now No. 6 on our gun. My duties are, to cut fuses and deal out ammunition, receiving my orders from sergeant T. D. Our line of battle runs nearly due East and West. When we first took this position our center was in advance of the wings. But now, after three day's skirmishing, our wings are slightly in advance of the center. Our Battery is on the right of the Left Wing. Near us, to the right, is the Georgia Central R.R. In our front is an open space of cleared ground, somewhat rolling, and dotted with clumps of sassafras bushes. These are occupied by our skirmishers and those of the enemy. Several of ours (of the 3d and 4th Divisions) have gradually reached the edge of the woods beyond the field. There is a very high hill on our front, called "Lost Mountain." The rebels have a strong force on its top. Right at the very top is a signal station; we see it plainly. They work it vigorously all the time. We felt for them yesterday; and one of our guns gave them a few rounds this morning. But we got no response, Except from the sharpshooters. Their movements are hidden by heavy timber. I believe we shall flank them out very soon. "Fighting Joe" Hooker drove them four miles on Tuesday, on our right, taking some prisoners. Yesterday our Left made an advance, capturing about a hundred men. Mud abounds, after recent rains. We have built three lines of works since Saturday, and tonight I think we shall build a fourth.

   I saw Gen. McPherson last evening; he looked pale and weary. He is far more popular with us than Blair. The latter we regard as a politician; besides, he is a hard drinker.[26] For that reason alone he should never have

   25. Transcribed in Thomas Christie reminiscence.
   26. Francis Blair came from a family with strong political ties. He served a term in Congress as a Free Soil Party representative from Missouri in 1856. His brother, Montgomery Blair, was a member of Lincoln's cabinet, and the two of them had been active supporters of the president's 1860 campaign. Further, both had important connections in two border states, Missouri and Kentucky, working to support pro-Union activities there. Although clearly a "political" general, Blair earned the respect of both Sherman and Grant for his military leadership. Warner, *Generals in Blue*, 35–36.

been given the command of our Corps. It is too bad that the men he is responsible for should suffer because of his vices. But God will make all things right in the end.

Things look brighter in the East, now that our old Grant is there. I saw lately a letter from a soldier in the Army of the Potomac to his brother here; he lost a finger in battle and is in the hospital. He says they are within four hours' march of Richmond. Grant and his army are doing well. We are proud of him as our first Commander . . .

∽

Thomas Christie to James Christie[27]

THE FRONT, NEAR KENNESAW MOUNTAIN, GEORGIA

JUNE 21ST, 1864

My Dear Father,

Some time has passed since I wrote you, but my excuse is a good one, Duty. We are all full of health and hope. At times we have to work very hard, and must always be on the alert. On an average we fire about 75 rounds a day from each gun. We are now in position on a ridge facing almost south-east parallel to the rail-road; this runs through the narrow valley between us and Kennesaw mountain. The mountain is occupied by the rebels; they have 3 or 4 guns on the top; ours point straight at them. Today we have fired enough at different points on the mountain to determine the range. Our part of the line is not doing much; we do not know the reason; we are not permitted to fire without orders. But to judge by the cannonading and mus-ketry there was heavy fighting on our right yesterday.[28] They say it was in front of Hooker. The great battle must soon take place, for the enemy is almost entirely surrounded; he cannot fall back quite so easily as he has done heretofore. Our line is so strong that they would make nothing in the attempt to break out. We have more guns than can be brought into posi-tion. Our battery always has a good place in the front. Everybody says we have well earned it. The Generals say they never saw better practice than we made on the 15th, 16th and 17th. We were firing at a battery at a distance of about 2,000 yards. Gen Gresham sent a note to Capt. Spear, our chief of

27. Transcribed in Thomas Christie reminiscence.
28. A number of probing attacks by Sherman's forces sought to outflank the Con-federate positions on Kennesaw Mountain. Foote, Civil War, III:392.

artillery, giving us a hearty compliment. My piece, "the Ranger," has fired since we came to the front 201 rounds of shell and shrapnel. 55 rounds were percussion shell, a splendid projectile, which bursts when it strikes. Perhaps I ought not to say it, but my gun has made the best average of all in firing. The battery with which we fought the duel was on a hill covered with green pines. Our Captain watched our firing for a long time—and then christened my piece "the Green Mountain Ranger." That rebel battery was the one in which Gen. Polk was killed on the 14th. An unexploded shell passed through his body, taking off both his arms. It was the day that sharpshooter sent his bullet through my breeches. I wrote you that day or the next; and had just finished the letter when a man was mortally wounded right at the end of the tarpaulin in which I was sitting. On the same day one of our fellows got a rap on the nose from a spent ball.

I am in the best of health. This is a mountain region, very different from the swamps of Louisiana and Mississippi. Our only trouble is, that we do not get half enough to eat, a little hard bread, a little coffee, and occasionally a very little meat—day after day that is all; so there is not much variety. This morning my gun detachment got together enough money to buy a fifty-pound box of hard tack; it cost us five cents a pound, but it tasted good.[29] Please send me a fiver, for if this thing continues I shall surely need it. Perhaps our half-starved condition is the secret of our good health; but it is not a pleasant medicine. To hold in your two hands all the food you are to have for two days; to know that if you eat all you want for one meal, you will have to make up for it by eating nothing for a whole day,—what say you to that sort of thing? Never mind! If only we can give these fellows a good beating before a month is over, I shall punish your mutton and potatoes and soft bread and milk and butter mightily this fall! . . .

Thomas Christie to Alexander Christie

THE FRONT, GA JULY 1ST / 64

Dear Brother,

Your letter with the account of the terrible drought you were afflicted with, was rec'd. on the 28th Ult. having been posted on the 23d, Pretty quick time from Clyman. But I was disappointed on reading it at the extremely

29. They probably made their purchase from a sutler, but one wonders how he came by it.

small space you devoted to the account of your late Expedition to Milwaukee, for I wanted a long letter on that subject alone, which I know would be interesting, and which I hope you will furnish us, if you have not already done so.[30]

Here, the position is still unchanged, except that our two wings have swung around toward each other, so the Johnstone is now in something of the scrape that Pemberton was the victim of at V'burg Our wings are very strong in men, but deficient in position, while the rest of the Line is in splendid position, but pretty thin in Men. Our Division is on the Left Centre, and is extended over almost twice the ground that it occupied in the first Line of Battle.

We do nothing beyond active skirmishing, the Batteries assisting our pickets when the Rebels get too saucy, and sometimes directing a shot at the heavy works on the Mountain, but in other parts of the Line the fighting has occasionally been very severe. One of these conflicts took place during the night of the 29th in which Davis' Division was engaged. The cannonade and roll of small Arms was very heavy, as heard by us, and we have since heard that the Rebels charged on our fellows, took them by surprise, and were in their pits before our chaps recovered themselves, when an awful hand to hand fight ensued in which the enemy were driven out, swept with Canister as they fell back, and in turn charged by our fellows who drove them over their own Rifle Pits, and intrenched in an advanced position, having taken 500 prisoners, and *Killed* as many more. I am told by an Officer who was over the ground yesterday morning, that the dead Butternuts lay more thickly than he saw them at Shiloh. But, of course you have heard of it, and of all our other doings on the Right & Left, so I will confine myself to more individual matters.[31]

30. In farm diary entries for June 1864, Alexander noted the extreme drought conditions: "Everybody allows this to be the driest time experienced in this country" (June 7, 1864). On his train trip to Milwaukee (June 9), he observed the parched fields and pastures, "dust flying on the latter in great clouds." He was largely unimpressed by the city, finding it "below my expectations," but he did purchase a good rifle for $27. On the day he wrote to Tom, June 23, he recorded the noon temperature as 102. Christie papers, box 45, vol. 20.

31. The action described here was not a major battle, but on June 27 Sherman attempted a full-scale assault on the Confederate positions around Kennesaw Mountain. The attack failed, and Sherman returned to his strategy of flanking movements. It is curious that Thomas makes no mention of this effort, since it started with an hour-long barrage by all Union artillery, during which morning reports show the battery fired 110 rounds. See Foote, *Civil War*, III:395–400.

We are all the same as usual, and our Guns are in the same positions as when I last wrote. Bullets fly around pretty thickly and many men have been killed & wounded close by us, but beyond some very narrow escapes the men of the Battery are not molested by the leaden messengers. Jesse, who, by the way, never felt better in his life, had a bullet put through his tarpaulin, which was full of his men at the time. Did you get that Rebel Newspaper I sent you yesterday yet? I told you in that that my position as Sergeant is secured by an order from Company HdQrs. I am the only one of the old Corporals who is promoted, the others who were comm'd'g Platoons as Sergts. having been reduced to their original positions, and some of the men who were acting Corporals have been reduced. It is as I thought it would be in that respect, the Capt. has delayed giving Warrants to us till he saw how we would do in the new positions, and now that we have been fairly tried he retains some permanently, and reduces others.

Southwick is put in as Qr. Master Sergt. the old Quartermaster,—Everts— having been assigned to the command of a Gun. Wiltse is confirmed as corporal, but O'Hara is reduced, for not doing his duty as Corpl. of the Guard recently, they say. My promotion does not elate me much, although of course it pleases me as it is a kind of acknowledgement that my Duty has been done as it should, and although I am a modest Kind of fellow, as *you know* and do not like to speak much of myself, yet I will indulge for once in a little self-praise by simply saying that if I have not done my duty while in the Service it was *not* because I have not tried. So that is the last piece of Egotism you may expect from me for some time.

My Gun broke an Axle band by recoil, is mending now, and that is why I have a little leisure. Remember me to all as I remember you and, accept this from your Loving Brother, Sergt. Christie

[margin note: first page] John Schaller and George Ehinger were well a day or two ago when I saw them. Send down a half dozen Pocket Handkerchiefs Good towel, rough & heavy, Had to leave all these things at H.V.

[margin note: back page] Will draw pay for the past 2 Months as sergt.

William Christie to Alexander Christie

IN THE FIELD IN SIGHT OF ATLANTA JULY 9TH, 1864

Dear Brother, I received a letter from you a day or two ago, in which I learned all about your trip to and from Millwaukee. I am glad you enjoyed yourself so much and has [gotten?] such a splendid rifle. But I do not like to hear of you wishing so much to be a soldier. just wait until fall when our Battery will discharge her old three years men and then you can join us that is if you see no better way of letting off your patriotism between now and then.

What shall I write about shall [I] go over the last two weeks after T.D. no, but I will go over the past two days, or three and then you may be sure we are having hot weather, hot work and excitement enough to keep us lively. we left our position on a hill about three thousand yards from the rebel lines, three nights ago, and moved off to the left of our own Division intoo the right of the fifteenth corps; so that we might be in the front, for you must know we are a crack battery, (Gen Grensham says we have the Best horses, the best men, [that?] we would fight and steal like h_ll and Da___tn.) and we are put forward in all hard places, we enjoyed our selves in our new fort very finely for the first night and second day, and just at close of day the rebs oppened out fourteen guns on our Battery, we had been ill using them all day, and they thought they had us at a disadvantage, and to tell the truth they had, for we were short of ammunition and the could only get four guns to bear on them, but we gave as good as we got and if all is true more for we killed some of them and they did not hurt us, not in the least, but they banged our fort in a most villanios manner, bursting shell all round us and in our embrasures; in the middle of the day they throwed over some shell and killed an Infantry man close by the end of our work. he was a fifer in the fifteenth Mich. in the time of the heavy firing in the evening the shell that flew over us killed a few men, besides mules and horses, indeed the cannonading was terrific, and between our batteries and [those] of Johnny Reb, the noise was deaffening. in the morning of the 7th we moved out of that position, and moved intoo our present one, in front of the other and too its right, and I am glad to say in front of our own Division. Iowa Brigade and the Boys are glad to have us with them, we are about six hundred yards from the skirmish line and nearly double that from the main works of the enemy, and are in front of every Battery on our line as far as I can hear, there is nothing in our front but the skirmishers of our Division, and [we] are under the cross fire of some of our other Batteries, and we find but little quiteness[32]

32. After maneuvering Johnston's army out of strong positions at Kennesaw Mountain and Smyrna, Sherman's army faced the Confederate Army of the Tennessee, placed in what the general called "the best line of field intrenchments I have ever seen," near

I suppose you have not crops in Wis. but it would be more vexing to see good crops spoiled as these are down here, by an invading force. By the by the rebs have been asking if our Battery has revolving guns; and think we abuse them by sharpshooting with them. Gen Gas, I hear you cry, but it's no Gas we are able to make the [prettiest?] kind of shooting as fine as Minnie rifle shooting, and my ears are now almost deaf with the discharge of our guns, and the cry is bully from our [?] and Infantry and our skirmishers cheer to see us pop it to the grey Backs.

I have nothing to say of much account, only that we are as a company in fine health, and T. D. and self as well as can be, and make our [rations?] disappear with wonderfull appetites: send us some Ink however as soon as possible, and be sure we nead it, it is almost imposable to get anything of writing material here, and then only at fabulous prices. Love to all, tell Sarah to write.

yours affectionally William G. Christie

[addendum]

ᏃᎥ

Thomas Christie to Alexander Christie

CHATTAHOOTCHIE TO CLYMAN: GREETINGS,

THE FRONT, GA. JULY 9TH 1864

My Dear Brother,

I finish Williams letter for the purpose of congratulating you on this your Birthday. Long may you live to see many more of them, & all brining as good health & happiness as I doubt not you are now enjoying. If you could see us this afternoon, sweltering with heat beside our smoking Guns, you would not think *we* could take half the pleasure, the "solid comfort" that we *do* appropiate. In the words of the immortal Skuddyhunk, "We still live," if we didn't you would not be reading this from yours truly.

I have a little business to write about, however, & must not defer it to the Postscript. It is briefly this, & is expressed in four words, I want a watch. I

Vining's Station on high ground just west of the Chattahoochee River. They were only eight miles from Atlanta, and the city was visible from parts of the Union line. On the day this letter was written, Yankee scouts would find an unguarded ford beyond the Confederate right flank, allowing Sherman once again to outmaneuver Johnston's army and begin the siege of Atlanta. See Foote, *Civil War*, III:401–6.

must have one, can't do without one in my present position, & it must also be a *good* one. The one I had did not posses the last important quality, & so I sold it, for __ I am ashamed to say how small a sum, all in Prommissory Notes, which is the only kind of currency in vogue in the Company, but to return to business, I want Father to send to the American Watch company at Waltham Mass, forward about 30 dollars & direct them to send by Mail to my Address a *good* article I forget the names of the different kinds of watches they manufacture, but I suppose the "Ellery" will be good enough, or what they call the "soldier's watch" would do If you could see one of their catalogues, you could select one of about the right price.[33] One thing is certain, & so Father should tell them in his letter, I want a *good* *timekeeper* for *use* & not to trade on, so I don't care about anything fancy, & I must also have it *soon*.

My Income will be 20 dollars per month since the 1st of May & I must "support the dignity of my position" Ah won't I cut a swell among you fellows about the middle of August, the "other stripe" Veteran Chevron & all the rest. It won't do, though, to anticipate too much though for we have a tremendous big job to do yet here, which may occupy us a month yet, but not more, I think We are under orders to be ready to repel an attack this afternoon, for some thing is going on that will develop "something" more. We are out in advance of the whole Line, the Post of Honor, inside good works & don't give a darn for anybody Be sure that Father attends to the watch business, & give my love to all the Grandmothers, & mother & Sarah, all the rest. Yours contentedly,

Thos. D Christie

～

Thomas Christie to Alexander Christie

BATTLEFIELD, NEAR ATLANTA, JULY 25TH 1864

Dear Sandy:

We got a Mail yesterday for the first time since leaving the Chattahoochee and among the letters were two from father, and one from you, telling about the Rifle and finding fault because I do not write longer letters, which

33. In the early years of the war, the American Watch Company of Waltham, Massachusetts, developed a line of good-quality, moderately priced watches for use by the military. These "soldier's watches" were popular and sold well, helping make the company one of the largest producers in the nation. Thomas, *Antique American Clocks*, 179.

is I think, a little ungenerous, seeing that I improve *every opportunity* to send you news of us. You must remember that my time is not my own, that I have duties to perform which I cannot neglect without injury to the service in which I am engaged and which duties, at present, take up very nearly *all* my available time.

There are hundreds of incidents occurring here daily that would be of great interest to you, and to myself in after years, if I could have the chance to record them in either diary or correspondence, but after all, this is only a little matter compared to the real earnest work which it is our business to perform. So don't grumble at short [letters?] but be thankfull you get *any*. My memory is pretty good, and with the assistance of my diary I will be able to give you many an interesting incident when I have a chance.

However, as we do nothing today of much account, having built our fort yesterday and as you have not yet had from us a recital of our adventures since leaving the Chattahoochee, I will give a brief resume of them up to the present. On the morning of the 16th we were roused at 2 O'clock with orders to withdraw the Guns from the fort overlooking the Chattahoochee, limber up and prepare to march. This was done, and at daylight our Corps was on the road to Marietta, our Division in the advance, stopped in the middle of the day, and rested till 5 in the afternoon, then resumed march and stopped for the night near Marrietta. Took up Line of March early next morning and passed through town on the Roswell road, which latter place we reached in the afternoon, pushed through it, crossed the River on bridge that the 16th Corps put in a week before and halted 4 miles this side, having made about 20 miles. On the 18th and 19th we made slow progress towards Decatur, camping on the night of the 19th within 4 miles. Next day passed through Decatur leaving the 16th Corps there, our Corps taking the advance, and when 2 miles from town on the Atlanta road formed Line of Battle and advanced slowly. At almost noon our Infty ran on a Rebel Battery and stopped. The Genl. sent back by all the other Batteries of the Division (we were marching in the Rear) and ordered us up to silence the Reb Guns. Advanced and took position on a hill, along which ran a road through the pasture at 1800 yards distance from the Enemy's Battery, unlimbered under their fire, got up the Hotchkiss shell from the Limbers and opened, as the boys say "for God's sake." They had the Range on us from the start, as they had measured the ground before falling back, and slapped the shells right into us from the first shot, while we had to fire several rounds before we could get the Elevation, as the ground is very deceiving, but we kept raising it till we knew what was wanted, and then you could have seen some fine practice. The Action continued for about 50 minutes, during which time each of our pieces fired about 40 Rds. [rounds] when the Johnnies could stand it no longer and withdrew, Genl. McPherson came up and told the Capt. he never saw a prettier Artillery duel, and told us also what we had not observed ourselves, that one of our shells knocked one of their Guns up on end which we afterwards found to be true when our fellows took the hill on which the Battery had been, and saw the broken "stock" of one of their pieces. I never want to see shells fly thicker than they did at us there, and it is a marvel that none of the men were seriously hurt.[34] Four of our fancy horses were killed and another wounded three of them by one shell, which burst under the Limber, throwing splinters and gravel right in the Captain's face, one piece struck the top of my Limber chest close to W. who was giving out Ammunition. A shell burst under the trail of the 5th Piece, tearing it badly and knocking down No. 3 who was serving vent another unexploded one ricochetted (pro. ricoshayed) and struck the wheel of my piece, doing no damage, but coming very close to Nos. 2 and 4 on that side. Another struck at the feet, almost, of my No. 1 and exploded, enveloping him in a cloud of dust. I was standing close by watching the effect of my shots and when the dust cleared I looked for O'Neal expecting to see him stretched out but he was erect in the position of "Ready," which command had just been given when the shell came among us. I admired his coolness so much that I immediately grasped his hand, with a "Bully for you old boy." I could not ask men to stand up under heavy fire any better than did the fellows of my Gun Detachment. I cannot recount half the "hair breadth 'scapes" we had, but you will see we had a hot time of it. When the Enemy's battery was withdrawn our 2 Divisions of Infty. advanced, and some skir- mishing took place in which Genl. Gresham was wounded in front of the Battery. On the night of the 20th we dug little works for the Guns but did not fire a shot next day, as they put other Batteries in position in front of us.

About 9 A.M. of the 21st our whole Line, (that is of the Corps) advanced, and charged the Rebel works, lost a large number of men in Killed and wounded, took a lot of prisoners and part of the enemy's works, and estab- lished a Line within close distance. John Shaller was wounded in this charge, in which his Regt. captured the 4th (?) Ga., but suffered severely. I

34. The Confederacy had difficulty manufacturing reliable ammunition, especially shells and case shot, which relied on fuses to explode when and where intended. See Ripley, *Artillery and Ammunition*, 277.

sent you and his wife particulars of the event and will only add that I saw him yesterday and both wounds were doing well, his appetite is good and so are his spirits. We are having beautiful weather for the wounded, cool days and chilly nights, which seems almost providential for it has been so *only* since the heavy fighting began. This charge I am telling about was right in front of us and we wanted much to assist our gallant Infantry fellows who were under a galling fire from the same Battery we had silenced in another place. If the Genl. had only let Clayton put us in position where he wanted to, we could have stopped the fire of the confounded scamps.[35]

But I must get on; that afternoon our Battery was moved out to the extreme Left of the Line, and we threw up slight works on the extreme flank, But we did not have enough Range for Rifled guns, so the Chief of Artillery ordered us out in the evening and the 2nd Regular Battery, with 12 pds, Light guns went into our works while we went back and took position in a fort in font of the hill from which we had silenced the Rebel Battery the day before, left our horses harnessed all night, and in the morning found the Rebs had left their works in front of us, where upon we unharnessed and the Infty advanced a half mile till the Enemy's Battery began shelling them. Then we had orders to harness and be ready to move to the front. Got ready and limbered up the guns, took and early dinner, and shortly after began to hear dropping shots *in our rear*. Were told that it was Wheeler's Cavalry playing smash with our Corps train. I jumped on my horse and rode out on the field in front where our fellows were scattered around looking at the bodies of the Killed, warned them all to their posts and spurred back, in time to see a Brigade and 2 Batteries of the 16th Corps come up on the double quick and form line in the rear of our Battery, *facing to the rear*. They had not more than got into position when our pickets were driven in and the Rebel Line advanced. The 2 Batteries, 14th Ohio, and Co. "H" 1st Mo. opened on them and the Infty line soon was engaged heavily; first the Rebs would yell and charge till they came within 50 yrds. of the Battery, when the fire would be too much for them and they would waver; then

35. The Army of the Tennessee had moved to the extreme left of the Union lines and was advancing on Atlanta from the east, taking Decatur, Georgia, and breaking the Georgia Railway, Atlanta's link to the Carolinas. On July 20 the Seventeenth Corps ran into resistance from Wheeler's Cavalry, supported by Patrick Cleburne's division, at a place called Bald Hill. Initial attempts to take this position failed, and General Gresham was seriously wounded. He was replaced by General Giles A. Smith. The corps succeeded in taking the position on July 21. Welcher, *Union Army*, II:456–61. For a detailed description of the Bald Hill attack, see Woodworth, *Nothing but Victory*, 531–36.

our chaps would cheer and charge with the bayonet, fall back again when the enemy rallied, and let the canister play into them, and so it went, till the last time the Johnnies charged, when they brought their flag out in plain sight of us, so close to the 14th Ohio that the smoke of their guns dashed over it, the canister thundered out twice as fast, our whole Line poured in a deadly volley, the standard bearer fell, the advancing Rebels faltered, our fellows sprang forward and there was a short hand to hand conflict over the fallen flag, the bayonets being locked and the muskets clubbed for a moment; then our chaps got the standard and the Enemy fled, leaving the field, with their heaps of dead and wounded and cords of muskets in our hands. This was only a small part of the field of Battle, for the Rebs charged on our Corps at the same time of this fight with part of the 16th, charged on the 15th and also on the 4th Corps, captured some Artillery, but lost the heaviest in Killed wounded and prisoners that they have since Stone River. This was the only part of the battle that we saw, and so I have described it to you, and you may imagine the rest of the field from it. The Iowa Brigade of our Division is badly cut up; they fought back to back at one time, when attacked in font and rear, and actually jumped over their slight works *seven times* to repel assaults form their rear; as soon as they would drive them off from one side the Enemy would come up on the other, when they would "change front to fire to the Rear," and jump over the protecting Earthworks. The 16th and 12th Wis. also were heavily engaged, but the Rebels did not succeed in breaking up a single Regt. of our old Corps, while whole Brigades of theirs were "wiped out," there being hardly a grease spot left of the Kentucky Brigade, which were the ones I saw fight. The Brigade of the 16th Corps that fought them and whose battle I have described is composed of the 66th Ills. (Geo. Ehinger's Regt.) 81st Ohio and 12th Ills. Genl. McArthur's old Regt. (I had a talk with George last night, and he is in splendid health and spirits. Is to answer the letter he got from Sarah soon) You may ask what was our Battery doing in all this time? We stood at our posts during the first part of the fight in our rear and the rest of the time we were led around by Genl. Blair into *6 different positions,* not being allowed to open at any of them. At last, when the heaviest of the fighting was over, a Rebel Battery, to cover the retreat, opened on our advancing skirmishers, when we were allowed to reply and after a few shots effectually silenced the Battery.

I forgot to notice that when the fighting at first was beginning to be serious, Genl. McPherson rode down by us, going to the place where the Brigade I have mentioned was forming; he rode right through the line, out to the front where the skirmishing was going on, and before he suspected, was right among the advancing Enemy. They told him to halt, but he wheeled to escape, when they fired on him and shot him through the breast. It was not 10 minutes after he passed us till he was hit. No language can tell the grief that fills the heart of every man in the Army of the Tennessee, and especially do we of his old Corps feel his loss. Not a man of us but would willingly have given his own life to save that of our much loved young Commander.[36]

Your Brother Thos. D. Christie

[margin note: top of fifth page] I send you a piece of handkerchief 2 stamps and a letter from Rebel Genl, Tyler to Col. Wall of the 15th Tennessee, all found in the pockets of the dead Colonel, not by me though, for that is a thing I have never done yet,—turn dead men's pockets outside in—This field over which the Rebs charged was an awful sight afterwards, and we did not get in all the wounded Rebels till night of the next day.

[margin note: first page] July 26th counldn't finish this yesterday, for we expected to move. All is quiet this M. [morning?] Rec'd a five from Father yesterday, much obliged.

ᵔ

Thomas Christie to James Christie[37]

NEAR ATLANTA, JULY 29, 1864

Dear Father,

Since I last wrote the Army of the Tennessee has made another move, from left to the right, and fought another battle. On the night of the 26th,

36. This was the Battle of Atlanta or "Hood's Second Sortie from Atlanta." General John Bell Hood, now in command of Confederate forces, had withdrawn Hardee's corps from his front line on the night of June 21 and sent them on a long flank march around the left wing of the Union Army. Fortunately for Sherman, part of the Sixteenth Corps of Reynold's Army had been positioned behind the Seventeenth Corps: these troops stopped the main Confederate attack on the morning of June 22. Other Confederate troops attacked the Seventeenth Corps front from the Atlanta lines. In consequence, the Fourth Division's lines on Bald Hill were attacked from front and rear at times, as described in the letter. Colonel Belknap's Iowa Brigade received particular notice for its fighting that day. Welcher, *Union Army*, II:465–74; Hurter, "Narrative," *Minnesota in the Civil and Indian Wars*, I:646–47; Woodworth, *Nothing but Victory*, 557–62.

37. Transcribed in Thomas Christie reminiscence.

the 15th, 16th and 17th Corps withdrew from before the enemy. The wheels of our guns and caissons were provided with leather washers to prevent noise. We marched all night, our Battery leaving the fort at midnight, and halted the morning of the 27th in rear of the 4th Army Corps; here we got some breakfast, and took a nap till 9 o'clock. Then we resumed our march, going about seven miles. At no time were we more than 3 miles from Atlanta; some of the boys said that Sherman was trying the Jericho plan. At dark that night we had our lines well established on the right of the 14th Army Corps. This brought us very near the railroad, south of Atlanta. The under-brush was so thick that we could not place the artillery; so the fighting yesterday was nearly all by the infantry. Yesterday morning the skirmishers advanced to the railroad; the line of battle fortified in a good position; and a few guns were planted, among them the left Section of our Battery.

About noon the Rebels, having massed 3 Corps in our front, made a furious attack on our two, the 15th and 17th. Our heavy line of skirmishers was driven like chaff before the wind. The Johnnies came on with a yell, in six lines of battle, and the action began in earnest. Our fellows never withdrew one inch; however, the enemy came up very close, several times planting their colors on our rude breastworks. At one time on the works of the Iowa Brigade there were 4 Rebel flags; our boys brought them all in, the color-guards with them. Never have we seen the enemy charge so fiercely and persistently. The battle raged at intervals all the afternoon; but when night fell we were still masters of the field. Our prisoners were many, our loss very small as compared with that of the enemy. Their dead and wounded lay literally in heaps upon the ground. Our men were partially under cover, while the Rebels came up in the open, and in so many lines that our bullets could scarcely miss hitting some of them. I never saw our gallant fellows in better heart that they were last night. The regular "three times three" that we gave after the fight was over were a good deal pleasanter to hear than the Indian yells with which the Johnnies advanced to the charge.[38]

38. This letter describes the Battle of Ezra Church. The Army of the Tennessee, now under the command of Oliver O. Howard, was moved from the far left of the Union forces to the extreme right in an attempt to cut the last railway connection to Atlanta from the south. To alleviate this threat, General Hood sent two corps of his army, under the command of Alexander Steward and Stephen D. Lee, to meet the Army of the Tennessee while it was still in motion, hoping to attack its flank near Ezra Church. However, Union troops were already in place before the Confederates advanced; the result was a bloody repulse of Hood's forces. Welcher, *Union Army*, II:474–80; Woodworth, *Nothing but Victory*, 569–76.

All the men of our Army know and feel that Northern courage, skill, and generalship are more than a match for the desperate efforts of the leaders in this Rebellion; we are only sorry for the poor ignorant rank and file whose lives are wasted in these encounters. Somehow or other, our men always fight with confident expectation of final success; this, no doubt, has a great influence upon the result. Have no fears for us then; we feel adequate to the undertaking that we have in hand; we only wish that our friends could see as well as we do how things are working.

The Battery is now in position on the right of the 14th Corps; except the Section which was engaged yesterday, and which is with our own Corps. One of our Colonels went out over the field yesterday, as he has been in the habit of doing ever since the War began, and found the body of his brother, a Colonel in the Rebel Army. I was present when he found him, and shall not attempt to describe the scene. Sergeants Heywood and Fall[39] are now Second Lieutenants.

Yours ever,

T.D.C.

∽

Thomas Christie to Alexander Christie

MIGHTY NEAR ATLANTA, GA. JULY 30TH 1864.

My Dear Sandy,

You grumble so much at my short letters that I must try this afternoon to give you a long one, and if it proves to be so long as to be tiresome you have yourself to blame. I begin this letter now, not yet having determined what I shall write about, but as I proceed the plan will develop itself, as the Novel writers say. In the first place I will have to remark on the extraordinary health we, in common with the rest of the Army, are enjoying. In the midst of hard work with spade and sponge staff, night marches an night labor, hot weather and short grub we are actually in better condition now than when we were at Vicksburg through the winter,—not a man from the Company in the hospital on account of sickness, and we are a fair sample of the whole of Sherman's Army. Everybody remarks on the ruddy cheeks and clear complexions of the men, their hearty appetites and jovial humor

39. F. L. Haywood (see page 183, note 15, Thomas to Sarah, Nov. 28th 1863) and James Fall both enlisted from St. Anthony. Fall was from New Brunswick. *Adjutant General's Report*, 783, 785.

and everyone seems to feel as if with such an Army, such leaders and such a cause we must be successful.[40]

(31ST) Was interrupted yesterday by orders to move, harnessed and hitched up, and left the woods in which we had stayed for 2 days, to proceed a half mile to the rear and go into park to rest a while and let other Batteries *that have not been engaged yet* go to the front in their turn. So we are now enjoying ourselves in the cool shade of our tarpaulins, our horses tied to the Picket Rope as in the old Garrison times, and everybody busy at washing 2 weeks dirt our of their shirts, mending the Campaign rents in our Huntsville-drawn breeches and reading, writing, and cooking of choice dishes by the Epicureans.

Our coming to the Rear, though did not add much to our security, for the Johnnies have got a good thing on this part of the Line with their big Guns. They have been shelling the woods in this vicinity regularly since the battle of the 28th, from their forts in town, and as a group of us were standing talking in the park last evening, a hundred pds Parrott percussion shell came along shrieking like mad, struck close to the 1st Caisson, ricochetted, broke one of the wheels of the caisson and exploded between the Ammunition chests, blowing up one of them and breaking another so that the tow on top of the powder inside took fire, but which we speedily extinguished with a bucket of water from a cook fire luckily near. There were 40 men within as many feet at the time of the explosion and several of us were within half that distance 2 men being so close that the powder burnt their whiskers and yet no one was seriously hurt, one or two being knocked down by splinters and some by the concussion. But the same thing might happen 20 times without so many narrow *escapes*. The splinters of the Ammunition chest, and the mess chest, which was also stove all to flinders, flew all around us, one of the men with whom I was talking getting a rap with a small fragment that knocked him flat, and some of the harness, on racks near by, was blown 50 yards. One of our mule drivers, close by the Caisson at the time of the terrific explosion was struck on the head by a splinter, and the concussion so crazed him that he got up and ran over two miles, so fast that three of our fellows who started after him thinking he was "clean murthered" had the greatest difficulty in catching him. He says this morning

40. Statistics support Thomas's perception. In July 1864, Sherman's forces had an illness rate of 19.9 percent compared to the overall U.S. Army average of 28.7 percent. Glatthaar, *March to the Sea,* 196–97. Further, the morning reports show only two men on the sick list for the entire month.

that all he wants now, is to fight a Duel with the Man on the Rebel Gun who pulled the Lanyard that fired it. Our Mule Drivers are unlucky—the only man we had wounded on the 22nd was the driver on the Battery wagon.[41] So you see there is as much safety at the Gun in these days of long-range Artillery as anywhere in the Rear. We may laugh about that accident yesterday, but it is a mercy that the whole camp was not filled with killed and wounded men. Genl. Leggett,[42] on seeing the place this morning said that we were a lucky set of men and that it was "better to be born lucky than rich," and so our fellows begin to think, for we have had most wonderful escapes, as you know.

I had a splendid view day before yesterday of the famous city of Atlanta with all its forts and defences, from the top of a tree into which I climbed with a Field Glass slung to me and by whose aid I could see the groups of Rebel women standing on the parapets of the big fort a mile and a half distant, looking out towards where the crack of our skirmisher's rifles proclaimed the advancing Yankees. Atlanta is a beautiful city being spread over a large extent of rolling ground, the smaller houses being completely hidden by the shade trees that grow all through the streets.

The city is directly East of where I am now writing and is very nearly surrounded by our troops, the wings of the Army being only about 2 miles apart. I think it is Sherman's plan to completely surround it and begin a regular siege. When I had the view of it, the gangs of impressed negroes were busy throwing up a rude rifle pit to connect the forts, so that it seems the last flank movement of the Army of the Tennessee was a surprise to old Gov. Brown[43] and the rest of them.

I see in the accounts of our fight on the 22nd published in the Louisville papers, the most glaring mistakes in regard to the different Corps engaged and for fear you do not understand how Sherman's Army is organized, I will tell you. Sherman's Grand Army is composed of the troops of three Departments of the Military Division of the Mississippi, each commanded by the Departmental commander, and all independent of each other, acting

41. According to the First Battery Company Morning Reports, "Prvt. Grant," probably Albert C. Grant, was wounded on this date.

42. Mortimer D. Leggett, an educator in Akron, Ohio, served first on the staff of General McClellan in 1861 and later commanded the Seventy-eighth Ohio. He distinguished himself as a brigade commander during the Vicksburg campaign in Logan's Division of the Seventeenth Corps and probably knew the First Minnesota Battery. At the time of this battle, he commanded a division in that corps. Warner, *Generals in Blue*, 278–79.

43. Joseph E. Brown, governor of Georgia. Wakelyn, *Biographical Dictionary*, 113.

under the supreme command of Genl. Sherman. These Armies are—The
Army of the Cumberland, Genl. Thomas; The Army of the Ohio, Genl.
Schofield; and our own Army of the Tennessee before the 22nd under
McPherson, then for a while under Genl. Logan, and now commanded by
Maj. Genl. Howard, one of the best men in Uncle Sam's Army.[44] Now each
of these Armies is composed of Army Corps,— the Army of the Cumber-
land of three—the 4th Corps, of Howard's (I do not know who commands
it now,) the 14th Corps—(Palmers) and the 20th Corps (Hooker's) The
Army of the Ohio has only one Corps here,—the 23rd—and Schofield commands it in person—The Army of the Tennessee has three corps, the 15th
(Genl Logan,) 16th (Genl. Dodge), and the 17th (Genl. Blair.) Each of the
Army Corps is composed of 2, 3, or 4 Divisions, and the Divisions are sub-
divided into Brigades, composed of three or four Regts. each. The two Divisions of our Corps that are present (3rd and 4th) are commanded now by
Genls. Legget and Giles M. Smith respectively, since our Genl. Gresham
was wounded on the 20th. Now you understand how Sherman's Army is
composed, better than two thirds of the Army Correspondents here.

{ 2– P.M.} Your letter of the 24th is come to hand and I am greatly
delighted with it, you need stirring up once in a while to move you from
your usual monotony of style, (you see I speak plainly, as becomes a friend
I think you must, or should appreciate this present epistle, for it has cost
me already, about 6 dollars, I will explain. I went out into the shade in the
woods to write, took out my pocket book to get a steel pen, laid it on the
ground beside me till I would want to return the pen, went to writing, got
interested, as I always do, was called off presently by the Capt to inspect
the Ammunition chests, put away the writing materials and come off, leaving the pocket book, containing 4 of the dollars Father sent me (I had paid
a debt with the other one in the morning) My gold pen, and a pencil. Of
course, when I missed it soon after, and went to look for it, it was gone,
some of the men having picked it up. I am not without hopes of having
it returned, but if it is lost it will be a good lesson to me. You need not

44. Oliver O. Howard, a West Point graduate, held various commands in the Army
of the Potomac, most notably that of the ill-fated Eleventh Corps routed at both Chancellorsville and Gettysburg. Despite these setbacks, he was well regarded for his personal
courage and had commanded the Fourth Corps in the Atlanta Campaign at the time of
General McPherson's death. His promotion to command the Army of the Tennessee
offended the more senior-ranking General Hooker, who resigned. Warner, *Generals in
Blue*, 237–38.

trouble sending any more for it is said we are to be paid soon. Now, as to yourself, I approve of your intention to enlist for but 2 years, as that will let you out when we come home, but as to your preference for the Infantry, I must tell you it is wrong, an I know from experience, *and as every foot soldier in this Army will tell you*. There is no branch of the Service that will compare with the Artillery for desireableness, or for opportunity to render distinguished services, and it will be a life-long regret to you if you join any other. If I had room I would give you the reasons. However, have patience till we go home, and spend our furlough with us, for before that you cannot get into the company on account of the fact that we have now 165 men and are only entitled to 156. When the now veterans go out in the beginning of October there will be a chance for a few Recruits. I spoke to the Capt. about it after the receipt of your letter, and he told me to have you wait till I go home when I will get authority to recruit and so save trouble and expense to you. Think of the duck hunting we will have with that famous rifle when you again see your Affectionate brother

    Thomas D. Christie

❧

Thomas Christie to Alexander Christie

NEAR ATLANTA GA, AUGUST 4TH 1864

My Dear Sandy;

Our Mail facilities are far better now than they have been before, since we came into the Service, for here we are getting letters almost daily, and of very late dates too. For instance, your and Sarah's letters postmarked the 28th July came to us yesterday, the 3rd, so that we are actually much nearer home now than we were at Corinth, our Line of communication being all Rail Road. A man could go from Atlanta to Clyman in about four days, so we are not very far from you here after all.

Well, as I was saying, the Mail came in last evening, bringing to W. a short letter from Newton Centre and an equally short harvest note of the 26th from yourself, and to me a nice long letter from the Clyman School Maurm,[45] for which you will please thank her in my name, and tell her I take back and eat up all the chiding words that began my letter of yesterday

---

45. Sarah Christie received her teaching certificate the previous summer: see Jean Christie, "Sarah Christie Stevens, Schoolwoman," *Minnesota History* 48.6.

to her, and also that I will give her time to read that last effusion—say three days—before I let her have another one. This correspondence with all you Home people is more of a comfort to us than you can imagine, especially when we get good letters, as was that one of Sarah's of the 27th. I was reading yours last evening when the heavy roll of the skirmisher's rifles immediately in our front and the infernal yelling of the Johnnies, told us that one of their "charges" was on hand. The letters were hurriedly shoved into blouse pockets, the command of "Cannoniers to your Posts" was given, Spherical Case and Canister was hurried up from the Limbers, and every Man stood with Equipments buckled on, waiting for the order to Commence firing, when the skirmish Line should be driven in on the Line of battle. But no such thing was done: our fellows in the Rifle pits in front were reinforced promptly by Genl. Belknap, comd'g Brigade, and held the Rebs gallantly at bay, so that we had no chance to fire a shot. And after standing to our posts for a half hour the fire in front died away to sullen shots at long intervals, when the Cannoniers were allowed to lie down and take off their boots, their Ammunition and tube pouches under their heads, and with orders to be up and have the horses harnessed at three in the morning. So this morning we were all ready for the Attack, but none came, and this forenoon everything is still, except once in a while a shot from our ever watchful Riflemen in the Rifle pits. There was very heavy fighting on our extreme Left yesterday afternoon, as we could tell by the musketry and cannonading, but nothing has been heard of the result, or whether the battle was defensive on our side or not. The thing is evidently working to a point, and we will have a "fight or a foot race," probably both, in this vicinity soon, after which I hope to date my letters by dropping the prefix "Near."

I see by Sarah's letter that you have written to Malmros,[46] and think it is right, but you must not be in too much of a hurry about enlisting for the reasons which I told you before. But, above all, do not be tempted to go in any of the new Regts. Now forming, for it will be *the very worst thing* you can do, and repentance will come too late. Trust to our experience when we tell you that our branch of the service is the most preferable *on every account*, and the advantages you will gain by coming into this old, tried organization

46. Oscar Malmros, the state's adjutant general and the chief official responsible for recruiting Minnesota soldiers. This contact was the beginning of Alexander's long and fruitless attempt to join the First Minnesota Battery. He eventually found a place in the Second Minnesota Infantry, also part of Sherman's Army. See introduction to Christie papers.

with us are more than I could tell you in the space of a short letter like this. When you come down you will see the difference. A man in the Infantry loses his Identity almost, he is only such a Number in the Rear or Front Rank, for their duties are all precisely alike, and if any soldier is a Machine it is the Infantry man, while in a Platoon in the Artillery no two men perform the same duties, and everyone is far more independent and self reliant than in an Infty Company.

Each of our Platoons, working a Gun, is a little Republic, of which the Sergeant is chief Magistrate and the two Corporals his Assistants Everything is done about the internal affairs of the Platoon without consulting any Commissioned Officer, the Sergeant and, the Boys themselves being considered fully competent for all the various duties without that dependence on shoulder straps which is the peculiarity of the Foot service. One great reason why our Battery has such a good reputation is because all the men work as much for it as if each one was Capt; they all feel personally concerned in preserving the good name of the Comp'y and never need to be dealt with as other men are to make them do their duty. You will understand this, when I tell you that fully seven eights of them are Americans of the best type too. As proof of this, I send you a list of my Platoon and you may see by the names that many are from Puritan stock. The *best* portion of our Army is American, no matter what your Irish neighbors may say, and for a good specimen of a Radical, Protestant set of men you must come to us.[47] There is one character in my squad by the name of Smith, a New England peddler, with a head seven & five eighths, and well filled with whom you would be delighted. The study of him alone would be an everlasting treat to you. But I must send this off. Thos. D. Christie

[enclosure]

List of Men in 3rd Platoon, 1st Minn, Battery

Christie, Thos. D.——Sergeant—Ireland

Gross——Corporal Maine

Foster——Corporal New York

O'Neal——Cannonier—No. 1 Ireland (O'Neal is the only Catholic]

Applebee Cannonier—No. 2 England

Christie W. G. " " " 3 Scotland

Wright " " " 4 New York

47. Note how Thomas, born and raised partly in Ireland, seems to identify himself as an "American," as though he were native born and a Yankee at that.

Farnum   " " " 5 Indiana
Smith, R. H.   " " " 6 New Hampshire
Griffing, J.   " " " 7 Massachusetts
Eagles——Driver No. 1 New Brunswick
Griffing, W. " " " 2 Massachusetts
Allen   " " " 3 Connecticut
Loud " " " 4 Maine
Salisbury   " " " 5 Michigan
Duryee " " " 6 New York
Blood   Supernumerary   Maine
Lathrop   "   New York
La Rue   "   Canada
Lee   "   New England

The other five men of the Platoon are merely attached to it for messing purposes being an Artificer, a Mule driver, the Farrier & c. all Americans and good fellows.

⤳

Thomas Christie to Sarah Christie

NEAR ATLANTA, GA. AUGUST, 5TH /64

My dear Sister:

I have to acknowledge the receipt of yours of the 27th Ult.—a very interesting letter—which I got on the 3rd while a very hard fight was going on on each side of us, especially on our Left.[48] I had to read it by piecemeal, as you might say, while getting my piece ready for Action, for we expected an attack on our part of the Line. This way of reading the letter perhaps make me think it better than it was, but I liked it Better than any other I have got from you in a long while. I must congratulate you on the approaching end of your Summer's work, school is out tomorrow I believe, and must also commend your resolution not to do any more of it for a while,—there is no use in driving yourself to death.

I send herewith something for your Photograph Album, being no less than a likeness of Lieut. F. L. Heywood of our Battery of whom you have

48. The Atlanta Campaign was becoming a regular siege at this point, with the city almost encircled. Sherman continued to extend the right flank of his army to sever the last rail connections to Atlanta. Skirmishing and probing attacks by both armies were frequent. See Welcher, *Union Army*, II:488–89.

doubtless heard me speak, and who went to see H. in Boston when on his Veteran furlough and who was our Orderly Sergt. for so long. The photograph does not do him justice, for he was sick when it was taken, but he promises that if he can get Leave of Absence this coming Fall he will show you the Original with all the late improvements in the shape of crimson shoulder straps & c. If he comes up with us we will have a good time singing some of the new pieces of the day, for he is an accomplished vocalist, as well as a performer on the Melodeon. Put him in the Album along with the rest of our Boys, and I hope to add a few more of "Ours" to the collection after we settle down again, on the fall of Atlanta, if they let us rest even after that.

I think Atlanta is not the chief object of Sherman's operation myself for the destruction or capture of the Rebel Army is worth more to us than a dozen Atlantas, and we will be kept on the move till that object is accomplished. We could go into the city at any time if we wanted to, but its occupation is not desired if it would endanger the main plan, which is for the annihilation of the Rebel host that man its defences. The desperate offensive fighting of the Enemy since we crossed the River, their baffled charges and night attacks, show that they know the end is nigh unless they can break our lines and stop the awful pressure on their contracting defences. Thanks to the fighting qualities of the Army of the Tennessee they have *not* broken into our lines,—day by day we move forward to new positions and day by day do we tighten the grip on this Aorta of the Confederacy.

They tried to break out last night through our line a little to the right of us, at about 10 O'clock, but after a half hour firing, during which they shelled us fiercely in support of the sally, they were repulsed and silence once more fell over the long dark lines of intrenchments. The firing began so suddenly and so close to us that we jumped up and ran to our posts in almost a state of nature, having taken off our clothes for the first night since we came into this position. However, as soon as we got things ready, and found that the attack was not coming our way immediately, we put on boots and breeches and stood ready for anything that might come on.

Everything shows that they are desperate—that is, the Leaders—as for the Men, they wish the thing ended anyway, and express the greatest joy when taken prisoners and are allowed to go to our Rear. Right in rear of where our Battery is now in position is the battle ground of the 28th July, and it is awful to see the long mounds of red dirt that show where the Rebel dead are buried, in trenches containing 30, 40, 50 and in one trench *240 bodies.*

You can have no idea of how the field looked before the detail for burying went on to it, and I would not have you know anything about it. Of one thing the people up North may rest assured; heavy as our loss has been since investing this city, it is nothing compared to that of the Rebel Army.[49]

But this is not very agreeable for you to read and as we write so much now I will stop for the present.

Write soon and don't forget—Tom—

ᕝ

Thomas Christie to Alexander Christie

NEAR ATLANTA, AUGUST 12TH/64

My Dear Brother:

I expected a letter from you before this time, but I suppose the Harvest work has prevented it. We have got nothing from home since the dates of 30th July, but as I have nothing pressing to do today I will give you a letter gratis, for which you will give me credit, of course. The usual health still accompanies us, and the worst season is now over, the weather getting cooler every day so we may anticipate no trouble from the effects of old Sol during the rest of this tiresome campaign. The most we have to dread are the effects of inaction upon the men—the Recruits especially,— as for the past 3 weeks we have done very little firing, and for the past two weeks very little moving. When the men have nothing to do but lie under the tarpaulins day after day, without anything to interest them except the whiz of a bullet or the shriek of a shell once in a while, they are very apt to neglect taking exercise enough, and therefore lose appetite and are very much afflicted with *Ennui*. Sometimes we have a variation to this dull life in the shape of a vigorous shelling from the enemy's batteries, which are concealed from us by the heavy timber in our front, and are not more than 900 yards from us. The Rebels are not near so sparing of their Ammunition as they used to be, and actually fire more now from Artillery than we do. I suppose they think there is no use of surrendering, as they did at Vicksburg, with Magazines all full, and so they give us the benefit of it. I was on Guard night before last, and had a good chance to see the effects of

49. During July, Sherman's forces lost about 8,000 killed, wounded, and missing, while Hood's Confederates lost 13,000 men. For the whole campaign to that point, Sherman's losses were around 25,000 and the Confederates' about 27,500. See Foote, *Civil War*, III:490–91.

what we have so often inflicted on the Johnnies—a night shelling. They opened their Batteries on us at 9 and kept up a slow fire till almost daylight getting no reply from us, although they made very good practice, bursting the shells close to our Guns and driving all the fellows who slept a little in rear up to the protection of our works. The effect as a view, was very fine. First, you would see the flash of the gun through the trees, and then, about the time the report reached you, here would come the shell, flying swiftly, its fuse burning bright as a candle, and dropping sparks. About the time it neared the works you would begin to think it was time to lie down, and then the fiendish shriek of the critter as it passed over, and a bright flash followed by a report, told you that you might assume the perpendicular again. All the damage they did was the wounding of one of my horses by a fragment of spherical case. We had another horse killed by a bullet the day previous.

My Gunner and I went out yesterday into the woods in front to try and find out something about the position of the Rebel forts, and to do this we passed outside of, not only the pickets, but the videttes[50] and got within 200 yrds of the little Rifle pit that protected the Rebel line of skirmishers. The Picket Officer went out with us to show us a point from which we could have a good view, and as we were crouched behind a stump taking observations, here comes a Rebel Officer in a fine grey Uniform, walking coolly along the Rebel pit. Our Picket Officer called the nearest vidette up and told him to shoot the Rebel, but before he could get his gun to bear the grey back had walked behind a point of brush out of sight. We went out still further and got a good view of the Rebel works,—they are very strong, protected by chevaux de frise[51] and two large forts have 9 Guns bearing on our part of the line. While still taking notes of the distance, Range, &c. to be useful when the Battery should have orders to open fire, we were a little startled by seeing 3 of the Butternuts get up in the pit, now not further from us than is the mouth of your house lane from the Pond Lot Bars,— take their Rifles and come over their little work, out towards the bush in which

50. Videttes were the "sentinels on the furthest outposts" placed closest to the enemy's lines in order to warn of an attack. Pickets were placed between the videttes and the primary defensive line. U.S. War Department, *U.S. Infantry Tactics*, 431.

51. A precursor to barbed wire, this obstacle consisted of a square beam, about nine feet in length, with sharpened stakes attached at right angles and typically placed in front of fortifications to impede infantry attacks. U.S. War Department, *U.S. Infantry Tactics*, 417.

we were hidden, with the obvious intention of cutting us off from our pickets as they had probably seen us. So we thought it was high time to adopt Sigel's[52] tactics and made a retreat in good order.

I find that I will have to do the same from the ink bottle and so, Au Revoir. Thos. D. Christie

> [margin note—first page] You will have to enlist before the 5th September I believe and so you had better see about it in time as I don't think we can get up there before that time. So follow the directions of Malmros[53] and come down about the last of the month if you can. That is, if you still hold your mind on the subject unchanged.

> [margin note—last page] Accept this as a scrap merely, written to pass away time, and give my love to all the "connection." What is the last you heard from Schaller?

∾

Thomas Christie to James Christie[54]

AUG. 15, [1864]

Our Junior First Lieutenant, William Koethe, was killed yesterday by a sharpshooter. We feel his death deeply; he was a universal favorite. It happened yesterday afternoon. We were not firing at the time. He was sitting between two of the men, talking with them. In his earnestness he leaned forward to put his hand on the knee of one of them. (He was persuading him to leave off drinking.) Just then the bullet came, from the direction of our right flank, and passed through his heart. He gave a piercing shriek, and fell forward dead. This is the worst position we ever were in; the enemy have a raking fire upon us. This bullet passed through my tarpaulin twice and another one twice, before it hit the Lieut. I was under my tarpaulin at the time, but lying down; so the bullet passed over me. We have now moved our tarpaulins close up beside the guns, and have built traverses; thus we shall be protected from flank fire. The enemy have a few picked sharpshooters

---

52. Probably General Franz Sigel, a German-born officer very popular with German Americans but with a poor reputation in the Union Army, particularly after his defeat at the battle of New Market on May 15, 1864. Warner, *Generals in Blue*, 447–48.

53. Alexander had written to the state adjutant general, hoping to join his brothers in the First Battery. See Thomas to Alexander, Aug. 4, 1864 (page 250).

54. Transcribed in Thomas Christie reminiscence.

armed with the terrible Whitworth rifle, with telescope sights; it carries a very heavy ball, and will kill a man at a distance of 2 or 3 miles.[55] It was one of these that gave me a rap on the ankle in June. The other night as we were coming up into position we passed a regiment lying in bivouac; the men were asleep. Just then we heard the whistle of one of those Whitworth bullets, and immediately the cry of a man who had been hit.

When the Lieut. was struck yesterday he was the only commissioned officer with us; the Capt. was in Marietta as Corps Inspector of batteries, and all our other Lieutenants were in the camp in the rear. So I took possession of all his effects, his watch &c.; and got a stretcher, on which his body was taken to the camp last night, and buried.

Among his things I found that Spanish Method which you sent him some time ago at my request. I shall keep it now as a memento of as brave a soldier and as interesting a man as I ever met. He was one of my best friends; we had been together ever since we both entered Clayton's Platoon at Fort Snelling as privates.[56] In the many discussions that made that big Sibley tent so interesting in the Arsenal Koethe was always prominent, and always original. At the battle of Corinth we were on the same gun, he as Number Three, and I as Number One. At Vicksburg he was chosen to be Second Lieutenant by the men. In some respects he was our best officer. Apparently his only fault was very hasty temper, which was a cause of great pain to himself, more than to anybody else; he never kept a grudge against any one. He was a man of very deep feelings. I remember how he cried on the 20th of July, when his horse was killed. We would not feel so badly about his death if [it] had occurred in the heat of action; to be shot down as he was while calmly conversing with one's comrades, looks too much like a case of cold-blooded murder. His only relatives live in a small village in Saxony. He was the only son of his father, a wealthy farmer. We fear that the news will nearly kill the father; his whole heart was set upon his boy. Again and again he wrote him to get out of the Army and come back to Germany. How far reached the dreadful consequences of this awful war!

55. Designed and developed by the renowned British engineer Sir Joseph Whitworth as a long-range weapon for the British Army, the Whitworth rifle was used largely by snipers. In the hands of a skilled marksman, it could kill at a range of over a thousand yards. The Confederates imported the Whitworth to equip their sharpshooter regiments. Edwards, *Civil War Guns*, 219–20.

56. Koethe's enlistment records show that he listed his place of birth as Germany and his residence as Missouri. He apparently first immigrated to that state and then came to Minnesota shortly before the war began. He does not appear on the state's 1860 census.

Far away in that German home how keen will be the anguish caused by that rebel bullet!

This morning a bullet went through my overcoat; but luckily for me the coat was hanging on the tarpaulin, and not on me. You will not blame us for not wishing to be killed while lying asleep on our bunks. Skirmishing is very lively now; it is said the enemy has received reinforcements. I know that we have: it is evident that we are soon to make another flanking movement. Deserters are coming in from the rebels by scores every day. Do not be impatient; we shall finish this thing before long.

Yours hopefully,

T. D. C.

❧

Thomas Christie to James Christie[57]

SEPT., 1864 [day not given]

We had good times during the recent movement. Our facilities for foraging reminded us of December, 1862, at Abbeville, in Mississippi. We lived on the best to be found in the country. Besides this, we had a chance to stretch our legs! Coming after our wearying confinement behind the breastworks, where exercise was impossible, and where our food was simply crackers and coffee, the change was very pleasant.

While we were down near Fayetteville, I "got on the Staff," as our fellows call being under arrest. We were on the extreme right of the Army. Our horses had no forage. After the skirmish on the 2nd I heard of a house about ½ mile to our right at which there was plenty of corn. So I obtained permission, took three of my drivers, and went over there on horse back. We tied up our horses near the house, filled our bags with corn, and got some of the finest honey I ever saw. Just then, Generals Belknap and Potts, with the Provost-Marshal, and a large guard arrived at the house. They arrested all of us, and took us to Division Headquarters, where we were kept under guard for a short time, and then questioned by General Smith. He was very kind to us, as he always is; but he told us not to go out upon the flank of the Army again, or we might be taken by the enemy. I informed him very respectfully that we had permission to go, as our horses were in need of forage; also, that there were no pickets between that house and the

---

57. Transcribed in Thomas Christie reminiscence.

Battery. Upon this he sent us home with our bags of corn. Then one of us went out and brought in the honey! As our officers got a share of this, they made no objection. I was reminded of the incident in which that big hog played such a part, on the Tallahatchie!

Yours Ever,

T. D. C.

⌒

Thomas Christie to James Christie[58]

CAMP NEAR ATLANTA, SEPT. 9, 1864

My Dear Father,

We have written nothing since the 25th of August, because all our communications with the railroad were cut off when we started on this last movement that has given us Atlanta; besides, we were hurried around so much, that nobody had any time to write. A great deal has happened since my last letter.[59] On the 26th of August, in the dusk of evening, we withdrew from the front of the enemy. All that night we marched towards Sandtown. There was much firing by heavy guns, probably those of the enemy; but our march was unmolested. In preparation for the movement we reduce baggage, taken [taking ?] rations for 20 days in the wagons, and sent off our knapsacks and all the sick to the river; this was done on the 25th. On the 27th we marched toward Fairburn on the West Point Railroad. We struck the line 3 miles above Fairburn on the morning of the 28th. Here some of us began fortifying, while the rest tore up the railroad for 15 miles. I saw General Howard and General Kilpatrick; they were talking about the raid recently made by the cavalry. In this place we stayed until the evening of the 29th, when we marched towards Jonesborough, our Division bringing up the rear of the Army of the Tennessee. That was a wretched night. We moved very slowly, and the halts were very numerous; nothing can be more disagreeable. In the forenoon of the 30th we came up with the rest of the Army, in position before Jonesborough. Then for 2 days we had continual fighting, sometimes very sharp. On the 2nd we began pursuit of the

58. Transcribed in Thomas Christie reminiscence.

59. The action Thomas describes here is Sherman's envelopment of Atlanta that sent Howard, Thomas, and Schofield's troops on a "grand left wheel," encircling the city from the west and cutting off all railroad communications. This movement forced General Hood to evacuate Atlanta on September 2.

enemy; they had fallen back the night before, going towards Macon. But near Fayetteville we ran upon them again, and had some slight skirmishing, in which the Battery also was engaged. The whole Army formed line of battle and threw up slight works. In this position we remained until the evening of the 5th, when we began to fall back by very short marches to our present position, about 2 ½ miles south of Atlanta. It is said that we are soon to move into the city. Near Fayetteville one or our veterans was wounded, the ball passing through his cheeks.

Last night at our bivouac near East Point we received our first mail since the movement began, something more than a bushel. In our present dirty condition mother's gift of the towels is most acceptable. we are soon to be paid, and shall rest for a month. The things which we left at Huntsville are soon to come to us. It is possible that some of us veterans will receive furloughs.

The campaign has been a long and wearisome one, and we are very glad that it is finished. You should have heard the tremendous cheering, day before yesterday. The complimentary orders from the President and General Grant were sent by General Sherman to be read to our three Army Corps. The splendid woods through which we were marching fairly rang with the cheers.

And now I shall hope to receive that new watch!

Yours Ever,

T.D.C.

7

"We Had a Lively Time for Awhile"
September 15, 1864–May 27, 1865

Thomas Christie to James Christie[1]

CAMP NEAR ATLANTA, SEPT. 15, 1864

My Dear Father,

At last we have settled down into the old routine of camp-life, roll-call twice a day, guard mount, feed-call, water-call, etc. etc. This morning we were inspected by Capt. Marvin, inspector Genl. On the Division staff. As always with us everything went off quite creditably. Just now we have great interest in Politics. Among our 150 men there are about 10 Fremonters, and half that number McClellanites; so once in a while you will hear very spirited arguments. O course our democrats are all in favor of the war, like the Chicago "Post"; nothing of the "Times" breed could live with us. It is curious that all the McClellan men are among our new recruits. In this whole Army you do not find many veterans on the side of the man who blundered so on the Chickahominy. But several of our old veterans, especially the Germans, are radical Fremonters.[2] All the rest of our men are in favor of our old Abe, "the Railsplitting Buffoon," as the New York "World" calls him. Our fellows say that the President has done very well, considering all the circumstances; and that it would be folly to put either of the other two into his place. We do not think it wise to favor a policy which would overthrow all that we have been fighting for during the past 3 years. No, we say,

1. Transcribed in Thomas Christie reminiscence.
2. General James C. Fremont, a favorite of radical Republicans, made an unsuccessful bid for the presidential nomination in 1864. He had been the party's candidate in 1856.

Lincoln's policy, while not always up to the mark, is on the whole, a good one; if we persevere under him for a while longer, as we have been doing, everything will yet come out right. Especially are we sound on the Negro question. Most of us would strike for Abolition more for the sake of the white than of the black. Our experience in the South has shown us that the owner suffers more than the slave from the evils of Slavery. It is plain to see that the great cause of the difference between North and South as to wealth, education, business enterprise, indeed everything that makes a people great and happy, in the curse of Slavery. It may be wrong, but nearly all the abolitionists among our soldiers are moved far less by philanthropy in general, than by a wish for the welfare of our own race. The most of us will tell you that we would like to see the blacks removed from the country altogether. They are not at all capable of self-government. One or two generations of freedom and education are needed to fit them for it. It is unjust to judge of the capabilities of these poor creatures by what we see they are now, when they are just emerging from the terribly debasing influences of servitude. Fifty years hence, probably, they can begin to do something as a people. I have not much hope of any thing from the present generation, or even the next. They are just like children as yet; they need an immense amount of teaching. Again, I do not see how the two races can live together without injury to both. The white will domineer over the black, and the black will debase the white. However, in the midst of these doubts and fears for the future, I still have faith that God has work for this race to do; and that all He requires of us is to treat them with kindness and justice. We are only instruments in God's hands; we shall be compelled to do our duty to the Negro whether we will or not. I am sure there never was an instance in the world's history when abstract right so well accorded with present self-interest as it does in the Abolition of slavery by our race. What astonishes us the most is that there should be found men at the North who oppose the measure. They have been brought up amid free Institutions; they know the contrast, there is in everything, between the free and the slave states; they can have not earthly interest in the preservation of slavery. Yet if this curse in interfered with, even as a war measure, you will hear them howl about the "Constitutional rights" of traitors in arms! Nevermind, we shall show them in Nov. what are the sentiments of the Army, what we think of their milk-and-water platforms and candidates. Have no fear for the Army. It is loyal enough and strong enough to save the Republic alone; but we shall not be alone in the great work; the majority of our people in the North are with us. They and we have suffered too much for these great principles to desert them now.[3]

It is not often that I trouble you with such things; but it seems right that on the eve of Election I should let you know where I stand It is possible that I am not radical enough on the Negro question to please you; but I think that is because I have seen more of the South than you have seen. I believe that the Negro is in need of three things, first Freedom, second education, and third a place where he can develop himself apart from the white race.[4]

We hear nothing more about pay or furlough; only there is a rumor that the former will come next week. Lieut. Hurter is soon to go to headquarters to Adj. Gen. Clark about our veteran furlough. Gen Blair starts for the North on a short leave tomorrow morning; one of our [boys?] (his cook) goes with him. The men of the 17th Army Corps have not a high opinion of Blair. He is a man who has almost destroyed himself by hard drinking. On the memorable 22d of July he was near our Battery so long that we observed him carefully; his conduct did not raise him much in our estimation. We all like our Division gen., Giles A. Smith. He also goes home for a week or two. In his absence Gen. Belknap will command the Division.

My watch has not yet come. I have written to the express agent at Chattanooga and at Marietta about it: no doubt it will soon come. Our old friend Strachan is now one of Gen Kilpatricks's orderlies. I saw him yesterday; he is having a good time in camp 4 miles to our right. We are having beautiful weather now; regular Indian summer. If we are paid soon I shall subscribe again for the "Independent." . . .

Thomas Christie to Alexander Christie

NEAR ATLANTA SEPT. 18TH 1864

My dear Brother,

By Father's letter of the 6th recd, this morning I am glad to see that you are home again, although the news was a surprise to me, I must confess, for by your note to me of the 30th as St. Charles I thought you were in for

---

3. Many soldiers in Sherman's army shared Thomas's views on the elections. See Glatthaar, *March to the Sea*, 48–49.

4. Direct contact with blacks seems to have influenced opinions about slavery and race for a substantial number of Sherman's troops, but not in a uniformly positive way. See Glatthaar, *March to the Sea*, 52–65.

it sure, and I was looking to see you join us at almost any time. I am really glad you did not do it though, and I think your short sojourn in Minnesota away from home and friends may have been a service to you in making you think more of those very desirable adjuncts to Life. I believe you got most thoroughly homesick and served you right too, But how you could think so lightly of the state of my adoption, as Father's letter indicates you do, is more than I can explain. Probably the hurried way in which you went through the country, and the troubled state of mind in which you were, prevented you from seeing its transcendent beauties. What did you think of the Bluffs back of Winona? and what of the great Prairies between St. Charles and Rochester? and above all what do you think of old Father of Waters? I await a letter, containing a full account of your adventures with much interest. Did you go to see Robertson and Clarkson? if you did not you were foolish, for Clarkson could have told you a great deal of interesting particulars. I'll wager, Alex, that your first rencountre with the world did not diminish, to say the least, your appreciation of Home delights. I know it did not with dis chicken. Trust me, my dear Brother, the home life is the best of all, *and the one with which come the fewest regrets and temptations.*

I am so glad to think you are still your own Master that I can't talk about anything else, for I was afraid the confounded Bookers would persuade you into joining the 11th Minnesota which they are now raising, and if you had gone into the Infty, I would never have forgiven you. To me, that was the most interesting portion of the letter, that spoke of you being at home, and of Father's playing a game of checkers with you. I hope you will now await our coming; before leaving home again.

As to that furlough; the case stands thus: we can get it at any time, so Capt. Clayton told us last night, but we don't wish to go home without anything in our pockets, and so we wait the motions of the Pay Master. There is something wrong with our veteran papers they say is the reason for the delay, and they have sent to Washington for Instructions. The matter is this: The Law says that a Mustering Officer must be of the Regular Army, and all the veterans of our Corps were mustered in by volunteer officers, so the Pay Masters refuse to recognize us as Vets, and from the veterans of our corps whom they have paid, the 14th Wis for instance, they have withheld the charges for transportation when, on their veteran furlough and mulcted them of the Advance Bounty they got when mustered in. The thing made quite an excitement for a while among the veteran Regts. of our old 1st Division and the 3rd Division, but I think they will fix the thing somehow, for the Govt. is not so foolish as to let go seven thousand old soldiers for a mere technicality.

Now I want you to write me a good long letter, if not done already, and tell us all about your trip to the "Etoile du Nord," And meanwhile, I remain, with much Love, Your Brother.

Thoms. D. Christie

[margin note—first page] Tell Mother that was rather a hard one on me when she said I was "always for myself" but I'll pay her for it when I am home and get at her Buttery. So, Bob McNulty and James Deverough have enlisted. I did not think Jim would have left his wife so soon.

[margin note—second page, in another hand] I kept my word to father to return home if I could into get into the 1st Battery. That was one of the "fiascos" in my life to be laughed at by light-headed, selfish people wanting in loyalty to truth. Alex. S. Christie Jan. 27, 1921.

Thomas Christie to James Christie[5]

SEPT. 24TH

Atlanta is not much of a place. There are a few business houses clustered around the great railroad Station, and the rest of the city is very scattering. They have a nice brick Court House, with a figure of Justice and her scales for a vane. Opposite this is a rather fine church. Only a few of the private dwellings are of much value. Sherman has ordered the removal of the citizens, and so nearly all the houses are empty. Many of these empty houses are being torn down to make the buildings needed by our Army. It seems hard to send away the people. But Wheeler's cavalry are always attacking our communications, and it cannot be expected that we should feed all these people; their friends went away without leaving them even a week's rations.

Our men who were captured during the past campaign are returning to us every day, they having been exchanged by special arrangement with Hood. Every train for Rough and Ready brings a load of them. No doubt you have read of the cruelties practices at Andersonville; but no one can form any just idea of them without hearing the narratives of these returned

5. Transcribed in Thomas Christie reminiscence.

prisoners, and seeing their emaciated bodies. The details of their treatment by the fiends who have charge of the stockade are so horrible that one can scarcely believe that beings in the shape of men could be guilty of such atrocities. Think of it: 35,000 men cooped up in an open stockade, without shelter from sun or storm, without water except from a stream that ran through the filth of the stockade, their clothing rotted off so that in hundreds of instances a meal-sack slipped on over the head serves for shirt, pantaloons, and boots; their only food ¼ ration of meal made by grinding the corn and the cob together; all of them liabel to be shot in mere wantonness at any time,—is it any wonder that many of our poor fellows have become insane, that many have died of a broken heart, and that many have committed suicide by wilfully passing the Dead-Line to be shot by the guards? May God keep me from falling into the hands of Jeff Davis and his myrmidons!

Yours Ever,

T. D. C.

~

Thomas Christie to Sarah Christie

ATLANTA GA. OCT. 19TH/64

My dear Sister;

Imagine my situation and pity me; compelled to stay in this old fort in this old desolate town of Atlanta while my comrades are in the field taking part in the great movements which are going on near Chattanooga. Here we are, without Mail, or newspapers for *over a month*, completely shut away from the rest of the world, our Rations shortened, and our horses dying for want of forage, furlough gone up and Pay ditto, is not our situation deplorable? And yet we have one thing to be thankful for; that in the midst of our troubles we still manage to keep in excellent health and spirits. The fact is, it is hard Killing us with care, or we would have Kicked the Bucket long ago, and so we manage to take things very coolly, and eat our solitary hard tacks with cheerfulness, and even *laugh* once in a while. We don't have any letters to read, and very few to write, so we employ ourselves in various other ways, make rings out of the fuze plugs[6] of the old shells that lie all around

6. Brass or wooden cylinders built into shells and case shot, into which fuses were inserted when the shells were fired. Gibbon, *Artillerist's Manual*, 305.

us, and wear the brass things as Relics; draw a little, tell stories a little, visit with the 20th Corps fellows a little (*very* little though, for we cant stand their continual bragging about the Army of the Potomac), and so we try to get through our time. You see we are all "Gentlemen of Leisure," rather too much leisure for me, for I am never contented except when on the move.

William is gone, and you of course have got news of him before this. He has sent no word to me since they went off, but I heard that our Corps was in Resaca on the 16th, and on the march for Chattanooga, as it was thought Hood intended to strike there somewhere. There was a Mail came to town a week ago for our Corps, but we could not get our letters, as it was sent right back to the Field, but we expect to get them back again soon from the Company, and look for them every day.

I hope you have been writing regularly whether you heard from us or not, for that is the way I have done, and if the Mail brings me only one or two letters I shall be angry with all of you.

I do not think we will join the Company for a month yet, for they will be busy up there trying to put an end to Hood, and will not settle down into camp for a long time, and as we have not horses enough for the two Guns we will have to wait till they can take us up by Rail. We *did* hear that the Army of the Tennessee had drawn forty day's Rations at Kingston and had started for Cumberland Gap, but I don't think they will go there till they drive Hood from the region around Chattanooga, and we expect to hear of fighting there soon, although the Rebels will not fight unless they are cornered, and can't help themselves. I think it looks as if Hood is trying to go East and reinforce Early or Lee, for both those worthies were in tight places when we last heard from them.

I only wish we were on the march along with the rest of the Boys. However, I suppose we are doing our duty by lying in this old fort as much as they are in fighting in the field, and so we must have patience.

I send you some specimens of my drawings, "taken from Nature," and will let you have some more in my next. I think they are not so bad for the very first efforts, and shall continue to improve if I can, without Books or teachers. One thing you may rely on, and that is that they are all true, which is more than can be said of those in the Illustrated papers, and now I hope you will answer this soon, and oblige your loving Brother Thos. D. Christie.

Thomas Christie to Alexander Christie

ATLANTA, GA. OCT. 25TH 1864

My Dear Brother:

When I wrote last to Sarah I was in hopes of having a letter to answer the next time I should take up the pen, but the letter has not yet come, and so I must write without it. It is a fact, that we poor fellows belonging to the Army of the Tennessee (several Detached Sections of Artillery and some Infantry convalescents) have not had a bit of Mail since the Army went away, although it has come to the 20th Corps here in Garrison with us several times. The Mail is not lost, only delayed at Company Head Quarters in the Field, so I am making big calculations on reading at least twenty letters when it does come down. We have not heard from our Corps since I wrote last, when it was at Resaca, which was on the 16th, I think, and I don't see why William has not written to me before this. The R.R. is now open to Chattanooga but how long it will stay so is doubtful. We get three fourths Rations yet, but manage by vigorous foraging on the country, to get plenty to eat, such as it is. I must tell you about a foraging Expedition that I went with on the 21st and which got in yesterday.

It was the third one that we had sent out and the most extensive one. Genl. Slocum[7] comd'g the Post takes this way to get food for the Men and Animals of his command, for we have drawn no forage for two weeks, and without this system of foraging our horses and mules would have been dead of starvation long ago. As it is; we reported 27 horses fit for service in the Section when we came into town, and today I report only 16, the rest having all died of want of food. But to return to our expedition: on the evening of the 20th I recd. Orders from Lieut. Ross,[8] comd'g our Section, to report at camp at Sunrise the next morning, (the camp and the guns where I stay with the Gun Detachments are a Mile apart.) to take charge of a detail of Men who were to go out with the Expedition.

At the appointed time I was on hand, mounted, armed with my Revolver loaded either for Rebels or their hogs, with my haversack and four day's Rations in it slung to my shoulder, and my Blankets strapped on to the cantle of my saddle. I found the men all ready, and so we started to where the train was to rendezvous, my command consisting of 14 men, most of

7. General Henry W. Slocum succeeded General Hooker as commander of the Twentieth Corps in July 1864. Warner, *Generals in Blue*, 452.

8. John D. Ross joined the battery in January 1864. *Adjutant General's Report*, 789.

them armed with pistols, 12 horses, 2 mules, and 2 wagons,—one of them drawn by 6 horses in Artillery harness, and the other by 2 horses and 2 mules—, so you see I had a pretty looking train compared with the fine Six Mule teams which composed our regular Army transportation.

Proceeded to the east of town, where the Rebs blew up their Ammunition trains, whose fragments strew the ground for a quarter of a mile along the Augusta R. R., and there found Lieut. Osborne, who was to command the trains of the Reserve Artillery of the Army of the Tennessee. Reported to him according to orders and he assigned me a place in the column, which was starting out, on the road to Decatur. We were very lucky in getting a position so near the head of the column, as you will see when I tell you that we had 940 wagons in the whole train, besides three Brigades of Infantry and six Guns for an escort, all of which had to travel on one road, so that, while it was seven A.M. when we started from Atlanta, it was noon when the Rear Guard went out. The Expedition covered 10 Miles of Road. Imagine the whole road between Watertown and Brockerway's corner full of moving teams, closed up so that you can hardly get through between them on foot, the white covered wagons looking very like the Prairie Schooners we used to see, only that the Schooners of the Emigrants had horses generally, and our army wagons are drawn by six Mules, driven by a single line; the driver being mounted on the near wheel mule. John Frank will be able to tell you about Mule driving for that was about all the soldier life he saw.

In such a large train as we had, you would naturally think there would be considerable wrangling about places and that every one would be trying to get ahead, but we manage things in a better way in the Army, and the vast column of wagons moved along as orderly and with as little interruption as would a body of well disciplined troops. Everything goes by system,— The whole train of wagons was under the command of one Officer, who assigned to each Quartermaster the position he would have in column. Each Quartermaster had under his charge from twenty to a hundred wagons, and these were divided again among the Wagon Masters. The Quartermaster of a Division, Brigade or Regiment is a commissioned Officer and the Wagon Master is a Non Commissioned Officer. Each Quartermaster is responsible to the officer in command that his wagons keep closed up, and he again holds his Wagon Masters to account if anything goes wrong in their respective trains. On this trip Osborne was acting Quartermaster of the Battalion of Reserve Artillery, and I, in command of two wagons, was acting Wagon Master. The way our train was guarded was this: on each side of the road and distant from it about 40 Rods, marched a single file of Infantry, the men five paces from each other, and besides these, there were Advance and Rear Guards of Cavalry, Infantry and Artillery. This force was necessary to guard to wagons, for the country we marched through is infested with Rebel cavalry, who tried hard, as it was, to cut off portions of our train.

Well, we moved out of the fortifications around the city, and over the Battle ground of the 22nd of July, dotted as it is by graves of both our poor fellows and those of the Enemy who died that day. Passed through the little village of Decatur about 10.30 A.M. and went into corral in a big field a mile east of it at 11. This corralling (pronounced correling, accent on the second syllable) is done by forming the wagons in solid Square, in several columns parallel to each other, and five of six paces apart, and is done every time the train stops for any length of time, in order to concentrate for safety. All the time we stopped in this corral, —three hours—the teams continued to come into their places, and when we left the rear had not come up.

While resting here we had to take out one of the team Horses, that had given out and put in one of the riding horses, while the tired one was put under the saddle. One of the men also picked up a Mule in Decatur, which he took to ride. From where we were at this place we had a fine view of Stone Mountain, 6 Miles east of us. It is a bare pile of rock rising to the hight of about of about 1200 feet, almost entirely devoid of vegetation, probably a half mile across on top, and sloping at an angle of 45 Degrees on the south, and perhaps 35 on the north side. It is one of the natural curiosities of the State, and before the war used to be visited every year by people from all parts of the Union. Perhaps I may send you a sketch of it and of the other famous Mountains in this vicinity—Kenesaw and Lost Mountains, for I have their outlines, as they appear from where our Guns are in position, all drawn out, But I am digressing. At 2 P.M. we left the corral and resumed the march in column on the road to Lithonia, which, as you will see by the Map, is a station on the Augusta R.R. beyond Stone Mountain.

We marched slowly this afternoon, halting frequently, and when we stopped for the night 3 miles from Lithonia it was 9 O'clock. During the afternoon I had shot a young Beef creature with my Revolver, one of the Men had got three fourths of a hog, and Corpl. Case had dug a sack of sweet potatoes with his fingers, besides all the corn for the horse's feed that had been got, so as soon as we got into corral for the night, which was in the edge of some timber, we went to work, the Drivers to unharness, water and feed their horses, and the others to make supper. Built a big fire of rails, carried water and put on 2 Kettles, to boil, one for coffee and the other for the potatoes, the latter being cleaned of Mother Earth by rubbing on a Gunnysack, Fried some of the fresh pork, and when all was ready we had the best meal of the season.

By the time we had supper it was half past ten, so we spread our Blankets in the bushes and lay down around the fire, but towards it in regular Bivouac fashion, for the night was very chilly. At four in the morning I roused the Men, it being still moonlight, but I knew that our best chance for foraging would be in the early Morning, and so as soon as Breakfast was over and the animals fed I started out for hogs and potatoes with two more of the Men, leaving a corporal in charge of the teams, with instructions to go out to Lithonia with the train and load with corn. We went to a house a half mile off and shot a tremendous hog, cleaned him and I took him to where I left the teams, on my horse, the others going to work to dig sweet potatoes, of which they brought in a sackfull. The teams had gone out to load with corn, so I left one of the men to stay by the stuff in camp while the rest of us rode out for more. While riding along through the timber, outside the pickets, I was fired on by a hidden Bushwacker,—the bullet clipping the leaves close to my head. The scamp must have instantly fled, for a Reconnaissance of the vicinity in company with some of our cavalry who came up behind me, discovered nobody. The Rebels were pretty numerous in the vicinity of our train, and showed no mercy to such of our fellows as fell into their hands,—our Cavalry reporting that they saw many of our men hung on trees and shot all to pieces. My other man, who went out mounted, in another direction came in at noon, and reported that as he and 7 others were scouting in the direction of Stone Mountain they were fired on by a squad of Rebels in ambush, and scattered. On coming together again they found that 3 of their number were missing. So you see this foraging business is not without its dangers. We managed to bring into the last nights camp a lot of meal flour, and Sorghum Syrup, besides some dried peaches and a lot of cured corn blades for the horses. At Sundown the wagons come in from beyond Lithonia, where they had loaded with corn and sweet potatoes, and we had only time to throw on what we had got, when the train started for Decatur. Marched 4 miles that evening and stopped for the night in a cornfield by the side of a creek. Got corn here for two or three feeds, so as not to touch that in the wagons, and when we had got supper, it was 11 O'clock. That night was very cold and we were covered with white frost in the morning. It was the night of the 22nd, just 4 months since McPherson fell.

Early in the next morning we were up, and three of the men set out to look for meat, taking my horse among the rest. I did not see these fellows again till we came into Atlanta, so I had to foot it in. On the afternoon of that day we traveled towards Decatur, but had so many stoppages that we did not camp till half past 11, and then we were still a mile east of Decatur. Yesterday we got into camp here in the forenoon, and the stuff we brought was found very acceptable.

Oct, 26th Another foraging Expedition went out this morning, and two wagons went from us. Slocum is bound to get the whole substance of the country around into his fortifications, so that if he is besieged there will be no danger of starvation. We are sorry our fellows went though, for this afternoon come orders to turn over all our horses, and report at the depot for transportation north. This cannot now be done for two days, till our men get in. It is said we are to go to Nashville. We are all very well pleased at this, and so am I in signing myself for the last time from Atlanta.

Yours Affectionately
Thos D. Christie

[margin note—first page] I think, by our being ordered north, that there is now some chance of our getting pay and furloughs. We will get 10 Months pay when it does come. I think we will spend the Holidays at home.

∽

Thomas Christie to James Christie[9]

ATLANTA, NOV.5, 1864

My Dear Father,

We are told that after tomorrow noon there will be no more mail received at this post for transmission north. So this will probably be the last line that you will receive from me for some time. You will have to depend on the Rebel papers for news from us. I think our plan will be, to take advantage of Hood's absence in Tennessee to rake the insides out of the Confederacy, in some direction. The move will probably be towards Montgomery, Macon,

9. Transcribed in Thomas Christie reminiscence.

and Mobile. Our two Corps, the 15th and 17th are certainly to take part in the movement; what other troops will do so I do not know. But you may be sure that Sherman will leave men enough north of the Tennessee to keep the rebels from getting to the Ohio. The plan will take us into the heart of our enemy's country for at least a month; but you need have no fears for us. Our good Uncle Billy knows where we are going, and how to get us there![10]

Our Corps was in Marietta yesterday, and would have been here today but for the rains of the past few days. Today the weather is fine, just what is wanted for campaigning.

We hear with sorrow of the death of General Ransom during the recent movement. He was a most worthy young officer. You remember that we served at Vicksburg in his Brigade. When he died he was in command of our Corps.[11] In the campaign up the Red River he was wounded. He was greatly liked by all of us. I hope they will soon give our old General McArthur a command in the field again; there is no man I would prefer to serve under. Today we took our two guns out of the fort, and put them into position on the inner line of defences, close to our camp. We are still busy refitting the Section for active service. Today we drew mules, harness, and 200 rounds of ammunition; tomorrow we are to get 27 horses. My candle-ration for five days is nearly burned out in the writing of this; so Goodbye for the present My next letter will come to you by sea!

Ever Yours

T.D.C.

∾

Thomas Christie to Alexander Christie

LINES BEFORE SAVANNAH, GA. DEC. 17TH 1864

My dear Brother:

Now that we have accomplished what I so often have prophesied the Army of the Tennessee would do, and have got within smell of the sea, I

10. In late October Sherman decided that he could leave General Thomas's army to check Hood's Confederates and turned his attention back to Georgia. It took several exchanges of telegrams to convince General Grant that the March to the Sea was worth the risk, but on November 2 Grant gave his consent to the move and Sherman immediately ordered his army to begin preparations. See Sherman, *Memoirs*, II:162–67.

11. Ransom died, apparently of typhoid fever, on October 28 during the pursuit of Hood. He was replaced as commander of the Seventeenth Corps by General Blair. See Sherman, *Memoirs*, II:161, 168.

must tell you all about *how* we have attained such great results, and how
it has come about that our Guns now thunder before the defenses of this
City of the Sea. I wrote a hasty note to father yesterday and propose now to
go into details more than I could then; Today also I have written to Lloyd[12]
in N. Y. Telling him to send one of his Military Maps of Georgia and Virginia to you, and one to me, that you may see the route we have taken from
Atlanta. To tell all the Business part of my letter at the start, I may also
inform you that I put into the hands of Samuel A. Frothingham[13] yesterday
the sum of three hundred and five dollars for him to either express or carry
home, as he is to leave us today.

For several days before we left Atlanta it was generally known that some
grand movement was afoot, on account of the preparations that we saw
going on to evacuate the city. The 14th, 15th and 17th Corps had marched
down from near Rome, after driving Hood gently across the Tennessee and
lay massed around Marietta; and the 20th Corps lay inside the works in
Atlanta. The Artillery had been reduced by sending Batteries to Chattanooga by R. R. till the Army had left only one Battery for a Division of
Infantry instead of three or four, the usual allowance. Orders were issued
by Genl. Barry, Chief of Artillery, by which four teams instead of three were
put on to the carriage, and by which it was forbidden for the cannoneers to
ride on the chests, or to carry anything on the carriages, except forage for
the horses, so that our connoneers were obliged to carry their knapsacks
like the infantry; a thing they had never before done;

Everything in the city was prepared for evacuation: the big Guns we had
captured were destroyed by knocking the trunnions off and bending the
chases, the Ammunition in the Ordnance Depots was either loaded on the
wagons of the ordnance train, or shipped by R. R. To Chattanooga; the forts
around the city were all mined ready for destruction and every Non Com-
batant, Sutlers, Christian Commission, Sanitary Commission &c. All were
ordered away so that the army, like a practiced wrestler, was stripped for the
contest. On the night of the 11th November the last train left the doomed
city, and early the next morning the troops began to destroy the R. R. and
the great depots. That morning, the 12th, I started on horseback to visit the
Battery near Marietta, and as I rode along the R. R. near the Chattahoochee,

12. Probably "Lloyd's Topographical Map of Georgia" (New York: James T. Lloyd,
1864). The firm published a series of war-related maps beginning in 1862.

13. Frothingham was mustered out on December 17, 1863, at the end of his enlistment. *Minnesota in the Civil and Indian Wars,* I:651.

I saw the Infantry of the different Divisions marching our of their camps, drawing up in line along the track, and stacking arms. Then they "went in," the ties were seized at one end and lifted bodily, rails and all to the perpendicular. Then the immense furrow began to fall over at one end, and as fast as it fell new track was torn up; so that the furrow would not be broken till perhaps 80 Rods of it was lying upside down, and all accompanied with tremendous cheers. After a Regt had turned over its "stent" of the road, the men went to work knocking the rails off the ties and piling the latter in large heaps to which they set fire, and then laid the rails on top, so that when the rails were heated they could be seized by a dozen men to each, and bent and twisted out of all shape around trees. This is the way we destroy R. R. and you must allow it is pretty effective; so that to be rebuilt requires everything new; ties, rails, spikes, chairs, &c. The whole R. R. from Stone Mt. to Chattanooga, from Atlanta to East Pt. And from near Macon to within 4 miles of Savannah, great part of the Augusta Road from Millen and some of the Mobile R. R. from here, has been destroyed in this way; the bridges, culverts, depots and warehouses all burned, and in some places even the road bed leveled, so that the *United States* could hardly repair the damage in a year, and as to the poor Confederacy doing it, without iron and without workmen; the idea is absurd. But I am leaving the Chattahoochee; Just as I came to the Bridge I saw a party of soldiers getting wood on to a wagon, and thought I recognized one of them. Rode up and accosted him with "Hallo Jo Monreau![14] how do you do?" Where at the aforesaid Joe paused in his labors and regarded me with a short look, then holding out his hand exclaimed, "Why, *Sandy Christie*," On being convinced of his mistake he became very communicative, told me he belonged to the 26th Wis., 20th A.C. that he was at Chancellorsville, Gettysburg, Missionary Ridge, &c. that most all his comrades had been "voonded," and that Show was in the 25th in our Corps.

Couldn't stay long with the garrulous Joseph, who appeared to be in the best of health, and so rode on to where the Battery was camped, where I found Wm and all the rest in good health. Got back the money I had sent by Loud, as the Non Vets, were not to go north then, and put it and Wms in my pocket book. Found that W. Had sent my letters to me by Mail, and that of course they were lost for I have seen nothing of them since; was

14. Joseph Morneau enlisted in the Twenty-sixth Wisconsin, Company D, from Watertown, very near Clyman. See *Roster of Wisconsin Volunteers*, II:322.

consoled by him with the assurance that there was no news in them, from which he drew the logical conclusion that they were not worth much, in which I did not agree with him in my letter hungry condition; Found all the men who had volunteered from my platoon to go out with the Battery, very anxious to get back, which, of course, was somewhat gratifying to my "Amour propre," On application to the Lieut Comdg. However, I could only get Wm back into the Squad, and the other boys are discontented yet. The next morning the troops had orders to march for Atlanta, and two orders from Genl. Sherman,[15] which you have doubtless seen, were read to us in which he announced that our 4 Corps had been organized into an Army for a special purpose, and that we were to forage liberally &c. All of which we recd. with loud cheers.

As soon as I saw the Battery into the Atlanta road, where they had to wait for the 4th Division to come up from Marietta, I rode ahead and went into the camp of our Section in Atlanta, with orders for Lieut. Ross. This was the 13th and next day the Battery passed by our Camp and camped between Atlanta and our old camp near East Pt. That evening we took the Section out to the Battery passing the whole 15th and 17th Corps in bivouac, their fires extending for miles in every direction.

We had left a corporal and a detail of men in the Section camp, and they joined us in the night, having burned nearly all of the Company tents, old harness, clothing &c. that we could not carry; according to orders. On the morning of the 15th we were roused at 3 o'clock, and preparations made for the march. Everybody reduced baggage, and burned what they could not carry. Wm & I overhauled our knapsacks destroyed several shirts pair of pantaloons and other clothing, besides both our Journals mine containing sketches of our life at Ft. Snelling, St. Louis, Pittsburg Landing, Corinth, Abbeville, Moscow, Memphis, Lake Providence and Vicksburg. I was sorry to burn it, but it could not be helped; it was too heavy to have W. carry on his back. I carried our Blankets and haversacks on my horse, while Wm strapped the knapsack on his back, in which was what little clothing we were allowed to take. It was announced that we were to draw half Rations of hard bread, and one third Rations Sugar and Coffee, but during the march we generally got only ⅖ Ration of crackers, living on sweet potatoes,

---

15. Special Field Orders 119 and 120 were issued on November 8. The first gave an overall description of the reorganization of the army and its "special purpose"; the second provided more details of how the army was to be organized and how it was to "forage liberally." See Sherman, *Memoirs*, II:174–76.

corn meal, and fresh pork, of which there was an abundance; so that what hard tack we got was seldom eaten.

At sunrise our Division marched, and taking a S.E. course over very rough country, and on new roads, blazed through the Oak and Beech woods we halted for the night only some 12 miles from Atlanta, although we had marched fast, but the way we came was very roundabout, and the horses at night were much jaded on account of the many hills we had to get over. Not much foraging done this day, as we were in country that had been pretty well stripped by our Garrison in Atlanta. On the 16th we kept the same general direction, made about 20 Miles and bivouacked for the night in a cornfield within a mile of the village of McDonough. At 3 P.M. today one of our Boys died in the ambulance, having been sick for some time. There was a singular coincidence connected with Davis S. King's death; At the hour he died he had been in the service just three years to an hour, and was a non-veteran. We buried him that night, poor fellow; and he was very much regretted by the whole Company.[16]

Nov. 17TH; Reveille sounded at 3 and we were on the road an hour before daylight, taking the Keyes Ferry road from McDonough; the ferry being on South River, which unites with the Yellow and another river to form the Ocmulgee. When within 2 Miles of the ferry we took the road for Jackson, further south, and marching 3 Miles on this road, bivouacked for the night, having made about 20 Miles, over some of the best country I ever saw, Fine rolling land, well cultivated, with barns full of forage, and plenty of hogs and sheep in the fields; The harvests were all in, the corn husked, and the corn fodder stacked in the fields or under cover in the Barns, so that we had plenty for man and horse. We felt very tired tonight though, for the marching of the past 3 days has been very severe, Crossed Tussahaw Creek this afternoon;

Nov. 18TH Left camp at 7 this morning and took the road for the Mills on the Ocmulgee, 6 miles distant. When within tree Miles of the River we halted to let the other Divisions of the Corps pass ahead. In the afternoon we took the road again, and at dusk stopped within a mile of the river. Here we went into park, unhitched and unharnessed, got supper, and at ten P.M. the Boots and Saddles sounded and we were again on the move. Moved along slowly till we came in sight of the Ocmulgee; a fine river; crossed on a pontoon Bridge laid above the dam at the Mills. The Ocmulgee Mills were

16. Davis King, born in Indiana, was another of the original enlistees from Winona. *Adjutant General's Report,* 785.

2 splendid buildings, which the Rebels had used night and day for the manufacture of cloth for the army: they were destroyed as soon as the army got over the Bridge. Our Quartermasters took the opportunity while we were crossing, to dismount every man that had no right to ride, in order to get mules and horses for the trains and in this way many of our cannoneers lost the nags they had picked up. After crossing we climbed one of the worst hills I ever saw and at 2 O'clock bivouacked 2 Miles from the river on the Monticello road.

∽

Thomas Christie to Alexander Christie

BEFORE SAVANNAH GA. DEC. 18TH/64

My dear Brother:

My letter of yesterday brought up the narrative of our March to the time we crossed the Ocumulgee, and I will now resume it. But first I must tell you that while I was writing yesterday a Mail came in, and with it 4 letters for us, two from you and 2 from father, of the dates of 6th and 13th Nov. There must be older letters yet to come, for in these you speak of John Sutton's buying a Sub. of Uncle Tom's being in the Army, and of Amot's being in Clyman: all new to me. How did Uncle get into the Heavy Artillery? Was he drafted, or did he volunteer?[17]

Your criticisms on Genl. Sherman show that, in common with the rest of the world, the Rebels included, you were not acquainted with his grand plan till it was put into execution: and therefore you could not see why he did not attack Hood up near Chattanooga, not knowing that "Old Billy" had bigger game in view when he was gently pushing Hood across the Tennessee. With all your smartness Alex, you are not quite able yet to instruct Genl. Sherman in Military Strategy. But to my Diary:

Nov. 19TH Marched at 10 O'clock, and passed through Monticello about noon; It was a pretty little village, with some handsome women in it, a great rarity in the South; A large quantity of Rebel Commissary Stores were found in the Courthouse and we loaded down our Caissons with shelled

17. "Uncle Tom" was Thomas D. Reid, the brother of Thomas Christie's mother, Elizabeth Reid Christie. He was in Company G of the First Wisconsin Heavy Artillery, a unit raised in 1864 that spent the remainder of the war guarding the fortifications of Washington, DC. *Roster of Wisconsin Volunteers*, I:277; Quiner, *Military History of Wisconsin*, 971.

corn in sacks for our horses; not caring if the sack were marked—"Capt. R. S. Jones, A. Q. M. C. S. A."—As we passed through the town the jail was burning, our Boys having discovered that our prisoners had been kept in it; so it was reduced to ashes, to the great terror of some of the women folks who thought we would destroy the town. We marched slowly all day and camped early, about 4 Miles south of Monticello. The weather, when we started from Atlanta was Cold and clear, but last night and today it has drizzled a little; and tonight is rainy.

On the 20th and 21st we continued our march, camping the latter day a mile west of Gordon on the Macon and Savannah R. R. The weather was very rainy, and the road pretty bad, especially near Gordon, where we first struck the regular "Piney woods," which stretch unbroken from there to Savannah. The soil very sandy, and the plantations few and far between; altogether a far inferior country to the rich "Cherokee Country" further north. At Gordon we saw the marks of Stoneman's unfortunate raid in the burnt depot, and the newly repaired R. R. and telegraph wire; which our Infantry soon demolished again. Heard considerable cannonading towards Macon on the 20th, 21st and 22nd. On the latter day we lay in camp till 11 O'clock, and then moved in an awful hurry, on acct. of not getting orders till very late, Marched through Gordon and on towards Irwinton halting at dusk, 9 miles from Gordon.

Nov. 23RD Took the road early, our Division in the advance, and passed through Irwinton soon after starting: Not a person to be seen in it, all had run on the approach of the dreaded yankees. We halted in the street some time and our fellows took a good many liberties with a Book store near by; found a large quantity of Rebel Mail, and I seized on a new Davie's Geometry and Trigonometry, which I brought along. I took it as part payment for the Ray's Algebra I lost at Shiloh. They shall not cheat me out of my Mathematics any how. On leaving Irwinton we marched through Toomsborough on the R. R. Here, again, we stopped quite a while, and took the opportunity to load our Baggage wagons with sacked corn:—Rebel commissary stores, One of the Inft'y dug up a pile of Rebel money and silver in an old citizens garden, and they also found about a half bushel of powder hid away, which the Boys put a fuze to fired it, making the whole town shake, While we stopped here, a man of the old 69th N. Y. who had been taken prisoner at Petersburg on the 30th July, came in to Genl. Smith Comdg. Division. He told a wonderful story of his escape from Savannah and his travel through the country by night toward Atlanta, assisted by

negroes, Of how he had got close to our advance when he was captured by
the Rebel cavalry and they were going to kill him, when our cavalry came
up and hauled in his captors: He told us there was a small force of State
Militia on the other side of the Oconee, and he lay in the swamp and
watched them haul up 4 old Guns and plant them, in readyness for us. This
man has come through safely with us, and is now on his way to join his
Regt. After a short halt in Toomsborough we marched for the R. R. Bridge
over the Oconee and when within two miles of it came up to where the
1st Ala. Cavalry had dismounted and left their horses while they went to
skirmishing. Here we went into park, the Infantry stacked arms, while
Gordon's piece was sent forward to shell the Johnnies out of a stockade
they were in on our side of the river. After a short time we heard the Rodman speaking to them and then the skirmishing ceased, and the piece
came back. The first shell had made them leave the stockade and as they
ran across the Bridge Gordon gave them a few shots lengthwise, as Dave
Waterhouse says. Our Infantry then went to destroying the R. R. and we
unhitched and also unharnessed. The weather today has been very cold, the
keen wind seeming to blow clear through overcoats and all:

All the next day, the 24th we lay in camp, only sending down two Guns
to touch up the Millish a little on the other side of the river. They had a Gun
mounted on a car in front of the Engine and our first shots were directed
for that, a percussion shell going through their smokestack made the critter back water in a hurry and Genl. Smith rub his hands with delight. We
stay here tonight. Heavy frost last night, Ice an inch thick this morning.

Nov. 25TH Roused at five O'clock and marched back to Toomsborough,
where we halted two hours. Then we took the road leading south east, and
after 3 miles march, the 1st Division of the 15th Corps came in on our Right,
and the two Divisions marched in the same road in two columns, side by
side for 4 miles. Halted for the night about dark and heard considerable
cannonading of the river in front where the pontoons were being laid under
cover of our artillery.

Nov. 26TH At One O'clock in the afternoon we moved, and crossed the
Oconee swamp and river the former on corduroy Bridge two miles long
laid by our Pioneers and the latter on the pontoons; the 15th Corps crossing on another Bridge to our Right and taking the same road with us for
two miles on the east side of the river and then branching off to the Right.
The Oconee is not so large as the Ocmugee, but the pine swamp on each
side is almost bottomless.

Halt for the night about 3 miles from the River. On the 27th, 28th and 29th we did not march very fast, keeping on the road almost parallel to the R. R. and passing through Irwins Cross Roads, and the small place called Spiers Turn out, not the Station but near it, where the wagon road crosses the road to the station of Spiers. Went through this place on the 29th and passed head of column of the 15th Corps and saw Genls' Osterhaus and Sherman. The latter marched with our Division that day for the first time since leaving Atlanta. Riding up beside Lieut. Ross Comdg our Section, accosted him with a pleasant "Good Morning," and then asked the Lieut if we found any difficulty in getting forage for the horses, at the same time laughing at the pile of corn fodder on Conner's Caisson in front of him. He told Ross that we had the finest column of horses he had seen on the march,—a well deserved compliment,— for our Drivers have always kept up the good reputation of the Battery for good looking horses, and on this trip our horses have actually gained flesh, while other Batteries have had to shoot animals every day. A little incident occurred today—the 29th, that shows how little "style" there is about Sherman. One of our Cannoneers— Griffing by name—was walking along by the side of his Gun talking to Small who was mounted; Genl. Sherman rode up behind Small who saw him and turned out of the way, unknown to Griffing who thought he was still by his side. So Joe continued the conversation, and kicking up the soil with his boot exclaimed, "This is pretty good land here," "Yes," says the Genl. "it is very good land, only a little too sandy." On hearing the strange voice Griffing looked up and saw that instead of Small being alongside, it was Old Billy himself looking as smiling as you please. Joe says that about that time he felt like getting into a very deep hole. A surprise awaited me on this day too. As we left camp in the morning we had to pass the train of the 1st Division of our Corps which was drawn up on the side of the road. While riding along at the head of my Piece, I heard my name called and looking round, who should I see but Ed O'Keefe mounted on a mule team in the 1st Division train. I could scarcely believe my eyes, but it was the veritable Ed although looking pretty rough. He is enlisted as teamster, and has seen some hard times by his story. Was looking well though. He was in Atlanta for two weeks before starting on this trip. I saw him once since, near the Ogeechee, but have had very little chance to talk to him; He saw Dave Waterhouse in Chattanooga who was soon to go home.

On the 20th we moved slowly and halted for the night a mile from the Ogeechee. Orders were read today breaking up the Artillery Brigade in our Corps, and assigning the Batteries to Divisions as heretofore. We are assigned to our old Division,—the 4th.

DEC. 1ST, This morning very foggy and dark. Started before daylight and crossed the Ogeechee on pontoon Bridge at the station of Sebastopol. Marched slowly down the east side of the R. R. and camped on Jones' plantation, 6 miles from where we crossed. The Infantry of our Division and the 1st tore up R. R. all day, while the 3rd Division marched with us on the wagon road and guarded the trains.

DEC. 2ND Marched to Millen, where we camped tonight. It is a very small place for such an important Junction; Infantry tearing up track all day. Since we crossed the Oconee we have traveled over strange country. I cannot describe it better that by saying it would be prairie were it not for the tremendous growth of pine, for it is as level as a floor, and perfectly devoid of underbrush; heavily timbered with pine and the soil nothing but sand, on which is a short thick growth of prairie grass. We have not had to lock the wheels of the carriages for the past 60 miles, (and I may say, we did not lock them yet except once at Paramara's Hill, near Millen.) As we approach the coast the country looks older, and we saw many fine old residences surrounded with the most splendid Live Oaks I have seen in the South. We also saw a great deal of the fan palmetto of which the most of ladies fans are made. Another peculiarity of this low flat country are the many springs ponds that cover the region, some of them quite large, and having small inlets and outlets. Our camps were always by the side of one of these, so that there was plenty of water for man and beast.

DEC. 3RD, Marched at 8 O'clock. Halted at 10.30 and waited till the rest of the Corps had passed, when at 3 P.M. we moved again, and brought up the rear of the Corps with our Third Brigade to Woods plantation near Scarborough Station, where we stop for the night close to a big corn crib that must have contained at least 5000 Bushels of corn. Our whole Army Corps is using from it tonight, and we will have to burn a pile of it in the morning. On the 4th we made about 15 miles and found the country better cultivated. Houses that look as if they might have [predated] the Revolution, surrounded by grand old groves of the green spreading Live Oak,—the King of shade trees. On the 5th we crossed the Little Ogeechee on wagon Bridge and went into camp on the south side. This is where the Chivalry tried to stop our advance, and got flanked out of their sand works. We got a number of *wooden* spades they had used, and burned them to cook our sweet potatoes by. Our foragers found today about a dozen horses and mules hid in a swamp, and brought them in to the Battery.

DEC. 6TH Weather very pleasant, Lay in camp all day while the Inf'ty were destroying R. R. and cutting down the Bridge over the Little Ogeechee. Our Pioneer Corps, now numbering some 600 negroes picked up on the marches, camped close to us, and I went down there today and bought some Rebel money for curiosities. Got some Rice in the bundles to feed our horses.

DEC. 7TH Left camp on the Little Ogeechee at 7 A.M. our division in the advance. Rainy this forenoon, and in consequence the road is pretty bad. Several swamps had to be corduroyed and in one of them we came near sticking with the whole Battery, for several horses fell down in the almost bottomless mud. The country gets lower as we approach the coast, and the spanish moss, so thick in the swamps of Louisiana, begins to appear. Got a Savannah paper of the 5th today, in which we see accts. of the capture of the Florida and other news, the first we have had since the 1st Nov. Genl. Sherman marched with us today, and tonight we bivouac close to his Hd Qrs. and those of Genls Blair and Smith, within 31 miles of Savannah.

DEC. 8TH Weather fair, On the road at 8 A.M. and marched very slowly on acct. of the numerous swamps we had to bridge. The country is low, sandy, piney, and very poorly cultivated. Heard heavy guns in front supposed to be from our fleet. Our fellows captured a Locomotive at Station 2 ½ and we saw it burning. within 21 Miles of the city tonight. Speaking of cannonading reminds me that at Millen we heard very heavy Guns at a distance on our left and were told by the citizens that they were at Charleston and that they heard them nearly every day.

Marched to the *rear* till we were 7 miles from the city when we turned south and halted for the night near the Ogeechee Canal. And here began the starvation period. Our Inf'ty came round tonight begging for ears of the corn we had to feed the horses while we were but little better off. (This was on the 11th and I am now entering on the 19th; *we drew our first hard tack from the fleet this forenoon,* so you can see we have not fatted up any in the past 8 days.)

DEC. 12TH Marched south, crossing the canal, till about a mile south of it, where we waited till dark, when we started to "man the Blockade," A Rebel Battery was within a half mile of the road we had to go and in plain sight of it, so that it was impossible to go by in the daytime and even in the night it was risky, so our trains had all been sent off by a very roundabout road while the Inftry of the Division and our Battery was to run by. The Column started; it was a high moonlight night and all was still except the heavy tramp of the Infty Battallions and the rattle of our Gun carriages: Just as we got to where the causeway commenced; looking over the low rice field to the left we saw two Rockets go up, one after the other; "Now" Thinks I, "we will catch it." Sure enough; we soon saw a lurid flash from the dark looking Rebel Battery, and then the boom of the Gun and the shriek of the shell came together. It ricochetted and went over us, "Steady Boys, hold your teams well in hand, Cannoniers march by your piece." and the column went steadily on. A half mile to go yet, and if they open their whole Battery on us it will go hard with us. Soon comes another flash, a short shriek, then a flash close to us, and the pieces of shell whistled by: no harm done: We began to breathe easier as we came near the end of the causeway without their opening more than one Gun; It fired 2 shots more, without hurting any one, and then we emerged from the bare Rice field and took the road through the safe woods, Camped that night two miles from the Rebel Battery, where the Beverly road joins the Savannah road, where we lay till the night of the 14th, when our Section moved back and went into a fort near the causeway, where we are now While the rest of the Battery is still in the old camp; We are in position close to an old frame building in which is machinery for cleaning Rice, and it has been pretty well riddled since we came here by rebel shot. We are spearated from the Rebel works by a sheet of water 700 yds. in width, the overflowing of the Rice field by the backing up of the water of the swamp by the tide. This is the way they have overflowed their rice land in times past, and it comes very handy to the Rebels now, for they have let the water in, and now keep the Sluice gates shut so it cannot get away again. These gates are on their side and our Genls, are offering a thousand dollars and a discharge to any man who will go over and cut the gates open; The Rebels opened on us here on the 15th and 17th and we had a lively time for awhile till some of our three inch messengers went into their port holes when they dried up. Genl. Blair gave us instructions to always have the last shot, and we have always *had* it. None of our boys were hurt, but 3 of the 12th Wis. Battery on our right were badly wounded on the 15th The Rebels have more artillery opposed to us than we have but they don't use it as well, as they generally fire over us, while at 1000 yds, which is the distance of their main fort, we can hit their Embrasure every time with our Rodmans.

Now, Sandy, I hope you are satisfied with my Diary of the march; It has taken the spare time I have had for two days to write it out, interrupted as I was several times by the roar of the Rebel Guns, when I would have to give my attention to the firing of my Gun. I wish you to save these letters, as I have only a pencil diary of the march, and that I shall not try to save. These 6 sheets ought to be enough I think to bring to my mind every incident of our memorable trip. Our Starvation period is now over, I think, for we drew stores today from the fleet on the Ogeechee, but while it lasted we had nothing but a little fresh Beef, some of which chased Hood north of Atlanta and what little rice we could pound out of the hull by hand. Since we came here we have run a rice mill that was used by steam; running it by hand in the old Building riddled by Rebel shells.

We have not yet seen salt water, but are pretty near it, within 20 miles of the open Ocean. This is very low country, and the tide backs up the water in the swamps and bayous all around us. I saw the Ft. McAllister prisoners day before yesterday, and they are a fine looking body of men.

That furlough will have to wait till Savannah is captured, and even then, if we march for Charleston I would not ask a leave of absence. Give my love to all, —Mother, Sarah—and all good friends, and I will sign myself as ever Your loving Brother

Thos D. Christie

༒

Thomas Christie to Alexander Christie

SAVANNAH, GA. JAN. 5TH 1865

My Dear Sandy:

As I know you love to read letters from us, and as I suppose it will be some time yet before I will have a letter from you to answer, and as it costs me only a little time, ink and paper, a three cent stamp and an Envelope to gratify you, I have determined to spoil a sheet of this new Hilton Head letter paper for your benefit. Contrary to our expectations, we did not break up camp today, and it is now thought that we will not leave immediately, even if the Infantry of the Division go, which they expect to do tomorrow. We hear that the 1st Division of the Corps is at Beaufort where it is thought we are to go when we leave here. We also have from Wilmington the news of Butler's landing there, above Fort Fisher.[18] It seems to me that we will push

18. In mid-December 1864, Union general Benjamin Butler led a force of sixty-five hundred men backed by a large fleet under Admiral Porter to assault Fort Fisher on the Cape Fear River, hoping to close the last open Confederate port, Wilmington, North Carolina. Butler's forces attacked on December 24 and 25 but were repulsed; Butler was sacked for his failure. See Foote, Civil War, III:715–20.

Charleston closely very soon as a diversion in Butler's favor. When the troops went on board the transports two days ago there were put on with them several Guns of the heaviest calibre captured here, which looks as if siege operations were to be commenced somewhere, and of course we naturally think of Charleston as the object of these forthcoming operations. No matter where we go, so that we are on the move, and *doing something* and we will be satisfied. Savannah is as tiresome to us now as ever Corinth or Vicksburg were, and we want to be at something new. Before the winter is out it is likely we shall be gratified.

Our life since we appeared before the city has been so full of interesting incident, that I have not been able to keep you posted on everything as I should. While we were in position on the lines outside the City we had several very exciting duels with the Rebel Batteries of 32 pdrs, and 10 pound Rifles, on the 15th Nov. they opened fiercely on us and our Cannoneers rushed to their posts, while I looked out a position from which I could observe the fire of my Gun. As the country was very flat, and the smoke of the cannonade hung low to the ground it was difficult to see the effect of our shots from our parapet. On the flank of our work, and close to it, was an old rice mill, of which you have heard before, and on the end facing the Enemy's Batteries was an old window in the upper story, some twenty feet from the ground, the blind of the window being thrown back against the side of the Building. I thought this would be a good spot from whence to get a view of the Rebel position, and so I went into the mill in order to go up the stairs into the upper story. On going inside however I found that the stairs had been taken down by the men for firewood, so I had to give up the project, as there was no other chance to get to the window. I had scarcely got to my piece again when a 32 pound shell from one of the Guns in front of us struck the old window-blind and burst just inside the mill, tearing off part of the roof above where it exploded and raising Ned generally. I could not but think that if those stairs had been all right in their place, I would have had a hard time of it at that old window. We dried up the Johnnies soon after, and had no more trouble till the 17th when they opened on us from both front and flank. They had a Battery on our left front, within 700 yards, with which they enfiladed us completely, sending the shells across in the rear of the Guns, through our Cook fires. We had been started up from our dinners to reply to the scamps, and as *I* was hungry, as I generally am about that time, I occupied myself in munching a cracker while directing the fire of the Gun. When my first hard tack was all nibbled up I bethought myself of getting another one, and looking round for the haversack, saw it hanging to the pole of the tarpaulin which was stretched immediately in rear of the Gun. Started for the haversack to get a cracker but when halfway to it, *something told me not to go.* A moment after, and a ten pound shot bounced over the low parapet on our left, passed close in the rear of Conner's Gun, and plunged right through my tarpaulin, making two holes in it that you might shove your head through: Of course I felt greatful to my inward Mentor for preventing my going to the haversack. The Tarpaulins that belong to my Gun have, always been specially unfortunate; The old one we turned over at Atlanta had 11 Ball holes through it, and now this new one is completely ruined for rainy weather by these shot holes through it. This thing of having a fellow's wigwam riddled with air holes, though fine for ventilation, is not very desirable when these Southern torrents pour on the canvas.

That was a rather hot place we were in by the old Rice Mill; a day or two after that close call of mine, a shot from the same flank Gun dashed through an Embrasure of the 15th Ohio,[19] in the same fort with us, and tore a man's shoulder and arm all to pieces; He has since died. When we passed through the line of Rebel forts on our way to the city on the morning of the 21st we had a good chance to see the effect of our shots; Their embrasures were completely torn to pieces, and two of their Guns had been dismounted by our Rodmans. I don't think you have much idea of the terrible accuracy of our kind of Guns, which the Rebels confess they dread far more than any other kind; Probably you think your rifle is pretty good at shooting, but what would you say to see a two foot square target, in the shape of an embrasure, hit twice out of three times at a *mile* distance. This we have done repeatedly, and we have *never* failed yet to have the last shot with either Batteries or sharpshooters.

If you enlist under the new call Sandy, and if no persuasions will keep you at home you must come to us. There is plenty of room now for 30 men and if Malmros will not enlist you for us, take 50 dollars in hand and come down to Savannah, or where the Corps may be. Lieut, Hurter will be glad to enlist you and his certificate will draw your Local Bounty anywhere. Never think of joining any other Company than ours. I have not space to

19. Fifteenth Ohio Light Artillery, also part of the Seventeenth Army Corps.

give you all the reasons that should influence you to this step, but if you come across any old soldier ask him about the different branches of the service, and see what he will tell you of the Infantry.

MORNING JAN. 6TH

We are under orders to march at 9 O'clock, for fort Thunderbolt— 5 miles south—where we are to take transports for Beaufort or some other place. Under these circumstances you must excuse me from finishing this sheet.

Yours hurriedly

Th. D. Christie

Hurrah for Sea sickness.

∽

Thomas Christie to James Christie

FT. THUNDERBOLT, NEAR SAVANNAH,

JANUARY 11TH 1865

My dear Father;

We moved down here on the 6th and have staid here ever since, waiting for our turn to embark for Beaufort. All our Corps is gone except our Battery, and we shall go today, most likely. The whole army is being transported to Beaufort, and as we have but about 8 transports it is very slow work. When we are gone the 15th Corps is all ready to follow and when we are all there it is thought the campaign will commence.

Ft. Thunderbolt, where we now are is on the St. Augustine River, which connects the Savannah with Ossibaw Sound, and is about 4 Miles south of the City. The river is more properly an arm of the sea and the tide rises here some nine feet. There are several large sea going vessels here, among them one or two regular Blockade Gunboats. All of them carry sail besides their steam power.

The seamen tell us that our Infty, who went some days ago, were awfully sea sick on the voyage, and the Pontiac, which carried the 53d Indiana of our Division, has not got her decks clean yet. We have had first rate times here, and I have been on the water every day. The second day I went out into the inlet in a boat, to where a vessel is sunk, which shows a good part out of water when the tide is out, and myself and two comrades got over a bushel of oysters which were sticking on the sides of the hulk. When the next tide was out that night, it being moonlight, we went out again and got a many more. I cut my hands all to pieces, though, in pulling the sharp clusters of oysters off the bed, and the soaking in Salt water don't make them feel any more agreeable. However, the next day I bought a boat load of Oysters that came from Ft. Pulaski, and got the boat—a fine yawl with 4 oars—in the bargain. Sold out the Bivalves to the Boys in the Comp'y and more than made my money back on them; Then we rigged a sail on the yawl and had a good time sailing all over the inlet, and up the different channels in the salt marsh through which the river flows. I have learned to pull an oar with the best of them now, although I caught a good many "crabs" when I first tried. Lieut. Fall[20] and myself with 6 others went out yesterday, and sailed more than two hours, the tide running in against a strong wind, which made the waves run almost "mountain high." We shipped one or two "heavy seas" and wet our Bow Oarsman to the skin. The wind blew so strong as to tear the sail out of the Bolt Ropes once, and those on shore thought we were to be capsized sure, but the Lieutenant, who had the helm, was raised on the coast of New Brunswick and can steer a boat as well as he can maneuver a Section of Artillery, while our stroke oarsman used to belong to a club on the Hudson, besides which, the rest of the crew were old Mississippi Raftmen, and of course, a boat with so much nautical skill aboard could meet with no accidents.

Capt. Clayton is in command of the Comp'y again, having given up his position as Inspector Genl. of Artillery in the 15th Corps.

JAN. 12TH Not off yet, and don't know when we shall be, as the Infty of the 15th Corps is going on the Boats, and it is said that we have to wait for a larger vessel than ordinary, on account of getting room for our guns and Caisson. We are too much used to such delays since we have been in the service to fret much about it, and we no doubt enjoy ourselves as much here as we would at Beaufort. There is not much temptation to spend money about Savannah at the prices they ask for things. 50 cts per doz. for little cakes—half a mouthful in each,— 10 cts. apiece for small half rotten apples, pocket-knives $5.00, combs, $1.00 handkerchiefs of the most common kind $3.00 apiece and everything else in proportion. It is surprising, but true, that at such prices the citizens find plenty of customers, especially for eatables, of which they cannot furnish enough for our hungry soldiers, whose Atlanta Greenbacks weight heavily in their pockets.

20. Second Lieutenant James Fall.

At such prices I will purchase nothing and so we will have to depend on you for another package, which I hope you have sent already, for we need a good many little things, such as *needles and thread,* combs, pocket mirrors & c. Such things do not last long where one's comrades are good at borrowing, and so we are rather destitute at present. I paid six dollars some time ago for a good pair of Buckskin Gloves, and am told they are not much cheaper up north. We have had weather lately, when I could not have done without them.

Has Alexander done anything about enlisting yet? I trust he will have good luck in getting Bounty, and hope he is coming to us when he does enter the Service. In that case I actually think our military life would benefit him, but the Infantry would be too severe for him.

I am very anxious to hear from home and shall, no doubt when we get to Beaufort, for a big Mail is there waiting for us, which came to Savannah 5 days ago, and then followed the Corps before we could get our part of it. We and the horses are on full Rations once more, and the latter are fast improving in flesh, but we shall have to get a good many more new ones before we can start on another campaign. give my love to Mother, Sarah and the Boys, and remember me as your loving Son

Thos. D. Christie.

[postscript] The weather, since we left the city, has been cold and rainy, making our big fires of Live Oak and pine feel very comfortable. Wind strong every day, and mostly from the north east. The health of the men is not as good as while on the march, a few cases of Chill fever being in the comp'y; but W and I are still rugged,—I think I weigh more now than ever before—149 pounds—and I am sure I never felt better inclined to enjoy myself. When we get to Beaufort it is intended to get a boat for the Comp'y to go oystering regularly. I have taken a passion for the shelly creatures, and can open their flinty habitation with as much skill as a Jarsey fisherman. We have cooked them every way, but I prefer mine raw to any other way and can put a few dozen out of sight with the greatest ease.

∽

Thomas Christie to James Christie[21]

CAMP NEAR POCOTALIGO, S.C.[22] JAN.17TH,1865

My Dear Father,

Tonight I put S.C. at the head of my sheet, as I have before this put several others. Here is the list, Minn, Wis, Ill, Mo, La, Miss, Tenn, Ala, Ga, and now S.C. Before the Army of the Tennessee finishes its work, you will no doubt see N.C. and Va, at the top of my letters. When you see such a large letter as this, you will think that I am back again at Corinth, with Halleck in command, and when old Billy had charge of only a Division. Those were the days of idleness, when we had time to write long letters. The war is conducted now on different principles; and your remark in a recent letter was true, that there will be no winter quarters for us this year. The new campaign is already begun. Charleston must see our flags before we take another rest.

I find the map of Georgia and Virginia by Lloyd, which I have carried from Atlanta, very useful. 19TH, I have been very busy preparing my men, horses, and the gun for active service. Several necessary things had to be drawn from the Quartermaster. So I have been too busy to write. But today it rains, and I am on guard and free from other duty; so now to finish my letter. Let me tell you about our sea voyage, and what I thought of the great Ocean. On the morning of the 14th we left Fort Thunderbolt in the small transport "Philadelphia." We had been up nearly all the night before getting the Battery on board; for we put a part of it on to another steamer, only to find that this was too small for us. At length we left the wharf, and steamed down against the rising tide into Warsaw Sound, passing several Rebel forts, that had so long kept our gunboats out of Savannah. I sat in the bow of the vessel and watched the porpoises. Soon I caught sight of the open sea, and of our blockading Fleet. The wind was pretty strong and the waves ran high; our little ship danced like an eggshell. The curious thing is that none of us were seasick. I cannot tell you how much I enjoyed the sight of the wide waste of tossing water, the white surf breaking on the low Georgia shore, and the scores of steamers and sailing vessels passing up and down. I stayed on deck all day looking at the Ocean. When we passed

21. Transcribed in Thomas Christie reminiscence.
22. Pocotaligo was a crossroads village a few miles inland from Beaufort. Its location, near the bridge where the Savannah and Charleston railway crossed the Combahee River and the junction of several roads, gave the spot strategic importance.

the opening of Tybee Sound we were out of sight of land for some time. In the afternoon we entered the harbor of Port Royal. Here were more than 50 vessels of all kinds, from the great 74-gun ship, the New Hampshire, to the smallest schooner. The Secretary of War had just arrived; so all the ships were decked out with flags, and the forts and the New Hampshire were firing a salute.[23] At the wharf of Hilton head we stopped only a few minutes, and then steamed up the inlet to Beaufort, 18 miles above, where we arrived at dark. When almost at the wharf, our old ship stuck hard and fast on a bar! There we stayed till the tide rose, at 10 o'clock. By the time we had taken off the Battery, hitched up, and marched half a mile to camp, it was past midnight. On the morning of the 15th, we drew some things from the Sanitary Commission, onions, tomatoes, and concentrated beef. The Quartermaster also gave us some clothing, which was very much needed. E.O.K. came to see me; he is a teamster; is soon to get his discharge and go North. He told me that all the conscripts from our town have run away. He wanted to know if he had been drafted. I remember now having heard that this was the case. Secretary Stanton I saw driving around in a buggy; the darkeys in the forts gave him a salute of 15 heavy guns. These black troops make a very fine appearance. Beaufort is a pretty place, and full of Union people.

On the 16th and 17th we marched out to this camp, half a mile from Pocotaligo Station, where our Corps Headquarters are. We do not think much of South Carolina; it seems to be all sand, pines, palmettos, and swamps.

Our Division drove the Rebels out of two lines of works near here, and our own lines now extend to the Coosawatchie.[24] It is said that we are to stay here for at least a week, so we have fitted up everything in good shape. All of us are in good health, except for slight colds, owing to the rain. I am on guard tonight; but a soldier must not grumble over the weather! However, I often dream of the time when I shall be able to sleep every night, and all night, undisturbed by guard, march, work, or fighting. While you are there, sitting comfortable in the house, here I am in these pine woods, squatted

23. Secretary of War Edward M. Stanton arrived at Savannah on January 11, 1865, to consult with Sherman and visited the troops at Port Royal on his way back to Washington. He was particularly concerned with matters regarding freed slaves. Sherman, *Memoirs*, II:243–53.

24. This partially tidal river runs from northwest to southeast a few miles west of Pocotaligo.

on my bed made of their needles, under an open fly through which the cold rain drops on this letter! Outside the storm is raging, and I have the consolation of thinking that I shall have to go out into it once every two hours tonight, to relieve the sentries. But after all, this life has its pleasures too. Take it all together, and probably the advantages overbalance the disadvantages. One thing is sure, if it does not make a *man* of a young fellow, teaching him self-reliance, self-denial, courage, endurance, and all the other Spartan virtues, it will be his own fault.

At Savannah the price of photographs, and very poor ones at that, was $7 a dozen. For this reason you will not receive any of ours.

Yours Affectionately,

T.D.C.

∾

Thomas Christie to James Christie[25]

FAYETTEVILLE, N.C., MARCH 12, 1865

My Dear Father,

A gunboat which came up this morning is to leave for Wilmington at 5 o'clock; so I take the opportunity of sending a line to tell you that W. and I are both well.

We have had for 6 weeks a most active campaign. As usual, nothing but success has attended us since we left Pocotaligo. I have no time to go into particulars, but here is a sketch. (When I write again I shall copy from the diary which I have carefully posted every day). On Jan. 26th we had Inspection, and marched directly from the field of review. That night Lieut. Hurter left us on recruiting service; I sent my last letter by him. Marching slowly, on the second of Feb. we struck the enemy in some force at the bridge over the Salkehatchie; on the next day we forced the passage, our First Division pushing the enemy in front, while ours, the Fourth, flanked them by crossing the river and swamp to the right. Our fellows waded across 27 streams, some of them waist deep, fighting all the way; General Smith and Belknap on foot with their swords drawn, at the head of their men. On the 4th we were all across the swamp. Rain day and night, bottomless mud, and the rebel rearguard, all combined could not stop us. On the

25. Transcribed in Thomas Christie reminiscence.

7th we struck the railroad at Midway Station, 10 miles west of Branchville. We destroyed the road for miles, and on the 9th marched for Orangeburg. That evening we reached the South Fork of the Edisto; our First Division swimming the river and driving the rebels off. On the 10th we lay all day in camp, while the trains and the troops of other Divisions were pouring over on the pontoon bridge. Seeing them pass one got an idea of the armed might of the North-West, and of the enthusiasm for the Union that propels this living stream against its enemies. Here, the 4th Division of the 15th Corps came up from Beaufort, and brought some letters from home. On the 11th we advanced to the North Edisto, where the Johnnies again disputed the passage. The next day we kept them amused by shelling them; till one of the regiments of our Division swam the river and flanked them out. They retreated hastily, setting fire to the town of Orangeburg as they left. That night we crossed, rode through the streets of the flaming city, and camped in the suburbs. On the next day, 13th, we took the road to Columbia, and until the 16th pressed swiftly on to the Capital. On the morning of that day we suddenly emerged from the woods on the west bank of the Congaree, and beheld the noble city spread out before us on the opposite shore. Our Division was in the advance. When we came in sight the rebels were still running trains in and out of the Station. Sharpshooters on the opposite bank opened fire and wounded two of our men. General Smith instantly ordered De Grasse's[26] guns and two of our section into battery. We fired on the trains and sharpshooters, and soon drove both away. We lay there that day, while the fifteenth corps marched passed us, laid a bridge over the Saluda, crossed, and massed between the Saluda and Broad.[27] Next morning the 13th Iowa of our Division crossed the Congaree in an old scow, while my piece was put in position on the bank to protect them. They had the honor of raising their flag over the State House. They were just in time, for just as they put up the flag the skirmish line of the Iowa Brigade of the 15th Corps was seen advancing at the double, to claim the honor of having captured the city, by hoisting the first flag. As soon as the flag was raised, the troops of our Division, who were all watching on the bank, gave a tremendous cheer. General Blair sent orders to Capt. Clayton to fire a salute, which

26. He probably refers to the guns of Captain Francis De Gress's First Illinois Light Artillery, who were equipped with longer-range, twenty-pound Parrott Rifles. U.S. War Department, *War of the Rebellion*, Series I, 44:87, 850.

27. The Saluda and Broad rivers combine to form the Congaree just north of Columbia.

my gun had the honor of doing.[28] I shall not linger over the description of Columbia, nor of the scenes I witnessed there on the night of the 17th.[29] On the 18th we were again upon the march. On the 22nd we passed through Winnsborough, having thoroughly destroyed the railroad all the way from Columbia. Here we first saw the 20th Corps, which with the 14th joined us from the left. From Winnsborough we struck eastward, through Liberty Hill, on the same rode used by the British when they left their winter quarters at W. to attack Gates at Camden. On the 3rd of March we reached Cheraw, where we found some 40 pieces of artillery and immense quantities of ammunition, which had been sent up from Charleston; all these we destroyed except one gun. This is a Blakely, a splendid piece, made in England. Gen. Blair gave it to the Capt. To present to the state of Minn.[30] We lay on the Great Pe-dee one day and then crossed, and marched by way of Bennettville and Flora College on this town. I have commanded, for some time, the foragers for our Battery; so I was in the advance yesterday morning when the "bummers" of our Division captured Fayetteville. We did not wait for the regular troops, but just formed line and charged on the double quick. We drove the enemy clear to the river. Then Gen. Smith hurried up his men, the flag was hoisted on the Courthouse, and our Battery sent a few shells across the river just to speed our departing friends. But we could not save the bridge; it was all ready for firing, and was partly destroyed before we reached it. This time it was the 14th Corps that was close at our heels. As you may imagine, the fellows of our Division are crowing over the rest of the Army; for this is the second important city that we have entered first.

So here we are, in communication once more with the North, for a gunboat came up from Wilmington this morning; it is said that more will come on Tuesday. While rambling through Dixie we got the latest news always

28. General Blair's campaign report mentions the crossing of the Thirteenth Iowa and its capture of the capitol buildings but includes nothing about the First Minnesota Battery. U.S. War Department, *War of the Rebellion*, Series I, 47.1:379.

29. Most of the city burned to the ground on the night of February 17, 1865. There has been much controversy over the role of Union soldiers in starting and spreading the fire.

30. Before Charleston's surrender, many of its Confederate military supplies had been sent to Cheraw to keep them out of Union hands. Wealthy Charleston families sent personal effects there as well: Sherman's men found quite a bonanza. See Sherman, *Memoirs*, II:290–92. The Blakely gun, also mentioned in later letters, was a rifled field gun of British manufacture imported to the Confederacy early in the war. A number of Blakeleys were in the Charleston garrison. See Ripley, *Artillery and Ammunition*, 149–51.

from rebel papers that we captured every day. In this way we heard of the fall of Wilmington the evacuation of Charleston, and the fighting at Richmond. The taking of Charleston we justly claim as another feather in the cap of Sherman's Army; for it was in consequence of our movements that the enemy were compelled to leave the much battered city.

On the whole, our campaign has been a pleasant one, with scarcely enough fighting to keep us amused. The foraging has been excellent. We have lived on the very best since we started, and have now more provisions in the wagons than we had then. The horses and mules are in splendid condition, the teams having been filled up by captured animals of the best description. Considering the season, the weather has not been very bad. But the swamps and the sandy soil were bad enough without any more rain than we had. However, nothing could stop our march; in the midst of rain and mud we pressed on almost as fast as in the finest weather. When we came to one of the numerous cypress swamps, the artillery and wagon trains would halt; the brigades of infantry would then advance into the swamp, each man carrying a rail on his shoulder; this he would throw down in the proper place, and pass on. In this way miles of fences were changed into corduroy roads, for the passage of our wheels. Lieut. Budlong and his Corps of Pioneers were most efficient.[31] I have often seen them standing in water up to their knees, chopping down trees for bridges.

We shall not stay here long; the grand campaign against Richmond must soon begin. Somebody is calling for the letters, and I must close. Goodbye till the next time.

T. D. C.

␣

Thomas Christie to David Christie

GOLDSBORO, N.C. MARCH 28TH 1865

My dear Brother Dave:

I received your most pleasant letter to me when we were in front of the enemy on the South Edisto River in South Carolina, and it gave me more pleasure than you can imagine,—It was just the kind of letter I shall always

---

31. Lieutenant David H. Budlong was the engineering officer for the Fourth Division of the Seventeenth Army Corps. According to his campaign report, engineers built 53,865 yards of corduroy road during the Carolinas campaign. U.S. War Department, *War of the Rebellion*, Series I, 47.1:413.

like from you,—telling about all the little things around home, which the rest overlook, forgetting that it is the *little things* that make home what it is.

I wish you to continue to write in the same manner, only leave out the buffoonery if you please, which you are too old now to indulge in. I got your last letter, to William, day before yesterday, and see by it that Charlie and Dolly have been trying on some of their tantrums again, you must look out for them, and not let them take you by surprise. I cannot see how you are to get along with the farm without a hired man nearly all the time this season for it is not right that you should work yourself so hard as you will have to do otherwise, nor should father have *anything at all* to do with the severe labour of the farm.

I have no news of anything more than when I wrote yesterday, for I have had no mail since the first one, the Recruits for the 2d Regt. have not been heard from yet, and the application for our furloughs which the Capt. sent to Head Quarters yesterday has not come back yet. Neither have I anything more to tell you about William than what I wrote to Father and Sarah.[32]

For the past 75 miles of our march I have been on regular detail as commanding the six mounted foragers of the Battery whose duty it is to supply the Company—150 men—with food, as we draw nothing from the Govt. In that capacity I met with a good many adventures and there was not a day that I did not ride 35 or 40 miles. One day we left the column early in the mourning and struck for Clinton toward which we were told the troops were to march. For 5 miles we rode along with the advance cavalry, but when they came to a big creek, found the Bridge destroyed by the Rebels and [the cavalry] went to work repairing it we "Bummers" could not wait, but took Sherman's plan of flanking the difficulty. On going down the creek through the swamp we found a place where we thought we could ford it and so to try the experiment I rode my little sorrel mare into the water and made for the opposite shore. She felt her way carefully through the swift current—the water getting deeper and deeper—till all of a sudden down she went into a hole, over the ears, the water coming up to my waist, with a chilliness that made me catch my breath. Amidst the cheers of my comrades the gallant little mare rose dripping and boldly struck out for the opposite shore. A few strokes and she again struck bottom, and we gained the shore without further difficulty, when the laugh was on the other side

32. William was captured by Confederate troops in the fighting at Bentonville, North Carolina, on March 21. First Battery Company Morning Reports, Mar. 1865.

as I was across and my men were not. They tried to make their mules take the water, but they—sagacious animals—had opinions of their own on the subject, and as is usual in such cases, they got the best of the argument. The next thing we did was to take a rope off one of the saddles, fasten one end to a mule's Bridle, tie the other end to a heavy club and throw it over to me. Two of the men then crossed the creek on a fallen tree and you can see how we got Mr. Mule over. In this way we got all safely across, mounted our animals, and set out for Clinton. But while on the road we heard that the Rebels had burned the Bridge over another, and larger steam in front, and of course we had more flanking to do. Galloped down to the right some seven miles to where I had heard of another Bridge, and arrived just in time to save it as the end next us was afire. Dashed over and struck for the plantations—We had thought we were the first of our fellows there, but found all our First Brigade foragers ahead, and had to ride four miles from there before we found fresh Country. When we had loaded three splendid carriages with hams, flour, meal, molasses &c. and had hitched enough mules from our party to haul them, we started for town in which we expected to find our column, But what was our surprise, on coming into Clinton to find it occupied by our Cavalry only, the main Column having turned to the left when within 6 miles of the place. After loading up we had come 10 miles to get to Clinton, and here was a 13 mile march before us yet—with the sun and hour high—Nothing daunted, we set out and after fording creeks, and hauling through miry swamps we arrived safely in camp at 11 O'clock, with enough supplies to last the Battery a week—I and all the men of the Company are very much amused by the picture Sarah sent me, of the "forager" but to make the likeness more striking and truthful the picture should represent a man, dressed in a nondescript suit part blue part home spun grey or Butternut, with a white hat and tremendous rents in his Breeches, and perhaps barefooted, with his Belt and cartridge box on, (for we always go well armed,) his trusty carbine by his side, and a revolver stuck in his Belt. When you have the man drawn out according to these directions, you must mount him in a splendid Buggy in which the aristocrats of the plantation used to take the air, attended by their sable coachman, in the "Good old times." The Buggy is to be hauled by the "Bummer's" old long eared, tail shorn mule accoutered as you please either in the magnificent silver mounted, ivory ringed harness that belongs to the Buggy, or in the cobbled up concern—the collars of braided cornhusks, the wooden harness tied together with rope, and the lines of the same material. Here you have the

forager and his conveyance—now for the plunder First and foremost you
will observe that the carriage is piled full of hams, (my foragers disdain any
other kind of meat,) and, on top of these you will see three or four sacks of
meal or flour, while around and behind hang clusters of turkeys, (chickens
are too difficult to catch, so we always take turkeys.) If you will enlarge your
picture so as to include three or four of these equipages with the same
number of mounted men in the [. . .] and a dozen darkeys bringing up
the rear mounted on captured horses and mules, you will have a very good
idea of how my train looks as it comes into camp at the close of each day. I
turned over so much forage during our march from Fayetteville to near
Bentonville that our Quartermaster Sergeant told me I must either stop
foraging, or else furnish another wagon to haul it. The next day I got him a
fine spring wagon loaded with supplies, and he put it in the regular train.

(Commence here on the interliniers)

I must tell you another adventure of mine,—The last day I was out I
left the column 20 miles from Olive Mount, on the Wilmington R. R. and
struck to the right, crossing the R. R. at Faisons. Near here we met a scout
of Genl. Sherman's coming from Kinston with Despatches from Schofield.
He had crossed the country afoot, and had many an adventure to tell which
I have not time to relate to you. Riding rapidly we came to Col. Hill's plantation 4 miles beyond Faison's, where we loaded a Buggy and wagon with
hams, flour, meal, and sugar, and then I sent them back to the station,
while I took one man with me, mounted a little darkey behind me for a
Guide, and set out into the interior to look for horses and mules. We were
the only Federals in that section of the country, and I felt pretty sure of finding live stock not far off. Rode 4 miles toward Wilmington, and came to a
plantation where there were two horses in the yard. These we transferred
our saddles to had the darkeys lead ours, and set out for the swamp, where
the Negroes said there were mules hidden. We had gone perhaps a Mile
from the house and had separated to look for mules, when I saw a Rebel
coming towards me, mounted.—He did not see me at first, but came very
leisurely over the plantation road on which we were, the distance being
about a quarter of a mile. My man was not is sight, but I knew that audacity would often win where numbers would fail, so unslinging my Breech-
loading carbine, (which, by the way, I captured in Columbia) and putting
spurs to my horse, I dashed on Mr. Johnny with a true Yankee yell. He
saw me, wheeled his horse, and ran as if a Regt. was at his heels. While I
was getting over a bad ditch in the field my comrade came in sight, and we

both set out in pursuit. In front of us—a mile distant, lay the swamp, and as it was merely a plantation road we were on I knew that we would have him there. On we rushed, yelling like Indians, the Rebel, keeping his distance, with hat off and long hair flying in the wind, and at every jump spurring his horse with the point of his naked Bowie Knife. It was the most exciting steeple chase you ever heard of, and perhaps you can imagine how we looked, flying over that old cotton field, the two contrabands bringing up the rear as they best could with the spare horses. The Rebel disappeared at the end of the road, and when we dashed up, there was his horse standing in the swamp, while he was in all likelihood up to the waist in water in the depths of the cypresses. We could not find him, and returned to our mule hunting with his splendid horse, saddle, and Blankets, as trophies. We were so lucky as to find three, excellent mules, which are now doing duty for Uncle Sam, and two more horses, so that we returned to our companions at Faison's with three mules and six new horses. Where we run the Johnny into the swamp there were two darkeys who told us he was a Rebel cavalry man, and that he was armed with two Revolvers, we did not know this till afterwards, or he would have had to come out of the swamp, sure. We rushed down to where the negroes were, shouting—"De Yankees, de Yankees" We got to camp that night at 10 O'clock, having passed through Mount Olive station on the road. The next morning we were on the march at three, as I wrote to father, so you see I had not much sleep that night.

One rainy, chilly day, soon after leaving Fayetteville, we had ridden till five in the afternoon without having got so much as a chicken, for the country was miserable pineland, inhabited altogether by poor people, from whom we hate to have to press supplies. We were then 8 miles away from the column, and it was raining hard, so the prospect for forage, you will perceive, was very slim. But I told the men that we had never gone to camp yet without something to show for the day's work, and that we must not then. So I enquired around, and found that there was a Grist mill in the neighborhood. We immediately made for it, took possession, and while I set the mill in running order, the men filled the sacks they always carry on their saddles, with corn from a crib within a mile. This was brought to the mill, several went to shelling into the hopper by hand, the Gate was raise, and there being a good head of water we soon had the thing progressing finely. I posted two men as pickets, and sent another to a house in the neighborhood to tell the folks to get supper for us, so that at dark he came back with a Basket full of cooked sweet potatoes, ham and "corn dodger," which were very acceptable, as you may imagine, to hungry fellows as we were. An hour after dark we stopped the mill, having shelled and ground over seven Bushels of meal, and filled every sack we had. The taking of this meal on our horses into camp,—nine miles—over a road scarcely to be seen through the woods in the daytime even, and now when the cloudy night was dark as pitch, all the way we could find the road was by our horses, was considerable of a job.

But you may be weary of this long talk about foraging, and so I will stop. If you can read this double letter in less than a week, I am very much mistaken. I shall write more home tomorrow. Give my love to all dear friends, and be as much of a help to father as Sandy was.

Write soon again and think sometimes of your loving Brother

Thos D. Christie

∼

Thomas Christie to Alexander Christie

GOLDSBORO, N.C. APRIL 3D 1865

My dear Sandy,—It is the greatest of disappointments to me to have to go north without seeing you,— I have been expecting your arrival every day and hour since I got news from home of your having left the State,—I know how hard it will seem to you to go into a strange Company, and to find on your arrival that William is in the hands of the Enemy, and that I am away on furlough for 45 days,—Cheer up, though, my dear Brother, and meet adverse and unpleasant circumstances with the manly fortitude that becomes a United States Soldier in the Field—you will find pleasant comrades in the Regt. you belong to—who I have known for three years— among them Sergt. Everts in Co. A. and Sergt. Thompson in Co. B,[33] who will be kind to you for my sake, if it were not in their generous natures to be kind to you naturally—Do not fail to visit my Battery after, for you will be very welcome I assure you. Southwick, whom you know is Q.M. Sergt. and he will introduce you to my friends. Enquire for Corpl. Gross, Corpl. Foster, Ed Rowley, Dan Wright, and for my platoon in particular. They are all good friends, and good Boys. and you will take much pleasure in talking

33. Edmund A. Everts and William R. Thompson. It is interesting that Thomas knew noncommissioned officers from the Second Minnesota, as the First Battery was never in the same division or army corps. The units may have served near each other at Vicksburg, Atlanta, or Savannah.

to them.—Geo. Ehinger is with me as I write this letter and promises to find you. His address is—Head Quarters 4th Div. 15th Army Corps, where he is an Orderly,—Another good friend of mine is Wm Hill Co. "B" 32d Ohio—in the first Brigade of our Div. but he has a detail now as Division postmaster and you will find him in Division H'd Qr's.

Southwick will give you the letters,—which I wish you to read and then return to him for William to read if he should come along.—You will also get from him all the Mail that may come for me or William and you may read all that are postmarked Clyman or Lowel,—I have taken the liberty or reading two letters from home to you, which came to your Company a week ago—Of course, I do not need to urge you to write to me in Clyman—and I shall take care, after learning your address that you shall not want for letters,—Now, a few words of advice, which I would make longer, but that I cannot doubt that I will see you in New Burn. Remember that a soldier will rust out sooner than wear out, so do not be afraid to take exercise enough even in camp,—On the march you will have enough to do at all times—but the more tired you are at night, the better—Be VERY *Careful of your stomach, for from derangement of it flows nearly all the ills that afflict the soldier,*—Eat regularly, and very little grease. Be always cheerful, and ready to join in any fun that is going on in Camp,—I would have died long ago but for my laughing propensities. And, above all—if you *do* get sick fight the thing out. Don't give up . . . sickness as long as you can stand on your legs,— I stood Guard at Shiloh when I could not walk my beat to save my life,— but I *whipped* nature into accordance with my will, and got well, while great, stout, fellows who were not half so sick as I, succumbed got discouraged,— and *died.*—You must shut your ears to a great deal of Obscenity in the con- versation of your comrades,—but this is a habit with some of them, and is no proof of extraordinary depravity.—May GOD bless you, my *dear* Brother and protect you till we meet again, is the heartfelt prayer of your aff'ctly

Thos D. Christie

[margin note—first page] I am in hopes of seeing you in Newburn or would have written more—Expect to start from here this evening, shall be in Clyman on the 12th at furthest—furlough for 45 days till May 19th.

[margin note—back page, in another hand] This letter brought to me by our old schoolmate Edward O'Keefe evening Apr. 3, 1865. Alex. S. Christie, Apr.15, 1921

∾

Thomas Christie to Alexander Christie

AT HOME—APRIL 13TH 1865

My dear Sandy—I have a great deal of pleasant news to tell you for which I hope you will be thankful.—I shall give it to you all in a bunch, first and then go into details—The news then is this,— William is at home on parole,[34] having been n Richmond, and has more adventures to tell of than would fill a volume,— Thomas Ried[35] is also with us, having got a furlough from his Regt. at Mobile,—also in good health, and getting fat fast after his experiences in Dixie—I got here all right night before last, and found *all well*. Dave and father busy putting in the Crop.—I shall not write much in this note, as I have not time, for Sarah is waiting on me to go with her to Watertown at 11:30 and it is now ten O'clock When we get back though you shall have a *very long letter* which I know will be acceptable,—If you see any of my company tell them to let the Capt. know that I had to leave the Gun in Baltimore,[36] and have written to the Gov. today. Of course you must be with your Regt. by this time—Everybody is well, and somewhat Jubilant over the good news from Grant, and our return—The only drawback to our enjoyment is the absence of yourself. Your letter to Willie from Wilmington has been recd, which is the latest from you—Calculate on a splendid letter in two days—Must excuse this short note, for I am awfully crowded at present.

—They all send their love—Yours aff'tly
Thos D. Christie

∽

Thomas Christie to Alexander Christie

CLYMAN WIS APRIL 20TH 1865

My dear Brother,—It is mail day—past eleven A.M. and you *must* have a letter from me,—father is writing at the same table to you also, for we are determined that you shall have letters enough anyhow to cheer your heart

---

34. In a form of prisoner exchange current in the nineteenth century, a soldier signed a document promising not to fight until traded for a prisoner from the other side. At this point in the war the agreement could not have meant much, as the Confederacy had few places to keep prisoners and no hope of getting men back.

35. A cousin serving in the Twenty-ninth Wisconsin.

36. The Blakely gun: see page 295, note 30, Thomas to James, Mar. 12, 1865.

in the new and strange life that is now your lot—You never saw so busy a chap as is "yours Respectfully," now and all the time I have been here—As if it were not enough for a poor fellow to do to run his legs off seeing every pretty girl in the neighborhood—besides some *not* in the neighborhood; and be dragged around by the collar, almost, by a sister who seems *determined* that if there is anyone in the *State* who will not know of my presence therein it will not be from want of physical, positive palpable, proof of the fact,—I say—as if all this exercise were not enough regular duty—father presses me into the service by insinuating allmost every morning, that— "there are some small stumps to be dug out or hauled off in the west lot," or "there are some stones on the southern part of the ridge, that should be transferred to the fence corners—" and forth with orders a detail from the 29th Wis.—and 1st Battery of Lt. Art. Min Vols.—to perform the indicated duty—Of course Tom Reid and W. and myself profess to be highly pleased with the prospect of doing a little work—as we really are, in all seriousness,—and to me have helped a little to earn our board—ever since our arrival. I must confess, after all, that there is an awful disparity between the value of our spasmodic labors on the farm, and that of the substantial products of the ditto, which daily disappear before our soldiers appetites,— I will tell you a portentous secret in this connection, which you are not to divulge under pain of the siverest penalties—we are all fatting up at father's expense—in fact we are filling up our supply trains with potatoes, fresh meet, salt ditto, chickens, eggs, milk and soft bread, preparatory to the next campaign.—But a truce to such nonsense—I am enjoying myself here *the best I have in my life*—and only wish you could be here with us—went over to Lowell day before yesterday with the team,—that is, W took the team and Sarah and Tom up, while Dave and I took the rifle and went by land, or rather by water, through the marshes, up the river, shot at several doocks, but failed in the desired requiseth of shooting through any,—Stayed then in Lowell and in Reeseville and in the town of Elba (where I went to see a comrade's family) till yesterday afternoon, when Jessie and Rosine came down with them, while I travelled home "en solo"—on the old hunting route—Shot off a duck's head in the river and the creature was so perverse as to float to the other shore, when of course, I had no alternative but to strip off plunge in, swim over, take Mr. Drake in my teeth and swim back again. This somewhat astounded the folks at home when I told them of it— but I told them I could not wait to corduroy, according to our plan with "Old Billy," so I had to do as our chaps did on the Salkehatchie—swim for it.

While at Lowell I saw Mrs. Henry Noyes,—who had to tell me all about how she managed everything in Henry's absence, who, you know, is now in the 53rd Wis. at Camp Benton Mo. I also saw Miss Catch at Uncle Daves and had a good visit with her and the two Miss Reese's,—The farm work is going on famously,—you remember the old, green elm stub, that the woodpeckers used to build in down in the west marsh—well, it is now *non est,* thanks to the labors of Will and I, and that is not half we have done of the kind. I feel regular old farmer like when I get to work in this style I assure you.

This is awful news from Washington. I can imagine how the Soldiers in the field will receive the news of Lincoln's death—the Johnnies will have to look out more that ever, for this murder has steeled the hearts of the nation. I shall leave here on the 12th proximo—So you may look out for me about the 24th, as I shall visit some down east—Must send off this to catch the mail—Yours truly T. D. Christie

∽

Thomas Christie to James Christie

CAMP NEAR WASHINGTON D. C.

MAY 25TH 1865

My dear father;

The grand Review is over and we once more settle down into the usual routine;[37] I am sure you have been looking anxiously for news from me, but I have not had a single moment since I arrived which I could devote to writing and even this now I have to do while I am watching my grazing horse.

To take up the thread of my narration, (the last instalment of which Sarah recd. from the Steamer on Long Island Sd.) The next morning after writing my letter of the 17th I found myself in the Metropolis, where I had to stay till ten A. M. getting transportation after which I took the ferry boat and went over to Jersey City, where I took the cars for Philadelphia. Did not see much worthy of note in crossing the Jerseys.

37. Following Johnston's surrender on April 26, Sherman's army had marched to Washington and joined the Army of the Potomac in a two-day Grand Review on May 22 and 23. The event was something of a contest between the two armies. See Foote, *Civil War,* III:1013–17.

Was in the Quaker City at noon and rode on the street cars clear through it from one depot to the other, a distance of *six miles*. It is a lovely city, the streets all regular and clean. When we got to the Baltimore depot we missed the train and had to wait till 2.30 for the next one. It was an express and we ran through from Philadelphia to Washington without change of cars. Crossed the Susquehanna at Havre de Grace on a ferry. Were in Baltimore in the night sometime, and in the Capital at 10.30 P.M. I stayed all night in the Soldiers Rest, and next morning walked through town to the Alexandria ferry boat, which I got aboard of and was soon on the "Sacred soil" in the dirty straggling city of Alexandria. Reported immediately to Capt. Taggart, Hd. Qrs. Army of the Tennessee, who told me the Corps would be close to town in the afternoon. Left my duds in the Soldiers Rest and went to see Uncle Thomas in fort Ellsworth whom I found well and hearty, only a trifle homesick. Saw all the Clyman chaps, who were perfectly delighted to see me.

Still going on the high pressure principle, that has characterized all my movements since leaving home, I only stayed two hours with Uncle and then went out is search of Sandy, as I knew his Corps was to be in that day. Uncle and Charley McQuivery went with me, and I had not gone far on the road leading out from the fort when I met an officer of my Division who told me that the 17th Corps was to bivouac 6 miles from the city that night. Went a little further and ran across Tom Gordon Laport and Lego, who had been in Washington for several days. Went with them to the provisional camp where I found 31 recruits for the Battery. Henry Murray and several old acquaintances who were awaiting the arrival of the army. Murray might as well have stayed at home till I left, as he had been all the time since coming to Washington, in the provisional camp with nothing to do.—From the camp we travelled out a mile further and found the 3d Division, 14th Corps going into camp. We struck their column on the flank, and happened to come up first to the Regt. just in advance of the 2d. When the 2d came marching along I discovered that they were marching with the left in front, which threw Co. A in the rear. When I saw the Capt of A, I spoke to him and asked if "Christie" was along. He said he supposed he was, for he was one of the very few who had never fallen out of the ranks yet, though they had made some tremendous marching. The Capt. was waiting for his Company to come up, as they had had to wade a creek a little distance back, which had strung the men out. I waited quite a while watching

the men as they came up the hill, but though the Regt was ordered forward
I see nothing of the Hero. As we were wondering what had become of him
I heard the Capt. calling to me and following the Company I found Sandy
on the other side of the hill he having gone around instead of over, and got
ahead of his company—I would give five dollars if you could see his photo,
as he appeared then. He was looking perfectly well and hearty, but rough
as a bear, dressed in old worn pants, shoes dusty with travel, torn Blouse,
low, broad brimmed black hat, and a shirt that looked as if it had seen
Raleigh since it had seen soap and water. Around his waist was the waist
belt for the cartridge box, in his hand his trusty Springfield, and from one
shoulder suspended his haversack, (alas—empty) while the other supported
his dog tent and rubber blanket, twisted together. He looked the perfect picture of an Infantry man in Light marching order. The Regt. moved on into
camp, but he got permission of his Capt. and stayed with us. So we had a
two hour's talk. He had had nothing to eat since morning, and had nothing
for supper, so I took out my of my pocket a large cake I got in Alexandria
for lunch, and it did me good to see him eat. You can imagine what a good
time we had there on the grass, talking of our mutual adventures. Sandy
smiled when I told him he took things too much in earnest, and that he
must laugh more. It is a fact, that he is entirely too sober, though not at all
melancholy. He laughed when he told me that he had discovered long since
that what I told him was true, that there was actually no *Romance* in the life
of a soldier.[38] You can't think how much pleasure I took in seeing him so
well, and in having a talk with him. He has a very high reputation in his
Company and his officers fully appreciate his good qualities. I could write
a dozen sheets about him, but must hurry.

On leaving Sandy we went back to where the road turned off toward my
Corps, when Charley took leave of us and I went out to find the Battery
accompanied by Uncle Thos. who went out with me some 3 miles and then
went back. After a tedious tramp over the muddy roads I found the Battery
just going into camp, and brought to them a large mail, the first they had
had since leaving Richmond, which of course made me doubly welcome. I
had the pleasure of reporting to Capt. Clayton at six P.M. of the 19th, the
very day my furlough expired, being the first of the absent who returned.
The Capt. had received a letter from the Governor who told him he had

38. See Thomas to Alexander, Mar. 5, 1864 (page 203).

ordered the gun from Baltimore; and should have the proper inscriptions put on it, and deposit it in the State House to be seen by everybody.[39]

I was immediately assigned to my old platoon. But found that my little mare had got stiffened up on the Raleigh campaign and had been traded off. I have a very fine roan mare now, however. Found Jesse Conner in camp, not very well, but he is better now. He had a thousand questions to ask about the folks in Clyman. Found that Bill Wiltse had met with an accident in Goldsborogh in being badly blown up and burned with powder, on acct. of which he had been sent to hospital north. Haywood, too had left at Raleigh, sick, and nothing has been heard of him since. Presume he is in the East.—All of the rest are well, I have not yet seen Geo. Ehinger as I have had no chance—On the 20th, as I was writing to you, who should come into the tent but Mr. Maull, the Agent of the Christian Commission at Vicksburg, now in business in Washington, who no sooner heard of the arrival of the 17th A. C. near Alexandria than he came out to see all of his old friends. So, all that day I went around with him through the camps looking up old chums of that happy winter in Vicksburg. Mr. Maull stayed with me all that day and night, and next day it rained, so he could not get away Till afternoon of Sunday, when I got him a horse, took one myself, and went to Alexandria with him. That same afternoon I visited the 39th Mass. in the 5th Army Corps, and had a talk with the husband of Mrs. Richardson with whom Helen is staying in Newton Center. To find him I had to traverse the whole Army of the Potomac, and did not get back to camp till ten P.M. having travelled all of 25 miles that afternoon.

On Monday we moved camp, passing through Alexandria, and camping close to the end of the Long Bridge, opposite Washington. On Tuesday we were busy making preparations for the Grand Review, and seeing what short time we had, you must allow we were busy. The harness was all washed and oiled, the brasses brightened up, the carriages well washed and brushed over with paint oil to make them shine; clothing was cleaned, and the Non-Commish had to put on their Chevrons and pantaloon stripes. Everything was got ready, and at 8 yesterday morning we marched across the Long Bridge, and went into bivouac till about ten, when our Corps passed in review. The Infantry was in Column of Companies and followed by all the

39. Governor Stephen Miller's papers show that he received letters from Thomas Christie and Thomas Simpson regarding the Blakely gun. Unfortunately, Miller's outgoing correspondence has not survived: it is not clear what action he took on this matter or what happened to the gun.

artillery of the Corps, our Battery in the advance with Battery front. In this order we marched for more than two miles, through Pennsylvania Avenue and the principal streets. The whole of this distance we were between living walls of spectators, who cheered us at every step. Near where we entered the Avenue there was hung over the street a great banner with the motto, "All hail our Western Heroes! Donelson, Shiloh, Corinth, Vicksburg," &c., all the names of our western battles. As we approached the reviewing stand, on which were the President, Genls. Grant, Sherman, Meade, and many more, the vast amphitheatre on either side of us rang with deafening cheers, and no wonder, for our Artillery Brigade presented a most magnificent spectacle. In front rode the Major Commanding attended by his staff. Then came our Captain mounted on his splendid grey. At an interval behind him followed the flag of the Battery presented to us by General Smith, the flag of crimson silk, with the name of the Battery and two crossed cannons, pierced by a blue arrow worked on it. This was carried by a mounted orderly, and guarded by Sergts. Conner and Grey with drawn sabres on either side. Close to the flag came on the front of our Battery, 24 horses abreast, and "dressed" in line to a hair's breadth, the Sergeants and Lieutenants abreast of their lead-drivers, with drawn sabres, the Guns and Caissons all moving as if on one axle, in a ponderous, rattling mass; the cannoneers (full detachments) all mounted on the chests with folded arms; Behind us followed by the other Batteries of the Brigade in the same manner and with the proper intervals. It was a sight seldom to be seen, and long to be remembered.

As the solid and well aligned head of column of our Battery passed General Sherman, he was noticed to turn quickly and smilingly to the Lieutenant General who sat near, and speak a few words. Grant smiled also, and answered him, and of course all our fellows have it that something complimentary to us passed between them. For my part, I can say that I never did a harder piece of work than I did in that two miles' march, and when I passed the reviewing stand I saw nothing except the line to my right, on which it was my duty to keep my piece "dressed." It required the most constant attention on the part of the mounted officers to preserve the distances and alignments, and this attention was faithfully given, which is the reason we did so well. It would have been far easier and more pleasant for us to have let the line take care of itself, while we looked around at the sights, but none of us had that intention, As I said, I did not see anything of the dignitaries on the Stand, and so, after we had marched to the lower part of the city and hauled out of the street to rest, I got permission from the Capt. and went back afoot to the stand, where I had good views of Pres. Johnson, Genls. Grant, Sherman, Meade, Hancock, Howard, Davis, Cadwallader, and all the rest, besides all of the Cabinet Officers, and foreign Embassadors.[40] I was there when the 14th Corps went by, and saw Sandy, but could not speak to him. After the thing was over our Corps marched out to its present position, where we are in camp near Fort Stevens, where they had the fighting last fall. The 14th went back across the river, so Sandy and I are now ten miles apart. There are a thousand rumors about our discharge but I am inclined to think we shall be kept till the thing is over for good, so don't look for me short of two months. They are all going out before the veterans. I think we will be paid off and perhaps given a sixty day furlough in our state till they can see whether we will be needed any further. Had a letter from W. in Benton Barracks. Have had nothing from home

Yours hopefully,

T.D.C.

[margin note—first page] The Orderly Sergt. is very sick and I am appointed to act in his place till he gets better, so am very busy with double duty. Southwick is well and sends his respects, Conner is much better and sends his thanks to S.

∿

William Christie to James Christie

BRIGHT NOON, D. C. MAY 27TH, 1865

Dear Father. I arrived in Washington on the day that "Buells" Army was reviewed, but could not see it, having to go through the "Circumlocution Office." So I and 91 other patriotic soldiers of these ere United States were held in durance vile, until the forenoon of the 23rd, and then we were allowed the privilege of finding our commands: after much travel, and sweating and many inquires as well as missdirections, I at length found the battery and had to run the gauntlet of nearly every old comrade in camp

40. General Sherman was immensely proud of his men and very pleased by the impression they made during the review: "Many good people, up to that time, had looked upon our Western army as a sort of mob; but the world then saw, and recognized as a fact, that it was an army in the proper sense, well organized, well commanded and disciplined; and there was no wonder that it had swept through the South like a tornado." Sherman, *Memoirs*, II:377–78.

about that forrage I went out after. I found T. D. in excellent health and enjoyed himself hugely while east. Receiving a warm Irish welcome among our old friends, and again [. . .] of the Sion Mills to me of many pleasant memories: He had very little to say to me about Minnie but she in the short time he stayed there, took him a sightseeing of Newhaven, giving him a very pleasant run off some very high hills near her place of residence.[41] It not being any of my business I have not asked him anything about what impression she made on him as to her personal or moral appearance, but to tell the truth it I think is favorable. I have not yet seen A. D. C. It rained so yesterday and rains so today that it is not fit to be out in, and besides we hear that the 14th Corps is moving camp, coming to this side of the Potomac, madam Rumor says they are now within two miles of us.

On Sunday afternoon I left St. Louis; and had a very pleasant passage over the Penn. C. R. R. being only three days on the road stoppages included, and I feel as though I had been paid for my trouble. I had a long travel through Baltimore, and allso through Pittsburgh, and the scenery over the Altoona mountains was very pleasing to the eye. I found the Boys all well except [. . .] so T. D. is now acting orderly. One of the Vets has not yet come back from furlough, he is the one that is such a Notorious Theif, and I would not be surprised if he was in Limbo somewhere for some trick of that kind on the road.

There [is] much questioning here among the troops about what is going to be done with the Vets: and Rummors are as thick as pigeons in a pigeon Roost, but there are none of them worth repeating so I will not bother you with any of them.

I have not yet seen much of the City, but what little I have seen does not much like what the Capital of the U.S. should do. The Capitol I have seen at a little distance, but owing to is Location it does not strike me as very imposing, or Grand, allthough I believe it is both. T.D. saw Sandy while on Review, but could not speak to him, so thats what it is to be in the army. My impressions are not favorable to a city life I saw enough of its dangers while round St. Louis: and the warnings I had was needed, I assure you, and were of use to me. I do not know why but it seems to me I can never see the better side of humanity anymore, the time was I could not [see] the dark side, but it seems to me now as though I had lost the faculty of seeing anything

41. Living in Connecticut were a number of Bertie cousins of Thomas Christie, the children of his mother's brothers and not directly related to William. See Christie papers, box 1.

but evil, and that [continually?]. It surely cannot be in myself this thing exists so much, that I am constrained to measure every one a peck out of my own bushel.

Tom saw Helen,[42] he says she told him she had quit corrosponding with me, he tels me she looks very healthy, and will be at home this July, so she talks in that strain at one time and then in a contrary one at others, and I verily believe she is like her Father very fikle minded. Tom had a first rate time, take it all round, and I am glad of it.

how is Sarah getting along with her school and what are you doing on the place, give my love to Mother, and do not forget to grand mother. I expect letters tonight, and if I get them, why I will just have another excuse for writing. I hope the folks are all well, and that everything looks as if you were going to have good crops; I have plavered all I can at present, so I must close. I am ever your affectionate son

William g. Christie.

42. Helen Alexander Christie, daughter of James Christie's brother William.

Bibliography

MHS   Minnesota Historical Society, St. Paul

Allen, Joseph M. Letters. MHS.

Brown, Dee Alexander. *Galvanized Yankees*. Urbana: University of Illinois Press, 1963.

Dictionary of American Biography. New York: Scribners, 1964.

Donald, Herbert David. *Lincoln*. New York: Simon and Schuster, 1995.

Dyer, Frederick Henry. *A Compendium of the War of the Rebellion*. New York: T. Yoseloff, 1959.

Edwards, William B. *Civil War Guns: The Complete Story of Federal and Confederate Small Arms*. Harrisburg, PA: Stackpole Co., 1962.

Ewen, David. *All the Years of American Popular Music*. Englewood Cliffs, NJ: Prentice-Hall, 1977.

First Battery Company Morning Reports. First Minnesota Light Artillery. Reports and Record. MHS.

Foote, Shelby. *The Civil War: A Narrative*. New York: Random House, 1958–74.

Fox, William F. *Regimental Losses in the American Civil War, 1861–1865*. Albany, NY: Albany Pub. Co., 1889.

Gibbon, John. *The Artillerist's Manual*. 2nd ed. New York: D. Van Nostrand, 1863.

Glatthaar, Joseph T. *The March to the Sea and Beyond: Sherman's Troops in the Savannah and Carolinas Campaigns*. New York: New York University Press, 1985.

Grant, Ulysses S. *Personal Memoirs of U. S. Grant*. New York: Charles L. Webster and Co., 1892.

Heaps, Willard A. *The Singing Sixties: The Spirit of Civil War Days Drawn from the Music of the Times*. Norman: University of Oklahoma Press, 1960.

Instructions for Field Artillery, prepared by a board of artillery officers. Philadelphia, PA: J. B. Lippincott, 1861.

Mathews, Mitford M. *A Dictionary of Americanisms, on Historical Principles*. Chicago: University of Chicago Press, 1951.

McPherson, James. *Battle Cry of Freedom: The Civil War Era*. New York: Oxford University Press, 1988.

———. *For Cause and Comrades: Why Men Fought in the Civil War*. New York: Oxford University Press, 1997.

Minnesota Adjutant General's Report of 1866. Reprint: Roseville, MN: Genealogical Books, 1997.

"Minnesota Biographies," *Minnesota Historical Society Collections* XIV (June 1912).

Minnesota in the Civil and Indian Wars. St. Paul, MN: Pioneer Press Co., 1891.

Minnesota Light Artillery, First Battery. Muster Rolls. MHS.

Monaghan, Jay. *Civil War on the Western Border, 1854–1865.* Lincoln: University of Nebraska Press, 1985.

Morgan, James. "'Green Ones and Black Ones': The Most Common Field Pieces of the Civil War." *Camp Chase Gazette* 23.7. http://www.civilwarhome.com/artillery .htm (accessed February 2006).

Munch, Emil. Papers. MHS.

National Park Service. "Civil War Soldiers and Sailors System." http://www.itd.nps .gov/cwss/ (accessed June 15, 2010).

Quiner, E. B. *The Military History of Wisconsin: A Record of the Civil and Military Patriotism of the State, in the War for the Union.* Chicago: Clark and Company, 1866.

Ripley, Warren. *Artillery and Ammunition of the Civil War.* New York: Van Nostrand Reinhold Co., (1970).

Sherman, William Tecumseh. *Memoirs of Gen. W. T. Sherman, Written by Himself.* 4th ed. New York: C. L. Webster and Co., 1891.

Thomas, Dean S. *Cannons: An Introduction to Civil War Artillery.* Arendtsville, PA: Thomas Publications, 1985.

Thomas, Richard. *Antique American Clocks and Watches.* Princeton, NJ: Van Nostand, 1968.

Todd, Fredrick. *American Military Equipage, 1851–1872.* New York: Scribner, 1980.

Trudeau, Noah Andre. *Like Men of War: Black Troops in the Civil War 1862–1865.* Boston: Little, Brown, 1998.

U.S. War Department. *Instructions for Field Artillery.* Philadelphia, PA: J. B. Lippincott & Co., 1861.

———. *U.S. Infantry Tactics.* Philadelphia, PA: J. P. Lippincott, 1861.

———. *The War of the Rebellion: A Compilation of the Official Records of the Union and Confederate Armies.* Series I, 10.2, 270. Washington, DC: Government Printing Office, 1880–1900.

Wakelyn, Jon L. *Biographical Dictionary of the Confederacy.* Westport, CT: Greenwood Press, 1977.

Warner, Ezra J. *Generals in Blue: Lives of the Union Commanders.* Baton Rouge: Louisiana State University Press, 1964.

Way, Frederick. *Way's Packet Directory, 1848–1994: Passenger Steamboats of the Mississippi River System.* Rev. ed. Athens: Ohio University Press, 1994.

Welcher, Frank Johnson. *The Union Army, 1861–1865: Organization and Operations.* Bloomington: Indiana University Press, 1989.

Wisconsin Adjutant General's Office. *Roster of Wisconsin Volunteers, War of the Rebellion, 1861–1865.* Madison, WI: Democrat Printing Co., 1886.

Woodworth, Steven E. *Nothing but Victory: The Army of the Tennessee, 1861–1865.* New York: Vintage Civil War Library, Vantage Press, 2006.

Index

abatis, 138

Abbeville, MS, 86–90, 92

absent soldiers, 70. *See also* deserters and desertion

accidents, 227, 308. *See also* injuries

age of recruits, 206n46

agriculture. *See* farming

ague, 159, 164, 166, 183, 199, 220

Aimer, Jesse, 36, 133, 192

Aimer, Maggie, 153

Aimer, Mary, 133n12, 153

Alabama, 15, 59n52, 225; letters posted from 219–27 passim

alcohol use. *See* drinking (alcohol)

Alexandria, VA, 17, 306, 308

Allatoona, GA, 228n23, 230n24

Allen, J. M., 80, 90, 103, 109, 117

alligators, 127, 128

American-born soldiers, 251–52

American Watch Company, 238n33

ammunition, 60–61, 143, 151, 212; care of, 220; Confederate, 240n34; "[doesn't] discriminate," 137; evacuation of Atlanta and, 274; explosions and, 167, 246; jewelry made from, 266–67; manufacture of, 33, 35. *See also* caissons

amputation of limbs, 56

Andersonville prison, 265–66

apples, 70, 178, 181–82, 195, 289

Archduke Ferdinand Maximilian. *See* Maximilian I of Mexico

Arkansas Post, 100

Arkansas River, 97

Armenian massacres, 18

Army of the Cumberland, 157n35, 248

Army of the Mississippi, 49n26

Army of the Ohio, 59n52, 248

Army of the Potomac, 67n59, 81, 85, 211, 214, 267, 305n37

Army of the Tennessee, 10, 37n32, 82, 147, 157n35, 225n17; Atlanta campaign and aftermath, 241n35, 243–73 passim; Washington, 306. *See also* Carolinas campaign

Army of Virginia, 59n51, 170

arrests, 258

arson, 76, 82, 165n46, 275–79 passim, 283, 294, 295n29; bridge burning, 298

artillery, 8–9, 43n11, 148; Atlanta campaign, 231–41 passim, 254–55; branch of army recommended by T. C., 27, 80, 249, 251; Confederate officer's ignorance regarding, 148; duels during March to the Sea, 284, 286, 287; on parade in Washington, 308–9; railroad transport of, 274; sea transport of, 286; Vicksburg, 130–31, 139, 142, 145, 163, 171. *See also* autonomy of artillerymen; caissons; guns; limbers; night shelling

Athens, AL, 219–24

Atlanta, GA, 247, 265, 266; evacuation of, 274. *See also* Bald Hill, Atlanta; Battle of Atlanta

Atlanta Campaign, 11, 15, 225n17, 228–60 passim; aftermath, 261–73; lead-up to, 218–28. *See also* Battle of Atlanta; Battle of Ezra Church; Siege of Atlanta

atrocities, 265–66, 271. *See also* black soldiers: massacre of

autonomy of artillerymen, 251

backpacks. *See* knapsacks
Bailey, Philip James, 159
baking. *See* bread baking
Bald Hill, Atlanta, 241n35
Baltimore, 16n23, 306
Banks, Nathaniel P., 59n51, 98, 99, 154, 224
Barry, William F., 274
baseball, 56, 111, 123, 211
"The Battle Cry of Freedom," 13, 106–7
battlefield descriptions, 45, 253–54
battlefield relics, 71, 79, 140, 243
Battle of Atlanta, 15, 237n32, 240–43
Battle of Bentonville, 16, 297n32
Battle of Big Black River Bridge, 180
Battle of Champion Hill, 180
Battle of Chancellorsville, 248n44
Battle of Corinth, 77–79, 80, 103, 107, 179–80, 257
Battle of Ezra Church, 243–44
Battle of Gettysburg, 248n44
Battle of Goldsboro Bridge, 16
Battle of Hatchie's Bridge. *See* Battle of Matamora
Battle of Island Number Ten, 114, 179
Battle of Kennesaw Mountain, 15, 234n31
Battle of Lexington, 35
Battle of Matamora, 82
Battle of Newmarket, 256n52
Battle of Nickajack Creek, 15
Battle of Raymond, 180
Battle of Shiloh, 10–12, 40–50 passim, 53n39, 55, 65, 80, 107, 168, 179; in epitaphs, 66
Battle of Wilson's Creek, 95
bayonet charges, 242
bayous, 102, 112n54, 117, 125, 128, 285
Beaufort, SC, 285, 288, 292, 294
Beauregard, P. G. T., 12, 44, 49
Beaver Dam (WI) *Sentinel,* 112
beds, 30, 110, 293
Belknap, William Worth, 243n36, 250, 258, 263, 293
Belleville, IL, 28
Beloit College, 18
Benton Barracks, MO, 8, 9, 28–33 passim, 305, 310
Bentonville, Battle of. *See* Battle of Bentonville
Bertie, David, 133, 157, 194, 305
Bertie, Janet, 36, 89, 124, 133n13, 178, 194, 212
Bertie, Jessie, 133n12
Bible, 150, 151, 160

Big Black River, 129, 169, 177, 212, 213–15. *See also* Battle of Big Black River Bridge
Big Shanty, GA, 15, 228n23, 231–32
birds, 40, 198. *See also* turkeys
Birge's Western Sharpshooters, 37
birthdays, 89, 90, 201, 237. *See also* Washington's birthday
bivouacs, 74, 76, 83–84, 86, 215, 221, 271, 276, 277; attacked by snipers, 257; in deserted houses, 100, 221; on levee top, 113–14
Bixler, Moses, 30n16
blacks, 58, 85, 89, 97, 136, 150, 157, 185, 262–63; assist escapee, 279–80; churches and, 156; as cooks, 208n48; as dockworkers 167, 174; employed to clean Vicksburg streets, 154; foraging expeditions and, 299, 300; impressed to construct rifle pits, 247; Meridian expedition and, 205; as Pioneer Corps, 283; schools for, 194; smell of (according to W. C.), 160; southern dialect and, 153. *See also* slavery; slaves
black soldiers, 120–22, 124, 155, 169, 170, 224, 292; massacre of, 217n7
Blair, Francis Preston, Jr., 16, 225, 226n19, 231, 242, 248, 273n11, 283; drinking of, 231, 263; taking of Columbia and, 294
Blair, Montgomery, 184, 231n26
Blakely guns, 16, 295, 303, 307–8
boats, 57, 98, 128, 289. *See also* gunboats; hospital boats; steamboats
bodies, dead. *See* corpses
body weight, 149, 156, 167, 181, 290
Bolivar, TN, 69, 79, 83
Bonaparte, Louis-Napoleon. *See* Napoleon III
bonus pay, 188n20
books, 87, 91, 110, 113, 159; as battlefield relics, 71; care for, 111; requests for, 191, 195, 201, 215; self-awareness regarding, 116; sent north, 119, 126, 157. *See also* Bible; dictionaries; libraries; travel books
bookstore pillage, 279
boredom, 254
Bormann fuse, 142
Brackett's Battalion, 5
Bragg, Braxton, 98, 157, 170
brass bands, 68, 190
brass jewelry making, 266–67
Bray, James, 164–65, 166
bread baking, 159. *See also* cornbread
breaking camp, 113
breastworks, 47, 49, 97, 138, 229, 241, 244, 260

bridges, 92, 296; Big Black, 213, 214; Chattahoochee, 239, 274; destruction of, 275, 283, 295, 297, 298; Edisto, 294; Little Ogeechee, 282, 283; Matamora, 82; Oconee, 280; Ogeechee, 282; Peedee, 295; pontoon, 222, 225, 277–78, 282, 294; Potomac, 308; repair of, 86; Salkehatchie, 293; Saluda, 294; Tuscumbia Creek, 62; Wolf, 91, 93. *See also* Battle of Big Black River Bridge; swamps: bridging of

Brown, John, 136

Brown, Joseph E., 247

Bruinsburg, MS, 127n9

brushes with death. *See* close calls

brush fires, 152

Buckland's Brigade, 10, 40

Budlong, David H., 296

Buell, Don Carlos, 44, 47–48, 59n52

buglers and bugling, 35–36, 68–69, 73, 83, 113, 114

bullying, 209–10

burials, 79, 160, 162. *See also* graves

Burnside, Ambrose, 85, 144, 170

Burnsville, MS, 76

Burrows, Eli, 30n16

Butler, Benjamin, 285, 286

"Butternut" (nickname), 58n49

Cairo, IL, 10, 15, 36, 44, 175, 199, 214–18 passim

caissons, 8, 44, 47, 113n55; accidents and, 227; chief of, 92; danger of, 76, 82, 246; foraging use, 278–79, 281; leather washers for, 244; positioning of, 75, 118; as shelter, 114; Washington march, 309

calliopes, 37

camaraderie: death and, 54

Camp Benton. *See* Benton Barracks, MO

campfires, 84, 222, 271, 276, 290. *See also* cooking: fires for

camping rough. *See* bivouacs

Camp Sumter. *See* Andersonville prison

Canada, 98

canals, 13, 96, 98, 100, 105, 112, 114

candles and candlesticks, 105, 110, 210, 273

cannons. *See* guns

Canton, MS, 205

Cape Fear River, 285n18

Cape Girardeau, MO, 36, 127

Carolinas campaign, 16, 291–302

carpentry, 189

Case, Douglas R., 270

casualties, 13–14, 55–56; Atlanta campaign, 234–36 passim, 240–44 passim, 253–57 passim; Corinth, 79, 103, 107n43; March to the Sea, 284, 287; Shiloh, 41–48 passim, 209n50; Vicksburg, 143, 145–46. *See also* death and deaths; friendly fire casualties; wounded soldiers

Catholicism, 123

cattle, 176, 222, 224, 270. *See also* cows

cavalry, 5, 40, 62, 83, 271; Atlanta campaign, 227; Carolinas campaign, 297; Confederate, 10, 62, 157n35, 213, 241, 265, 270, 280; foraging and, 270; horse artillery and, 148n25; Vicksburg, 116

caves, 153, 162

cease-fires, 130

cemeteries, 158

Chambers, Alexander, 121, 209–10

Champion Hill, Battle of. *See* Battle of Champion Hill

Chancellorsville, Battle of. *See* Battle of Chancellorsville

chaplains, 109, 195, 215

Charleston, SC, 59, 158, 283–86 passim, 291, 295, 296

Chattahoochee River, 237n32, 238, 239, 274, 275

Chattanooga, TN, 157n35, 170, 266–68 passim, 274, 278

Cheatham, James, 208

Cheatham, Nelson, 208

checkers and chess, 183, 264

Cheraw, SC, 295

chevaux-de-frise, 255

Chewalla, TN, 12

Chicago, 28, 218

Chickamauga, GA, 170n52

children as war victims, 137, 161

choirs, 190, 191

Christian Commission, 15, 215, 274, 308

Christian hymns, 106, 109, 110, 111, 115

Christianity, 102, 109, 207. *See also* Catholicism

Christian missionary work, 18

Christie, Alexander D. (brother), 3, 17; advises against brothers' reenlisting, 193; desire to enlist, 202–3, 227, 236, 249, 250, 256, 287, 290; letters to, 6; math and, 141, 152, 168, 187, 197; T. C. letters to, 27–28, 32–33, 63–65, 103–5, 133–35, 173–75, 187–89, 197, 202–5, 210–12, 216–18, 233–56 passim, 263–65, 268–88 passim, 301–5; T. C. mistaken for, 275; T. C. reunited with, 306–7, 311; travels of,

234, 235–36; 263–64, 268–72; twentieth-century annotations by, 265, 302; W. C. letters to, 49–50, 57–60, 65–67, 97–101, 125–30 passim, 135–46 passim, 154–71 passim, 178–87 passim, 192–94, 235–37
Christie, Carmelite, 22
Christie, David (brother), 4, 18, 60, 90, 146, 160, 218, 219, 303; T. C. letter to, 296–301
Christie, Elizabeth ("Eliza") Reid (step-mother), 3, 4, 6, 67n59, 124n2, 278n17
Christie, Elizabeth Gilchrist. *See* Gilchrist, Elizabeth
Christie, James (father), 3–6 passim; farm work and, 69, 297, 303, 304; proposed visit south, 218; T. C. letters to, 25–27, 36–48 passim, 53–62 passim, 70–71, 77–79, 86–87, 96–97, 112–15, 120–22, 127–28, 147, 195–96, 200–202, 206–7, 213–19 passim, 224–33 passim, 243–44, 256–66 passim, 272–73, 288–96, 305–10; W. C. letters to, 31–34 passim, 42–44, 51–52, 83–91 passim, 117–20, 130–33, 150–51, 161, 205–6, 221–24, 231–32, 310–12
Christie, Janet Smith. *See* Bertie, Janet
Christie, Mary. *See* Nute, Mary Christie
Christie, Mary Aimer. *See* Aimer, Mary
Christie, Sandy. *See* Christie, Alexander D. (brother)
Christie, Sarah (sister), 5, 6, 21, 36, 50, 59, 120; Amos Noble and, 165; birth, 3; debts of, 183; on farming, 4; Fox Lake Seminary attendance, 67, 89n20, 79, 112, 116, 126; George Ehinger and, 242; German language study, 103; James Dempsey and, 78n10; Jesse Conner and, 310; letters to, 6; portrait of, 220; religion and, 13, 102, 109, 123–24; as "School marm," 67–68, 133–34, 183, 220, 249, 252; T. C. furlough and, 304; T. C. letters to, 29–31, 67–69, 73–83 passim, 91–96 passim, 103–17 passim, 123–24, 138–40, 147–49, 175–84 passim, 190–92, 198–200, 207–10, 219–21, 252–54, 266–67; Tom Reid and, 137; W. C. letters to, 93–94, 125–27, 151–54
Christie, Thomas D.: as acting sergeant, 220, 231, 235; arrest of, 258; birth, 3; Blakely gun and, 16, 295, 303, 308n39; daughter of, 22; as editor and transcriber, 22–23; enlistment of, 5, 25–26; farming and, 4; health of, 52; illness of, 159, 214, 220; near wounding of, 229–30; opinion

of infantry branch, 124, 249, 251, 264, 288, 290; postwar life, 18–19; promotion of, 92; promotion declined, 226; romanti-cization and, 9; wounding of, 11, 40–41, 43, 47
Christie, William, birth, 3; capture and parole of, 297n32, 301, 303; enlistment of, 5; farming and, 4; grammar and punctuation of, 4, 23; illness of, 200, 208; postwar life, 18, 19; reunited with T. C., 303, 304, 311; self-analysis, 132, 193; T. C.'s correspondence with Sarah, 151–52; wounding of, 11, 40–41, 43
Christie, William (uncle), 60, 170, 187
Christmas, 31, 87
churches and church services, 156, 163, 188, 190, 195. *See also* prayer meetings
cigars, 135
Cincinnati Gazette, 59
City of Madison (steamboat), 166–67
civilians, 54, 64, 74; theft of food by, 155; Vicksburg cave system of, 153; as war casualties, 137
Clarkson, Janet, 126, 153
Clarkson, John, 89
class and war, 150, 207
Clayton, William Z., 7, 25, 61, 70–71, 75, 76, 214; Alexander Christie and, 249; Blakely gun and, 307–8; Carolinas campaign and, 294, 295; Chambers incident and, 209–10; as commander, 80, 90, 289; furloughs and, 120, 124, 126, 196n30, 225, 264; health of, 159, 164; in Marietta, 257; recruiting by, 5, 7, 15, 196n30, 199; Sarah Christie and, 96; wounded at Shiloh, 43, 55, 61
Cleburne, Patrick, 241n35
Clifton, TN, 218–19
Clinton, NC, 297, 298
close calls, 46–47, 229–30, 231, 233, 235, 240, 246–47, 258, 284, 286; river fording and, 297–98
clothing, 76, 95, 118–19, 292; of Alexander Christie, 307; burning of, 276; drilled by a bullet, 258; a forager's, 298; mended and washed, 246; removed for a change, 253; Shiloh loss of, 44, 94, 118; vermin-infested, 154. *See also* inspections
clothing allowance, 94n31
Clyman, WI, 3–4, 5, 12, 50n30, 66, 146n21
coal and coals, 29, 30, 173–74
coffee and tea, 59, 92, 104, 176
Coleman, Joseph, 175–76
college. *See* Fox Lake Seminary

Columbia, SC, 16, 294–95
commerce, 64, 181–82, 289. *See also*
   hawkers and peddlers
commissions, 124
Confederate Army of the Tennessee,
   236n32
Confederate battlefield relics. *See* battlefield
   relics
Confederate letters. *See* letters, Confederate
Congaree River, 294
Connecticut, 108, 311
Conner, Jesse, 43, 55–56, 123–24, 189, 192,
   211, 221, 308–10 passim; close calls of,
   235, 287
conscription, 69, 194, 206, 207n47
consumer goods: prices, 64, 289, 293
cooking, 67, 70, 104, 246, 290; on bivouac,
   75; fires for, 118, 282, 286
cooks, 58, 104, 208n48, 221, 263
Coosawatchie River, 292
copperheads (people), 114, 166, 179, 186,
   189, 207, 216
Corinth, MS, 10, 12, 45–85 passim. *See also*
   Battle of Corinth; Siege of Corinth
corn: begged for, 283; on Christie farm, 186;
   foraged, 88, 258, 259, 270, 271, 277–82
   passim, 300–301; grown in South, 58, 65,
   115, 128–29
cornbread, 88
cornmeal, 89, 277, 301
corpses, 39, 79, 153, 234, 242, 244; colonel
   finds his brother's body, 245. *See also*
   burials
corrupt practices, 14, 51, 56
cotton, 58, 65, 81–82, 94, 115, 118
Cotton, George C., 146, 182
cotton mills, 277–78
The Course of Time (Pollok), 159
courts-martial, 69
cows, 217
cricket, 118, 123, 211
Crimean War, 86, 87, 146n20
Crocker, Marcellus, 215n5, 226
Croover, Martin, 95
Cumberland, Army of the. *See* Army of the
   Cumberland
Cumberland Gap, 267
cursing, 68, 113, 134, 145, 157, 302

Davis, C. S., 53, 56
Davis, Jefferson, 179, 234, 266
Dawley, Richard L., 5
death and deaths, 13–14, 53–54, 179, 198;
   Atlanta campaign, 234–36 passim,

240–44 passim, 253–57 passim; caused
   by disease, 10, 33n20, 34, 53, 208, 277,
   302; caused by friendly fire, 32, 143;
   discouragement and, 302; drunkenness
   and, 96, 164–65, 166; fear and, 166;
   March to the Sea, 287; Shiloh, 41–48
   passim; of T. C., 19; Vicksburg, 143; of
   W. C., 18. *See also* close calls; corpses;
   suicide
debates, 85, 182, 191
debt, 32, 59, 67, 89, 115, 183. *See also* loans
Decatur, AL, 224–27, 228n20
Decatur, GA, 239, 241n35, 270–72 passim
De Gress, Francis, 294
dehumanization of infantrymen, 251
Dempsey, James, 59, 78–79, 81, 84
Dempsey, Michael, 36
Department of the Mississippi, 12. *See also*
   Army of the Mississippi
Department of the Ohio, 144n18. *See also*
   Army of the Ohio
Department of the Tennessee, 12. *See also*
   Army of the Tennessee
deserters and desertion, 35–36, 62, 258
desolation, 116, 161, 180, 217, 266
Devereaux, James, 265
Devereaux, William, 191
diaries, 45, 239, 293; destruction of, 276
diarrhea, 89, 103, 181
dictionaries, 199
diet. *See* eating; food
dinner calls, 104
dinners. *See* eating
disease, 10, 13, 32–35 passim, 56, 60, 208;
   inaction and, 211. *See also* malaria
Dodge, Grenville M., 248
Dodge County, WI, 3–4
dogs, 58, 206
draft. *See* conscription
drawings, 267, 270
dreams, 206
drilling of troops, 8, 27, 31–36 passim, 52,
   85, 118, 200, 207
drinking (alcohol), 15, 32, 50, 153, 164,
   231–32. *See also* drunkenness; whiskey
drinking water, 61, 64, 282
drought, 233, 234n30
drownings, 96, 201
drumming. *See* fifing and drumming
drunkenness, 96, 101, 164, 209–10
Dundee, Scotland, 3, 156
Dunn, James Taylor, 21
Duryea, Dave, 208
dust, 52, 62

Early, Jubal Anderson, 267
earthworks, 242
eating, 82–83, 104, 107–8, 143, 271, 300–301; artillery duels while, 286–87; breakfast, 114; imaginary, 71, 233; of oysters, 290; T. C. advice regarding, 302; of T. C. on furlough, 304. *See also* dinner calls; food; malnutrition; restaurant meals
Edisto River, 294
education, 52, 68, 116, 191, 194; blacks and, 262, 263
Edward Walsh (steamboat), 167
Ehinger, George, 235, 242, 302, 308
Eighteenth Illinois Infantry, 69n63
Eighteenth Missouri Infantry, 50n29
Eighteenth Wisconsin Infantry, 13, 41, 69n64, 80, 88, 107, 109
Eighth Indiana Infantry, 216
Eighth Iowa Infantry, 43
Eighty-first Ohio Infantry, 242
elections, 155. *See also* presidential elections
Eleventh Army Corps, 248n44
Eleventh Illinois Infantry, 62, 143, 155
Eleventh Iowa Infantry, 62, 212
Eleventh Minnesota Infantry, 264
Emancipation Proclamation, 97
embrasures, 101, 135, 139, 229; permit entrance of fatal shot, 287
Emma (steamboat), 173
Emperor Louis Napoleon. *See* Napoleon III
enclosures in letters: clover and grass sprigs, 152; myrtle, 157; Spanish moss, 95–96, 97. *See also* battlefield relics
England, 161
enlistment, 5–6, 25–26. *See also* Christie, Alexander D. (brother): desire to enlist; reenlistment
Ennisson, Joseph, 69
Ennisson, William, 153
Ennisson family, 60, 67
ennui. *See* boredom
epitaphs, 66–67
erysipelas, 33
escaped prisoners, 279–80
Evansville, IN, 57
Everts, Edmund A., 301
Everts, Rezin, 92, 235
evil, 311–12
Ezra Church, Battle of. *See* Battle of Ezra Church

Fall, James, 245, 289
farming: accidents, 202; Alexander Christie and, 186, 197, 202, 203; of Christie

brothers, 4, 5, 153n33, 304, 305; clover cutting, 61; horses and, 168, 186, 226, 297; James Christie and, 69, 70, 168, 170, 202, 203, 226, 297, 303, 304; in the South, 14, 65, 237; T. C. asks about home farm, 175
Farragut, David, 143
fatality and fatalities. *See* death and deaths
Fayetteville, GA, 260
Fayetteville, NC, 17, 295; letter posted from, 293–96
fear, 131–32, 166, 189
fearlessness, 230
Feber, Henry, 50
Ferdinand Maximilian. *See* Maximilian I of Mexico
ferries, 28, 128, 277, 305, 306
fifing and drumming, 83, 155
Fifteenth Army Corps, 244, 273, 274, 276, 280, 288, 289, 294
Fifteenth Iowa Infantry, 121, 212
Fifteenth Michigan Infantry, 68, 77, 88, 236
Fifteenth Ohio Light Artillery, 287
Fifth Ohio Cavalry, 40, 62, 93
Fifty-second Illinois Infantry, 106
Fifty-third Indiana Infantry, 219n11, 288
Fifty-third Wisconsin Infantry, 305
fighting with fists. *See* fisticuffs
firearms. *See* pistols; rifles
fires. *See* arson; brush fires; campfires
First Alabama Cavalry, 280
First Illinois Light Artillery, 50n27–28, 294n26
First Kansas Colored Infantry, 85, 88, 95, 96, 101, 169
First Kentucky Brigade, 242
First Minnesota Heavy Artillery, 42n9
First Minnesota Light Artillery, 3, 7, 26–27; Alabama and Georgia, 15–16, 219–28; health of, 158; Mississippi and Louisiana, 12–15 passim, 47–81 passim, 87–212 passim; St. Louis, 28–36 passim; steamboat transport of, 36–38, 216–17; Tennessee, 11–12, 39–47 passim, 81–86, 218–19; training of, 8–10, 27; Virginia and Washington, DC, 17, 305–12 passim. *See also* Atlanta campaign; Battle of Corinth; Battle of Shiloh; Carolinas campaign
First Missouri Light Artillery, 88, 101, 143, 175, 241
Fischer, James, 157
fishing, 68, 102
fisticuffs, 96, 101

flags, 107, 188, 294, 309; Confederate, 140, 242, 244

Flemming, Francis B., 58, 62n54

flintlock rifles, 64

floods, 13, 14, 37, 96, 115, 216. *See also* tents: leaking and flooding of

fog, 99

food, 40, 70, 88–89, 104, 107, 258, 271; aboard steamboats, 173, 176; baked peas for breakfast, 143; expenditures for, 119; imaginary, 65, 71, 227, 233; at literary association social, 192; price of in Savannah, GA, 289; purchased, 59, 64; from Sanitary Commission, 292; "we draws nothing from the Govt.," 297. *See also* apples; cooking; eating; foraging; hardtack; honey; hunger; milk; peaches; pork; rations; rice; sweet potatoes

foraging, 16, 40, 70, 75, 88, 222, 268–72, 282; army policy regarding, 54, 70; of berries, 59; country "pretty well stripped," 277; dinners after, 104, 107; during Carolinas campaign, 295–99 passim; a forager depicted, 298; of oysters, 288–89; poor southerners and, 300; T. C. arrest and, 258–59

Ford, John, 192, 194

fording of rivers, 227, 294, 297–98

Forrest, Nathan Bedford, 217

Fort Donelson, 37

Fort Ellsworth, 306

Fort Fisher, 285

Fort Henry, 37

Fort McAllister, 285

Fort Pickering, 177

Fort Pillow, 217

Fort Pulaski, 289

forts, 137, 138–39, 144; Atlanta evacuation and, 274

Fort Snelling, 5, 6–7, 17, 25–28 passim, 71, 178

Fort Stevens, 310

Fort Thunderbolt, 288–90, 291

Forty-seventh U.S. Colored Infantry, 55n43

Fosket, Horace B., 215n3

Fourteenth Army Corps, 244, 248, 274, 276, 295, 306–11 passim

Fourteenth Illinois Infantry, 224

Fourteenth Iowa Infantry, 43

Fourteenth Ohio Infantry, 241, 242

Fourteenth Wisconsin Infantry, 77, 80, 88, 107, 205, 264

Fourth Division, 15, 215n5

Fourth Minnesota Infantry, 7, 27n9

Fourth of July. *See* Independence Day

Fourth Wisconsin Cavalry, 216, 217

Fox Lake, WI, 76

Fox Lake Seminary, 67, 89n20, 94, 112, 185

France, 161

Frank, John, 165, 269

fraternization with enemy, 127, 130, 137, 148, 150, 153, 237

Fremont, John C., 35, 59, 261

friendly fire casualties, 32, 143

Frothingham, Samuel A., 274

Frye, Sylvester, 52

funerals, 53–54, 109

furloughs, 27, 205, 216–20 passim, 260, 263, 272, 310; application for, 167, 297; attempts to gain, 58; Clayton and, 120, 124, 126, 196n30, 225, 264; hopes for, 25, 164; impossibility of, 226; lotteries for, 156–57; reenlistment and, 15, 188, 195; sick leave, 60; T. C.'s finally achieved, 17, 301–7

gabions, 139, 229

Gage, Joseph B., 182–83, 197

"galvanized Yankees," 204

gambling, 15, 58–59, 158, 217

game, 63. *See also* turkeys

games, 110, 199. *See also* baseball; checkers and chess; cricket; quoits

gardens, 94, 115–16, 162

Georgia, 15, 16, 170, 224

German American soldiers, 56n46, 111, 165, 166, 256n52, 257–58, 261

Germantown, TN, 93

Gettysburg, Battle of. *See* Battle of Gettysburg

gifts, 99–100, 186, 187, 201

Gilchrist, Elizabeth, 3

glory of war (alleged), 161

gloves, 290

God, 99, 114, 126, 132, 161, 180, 193, 215, 232; close calls and, 230; race relations and, 262; in Robert Pollok's poetry, 159; as sender of war, 223

Goldsboro, NC, 301–2, 308

Goldsboro Bridge, Battle of. *See* Battle of Goldsboro Bridge

Gordon, GA, 279

Gordon, Thomas, 87, 92, 119, 212, 280, 306

gossip, 103, 152

grammar, 155

Grand Gulf, MS, 128

Grand Junction, TN, 81–86, 88, 106

Grant, Albert C., 247n41

Grant, Ulysses S., 10, 13, 14, 37n32, 91, 135;
Atlanta and, 225n17, 260; Blair and,
231n26; canal plan and, 13, 96n37,
112n54; confidence in, 155; eastern
theater and, 223, 232; McClernand and,
79n12; in Mississippi, 12, 14, 47, 96n37,
127n9, 130, 180n9; reviews troops in
Washington, 309, 310; Richmond and,
211; Shiloh and, 11; unpretentiousness of,
135, 146; Vicksburg surrender and,
147n23
graves, 79, 153, 158, 179, 253, 270;
unearthed by rain, 39
Green, James, 149n28
Green, Martin E., 149
Gresham, Walter Q., 219, 224, 226n19,
232–33, 236, 241n35, 248; wounded,
240
grist mills, 300–301
guard duty, 9, 32, 33, 34, 35; aboard
steamboat, 176–77
guerrillas, 16, 69, 169, 176, 177n7, 207;
boats and, 96, 99, 112, 174, 176, 217
gunboats, 31, 36–37, 44, 79, 96, 100n39,
101, 116, 177, 217; roar of, 137; Savannah,
GA, 288
guns, 8–16 passim, 43n11, 171, 205, 213;
Atlanta campaign, 232–41 passim,
246; destruction of, 274, 295; "exactly
in a line," 118; fired on Washington's
birthday, 201; names of, 233; names of
parts, 199, 211–12; operation of, 8, 78,
139, 142; Shiloh, 44; as site of bird's nest,
198; sound of, 78, 127, 129, 131, 137, 143,
237, 246, 255, 284; Vicksburg, 149, 163;
wheels silenced, 244. See also Blakely
guns; howitzers; James rifles; mortars;
ordnance rifles; Parrott rifles

Halleck, Henry Wager, 12, 49n26
ham, 298–300 passim
Hamburg, TN, 68, 70
Hamilton, Charles S., 86
hand grenades, 144, 145
hand-to-hand fighting, 234, 242
handwriting, 63, 103, 152, 192
Hanks, Norman K., 35, 53
Hardee, William J., 41, 243n36
hardtack, 40, 220, 226, 230, 266, 276, 283,
287; "adamantine," 107; breakfast of, 114;
enjoyed, 125; purchased, 233
Harper's, 133, 135
Harvey, Cordelia Perrine, 201
Harvey, Louis Powell, 201

Hatchie River, 82
hats: apparently slept in, 135; burned by
steamboat coals, 173; criticized during
inspection, 196
haversacks. See knapsacks
hawkers and peddlers, 30, 175
hay and haying, 68, 88, 166, 176, 202, 212
Haywood, F. L., 183, 221, 245, 252–53, 308
health, 18, 32, 40, 46, 52, 60, 92, 158, 290,
292; in Atlanta campaign, 245–46;
drinking and, 48. See also body weight;
disease; illness
Helena, AR, 100, 140, 217
Helper, Hinton Rowan, 149
Hickenlooper, Andrew, 69, 79
Hill, William, 302
hogs. See pigs
Holly Springs, MS, 81, 83, 84, 91, 92–93,
106
home life, 164, 304
homesickness, 204, 264
homesteading, 18, 189
honey, 258, 259
Hood, John Bell, 15, 243n36, 244n38,
259n59, 267, 272, 274
Hooker, Joseph, 85, 231, 232, 248, 248n44,
268n7
Hope (schooner). See USS Hope
hopefulness, 89, 203
Hoppin, Henry C., 53
horsehair chains, 187
horses, 32, 226, 229, 273, 290; Cairo, 214;
care of, 211, 220, 227, 281; falls from,
196; falls upon riders, 52; farm work and,
186, 226, 297; foraging and, 266, 268,
270, 300; inspections and, 196; jaded on
account of hills, 277; killed at Shiloh,
42–47 passim, 50; killed in Atlanta
campaign, 240, 255; limbers and caissons
and, 8; orders to give up, 272, 278;
providers of lullaby, 114; rain and mud
and, 74, 100, 116, 283; replaced, 308;
Sherman compliments regarding, 281;
steamboat travel and, 37, 39; stolen by
deserters, 62; tears over death of, 257;
topic of discussion, 168; at Vicksburg,
131, 134
horseshoes (game). See quoits
hospital boats, 103
hospitals, 32, 56, 62, 69, 124, 125, 168;
Cordelia Harvey and, 201n37; St. Louis,
52, 55, 56; stench of, 154
Hotchkiss, William, 26n7
Hotchkiss shells, 60–61, 80

houses, 74, 115–16, 282; bivouacked in, 100; burned, 116, 136, 180; damaged in Vicksburg, 153; emptied and destroyed, 265
Howard, Oliver O., 244n38, 248, 259, 310
howitzers, 43n11, 50, 62, 64, 139, 142, 171; ammunition and, 212; bird considers nesting in, 198; misplacement of, 131; sound of, 129
Huff House Hotel, 5
humor: T. C. on, 302
hunger, 75, 151, 226–27, 230, 233. See also starvation
Hunter, David, 31
hunting, 40, 63, 66, 218, 249, 304
Huntsville, AL, 15, 218, 219, 224
Hurlbut, Stephen A., 82, 226
Hurter, Henry, 196, 197, 226, 263, 287, 293
hymns, Christian. See Christian hymns

Iatan (steamboat), 114, 216, 217
illness: attitude and, 302; Benton Barracks, 32–34 passim; Corinth, 52n35; "idleness and dirt" as cause of, 56; of Joseph Allen, 103; of T. C., 159, 214, 220; transport of the sick, 65; Vicksburg, 156, 165, 177, 183; of W. C., 200. See also diarrhea, rheumatism; typhoid fever
The Impending Crisis (Helper), 149n149
Independence Day, 59, 60–61, 63, 66, 147
inequality, 169n50. See also rich and poor
infantry: T. C. opinion of. See Christie, Thomas: opinion of infantry branch
ingenuity, 86–87; examples of, 105, 110, 266–67
injuries, 196, 227
inspections, 104, 195–96, 211
Iowa Brigade, 15, 88, 118, 169, 294; Atlanta campaign, 236, 242, 243n36, 244
Ireland, 3, 117n60
Irish American soldiers, 85, 88, 123, 126, 136, 150
iron: in water, 52, 64; pig iron, 222
Island Number Ten, 174. See also Battle of Island Number Ten
isolation, 14, 53, 54
Iuka, MS, 12, 73, 75n4, 76, 179, 209n50

Jackson, MS, 147n24, 226
jails: burning of, 279
James rifles, 10, 15, 43n11, 142n17, 171, 205
Janesville, WI, 165, 166
J. C. Snow (steamboat), 216–17
Jeannie Deans (steamboat), 94, 101

Jerrold, Douglas William, 191
jewelry making, 266–67
Johnson, Andrew, 309, 310
Johnson, Joseph, 43, 85
Johnston, Albert Sidney, 10, 147
Johnston, Joseph, 154, 157, 228n23, 230n24, 234, 236n32, 305n37
Jonesboro, GA, 259
journals. See diaries; magazines (periodicals)

Kane, Lucille, 21
Kankakee, IL, 55
Kansas First Infantry. See First Kansas Colored Infantry
Kelly, Murray, 111, 177, 183
Kennesaw, GA. See Big Shanty, GA
Kennesaw Mountain, 232–35 passim, 236n32
Kennesaw Mountain, Battle of. See Battle of Kennesaw Mountain
Kentucky, 10, 231n26
Kentucky Brigade. See First Kentucky Brigade
Kilpatrick, Hugh Judson, 259, 263
King, Davis S.
Klink, Peter, 121, 124
knapsacks, 62, 276; bloody, 79; close calls and, 229, 231, 287; drilling with, 27; found in woods, 63; given up, 225, 259; hasty packing of, 113; inspection and, 195, 196; marching with, 28, 73, 274; overhauling of, 276; in tents, 110, 111
knives, 63
Koethe, William, 196, 256, 257
Kossuth, MS, 64

La Crosse, WI, 28, 107n43
Lafayette, MS, 93
Lake Providence, LA, 12–13, 102–24, 156, 165
Lammers, George C., 56
leaves of absence. See furloughs
Lee, Robert E., 98, 161, 267
Lee, Stephen D., 244n38
Leggett, Mortimer D., 205–6, 215, 226n19, 247
legislators, 30
letters, Confederate, 91
levees, 13, 30, 97, 113–14, 117; used as highways, 128
Lexington, Battle of. See Battle of Lexington
libraries, 185, 191, 201, 215, 216
lice, 157
limbers, 8, 43–44, 75, 118

Lincoln, Abraham, 31n18, 97, 121, 122, 184, 260–62 passim; assassination, 305
Literary Association of Vicksburg. *See* Vicksburg Union Literary Association
literature. *See* poetry; Shakespeare, William
Lithonia, GA, 270
live oaks, 282, 290
livestock, 65, 155, 205, 296, 299. *See also* cattle; horses; mules; oxen; pigs
living quarters. *See* quarters
loans, 34, 126. *See also* debt
locomotives: destruction of, 205–6, 283
Logan, John A., 86, 104, 112, 114, 130, 144, 147, 215, 248
lotteries, 156–57, 182
Louisiana, 12–13, 94–99, 114, 128, 224
Louisiana State University, 23
Lowell, WI, 304
luck. *See* close calls

Macpheeters, Jim, 101
magazines. *See* powder magazines
magazines (periodicals), 133, 182, 190–91
magnolia trees, 93
Maine, 7, 42n8, 186
malaria, 116, 214
malingerers, 58
Malmros, Oscar, 250, 256, 287
malnutrition, 40, 159
malpractice, surgical, 51, 56
Mankato, MN, 21
manuscript collecting, 21–23
maps, 274, 291
March to the Sea, 16, 273
marching, 57; Carolinas campaign, 293; during foraging expeditions, 269, 270; Louisiana, 125; Mississippi, 73–76 passim, 86, 91–93, 179, 180; "the more tired you are at night, the better," 302; preparation for, 276; St. Louis, 28, 29; singing and, 106, 125; Sixteenth Wisconsin prowess, 213; Tennessee, Alabama, and Georgia, 82, 93–94, 222–27 passim, 228n20–21, 239, 277–85; Washington, 17, 308–10; yearning for, 267. *See also* March to the Sea; night marching
Marietta, GA, 228n23, 239, 273, 274
marriage, 221
Matamora, Battle of. *See* Battle of Matamora
math, 141, 152, 167, 187, 197, 279
Mattoon, IL, 28
Maximilian I of Mexico, 161n43

McArthur, John, 73, 82, 94, 121–23 passim, 201, 242, 273; literary association and, 188–89, 190
McClellan, George B., 51, 65–66, 85, 91, 247n42, 261
McClellan Rifles, 5n4, 6–7, 26
McClernand, John Alexander, 79, 84, 100n39, 135
McDonough, GA, 277
McGuinness, William, 126n6
McKean, Thomas Jefferson, 45
McNulty, Robert, 149, 265
McPherson, James, 15, 86, 121, 122, 130n10, 188, 240; popularity of, 231; rumor of death of, 202; shot and killed, 242–43; takes over Army of the Tennessee, 225n17, 248; unpretentiousness of, 135
Meade, George, 154, 309, 310
meal. *See* cornmeal
meals. *See* eating
medical care. *See* hospitals; surgeons
Memphis, TN, 12, 37, 51, 83, 90, 93–94, 104, 149, 217; description of, 175; T. C. journey to, 173–77
mending equipment. *See* needles, needle cases, etc.
Meridian, MS, 202n38, 205
Mexico, 161
military draft. *See* conscription
military occupation, 14, 66, 144n18
military recruiters. *See* recruiters and recruiting
military training. *See* training
militias, 7, 280
milk, 217
Millen, GA, 282
Miller, Stephen, 307–8
Milliken's Bend, LA, 125
mills, 3, 277–78. *See also* grist mills
Milwaukee, 234, 235–36
Minneapolis, 26n3, 42n8
Minnesota Historical Society, 21–23 passim
Minnesota Light Cavalry, 5
Minnesota Mounted Rangers, 90
missionary work. *See* Christian missionary work
Mississippi, 12, 13, 128. *See also* Corinth, MS; Vicksburg, MS
Mississippi, Army of the. *See* Army of the Mississippi
Mississippi River, 7, 79, 85, 97–101 passim, 112–13, 117–18, 128; ferry across, 28; flooding, 13, 14; ice in, 197; partial fording of by pigs, 174; at St. Louis, 30, 31;

steamer travel on, 10, 36–37, 95; at Vicksburg, 149, 156
Missouri, 29, 35, 231n26. *See also* St. Louis, MO
Missourians: nickname for, 58n49
mistaken identity, 41n5
Mitchel, Ormsby M., 59n52
Mobile, AL, 79, 303
Monahan, George W., 21
Monahan, Jean Ritchie, 21, 22
money, 58–59, 64, 67, 132–33; accounting for, 118; burned on the *Ruth*, 165n46; Confederate, 283; lost, 248; sent north, 120, 124–26 passim, 137, 165, 183, 199, 204, 274, 275; sent to T. C. by his father, 243, 248; substitutes for, 108. *See also* consumer goods: prices; gambling; pay
monotony, 203, 204, 211
Monticello, GA, 278–79
morale, 97, 98, 145, 215, 245–46, 266; Confederate, 207
Morgan, John Hunt, 157
Morneau, Joseph, 275
mortars, 44
Moscow, TN, 12, 91–93
moss, Spanish. *See* Spanish moss
mountains, 227, 232–33, 270, 311
Mourne River. *See* River Mourne
mud, 65, 100, 217, 218, 229, 231; Benton Barracks, 31, 32; gardens trampled into, 116; marching through, 74, 125, 283, 293
mules, 65, 68, 268–73 passim, 278, 298–300 passim
Munch, Emil, 7, 11, 30n16, 41, 42n9, 55, 70; resignation of, 90
Munch, Paul, 80
Murfreesboro, TN, 149, 219n10
Murray, Henry, 306
music, 13, 37, 83–84, 88, 155, 157, 164, 253; at Corinth, 68; flute, 59. *See also* brass bands; buglers and bugling; fifing and drumming; sheet music and music books; songs and singing

Napoleon III, 161n43
narrow escapes. *See* close calls
Nashville, TN, 272
Natchez, MS, 155, 165, 170
navy, 143, 285n18, 291–92
near misses. *See* close calls
needles, needle cases, etc., 137, 140, 165, 201
Newburn, NC, 302
New Hampshire (steamship). *See* USS *New Hampshire*

New Haven, CT, 311
Newmarket, Battle of. *See* Battle of Newmarket
New Orleans, LA, 37
newspapers, 31, 59, 91, 125, 158; absence of, 97, 100; Army of Potomac coverage, 85; Corinth campaign coverage, 77; desire for, 174–75, 191; hawked in Memphis, 175; literary association, 185; northern, 112, 115, 128, 133, 170, 211, 261; publish governor's reports, 65n58; southern, 54, 149, 235, 283, 296; useless at Shiloh, 45
New Ulm, MN, 7, 111
New York City, 305
Nickajack Creek, Battle of. *See* Battle of Nickajack Creek
night marching, 76, 244, 245, 259, 283–84
night shelling, 255, 284
night sky, 62, 91, 109, 164, 169
Nineteenth Wisconsin Infantry, 107
Ninety-fifth Illinois Infantry, 85, 88, 191
Ninth Army Corps, 144n187, 147n24
Nisswa, MN, 21
Noble, Amos, 69, 80, 165, 168
North Carolina, 16
Norton, Charles, 210
Norwegian American soldiers, 41n4
Noyes, Henry, 305
Noyes, Luther, 69
Noyes, Osgood, 212
Noyes, Persis, 4
Noyes, Samuel, 135
Nute, Cyril, 22
Nute, Mary Christie, 22

ocean voyages, 291–92
Ocmulgee River, 277
Oconee River, 280
officer commissions. *See* commissions
Ogeechee River, 281, 282
O'Hara, Joseph, 111, 189, 198–99, 211, 235; marriage of, 221
Ohio, Army of the. *See* Army of the Ohio
Ohio River, 36–37, 215–18 passim, 273
O'Keefe, Ed, 281, 302
Olmsted County, MN, 4n2, 18, 43n15
Olmsted, Frederick Law, 223
120th Illinois Infantry, 156
124th Illinois Infantry, 215
Orangeburg, SC, 294
orchards, 52, 70, 229
Ord, Edward O. C., 75, 148n24
ordnance rifles, 15, 171, 205, 213, 280, 284, 287

Orphan Brigade. See First Kentucky Brigade
Osterhaus Peter Joseph, 281
ovens, 159
oxen, 168, 170
Oxford, MS, 91, 92
oysters, 288–89, 290

Paducah, KY, 37, 140
Palmer, John M., 248
Palmquist, Bonnie, 22
Parke, John, 147n24
Parrott rifles, 142, 148, 201, 294n26
pay, 35–36, 95, 115, 120, 238; awaited, 86,
    205, 264, 272; of black soldiers, 169; for
    foraged items, 64, 70; to forego military
    service, 150, 194; Sarah Christie and, 6; at
    sergeant level for T. C., 235. See also
    bonus pay
peaches, 52, 70, 271
peach trees, 52, 70, 114, 205
Pease, Russell, 62n54
peddlers and hawkers. See hawkers and
    peddlers
Peebles, Ferdinand E., 43, 55, 70, 90, 122
Pee Dee River, 295
Pemberton, John C., 147, 180n9
Pfaender, William, 42, 69, 70, 90
Philadelphia (steamship). See USS
    Philadelphia
Philadelphia, PA, 305–6
photographs, 198–99, 252, 293
pickets, 255
pigs, 40, 66, 174, 270, 271, 277. See also
    pork
pillage. See plunder
pine woods, 279, 282, 291
Pioneer Corps, 283, 296
pistols, 63
Pittsburgh, PA, 57
Pittsburg Landing. See Battle of Shiloh
plates: sharing of, 104
plunder, 82, 279, 299. See also foraging
Pocotaligo, SC, 291–93
poetry, 66–67, 71, 91, 116, 159, 198
Polk, Leonidas, 229n23, 233
Pollok, Robert, 159
Pontiac (gunboat). See USS Pontiac
Pope, John, 49, 59
pork, 66, 70, 88, 180, 220, 271, 276; salt
    pork, 40
Porter, David, 146, 285n18
Port Gibson, MS, 127, 180
Port Hudson, LA, 98, 99, 143, 154
portraits, 115, 198–99, 200, 220, 252–53

Port Royal, SC, 292
postage stamps, 133, 134, 138; Confederate,
    243; requests for, 57, 82, 86, 106, 165,
    224
Potomac, Army of the. See Army of the
    Potomac
Potts, Benjamin F., 258
powder horns, 64
powder magazines, 49
prayer meetings, 109, 207, 215
prayers, 182, 190, 207
Prentiss, Benjamin M., 40n2, 43, 44,
    45n17, 47
presents. See gifts
presidential elections, 261–62
Price, Sterling, 29, 73, 75n4, 76, 84, 179
prices of consumer goods. See consumer
    goods: prices
prisoners, 40, 45n17, 83, 88, 127, 279;
    Andersonville, 265–66; Atlanta
    campaign, 231, 234, 240, 242, 265;
    Benton Barracks, 35; exchange of, 265,
    303n34; Fort McAllister, 285; joyful, 253;
    Vicksburg, 147n23, 150, 160. See also
    escaped prisoners; "galvanized Yankees"
private property, 54. See also houses
prodigality, 9, 32, 58
profanity. See cursing
promotions, 90, 92, 192n24, 235;
    anticipated, 201; declined, 226

quartermasters, 100, 235, 278, 291, 292;
    foraging and, 54n40, 269, 299
quarters: Camp Benton, 30. See also tents
quoits, 52, 56–57, 123, 208–9, 211

race relations, 262–63
railroads, 59, 91–93 passim, 230n24, 231,
    241n35, 267, 268; destruction of, 259,
    274–75, 279–83 passim, 295; repair of,
    81, 86, 87, 279. See also trains
rain, 58, 100, 311; at Benton Barracks, 32;
    camping in, 217, 218; health and, 116,
    292; holey tarpaulin and, 287; marching
    in, 74, 125, 222–23; river color and, 213;
    steamboat travel and, 101; T. C. on, 86,
    103–5 passim, 229, 292–93; unearths
    graves, 39; W. C. on, 65, 66, 93, 94, 110,
    168, 169. See also mud; tents: leaking and
    flooding of
Ramsey, Alexander, 61, 64, 65, 66, 70–71,
    170
Ransom, Thomas E. G., 128, 135, 145, 155,
    177; death of, 273

rations, 220, 290; of candles, 273; letters more than equivalent to, 230; reduced, 151, 225–27 passim, 266, 268, 276; used up, 74. *See also* hardtack
Raymond, MS, Battle of. *See* Battle of Raymond
reading. *See* books; literature; magazines (periodicals); newspapers
rebel yell, 241, 244, 250; matched with a "Yankee yell," 299, 300
recruiters and recruiting, 7, 69, 196, 199, 293
recruits, age of. *See* age of recruits
Redbone, MS, 183, 199
Red River, 112n54, 205
reenlistment, 15, 186, 187–88, 191, 193, 195, 199
Reid, Elizabeth. *See* Christie, Elizabeth ("Eliza") Reid (stepmother)
Reid, Helen, 36, 151, 152n31
Reid, Robert, 124n2
Reid, Robert K., 124
Reid, Thomas D., 67, 100, 125, 140, 178, 192, 210, 278; furlough of, 303, 304
Reimers, Roemer, 181
reinforcements, 213; Confederate, 98, 229, 258, 267; Shiloh and, 11; Union, 107, 144n18, 148n24, 157n35, 250, 258; waiting for, 83, 229
relics, battlefield. *See* battlefield relics
religion, 13, 102, 109, 123, 156; reenlistment and, 193. *See also* Christianity; God; prayers
Republican Party, 149n28
Resaca, GA, 230, 267
restaurant meals, 175–76
Reynolds, Alexander W., 243n36
rheumatism, 18, 32, 52, 181
rice, 283–86 passim
rich and poor, 150, 206–7, 300
Richmond, LA, 140
Richmond, VA, 16, 51, 57, 59, 65, 67, 211, 232, 296; W. C. in, 303
rifles, 234n30, 236, 238. *See also* flintlock rifles; Whitworth rifle
Ringgold, GA, 224
Ripley, MS, 62
Rippe, Henry, 35–36
river fording. *See* fording of rivers
River Mourne, 117, 118
roads, 62, 74, 93, 125, 141, 213, 222, 277; corduroy, 296. *See also* railroads
Roddey, Philip Dale, 220, 221, 227
Rodman guns. *See* ordnance rifles

Rogers, Albert T., 92, 189, 195
Rogers, William P., 79
Rome, GA, 225, 227–28, 274
Root, George F., 106n42, 115n57
Rosencrans, William S., 75, 157n35, 170, 179
Ross, John D., 228n20, 268, 276, 281
Roundaway Bayou, 125
Rowley, Ed., 301
rumors, 59, 91, 99, 125, 170; of Atlanta campaign, 224; of Confederate troop movement, 51, 83; of discharge, 310; of McPherson's death, 202; of pay, 263; of Port Hudson, 143, 154; of Union troop movement, 116, 211, 214, 218, 311
Ruth (steamboat), 165

St. Anthony, MN, 111n49, 175n3
St. Augustine River, 288
St. Charles, MN, 263, 264
St. Louis, MO, 8–10, 28–36 passim, 56, 65, 311
St. Louis Arsenal, 10, 33–36, 38
St. Paul, MN, 65
St. Paul Press, 128, 133, 191
Salkehatchie River, 293
Saloman, Edward, 135
Saluda River, 294
Sanborn, John Benjamin, 27
Sanitary Commission, 201, 274, 292
Savannah, GA, 16, 286–92 passim; escapee from, 279–80; letters posted from, 273–90
Savannah, TN, 36–38, 39, 201n37, 219
Schaller, John, 80, 165, 168, 183, 199, 220, 235, 256; wounding of, 240–41
Schofield, John, 248, 259n59, 299
Schuler, Henry, 166
Scotland, 3, 156
scouts, 299
seasickness, 288, 291
Second Battle of Corinth. *See* Battle of Corinth
Second Illinois Light Artillery, 67, 127, 139
Second Minnesota Infantry, 17
Second Minnesota Light Artillery, 5n4, 7, 26
Second Tennessee Cavalry, 219
self-analysis, 132, 193
sermons, 102, 195
Sevastopol, 146
Seventeenth Army Corps, 215n5, 224n15, 226n19, 273–76 passim; Atlanta campaign, 241n35, 244; commanders,

130n10; corduroy road and, 296n31;
Vicksburg, 157, 205n43, 247n42;
Washington, 306, 308
Seventeenth Wisconsin Infantry, 12, 45, 59,
78, 85, 107, 120–21, 177–78, 191n23;
Natchez, 165; Vicksburg, 137, 145, 164–
65, 166
Seventh Connecticut Infantry, 124n2
Seventy-eighth Ohio Infantry, 247n42
Shakespeare, William, 35, 221
Shaller, John, 80
sheet music and music books, 13, 94, 112,
115, 123, 165, 183
Sherman, William T., 10, 11; Alexander
Christie criticism of, 278; Arkansas Post
and, 100n39; Atlanta campaign and, 15,
225n17, 230n24, 232n28, 234n31, 236n32,
252n48, 259n59; Blair and, 231n26;
foraging and, 54n40, 276; Jackson campaign, 147n24; locomotive destruction
and, 205–6; March to the Sea, 16, 273,
281, 283; march to Washington, 17;
McClernand and, 79n12; organization of
army, 247–48; reviews troops, 309, 310;
Stanton and, 292n23; unpretentiousness
of, 281
Shiloh, Battle of. See Battle of Shiloh
Shiloh Chapel, 10, 39, 69
ships. See steamships
shot manufacture, 33, 35
sickness. See illness
sidearms, 101, 110. See also pistols; swords
Siege of Atlanta, 252–60
Siege of Corinth, 45–50 passim
Siege of Vicksburg, 14, 129–47, 247n42
Sigel, Franz, 29, 256n52
Sill, Joshua W., 59
Simpson, Thomas, 308n39
singing. See songs and singing
Sion Mills, Ireland, 3, 117n60, 311
Sixteenth Army Corps, 241
Sixteenth Iowa Infantry, 209n50, 212
Sixteenth Wisconsin Infantry, 85, 88;
Atlanta campaign and, 242; Big Black
River, 213; consolidation, 80; Corinth, 73,
77; Shiloh, 41, 42; Vicksburg, 156, 165,
169, 199
Sixth Division, 11, 12, 40n2, 45, 76; black
soldiers and, 120–22
Sixth Missouri Infantry, 127
Sixty-ninth New York Infantry, 279
Sixty-sixth Illinois Infantry, 242
sketches. See drawings
sky at night. See night sky

slavery, 14, 25–26, 52, 223, 262; biblical
argument for, 150, 151; John Brown and,
136; poor whites and, 207; soldiers'
opinion of, 85, 97, 124, 150; "sum of all
villanies," 51, 161
slaves, 66, 292n23
sleep deprivation, 227
Slocum, Henry W., 268, 272
Small, John, 200
smells, foul. See stench
Smith, Giles A., 241n35, 248, 258, 263, 280,
283, 293–95 passim
Smith, Janet. See Bertie, Janet
Smith, R. H., 251
smoking, 135, 145
snipers, 55, 149n26, 256–57
snow, 44, 100, 119
snuff, 223
social class and war. See class and war
songs and singing, 13, 88, 94, 105–7, 115,
123, 183, 253; literary association and, 182,
190, 191; W. C. hollers and screams, 165;
while marching, 106, 125. See also choirs;
Christian hymns
sounds, 83–84, 150, 164; of cannonading,
78, 127, 129, 131, 137, 143, 237, 246, 255,
284; of rifles and bullets, 134, 139, 229.
See also buglers and bugling; dinner calls
South Carolina, 16, 292. See also Carolinas
campaign
southern dialect, 58, 153
southerners: rich and poor, 150, 206–7,
300; "a sorry looking lot," 223; women,
223, 278, 279
Southwick, Charles W., 152, 181, 189, 192,
301, 302, 310; enlistment of, 26; literary
association and, 190; made quartermaster, 235; marriage of, 221; sister of, 108;
wounding of, 149
Southwick, Minnie R., 108, 116, 311
Spanish moss, 95–96, 97, 283
Stanton, Edward M., 292
starvation, 265–66, 272, 283
stationery, 29, 44, 45, 99–100, 111, 248, 285
steamboats, 101, 118, 149, 150, 216; burning
of, 165; explosion of, 166–67; travel on,
36–39, 63–64, 94–97 passim, 114, 173–
77, 216–17
steamships, 288, 291–92
stench, 154
Stevens, W. L., 21
Steward, Alexander, 244n38
Stewart, George, 89
Stinson, Colby, 42, 48

Stokes, George, 109n44
Stoneman, George, 279
Stone Mountain, 270
Strachan, James, 5, 126, 140, 149, 263
suicide, 266
supply depots, 68n60
surgeons, 14, 51, 56
surrenders, 147n23, 217n7
sutlers, 9, 32, 233n29, 274
Sutton, John, 278
swamps, 73, 74, 83, 93, 97, 115, 280, 293,
    300; bridging of, 280, 283, 296
swearing. *See* cursing
sweet potatoes, 104, 107, 270, 271, 276, 282
swimming, 68, 294, 304
swine. *See* pigs
swords, 31, 34, 36

Tallahatchie River, 84, 86
target practice, 60–61, 63–64
tarpaulins: employed as shelters, 221, 246;
    pierced by shells, 230, 235, 256, 287
Taxdahl, Ole J., 41, 46, 47, 48, 78n7
Taylor, Ezra, 50
Taylors Falls, MN, 7, 58n50, 103n40,
    166n47
tea and coffee. *See* coffee and tea
tedium. *See* monotony
Temperance Advocate, 112
Tennessee, 10, 39–47, 219n9–10; Army
    of the Ohio and, 59n52; Burnside and,
    144n18; marching through, 82, 93–94,
    222. *See also* Grand Junction, TN;
    Memphis, TN; Nashville, TN; Savannah,
    TN
Tennessee, Army of the. *See* Army of the
    Tennessee
Tennessee River, 10, 15, 37, 44, 68, 114,
    201n37, 218, 219
Tenth Ohio Light Artillery, 88, 182, 217
tents, 33, 39, 41, 44, 83, 87, 109–11; burning
    of, 276; as dining rooms, 104; given up,
    100; heating of, 86, 87–88, 197; leaking
    and flooding of, 92, 94, 103, 105, 110–11;
    leveling of, 113; naming of, 67, 111;
    "puppy-tents," 85–86, 307
theater, 176, 192
theft, 56, 62, 155; called "confiscation," 157–
    58, 202
Third Michigan Cavalry, 32
Third Minnesota Infantry, 5, 6–7
Third Wisconsin Infantry, 67
Thirteenth Army Corps, 79n12, 148n24
Thirteenth Illinois Infantry, 155

Thirteenth Iowa Infantry, 212, 294
Thirtieth Illinois Infantry, 224
Thirty-ninth Massachusetts Infantry, 308
Thirty-second Ohio Infantry, 224, 302
Thirty-sixth Massachusetts Infantry, 144
Thomas, George Henry, 248, 259
Thomas, Lorenzo, 120–22
Thompson, M. Jeff, 177
Thompson, William R., 301
Tilson, Richard O., 26, 41, 47, 48
tobacco. *See* cigars; smoking; snuff
Toomsboro, GA, 279–80
Torrey, John W., 126
towels, 32, 235, 260
training, 8, 13, 27, 31, 36; dreams of, 206
trains, 28, 30, 47, 210, 294; evacuation of
    Atlanta and, 274; fares, 218. *See also*
    locomotives
train trips, 234, 305–6, 311
travel books, 223
trees, 114, 129, 162–63, 233, 277; climbed
    for view, 247; close calls and, 230; felled
    for bridges, 296; used for making
    embrasures, 229; used for target practice,
    60–61. *See also* abatis; live oaks; magnolia
    trees; orchards; peach trees; pine woods
trenches: as graves, 79, 153, 253; Vicksburg,
    142, 145, 146, 151, 153, 159, 163, 164
Tunnel Hill, GA, 224
Turkey, 18
turkeys, 70, 75–76, 299
Tuscumbia Creek, 62
Twelfth Illinois Infantry, 242
Twelfth Iowa Infantry, 43
Twelfth Michigan Infantry, 42
Twelfth Wisconsin Infantry, 135, 139, 242,
    284
Twentieth Army Corps, 267, 268, 274, 295
Twentieth Wisconsin Infantry, 165
Twenty-fifth Missouri Infantry, 42, 50n29
Twenty-first Missouri Infantry, 50n29
Twenty-ninth Wisconsin Infantry, 99, 100,
    125, 165
Twenty-sixth Wisconsin Infantry, 275
Twenty-third Wisconsin Infantry, 125
typhoid fever, 273n11

Union Literary Association of Vicksburg.
    See Vicksburg Union Literary Association
U.S. Christian Commission. *See* Christian
    Commission
U.S. Sanitary Commission. *See* Sanitary
    Commission
USS *Hope,* 217

USS *New Hampshire*, 292
USS *Philadelphia*, 291–92
USS *Pontiac*, 288

valentines, 211
Van Dorn, Earl, 12, 80, 91, 179
veterans, 187, 210, 264–65, 311
Vicksburg, MS, 12–15 passim, 91, 96–99
    passim, 116; battle anticipated, 85, 114;
    cave system, 153, 162; departure from,
    215–16; described by W. C., 162–64;
    letters posted from, 128–212 passim,
    215–18; march to, 125–28; McClernand
    and, 79, 84; "natural protections of,"
    129, 163–64. *See also* Siege of Vicksburg
Vicksburg Union Literary Association,
    182–95 passim, 201
videttes, 213, 255
Vining's Station, GA, 237n32
Virginia, 17, 57. *See also* Army of Virginia;
    Richmond, VA
virtues, 293
Visgar, Charley, 41, 80

wagon trains, 269–71
Wallace, W. H. L., 48
Walpole, Horace, 159n40
Washington, DC, 17, 305–12
Washington's birthday, 201
watches (timepieces), 237–38, 260, 263
water for drinking. *See* drinking water
Waterhouse, Allen C., 50
Waterhouse, Dave, 280, 281
waterproofing, 110, 111
Watertown, WI, 80, 119, 191n23
weather, 44, 91, 117; "always something
    wrong with [it]," 166; "beautiful . . . for
    the wounded," 241; clement, 84, 88, 94,
    97, 118, 157, 198, 205, 263; cold, 32–35
    passim, 183, 184–85, 197, 207, 272, 280;
    dry, 52, 61–62; fickle, 86, 184, 279; hot,

58, 61–62, 116, 138, 144, 151–55 passim,
    160, 162, 236, 237; "must not grumble
    over," 292; "none of the finest," 98. *See
    also* drought; rain; snow
Webster, Joseph Dana, 44
Wechsler, Mathias, 34
Welch, Billy, 95
wells, 64
Westmoreland (steamboat), 176
Wheeler's Cavalry Corps, 241, 265
whiskey, 48, 153, 158
White River, 97
Whitworth rifle, 257
wild game. *See* game
Wilmington, NC, 285, 293, 296
Wilson's Creek, Battle of. *See* Battle of
    Wilson's Creek
Wiltse, William H., 126, 177, 189, 211, 221,
    235, 308
Winnsboro, SC, 295
Winona, MN, 5, 26n4, 52n34, 55n45,
    92n27–29, 111n50, 126n7, 176n5, 189,
    211, 277n16
"Winona" (tent name), 111
Winona County, MN, 4, 221
Wolf River, 91, 93
women: Joseph O'Hara and, 199, 221;
    present at literary association sociable,
    201; southern, 223, 278, 279; T. C. fur-
    lough and, 304; as war victims, 137, 161
wool, 61
Wooley, Sam, 176, 181–82, 189, 192, 221
Work, Henry Clay, 105n41
wounded soldiers, 65, 149n26, 227, 275,
    284; Atlanta, 240–41; Corinth, 103;
    Shiloh, 11, 40–41, 43, 47, 55–56
Wright, Dan, 208–10, 301

"Yankees" (label), 127
Yazoo City, MS, 133
Yazoo River, 94, 96, 102, 116n59, 149

Brother of Mine is set in the Scala typeface family.

Book design and typesetting by BNTypographics West Ltd., Victoria, B.C. Canada.

Printed by Sheridan Books, Ann Arbor, Michigan.